P9-DMV-262

THE UNITED STATES AND WORLD WAR II

Volume II

The

New American Nation Series

EDITED BY

HENRY STEELE COMMAGER

AND

RICHARD B. MORRIS

THE UNITED STATES AND WORLD WAR II

Volume II

By A. RUSSELL BUCHANAN

ILLUSTRATED

HARPER & ROW, PUBLISHERS
NEW YORK, EVANSTON, AND LONDON

The maps in this volume are from *The War in Maps: An Atlas of the New York Times Maps, Fourth Edition,* by Francis Brown, Lucas Manditch, and others. Copyright 1946 by Oxford University Press, Inc. Reprinted by permission.

LIBRARY OF CONGRESS CATALOG CARD NUMBER: 63–20287

Contents

VOLUME II

Illustrations

These photographs, grouped in a separate section, will be found following page 412

Maps

THE UNITED STATES AND WORLD WAR II

Volume II

CHAPTER 14

The Statesmen at War

TWO basic themes feature the diplomacy of the United States during World War II. One, winning the war, naturally dominated earlier international conferences, but as the conflict drew to a close the second, winning the peace, assumed a primary position. Both themes, however, were present in the first international meeting held after formal entry of the United States into World War II, the so-called Arcadia Conference, instigated by Prime Minister Churchill and held in Washington.

Coming by vessel to the United States, Churchill, his Chiefs of Staff, the Minister of Supply, and an entourage of assistants arrived in Washington December 22. The Prime Minister moved into the White House, and informal and formal discussions followed until January 14, 1942. This conference established much of the pattern for subsequent negotiations, a pattern of diplomacy at the top level in which Roosevelt and Churchill assumed active and enthusiastic leadership. Among the President's advisers the military leaders overshadowed State Department officials, and Harry Hopkins emerged not only as an intimate adviser of the Chief Executive but as head of one of the most powerful agencies of the wartime government. Cordell Hull, on the other hand, despite his position as Secretary of State, became a relatively less important figure left out of the top discussions, who concerned himself primarily with planning for an international organization.[1]

[1] Hull felt that as Secretary of State he should have been included in the

The Arcadia Conference produced several significant results, one of which was political and had been initiated by the State Department, although it underwent numerous changes during the discussions in Washington. The State Department went to the conference with two proposals, but one recommending a war council of the leading Allies failed to gain support.[2] The other emerged as an important document in the history of international organizations. This Declaration of the United Nations was a joint statement signed not only by the United Kingdom and the United States but also by the other enemies of the Axis, promising full support to the war effort and pledging each state not to make a separate peace.[3] The immediate purpose of the declaration was to demonstrate to the world that a united front faced the enemy. The ultimate significance of the document was that as other nations declared war on the Axis they added their names to the list, and it was inclusion on this roster which later entitled a state to membership in the United Nations. The order of listing the first signatories was also of importance, for it clearly indicated the dominance of the great powers. The smaller states were listed alphabetically but after the four great powers, the United States, Britain, the USSR, and China. The suggestion that the United States head the list came from the American representatives, and the British acquiesced, apparently convinced that this minor sop to American prestige was counterbalanced by other more substantial gains in the conference.[4] At Roosevelt's insistence also, China was included as one of the "Big Four," although Chiang Kai-shek's government hardly measured up to this distinction. Roosevelt, however, was thinking of the importance to the Far East of a politically strong China.[5] There was a continuing difference on this point with Churchill, who felt that a policy relying on China was an illusion.

Portentous though the United Nations declaration was for the future, it consumed much less time in the conference than did military

---

war councils. Cordell Hull, *The Memoirs of Cordell Hull* (New York, 1948), II, 1109–1110.

[2] *Ibid.*, II, 1121.

[3] *Ibid.*, II, 1124.

[4] Winston Churchill, *The Second World War: The Grand Alliance* (Boston, 1950), III, 666.

[5] Harry Hopkins made the suggestion to President Roosevelt. Robert E. Sherwood, *Roosevelt and Hopkins: An Intimate History* (New York, 1948), p. 448. See also p. 408 for a comparison of Roosevelt's and Churchill's ideas on China.

problems. The British arrived in Washington with a great deal at stake. Heavily dependent upon the United States, British leaders feared the immediate consequences of the war against Germany if the United States under the impact of the Pearl Harbor attack should insist on waging major war in the Pacific or on turning the flow of production away from Lend-Lease support to the Allies to the development of its own armed forces. The Americans quickly made it clear that they contemplated neither move, and as a result compromise became easier on lesser issues.[6]

There were so many military problems of immediate urgency that the conference came to no agreement on long-range strategy. In the Pacific it was necessary to divert ships and cargoes to aid in establishing a life line between the United States and Australia.[7] In the Atlantic, partly as a stimulus to morale and partly to relieve British troops for service elsewhere, the United States dispatched troops to Northern Ireland to complete their training.[8] Churchill in the summer of 1941 had suggested the invasion of North Africa and he revived the proposal at the Arcadia Conference.[9] Roosevelt was definitely intrigued by the idea, but military advisers noted that preparations for an invasion in the spring of 1942 would force cancellation of other military activities, and the plan remained on the record without any specified date for implementation.[10] Churchill also spoke of large-scale raids on the coast of Western Europe, possibly by 1943. These would feature armored attacks and support by the local population. No action was taken at the conference on this idea.

Although the conference failed to produce a long-range strategic plan, it did move toward the creation of agencies which would make such planning possible. General Marshall strongly urged adoption of the principle of a supreme commander in each theater of military operations. The conference took the idea, which met vigorous initial opposition, and agreed on a supreme commander who would, however, be subject to higher authority. That authority was the newly

[6] Churchill, *The Second World War,* III, 643.

[7] Maurice Matloff and Edwin M. Snell, *Strategic Planning for Coalition Warfare, 1941–1942* (*United States Army in World War II: The War Department*) (Washington, 1953), pp. 114–119.

[8] *Ibid.,* pp. 108–111.

[9] *Ibid.,* pp. 102–105; Churchill, *The Second World War,* III, 649, 684–685.

[10] Matloff and Snell, *Strategic Planning,* pp. 112–114.

created Combined Chiefs of Staff of the British and American military forces, an agency which assumed an increasingly important role as the war progressed.[11]

Vital to strategic planning was control of priority assignments of munitions and other war materials, for without this authority planning was meaningless. The United States, which was producing the bulk of the materials, did not wish to relinquish control of their assignment, while the British fought for a share of control in order to retain some voice in military policy. As a temporary solution, in response to a last-minute American suggestion, the conference created two Munitions Assignments Boards, one in Washington and the other in London. The Washington Board concerned itself with American-made munitions, and the London office with British-made munitions. The vastly greater production in the United States inevitably made the London Board subsidiary to that in Washington. Despite the fact that the boards were established as a temporary experiment for one month, they continued and operated with reasonable effectiveness throughout the war. Lord Beaverbrook was in charge of the London Board, and Harry Hopkins became the head of the powerful Washington Board.[12]

In addition to producing the United Nations declaration, making immediate decisions on military matters, and creating agencies for control of military strategy and logistics, the Arcadia Conference did much to further Anglo-American accord. Both in informal discussions and in public addresses Roosevelt and Churchill made ideal foils; Roosevelt's messages stirred the people, and Churchill's sparkling performances before the United States Congress and the Canadian Parliament, which he visited briefly, captivated the North American radio audience.[13]

During 1942, Anglo-American bonds became even tighter as the two nations pooled their resources, efforts, and ideas for the prosecution of the war. On January 26, Roosevelt and Churchill announced the formation of a number of joint boards, including the Combined Munitions Assignment Board, the Combined Raw Materials Board, and the Shipping Adjustment Board.[14] Lend-Lease faced readjust-

[11] Churchill, *The Second World War,* III, 686–687.

[12] Sherwood, *Roosevelt and Hopkins,* pp. 470–474.

[13] *Ibid.,* p. 444; Churchill, *The Second World War,* III, 671–673, 678–680.

[14] Richard M. Leighton and Robert W. Coakley, *Global Logistics and Strat-*

ment when the United States became an active belligerent. After a temporary stoppage of all Lend-Lease shipment which alarmed the would-be recipients, the flow resumed on an even larger scale.[15] As American forces began to move into Allied countries, a system of mutual aid developed; Britain, for example, provided barracks and locally produced foodstuffs, and gradually Mutual Aid Agreements came into being as a counterpart to the Lend-Lease agreements.[16] The original Lend-Lease act had indicated some type of repayment, in goods, services, money, or other benefit. In June, 1942, President Roosevelt reported to Congress a new concept of Lend-Lease, which recommended that nations contribute according to their ability to pay rather than in proportion to the amount of Lend-Lease materials they had received. If each country gave the same percentage of its national income to the war effort, the financial burden of the war would be equitably divided. The Lend-Lease program with the USSR was different in that geographical factors alone made any mutual aid impossible, and the United States signed separate protocols for Lend-Lease with the Soviets.[17] Canada was also an exception to the usual rule, for since there was roughly a financial balance between the United States and its northern neighbor, Lend-Lease rules did not apply, and trade was on a cash basis during the war. Although there were inevitable frictions, waste, and inefficiency, the United States moved with its allies toward tremendous war production and distribution. Unity for the winning of the war approached much nearer reality in the economic than in the political or military spheres.

Throughout many of the diplomatic discussions of 1942 ran the subject of a second front in Europe. The Americans were the protagonists of invasion of France, even with a small force, in 1942, and in late March Roosevelt dispatched Hopkins and General Marshall to England to present the proposal to the British. On April 14, the British Chiefs of Staff agreed to start planning for a main assault in 1943 and emergency landing in 1942 in case of imminent German collapse or threatened defeat of the Russians. Churchill was unenthusiastic

---

egy, 1940–1943 (*United States Army in World War II: The War Department*) (Washington, 1955), pp. 252, 255; Sherwood, *Roosevelt and Hopkins,* p. 470.

15 Leighton and Coakley, *Global Logistics and Strategy,* p. 247.

16 *Ibid.,* pp. 257–259; Edward R. Stettinius, Jr., *Lend-Lease: Weapon for Victory* (New York, 1944), pp. 274–285.

17 Leighton and Coakley, *Global Logistics and Strategy,* pp. 551–597; Matloff and Snell, *Strategic Planning,* pp. 205–206.

about early cross-Channel attack and soon worked for invasion of North Africa instead.[18] In July, Roosevelt sent Harry Hopkins, General Marshall, and Admiral King to London to try to reach accord with the British on war plans. From the discussions which followed came agreement to invade North Africa and not France in 1942.[19]

The next important top-level conference was at Casablanca, January 14–25, 1943, and since Stalin declined to attend, it was an Anglo-American meeting. Roosevelt and Churchill at this time were thinking of the war rather than of the peace to come, and the major points of discussion and agreement, whether military or political, were directed toward winning the conflict. Top priority went to the Battle of the Atlantic against the submarines since victory at sea was a prime requisite for any campaign in Europe. The United States agreed to the British plans for further operations in the Mediterranean, especially against Sicily, and the British leaders assented to the American plan for a limited offensive in the Far East. At the conference, refraining from definite commitment on the cross-Channel attack, the Combined Chiefs of Staff provided for an organization to prepare for possible invasion in 1943 and actual invasion in 1944. This was the office of "Chief of Staff to the Supreme Allied Commander (designate)," later to be known as Cossac. To this post they appointed British Lieutenant General Sir Frederick Morgan, who collected a staff from the American, British, and Canadian armed forces. The leaders at Casablanca were unable to reach satisfactory results on political matters. They failed to solve the complicated problem of the French in North Africa, President Roosevelt enunciated the "unconditional surrender" principle, and the United States gave Britain a free hand in what proved to be an unsuccessful attempt to draw Turkey into the war as an ally.[20]

Since many of the agreements at Casablanca were unclear, it was inevitable that another conference follow, and it came in Washington May 12–25, 1943. In this Trident Conference Marshall pressed successfully for a firm British commitment to cross-Channel invasion, and a reluctant Churchill agreed to Operation Overlord, a projected

[18] Sherwood, *Roosevelt and Hopkins,* pp. 523–538. See also above, I, 143–146.

[19] *Ibid.,* pp. 606–612; Matloff and Snell, *Strategic Planning,* pp. 266–293.

[20] Sherwood, *Roosevelt and Hopkins,* pp. 667–697; Churchill, *The Second World War,* IV (1950), 674–695; Herbert Feis, *Churchill, Roosevelt, Stalin: The War They Waged and the Peace They Sought* (Princeton, 1957), pp. 105–113; Leighton and Coakley, *Global Logistics and Strategy,* pp. 661–686.

invasion of France set at that time for May 1, 1944.[21] The Prime Minister still favored the Mediterranean approach and he invited General Marshall to meet him in Algiers. The two conferred with General Eisenhower, and although no specific agreements resulted, Eisenhower promised to work on plans to take advantage of a victory in Sicily, presumably by invading Italy.[22]

While the military discussions in Washington and Algiers solidified the war efforts of the British and the Americans, they produced a great strain on relations with Russia. The United States leaders had preferred a firm British commitment to cross-Channel invasion in 1944 to a vague promise of one in 1943. Stalin, on the other hand, bitterly resented this delay in plans to open a second front and accused his allies of broken pledges. Churchill retorted with a hot cable of denial, and although Roosevelt attempted to restore calm, Stalin manifested his displeasure by recalling temporarily his ambassadors from London and Washington and postponing indefinitely a meeting with Roosevelt. There were even rumors of separate negotiated peace with Germany.[23]

The collapse of Mussolini late in July revived Churchill's hopes for increased Mediterranean action and he instigated another Anglo-American conference, held at Quebec from August 14–24, 1943. While staff officers conferred in this so-called Quadrant Conference, Churchill went to Washington and remained until September 12. Plans for cross-Channel invasion, however, were gaining in strength, and the Combined Chiefs of Staff approved the Cossac plan but added a supplementary invasion of southern France and laid down as conditions prerequisite to European invasion the reduction of German fighter air strength, the existence of not more than twelve mobile

[21] Gordon A. Harrison, *Cross-Channel Attack* (*United States Army in World War II: The European Theater of Operations* (Washington, 1951), p. 69; Ray S. Cline, *Washington Command Post: The Operations Division* (*United States Army in World War II: The War Department*) (Washington, 1951), pp. 219–222.

[22] Churchill, *The Second World War,* IV, 810–826; Dwight D. Eisenhower, *Crusade in Europe* (New York, 1948), pp. 166–169.

[23] Sherwood, *Roosevelt and Hopkins,* p. 734; Feis, *Churchill, Roosevelt, Stalin,* pp. 131–136. Foreign Commissar V. M. Molotov visited London and Washington May, 1942; he got no promise from the British on a second front and only a statement from Roosevelt that the Americans were consulting with the British and "We expected to establish a second front." Quoted in Sherwood, *Roosevelt and Hopkins,* p. 575; Matloff and Snell, *Strategic Planning,* pp. 231–234.

German divisions in France, and solution of technical problems relating to the artificial harbors. Churchill assented to the decision and suggested Marshall's name as Supreme Commander. The conference also created a new command in Southeast Asia, headed by Lord Mountbatten.[24]

In 1943, postwar planning assumed greater significance. One of the first moves was in the direction of relief, since it was apparent that without careful planning even Allied victory would result in widespread starvation during the immediate postwar period. In August, 1940, Churchill had appointed the Leith-Ross Committee to store agricultural and other surpluses for postwar distribution, but the exigencies of war had dissipated most of these stores by 1943. In November, 1942, the United States created a comparable committee, the Office of Foreign Relief and Rehabilitations Operations, headed by Herbert Lehman, former Governor of New York. The need for an international approach to the problem was apparent, and in May, 1943, the United States, Britain, Soviet Russia, and China submitted to forty other nations a draft UNRRA (United Nations Relief and Rehabilitation Administration) Agreement. Minor suggestions made by some of the smaller powers were accepted, and the revised agreement was made public in late September and received the signatures of all the powers November 9, 1943. The agreement provided for an international relief administrative body to distribute postwar relief but left details to an UNRRA Council, which held its first sessions at Atlantic City, New Jersey, November 10—December 1, 1943. The draft agreed on payments by participating nations on the basis of one percent of the national income, and on distribution without regard to race, color, or creed. Herbert Lehman became Director General of the new agency.[25]

Planning for immediate postwar relief was far simpler than preparing a blueprint for world order. Americans like Roosevelt and Hull envisaged a world organization of independent states along the lines of a revised League of Nations which would preserve peace by legal means if necessary through the use of a police force against delinquent members. The Soviet leaders, presumably, looked to a

[24] Sherwood, *Roosevelt and Hopkins,* pp. 744–750; Cline, *Washington Command Post,* pp. 222–226.

[25] William Hardy McNeill, *America, Britain, and Russia: Their Co-operation and Conflict, 1941–1946* (*Survey of International Affairs, 1939–1946*) (London, 1953), pp. 313–315.

world of a Communist nature. The British could see in the American idea a development of the self-determination of nations which might destroy the British Empire, and Churchill advocated regionalism as a necessary corollary to world organization. He expressed his ideas in the Trident Meeting in May, 1943, but during the ensuing months Secretary Hull challenged these concepts.[26] By August, 1943, President Roosevelt favored a world organization, but one which would be dominated by the great powers. Churchill, meanwhile, had come to doubt the possibility of regional organization of Western Europe to control the balance of power between the United States and Soviet Russia, which clearly would emerge from World War II as the leading powers in the world. Seeing the advantages of close Anglo-American accord, he accepted American postwar plans as presented to the Quadrant Conference.[27] At that time Secretary Hull presented a draft declaration of a world organization to be formed even before the end of the war, and the British accepted this plan as the basis for negotiations with the Russians.[28] During 1943, the Russians also apparently underwent a change of attitude. While the issue on the Eastern front continued in doubt, the Russians were highly suspicious of the motives of the United States and Britain and felt that they were deliberately refraining from opening a second front until both Germany and Russia were exhausted and that they planned then to intervene to the detriment of both sides. At that time, consequently, a negotiated peace with the Germans held some attraction for the Russians. By summer, however, Stalin had come to feel confident of victory, and alliance with the Western powers might hasten that end and at the same time aid Russia's expansionist interests.[29]

Roosevelt had long sought a conference with Stalin, since as a firm believer in the personal approach and in his own persuasiveness he felt that such a meeting would improve relations. Stalin agreed to a meeting of ministers as a preliminary to a later conference of the Big Three, and Secretaries Eden and Hull joined Molotov in the Moscow Conference of Ministers, October 18–30, 1943.[30] Hull refrained from discussing military problems and turned such matters over to General John R. Deane, who had accompanied him. The Rus-

[26] *Ibid.*, pp. 315–321.
[27] *Ibid.*, pp. 322–323.
[28] Hull, *Memoirs,* II, 1238–1239.
[29] McNeill, *America, Britain, and Russia,* pp. 323–326.
[30] Hull, *Memoirs,* II, 1274–1318.

sians agreed "in principle" to shuttle bombing using Russian bases, weather stations, and improved air transport but subsequently placed practical obstacles in the way.[31] There were also discussions of Italy and Turkey, but Hull was primarily interested in postwar plans, and carried with him a State Department draft "Four-Power Declaration on General Security." Molotov objected at first to the inclusion of China among the signatories but later he acquiesced, and on October 30, 1943, representatives of the United States, the United Kingdom, the Soviet Union, and China signed a statement that they would cooperate in fighting the war to the end and that they recognized "the necessity of establishing at the earliest practicable date a general international organization, based on the principle of the sovereign equality of all peace-loving states, and open to membership by all such states, large and small, for the maintenance of international peace and security. . . ."[32] This declaration indicated the willingness of Soviet Russia to cooperate with the Western powers and also the intention of the United States to participate in international organizations. The Senate of the United States a few days later, on November 5, 1943, underlined this intention by passing by a vote of 85 to 5 the Connally Resolution which stated that the United States should join the free nations of the world to establish and maintain an international association "with power to prevent aggression and to preserve the peace of the world." In adopting the Fulbright Resolution September 21, 1943, the House of Representatives had already expressed a similar view.[33]

At Moscow, the ministers followed Eden's suggestion and created a European Advisory Commission with headquarters in London and later referred to it for further study the problem of partition of Germany, although the ministers did agree on complete disarmament of Germany after the war. Hull failed to make headway on two subjects, a liberalization of world trade and the substitution of the trusteeship principle for colonialism. On another point, however, there was agree-

[31] John R. Deane, *The Strange Alliance: The Story of Our Efforts at Wartime Cooperation with Russia* (New York, 1947), pp. 20–21.

[32] Hull, *Memoirs,* II, 1299, 1306–1307. The declaration may be found in Ruhl J. Bartlett, *The Record of American Diplomacy: Documents and Readings in the History of American Foreign Relations* (New York, 1947), p. 658.

[33] *Ibid.,* pp. 673–676; H. Bradford Westerfield, *Foreign Policy and Party Politics: Pearl Harbor to Korea* (New Haven, 1955), pp. 155–159.

ment, and the ministers issued a joint statement favoring the principle of trial and punishment of Nazi war criminals.[34]

Stalin's refusal to move out of telephonic contact with his commanders in the field complicated the selection of a meeting place of the Big Three since for reasons of prestige Roosevelt declined to go to Russia. Early in September, Stalin suggested Persia; Roosevelt delayed but on November 10 agreed to go to Teheran (also spelled Tehran).[35] Another complication arose from the President's desire to confer with Chiang Kai-shek and Stalin's refusal to meet the Chinese since Soviet Russia and Japan were not at war. Chiang Kai-shek, further, insisted on meeting Roosevelt and Churchill before the Teheran Conference.[36] The result was not one conference but three: in Cairo, Teheran, and again in Cairo.

On November 13, 1943, Roosevelt, Hopkins, Marshall, Leahy, King, and many advisers sailed from Hampton Roads on the new battleship, *Iowa*. The trip was uneventful, aside from an incident in which an escorting destroyer accidentally discharged a torpedo which missed the *Iowa* by some six hundred yards. The party left the ship in Oran, and Roosevelt met Eisenhower, whom it later appeared he was considering for appointment as Supreme Commander of Overlord (cross-Channel invasion). The Americans then flew the remainder of the distance to Cairo and with the British and Chinese began the first Cairo Conference, November 22–26, 1943.[37] Roosevelt, Churchill, and Chiang Kai-shek reached little agreement. Interested in keeping China in the war, the United States advocated action in Burma, including an amphibious operation in the Bay of Bengal. Churchill on the other hand wished to divert the craft which would be used in such a venture to use in the eastern Mediterranean, and Chiang Kai-shek

[34] Hull, *Memoirs,* II, 1283–1291. Ambassador John G. Winant represented the United States on the E.A.C. W. B. Smith, *Moscow Mission, 1946–1949* (London, 1950), pp. 7–9.

[35] Winston Churchill, *The Second World War: Closing the Ring* (Boston, 1951), V, 317–318; The White House took the initiative in American planning to the Cairo and Teheran conferences, and the State Department knew only in a general way of developments. Herbert Feis, *The China Tangle: The American Effort in China from Pearl Harbor to the Marshall Mission* (Princeton, 1953), p. 103.

[36] Charles F. Romanus and Riley Sunderland, *Stilwell's Command Problems* (*United States Army in World War II: China-Burma-India Theater*) (Washington, 1956), pp. 52–53.

[37] Sherwood, *Roosevelt and Hopkins,* pp. 766–771.

shifted ideas and positions from day to day. Unable to secure agreement, Churchill and Roosevelt went on by air to Teheran, and Chiang Kai-shek returned to China thinking that the Burma campaigns would go on.[38]

Arriving in Teheran on November 27, Roosevelt went to the American Legation, located some distance from the Russian and British legations which were near each other. On the following day, for security reasons and for ease of communication, the President and his party accepted Stalin's invitation to transfer to the Russian Legation. At Teheran Roosevelt, Churchill, and Stalin met for the first time, and during the next few days there were times of great tension, of conviviality, of debate, of calm discussion, of disagreement, and of concord.[39]

On the major military issue the Russians and the Americans were in agreement. Stalin strongly endorsed the Overlord attack which the United States had been urging and like the Americans wanted a firm commitment on the operation. The Soviet leader more than once pressed Roosevelt for the name of the Supreme Commander and indicated his own respect for General Marshall, who was at Teheran.[40] The President, however, stated that he needed a few more days in which to reach a decision.

One of Roosevelt's primary purposes was to win Russian goodwill and he strained so hard in this direction that he affronted Churchill by declining to hold a private discussion with him. On the other hand, he met Stalin privately on several occasions and by this action led Churchill to follow the same tactics.[41] In much of the conference the alignment seemed to be the United States and Soviet Russia against the United Kingdom. In his memoirs, Churchill denies that he was hostile to cross-Channel invasion and insists that he was interested in Mediterranean action as opposed to the projected Burma operation.[42] Whatever the Prime Minister's real attitude may have been, Americans went to the conference believing Churchill and the British

[38] For appraisals of the Cairo Conference, see *ibid.*, pp. 771–775; Romanus and Sunderland, *Stilwell's Command Problems,* p. 82; Feis, *The China Tangle,* p. 109.

[39] Sherwood, *Roosevelt and Hopkins,* pp. 776–799.

[40] *Ibid.*, pp. 787, 791.

[41] *Ibid.*, pp. 784–793.

[42] Churchill states that he never asked for more than one-tenth of "our realisable strength" to use in the eastern Mediterranean. Churchill, *The Second World War,* V, 328, 345.

military leaders to be less than enthusiastic regarding Operation Overlord, and one United States Army planning note stated that on this subject Britain must "fish or cut bait."[43] Stalin's insistence on a second front no doubt helped the British to decide to "fish." The main military decision of the Teheran Conference, therefore, was a firm agreement by the Big Three to invade France with a major force in Normandy and a minor one on the southern coast, beginning in May, 1944. Stalin promised a strong Russian offensive at the same time to aid the invasion.[44]

Many other matters came up for discussion. Roosevelt in a separate conversation with Stalin advanced his ideas on postwar international organization. Stalin asked questions, did not commit himself, but indicated concern with the possibility of German rearmament and the inadvisability of considering China as a major power. At various times the Big Three discussed such matters as Poland, Germany, and the Mediterranean. There is some indication that the attitudes of Churchill and particularly Roosevelt may have strengthened Stalin's determination to seek territorial expansion at a later date. Roosevelt, for example, expressed his belief that Soviet Russia should have a warm-water port in the Pacific, and in his discussion with Stalin on postwar organization he stated that, although the United States might contribute naval and air power to an international police force, he did not foresee United States land armies serving in Europe. After making the great decision to proceed with Overlord, the conference moved toward a more relaxed and congenial conclusion, and during this period Stalin declared that without American production Soviet Russia would have lost the war.[45]

The apparent Allied solidarity achieved at Teheran affected the renewed discussions in Cairo. Partly to placate Churchill for his uncomfortable position at Teheran, Roosevelt discarded the proposed amphibious operation in Burma and agreed to diversion of a few landing craft to the eastern Mediterranean provided Churchill could persuade Turkey to enter the war, an objective which he failed to accomplish. After Cairo, China declined in importance as an ally of the Western Powers.[46]

[43] Cline, *Washington Command Post,* p. 227.

[44] Churchill, *The Second World War,* V, 382–383.

[45] Sherwood, *Roosevelt and Hopkins,* pp. 777–799.

[46] *Ibid.,* pp. 799–802; McNeill, *America, Britain, and Russia,* pp. 370–371; Romanus and Sunderland, *Stilwell's Command Problems,* pp. 70–71; Maurice

At Teheran, since the Big Three had a common military objective in Europe, the defeat of Germany, they were able to decide on military strategy, and it was a strategy which ultimately brought victory. On matters of postwar concern, however, since motives were different and since the time was not yet imminent, Churchill, Roosevelt, and Stalin discussed matters, and exchanged ideas, sometimes frankly and sometimes not, but reached no agreement on important matters of policy.

The Teheran and Cairo conferences were the last top-level wartime meetings in which the primary question was military planning for winning the war.[47] The grand strategy was firmly set, a great pincers movement of the Russian armies in the East and Allied invasion of France in the West. The Combined Chiefs of Staff, of course, continued scrutiny of war planning and operation, and Churchill did not abandon hope for Mediterranean operations. The Prime Minister saw Soviet Russia emerging as a dominant world power and he sought to recover some of Britain's former position in the Mediterranean. Growing American military strength, however, gave United States leaders power to insist on adherence to the original concept of defeating Germany first and also on the principle of a decisive military war. To that end General Marshall had fought the decision to invade North Africa and when he lost, had struggled to link all activities in North Africa and the Mediterranean to the invasion of Western Europe. The withdrawal in 1943 of seven divisions from the Mediterranean to England was in line with this view, and the conflict between the British and Americans over invasion of southern France resulted in another victory for the principle of a decisive military war.

The United States military staff feared that a peripheral war against Germany would be more costly in time and manpower than would be a direct thrust against Germany and that it would disturb the balance which so far the nation had been maintaining between war production and a high standard of living.

Churchill was interested in the political implications of the war and was alarmed at American insistence on fighting purely a military war. The United States military staff knew what some of the political consequences of the war might be. In July, 1944, it informed the Secretary of State that a defeat for Germany would "leave Russia in a position

---

Matloff, *Strategic Planning for Coalition Warfare, 1943–1944* (*United States Army in World War II: The War Department*) (Washington, 1959), p. 373.

[47] Cline, *Washington Command Post,* pp. 231–232.

of assured military dominance in Eastern Europe and in the Middle East." The same memorandum noted that, although Britain and the United States would control Western Europe, their strength in the area would decline as troops were withdrawn for the Pacific war or for demobilization. It further predicted that "whether or not she enters the war" Russia would gain a "dominant position" in the Far East upon the fall of Japan. Looking ahead, the report visualized the United States and Russia as "the only military powers of the first magnitude." Obviously unaware of the atomic bomb, the staff then predicted that "the relative strength and geographical positions of these two powers preclude the military defeat of one of these powers by the other, even if that power were united with the British Empire."[48]

Seeing signs of growing and increasingly serious differences between Britain and Soviet Russia and fearing that these differences might hurt the war's progress, the United States staff proposed that territorial settlements be postponed until after the military war had been won. By this time the British-American coalition had developed an efficient war machine. The American view prevailed, and this war machine concerned itself with winning the war and let political leaders deal with questions relating to political and territorial settlement.

The war in the Pacific was seen as primarily an American problem, and direction of military operations came for the most part under the American Joint Chiefs of Staff rather than the Anglo-American Combined Chiefs of Staff, although the British and Chinese were largely responsible for advances on the Asian Continent.[49]

On his return from Teheran President Roosevelt contracted a respiratory ailment which kept him from paying full attention to his duties until May, 1944. Hopkins, seldom well, became ill during the Teheran Conference and partly for reasons of ill health ceased to be an influence with the President for a number of months.[50] Secretary Hull, in his seventies, became ill in October and delayed resignation only because of the coming election. In this election Roosevelt sought an unprecedented fourth term. The war did not become an issue in the campaign, but neither could the administration forget that there was an election coming. Roosevelt, for example, moved with extreme caution on the Polish question in order not to offend persons of Polish

[48] Quoted in Matloff, *Strategic Planning,* pp. 523–524. Matloff analyzes carefully shifting power in the coalition. *Ibid.,* pp. 521–524.

[49] Matloff and Snell, *Strategic Planning,* pp. 166–167.

[50] Sherwood, *Roosevelt and Hopkins,* p. 804.

background in the United States.[51] Cordell Hull spent much time, not on foreign affairs, but on efforts to remove the war as an issue in the campaign. Some persons feel that Harry Hopkins' temporary eclipse from friendship with Roosevelt came from the President's view that such friendship was a political liability during an election year.[52]

The United States, for the reasons just indicated, tended to remain aloof from the maneuvering of its allies regarding a number of specific European issues. Dissatisfied with developments in Italy, Churchill in February, 1944, suggested a meeting with Roosevelt, but the latter, ill and uninterested in changing agreements already made, declined the invitation.[53] Later Roosevelt failed to support Churchill on the Polish question, and matters became more strained over the government of France. Anglo-American relations then improved with Roosevelt's health in the spring of 1944, and in April the President sent his new Under Secretary of State, Edward Stettinius, to London for a consideration of political and economic problems. The British and Americans came to no agreement, but at least the situation was eased.[54]

The Russian Army's rapid drive across the Ukraine into Rumania aroused Churchill's fears, despite statements of the Soviet leaders that they did not intend to retain permanent possession of Rumania. He negotiated a British-Russian deal in which Soviet Russia would dominate Rumania and Bulgaria and Britain would have paramount interests in Yugoslavia and Greece. The Prime Minister did not notify Roosevelt of his actions until they were completed, and the President responded by recommending a consultative committee for Balkan affairs instead of the projected spheres of influence. Churchill rejected this relegation of matters to a board in favor of continued personal diplomacy at the top level and he suggested that the Anglo-Russian deal might be given a three months' trial. Roosevelt assented, but

[51] Roosevelt was informed of Allied discussions on the Polish question but remained aloof. On October 22, 1944, he sent a message to Churchill stating, "I am delighted to learn of your success at Moscow in making progress toward a compromise solution of the Polish problem.

"When and if a solution is arrived at, I should like to be consulted as to the advisability from this point of view of delaying its publication for about two weeks. You will understand.

"Everything is going well here at the present time." *Foreign Relations of the United States: Diplomatic Papers: The Conferences at Malta and Yalta 1945* (84th Cong., 1st Sess., House Document 154) (Washington, 1955), p. 207.

[52] Sherwood, *Roosevelt and Hopkins,* p. 814.

[53] McNeill, *America, Britain, and Russia,* p. 416.

[54] *Ibid.,* p. 421; Hull, *Memoirs,* II, 1428–1431.

knowing Hull's aversion to spheres of influence neglected to inform his Secretary of his action.[55] When Hull discovered the spheres of influence deal, he protested to the British, only to find that his chief had already given his approval.[56] Meanwhile, the United States and Britain differed on Italian and French developments. In the case of Italy, American pressure to recognize the new Bonomi government succeeded,[57] but the United States found itself forced reluctantly to acquiesce in de Gaulle's assumption of authority in France.[58]

[55] McNeill, *America, Britain, and Russia,* pp. 421–423.
[56] Hull, *Memoirs,* II, 1455–1456.
[57] *Ibid.,* II, 1568–1569.
[58] *Ibid.,* II, 1435.

CHAPTER 15

The Home Front

THE United States went into World War II with a Democratic President and a Democratic Congress. The attack on Pearl Harbor obliterated party lines for the moment, but differences soon arose over the manner in which the war should be run. Politics did not adjourn, elections were held, and each party sought, not necessarily to gain by the war, but at least not to lose by it. The Democrats had the advantage of leadership, which they could not exercise for partisan purposes, and the handicap of being unable to take credit for winning the war but being assured discredit for mistakes. The Republicans had to overcome their isolationist record, yet they had the potential advantage of profiting from Democratic errors in a postwar reaction.[1]

During World War II, the executive branch of the government expanded its power at the expense of the legislative and judicial branches through a delegation of authority which was not necessarily automatic and which excited sharp criticism. Some months before the attack on Pearl Harbor, Republican Senator Arthur H. Vandenburg of Michigan introduced a resolution to create a "joint congressional committee on the conduct of national defense." Defeating the resolution, the Democratic majority made it clear that it planned to leave defense administration and military control in the hands of the President. Senator Tom Connally of Texas said, "I am not in favor of Congress undertaking to put on shoulder straps, epaulets, and big hats, and

[1] Roland Young, *Congressional Politics in the Second World War* (New York, 1956), pp. 11–16.

saying, 'We are going to run the Army: we are going to run the war.' "[2] Senator Henry Ashurst of Arizona drew attention to the Congressional committee which had hampered the Union forces in the Civil War. After entry into the war, Congress rejected another resolution for a joint committee to advise the President on war matters. However, although it failed to create a special committee for the purpose, Congress through many committees did participate extensively in the war. In addition to such standing committees as the House and Senate Committees on military affairs and on naval affairs, there were numerous special investigative committees.

Among the most important was the Special Committee to Investigate the National Defense Program, headed by Senator Harry S. Truman of Missouri. This Truman Committee, with wide investigatory powers, was created to check extravagances in the huge defense spending and to guard against permanent changes in the American business system.[3] An investigative body with no supervisory power, the committee strove effectively to avoid partisanship by concerning itself with fact-finding, not "witch-hunting" on the strength of hearsay, restricted its probes to logistical matters, and did not interfere with military strategy or tactics. It gained a reputation for integrity and hard work and was on the alert against illegal action or misuse of power by either the armed forces or business. It supported civilian rather than military control of war production and backed legislation leading to the creation of the powerful Office of War Mobilization and Reconversion. As the war drew to a close, the committee advocated limited rather than drastic cutbacks in war production to facilitate the economic shift from war to peace.[4] The spotlight the committee turned on lack of coordination in economic matters among the armed services may have contributed to the postwar move toward unification of the armed forces. One of the activities which the committee scrutinized carefully was the so-called Canol Project, designed to exploit the oil reserves

[2] *Congressional Record,* 76th Cong., 3d Sess., LXXXVI, Part 6, 6591, quoted in Louis Smith, *American Democracy and Military Power: A Study of Civil Control of the Military Power in the United States* (Chicago, 1951), p. 212.

[3] *Congressional Record,* 77th Cong., 1st Sess., LXXXVII, Part 2, 1615 (Mar. 1, 1941).

[4] Smith, *American Democracy and Military Power,* pp. 212–226; Eliot Janeway, *The Struggle for Survival: A Chronicle of Economic Mobilization in World War II* (New Haven, 1951), pp. 307–310; Donald M. Nelson, *Arsenal of Democracy: The Story of American War Production* (New York, 1946), p. 412.

in the Yukon Territory and build a pipeline to supply forces in Alaska. Investigation showed the venture to have been ill-advised; it cost $200 million instead of the anticipated $25 million and after the war went to a Canadian oil company for $2 million.[5]

As its prestige increased, the Truman Committee became more than merely a recommending, investigative body and in effect acted to regulate administrative agencies and departments. As the most important legislative committee dealing with the war, the Truman Committee was significant in the recovery of some of the tremendous power which Congress had delegated to the executive. Although the committee prided itself on its nonpartisanship, it enhanced the prestige of its chairman and paved the way for his accession to the presidency. The Truman Committee represented only one facet of Congressional interest in the war.[6] Other special committees investigated such matters as small business and gasoline and fuel-oil shortages.

On the outbreak of war Congress rushed through the first War Powers Act, which extended to President Roosevelt the same powers that the Overman Act had given President Wilson in World War I. Then, more prudently, it passed a second War Powers Act, a much more detailed piece of legislation which included such miscellaneous items as increased penalties for priorities violations and a grant of free postage for military personnel. Using his delegated powers, the President through his regular departments and newly constituted agencies began to take charge of war administration, but always under the jealous eyes of Congress.

Financing of World War II in the United States was similar to that of World War I, but was much more extensive and complicated. About one-fourth of the nation's annual production went toward the costs of the first conflict, about half toward World War II. The government imposed taxes to raise roughly 46 percent of the war costs and resorted to borrowing for the remainder.[7] From July 1, 1940, to June 30, 1946, the Federal Government spent $389 billion; of these

[5] Smith, *American Democracy and Military Power,* pp. 218–223. For a different version, see John D. Millett, *The Organization and Role of the Army Service Forces* (*United States Army in World War II: The Army Service Forces* (Washington, 1954), pp. 391–394.

[6] Young, *Congressional Politics,* pp. 20–22.

[7] A convenient summary of World War II financing in the United States is in Paul Studenski and Herman E. Kroos, *Financial History of the United States* (New York, 1952), pp. 436–458.

$360 billion went for defense and war. In 1945 alone the United States spent $100 billion, or more than ten times prewar annual expenditures.

During the war, the administration asked for increased taxes, but in the three revenue measures passed Congress responded only in part to the requests. The tax measure of October 12, 1942 reduced personal income exemptions, this time to $1,200 and $500, and increased a variety of tax rates. This act reflected a controversy over a plan to revise the method of income tax collection proposed by Beardsley Ruml, treasurer of R. H. Macy and Company and chairman of the Federal Reserve Board of New York. Under the existing method many workers would not pay for their 1943 earnings until 1944. Since earnings would be higher in 1943 than in 1942, Ruml suggested canceling the tax on 1942 earnings and placing everyone on a pay-as-you-go basis for 1943. Returns would be greater, administration simpler, and inflation checked by this curb on free spending. On the other hand, by canceling the 1942 taxes, the government, theoretically at least, would be losing a long-time tax benefit, but arguments on this point soon became mathematically complicated, although one could easily see that individuals who had already saved their 1942 income taxes would profit from the Ruml Plan. Congress took up the debate and emerged with a compromise bill which canceled three-fourths of the 1942 taxes and all remaining amounts under fifty dollars, and taxpayers had two years to pay the remaining fourth of the 1942 tax. Ingenious as the plan may have been for increasing current revenues, it did not alter the tax rates nor did it produce additional revenue.[8]

Exhausted by the debate over the Ruml Plan, Congress was in no mood to levy additional taxes, but the need forced action. Accordingly in 1944, it passed a bill designed to raise far less money than the Treasury Department had requested. The President had opposed the bill and rejected it in a veto message so strongly worded that Senator Alben W. Barkley responded violently and resigned as Majority Leader of the Senate.[9] The President attempted to placate Barkley in a "Dear Alben" letter;[10] the Senate, however, re-elected Barkley to his post, and Congress with considerable haste then overrode the presidential veto. Congress did not attempt again during the war to raise taxes; its tax law of 1945 was designed to rebate taxes to aid in the postwar

[8] Young, *Congressional Politics,* pp. 130–136.

[9] Franklin D. Roosevelt, *The Public Papers and Addresses of Franklin D. Roosevelt* (New York, 1950), XIII, 80–83.

[10] *Ibid.,* XIII, 85–86.

recovery. A summary of war financing shows that between 1941 and 1946 the government collected $155.8 billion in taxes. The sharp increase is indicated by the rise in the annual tax return of $76 billion in 1945. As in World War I, World War II had stimulated direct taxation. Individual and corporate income taxes, which had provided 30 percent of the tax return during the Great Depression and 40 percent later in the 1930's, rose to a peak of 76 percent in 1944 and provided 70 percent in 1946.

Extensive governmental borrowings during the same period increased the gross national debt from $43 billion on June 30, 1940, to $269.4 billion on June 30, 1946. The per capita debt of about $2,000 contrasted sharply with that of $240 in 1919 and $75 in 1865. By providing various types of bonds, the government secured about 40 percent of the funds which individuals had available for investment. For the general public, the government conducted seven war loan and one victory loan drives, the largest such ventures in history, which sold a total of $156.9 billion of war bonds to an estimated 85 million investors. War financing increased the supply of money in circulation from $9.6 billion in 1941 to $28.2 billion in 1946. War also decentralized the structure of American banking, as banks both large and small grew throughout the country.

One of the most remarkable financial phases of the war centered about atomic research and production. Appropriations for the Manhattan Project first appeared unspecified under the guise of engineering or other listings. When General Marshall was asked by the House Committee on Appropriations to explain the great discrepancy between the huge requests and the designated use of the funds, he at first declined to comply and finally stated that both the United States and Germany were working on experiments and that if Germany solved them first she would win the war. On the basis of this meager explanation, the House subcommittee approved the addition of funds hidden in subsequent appropriations bills. When the sum reached $2 billion, however, the subcommittee balked and refused to proceed without further clarification. Secretary Stimson and Dr. Vannevar Bush then informed several key Senators and Congressmen of the nature of the project. These men assumed responsibility for securing appropriations from Congress without compromising the security of the program. Senator Truman's committee became interested in vanishing funds and unusual war plants, but when informed by Secretary Stimson that the project was top secret and of the utmost importance the chairman kept his committee from investigating the plants concerned.[11] The result was undoubtedly one of the best-kept major secrets of the war.

Another difficult problem confronting Congress was that of manpower. It had passed the Selective Service Act in 1940, but what was the extent of governmental control over the civilian who was not drafted? Congress resisted pressure to change the forty-hour week; however, continued strikes and the altered character of Congress after the 1942 elections led to enactment over a presidential veto in 1943 of the Smith-Connally Act, which authorized the government to seize strike-bound plants and supervise prestrike plebiscites to reduce strikes.[12] A curious development from this act came in the case of Montgomery Ward and Company, which the government seized not because of a strike but because of refusal of company officials to obey a War Labor Board order.[13]

Within a year after entrance into the war, the Army told Congress that it needed more men. Congress chose to lower the draft age to eighteen rather than call up young fathers and enacted the necessary legislation in October, 1942. There was considerable pressure for a year's training of such recruits before assignment to combat duty. Congress heeded the protests of military leaders against having their authority restricted in this way, but late in the war, after many young soldiers had lost their lives in the Battle of the Bulge, Congress imposed such a rule.

A long struggle developed over farm labor, and in September, 1943, Congress amended the Selective Service Act in such a way that two million farm workers were deferred. Later Congress approved the drafting of fathers, but gave them a low priority. Throughout the war there was agitation for national legislation which would enable the government to tell men where they should work. Secretary Stimson ad-

[11] Young, *Congressional Politics,* pp. 44–47; Henry L. Stimson and McGeorge Bundy, *On Active Service in Peace and War* (New York, 1948), pp. 614–615; Harry S. Truman, *Memoirs by Harry S. Truman* (New York, 1955), I, 10–11.

[12] After some 400,000 miners had gone on strike by May 1, 1943, President Roosevelt ordered the Secretary of the Interior to take over and operate the mines. The strikers did not return to work until June 23, after receiving instructions from union officials. Private operation of the mines was resumed October 12, 1943. Young, *Congressional Politics,* p. 63.

[13] The case became a national sensation when news photographs showed the head of the company, Mr. Sewall Avery, being literally carried from his office by two soldiers.

vocated such legislation, and President Roosevelt made mild overtures toward it, which Congress failed to support.[14]

During the American Civil War, some of the states had provided for "voting in the field" by citizens in uniform,[15] and there had been a similar practice in World War I. The occurrence of a Congressional and a Presidential election during World War II gave special significance to the question of military voting privileges and prompted national legislation. Over strong Southern opposition to an amendment waiving the poll tax, Congress passed a soldier voting law so late in 1942 that only 28,000 soldiers took advantage of its provisions to vote in the elections of that year. The argument settled down to one of state or federal ballots. The bill which emerged from a joint Congressional committee was a victory for the states' rights cause and made possible only limited use of a federal ballot. In the 1944 election, service personnel cast over four million state absentee ballots and only 111,773 federal ballots.[16]

Inflation accompanied each of America's principal wars. During the War of 1812, wholesale prices rose more than 40 percent; during the Civil War they advanced 120 percent and during and shortly after World War I they soared to about 170 percent of the prewar figures.[17] In World War II, wholesale prices advanced 115 percent and cost-of-living items went up 76 percent. In July, 1941, the President asked Congress for authority to impose price ceilings, but Congress, willing to see some advance in prices, was slow to act. In January, 1942, however, it passed an act providing for a general price freeze by the Office of Price Administration. There were restrictions on freezing farm prices and, despite provisions of the act, prices continued to rise until Congress provided a plan which froze the price of consumer commodities essentially at the figures for March, 1942, and which also extended the range of rent controls.[18]

Farm prices continued to rise, but Congress hesitated to act since

[14] In his annual message to Congress, January 11, 1944, Roosevelt recommended that Congress adopt "a national service law—which, for the duration of the war, will prevent strikes, and, with certain appropriate exceptions, will make available for war production or for any other essential services every able-bodied adult in this nation." Roosevelt, *Public Papers,* XIII, 37.

[15] Josiah Henry Benton, *Voting in the Field: A Forgotten Chapter of the Civil War* (Boston, 1915), *passim.*

[16] Young, *Congressional Politics,* pp. 82–89.

[17] Lester V. Chandler, *Inflation in the United States* (New York, 1951), p. 1.

[18] Young, *Congressional Politics,* pp. 90–93.

the costs of farm labor were also advancing. In the fall of 1942, a disgruntled Congress under very strong pressure from the White House passed an act to lower the ceiling on farm prices.[19] Acting on the order, President Roosevelt created a new Office of Economic Stabilization, headed by James F. Byrnes, who resigned from the Supreme Court to take this first of many administrative assignments. The President also prohibited salaries in excess of $25,000 a year.[20]

During the next year relations between Congress and the administration became increasingly strained. The war was not an issue in the 1942 Congressional election, but the government's management of the war was. The result of relatively light voting was marked gains for the Republicans but not victory; they secured 208 seats in the House to 218 for the Democrats, and 38 Senators to 57 Democrats and one Independent. There were enough Republicans to join with conservative Southern Democrats to jettison a number of New Deal agencies, including the Works Progress Administration, the Civilian Conservation Corps, and the National Youth Authority. Congress blocked presidential nominations, especially that of Edward J. Flynn, chairman of the Democratic National Committee and a New York political boss, as Minister to Australia.[21] This Congress showed its recalcitrance in other ways; it refused the President's request for a third War Powers Act, it repealed the $25,000 limit on annual salaries, and only reluctantly adopted national gas rationing. It carried on intermittent war against the Office of Price Administration and in effect forced the resignation of its head, Leon Henderson, whose successor, former Senator Prentice M. Brown, found his duties carefully scrutinized by the "Special Committee to Investigate Acts of Executive Agencies Beyond the Scope of Their Authority," headed by hostile Democratic Representative Howard W. Smith of Virginia.[22]

Confronted by a continued rise in prices, the administration initiated a subsidy program without specific authorization from Congress and which provided funds for the purchase of certain commodities and

[19] Roosevelt, *Public Papers,* XI, 364.

[20] Executive Order No. 9250, Oct. 3, 1942, in Roosevelt, *Public Papers,* XI, 396–404; James F. Byrnes, *Speaking Frankly* (New York, 1947), pp. 17–19.

[21] See letter, Roosevelt to Flynn, Feb. 1, 1943, accepting the latter's request that his name be withdrawn. Flynn later accompanied the President to Yalta and went on missions for him to Rome and to Moscow. Franklin D. Roosevelt, *F.D.R., His Personal Letters,* ed. by Elliot Roosevelt (New York, 1950), II, 1395.

[22] Young, *Congressional Politics,* pp. 91–103, 107–108.

their resale at less than the purchase price in order to prevent the rise of consumer prices. Congress at first opposed this procedure but reversed itself mainly since farmer groups came to support it. Relations with the Office of Price Administration also improved when Chester Bowles, a well-known and highly regarded New York advertising man, became its head.[23]

Although Congress did not participate in military planning, it was actively concerned with preparations for the postwar world. That interest is related elsewhere, but a summary of Congressional participation may be in order here. The Senate was jealous of its rights in the treaty-making process, and much of the debate over Lend-Lease was inspired by fear that the President might make important international commitments without senatorial approval. Senatorial sensibilities were irritated by the State Department's decision to prepare the UNRRA Agreement as an executive agreement rather than as a treaty, and as a result of protests a joint resolution was passed giving the new organization requisite funds and Congressional approval.[24]

During the war, the administration invited members of both parties in Congress to participate in postwar planning conferences. In March, 1943, four Senators, Joseph H. Ball, Republican from Minnesota, Harold R. Burton, Republican from Ohio, Lester Hill, Democrat from Alabama, and Carl A. Hatch, Democrat from New Mexico, introduced a resolution urging the United States to take the lead in creating a United Nations organization. The following June, the House passed a similar resolution, sponsored by J. William Fulbright, Democrat from Arkansas. After Secretary Hull's return from the Moscow Ministers' Conference, the Senate by-passed its earlier resolution in favor of one introduced by Senator Tom Connally of Texas that the United States "acting through its constitutional processes," including Senate approval of any treaty, should join the free and sovereign nations of the world after the victorious conclusion of the war "in the establishment and maintenance of international authority with power to prevent aggression and preserve the peace of the world."[25] In January, 1945, internationalism gained a significant advocate when former iso-

[23] *Ibid.*, pp. 109–122.

[24] Arthur H. Vandenberg, *The Private Papers of Senator Vandenberg,* ed. by Arthur H. Vandenberg, Jr. (Boston, 1952), pp. 66–74; Ruth Russell, *A History of the United Nations Charter* (Washington, 1958), pp. 70–71.

[25] The Fulbright-Connally resolutions are in Henry Steele Commager (ed.), *Documents of American History* (New York, 1949) (5th ed.), Doc. No. 555.

lationist Senator Arthur H. Vandenberg of Michigan publicly announced his conversion and joined Senator Connally to become conspicuous champions of bipartisanship in the Senate and at the San Francisco meeting of the United Nations. Finally, the Senate, on July 28, 1945, by an overwhelming vote endorsed the United Nations Charter. Congress also gave thought to the problems of postwar readjustment within the nation, not only in standing committees but in two special committees as well.[26] In 1944, Congress passed a Contract Settlement Act and a Surplus Property Act and in the same year created the Office of War Mobilization and Reconversion to administer these acts.

An important related problem was the future of the men and women in uniform. Congress first moved by authorizing mustering-out pay, varying from $100 for those serving in the United States to $300 for those who had seen duty outside continental United States and Alaska. Debate was more protracted on bills to provide subsidies to veterans for further education or unemployment relief. Pressured by veterans' groups and not unaware that veterans were also voters, Congress unanimously passed the Rankin-Barden bill, which became law June 22, 1944.[27] This measure provided unemployment compensation for fifty-two weeks at twenty dollars weekly, guaranteed 50 percent of loans not in excess of $2,000 for veterans' homes or businesses, and appropriated $500 million for hospitals and to help the United States Unemployment Service find work for veterans. A popular feature of the act was the provision giving veterans attending college $500 annually for tuition and books and providing monthy subsistence funds of $50 for single veterans and $75 for those who were married. This so-called "G.I. Bill of Rights" resulted in the largest entry of the federal government into education since the Morrill Land Grant Act of 1862 and was one of the most significant acts of the war for it made possible intelligent readjustment from war to peace by millions of young men and women who might otherwise have found frustrating bars to employment and further education. By 1951 some eight million veterans had received aid under the terms of the act. Of

[26] The committees were the George Committee, whose chairman was Senator Walter F. George of Georgia, and the Colmer Committee, headed by Democratic Representative William M. Colmer of Mississippi.

[27] Significant extracts from the "G.I. Bill of Rights" are in E. W. Knight and C. L. Hall, *Readings in American Educational History* (New York, 1951), pp. 609–612.

these, 2,350,000 had received college training, 3,430,000 had attended other schools, and 2,390,000 had taken on-the-job training.[28] So successful was the venture that in 1952 Congress passed a somewhat revised "G.I. Bill" for veterans of the Korean fighting.

To summarize legislative activity during World War II, one may say that Congress delegated wide authority to the President and the administrative agencies, new and old, of the government. It regained some of this authority by exercising control through appropriations, legislation on policies, and supervision through standing and special committees. Furthermore, it granted powers only for the war and afterward regained a good deal of its authority. Nevertheless, in the main the executive branch gained in strength at the expense of the legislative and retained much of that power in the postwar period.

The war years also witnessed a diminution in the strength of the judicial branch of the government, primarily through court decisions acquiescing in executive leadership. Early in the war, in the case of *United States* v. *Pink,* recognizing certain Russian decrees as binding on property located in New York, the Supreme Court's decision raised an executive agreement to the status of a treaty and increased the President's power to by-pass the Senate in making international agreements.[29]

On June 27, 1942, a German submarine landed four saboteurs on the shores of Long Island, and four nights later another submarine deposited four more on the Florida coast. The Coast Guard and Federal Bureau of Investigation were alert and soon had the eight men in custody. President Roosevelt immediately appointed a military commission of seven Army generals to try the men and, in addition, issued a proclamation closing the courts of the United States to enemy aliens who entered this country to commit sabotage. An attempt was made to obtain civil trials by resurrecting *Ex parte* v. *Mulligan,* a post-Civil War case which questioned the validity of military trial of persons far removed from the field of battle.[30] The Supreme Court considered the matter sufficiently important to cancel its summer recess and reconvene. Its decision upheld the jurisdiction of the military commission, and within a few days six of the men were executed, a seventh received life imprisonment, and the eighth, who had not appealed, began a

[28] R. Freeman Butts and Lawrence A. Cremin, *A History of Education in American Culture* (New York, 1953), p. 582.

[29] United States *v.* Pink, 315 U.S. 203 (1942).

[30] Ex parte Mulligan, 4 Wallace 2, 109 (1886).

thirty-year term. The practical result of the case was that the Supreme Court had signified its approval of military tribunals during the war.[31]

Inevitably, restrictions upon American citizens of Japanese parentage came to the attention of the Supreme Court. The first case involved Gordon Kiyoshi Hirabayashi, an American citizen who had violated the curfew set by General De Witt on the West Coast. The court upheld De Witt's action in setting a curfew, but such was the concern over the implications that there were three concurrent opinions. Chief Justice Stone, who wrote the majority opinion, noted that "in time of war residents having ethnic affiliations with an invading enemy may be a greater source of danger than those of a different ancestry." The principal issue was the war power of those charged with the nation's defense, and stating specifically that the Court was not attempting "to define the ultimate boundaries of the war power," Stone pronounced the Court's opinion "only that the curfew order as applied and at the time it was applied, was within the boundaries of the war power."[32] There was much less agreement on the Court in the *Korematsu* case, when it assented to the relocation order which removed Japanese and Americans of Japanese parentage from the West Coast to relocation centers.[33] Justice Frank Murphy denounced the removal as "one of the most sweeping and complete deprivations of constitutional rights in the history of this nation in the absence of martial law." The crux of the problem confronting the Court was to determine the dividing line between the constitutional rights of the citizen and the nation's power to defend itself. Early in the war the

[31] A. T. Mason, *Harlan Fiske Stone: Pillar of the Law* (New York, 1956), pp. 653–666; Smith, *American Democracy and Military Power,* pp. 270–271.

[32] Hirabayashi *v.* United States, 320 U.S. 81 (1943), reprinted in Commager, *Documents of American History,* Doc. No. 549. A West Coast district court (Ninth Circuit) declared that another American of Japanese ancestry had renounced his U.S. citizenship by violating the curfew. Although holding this to be a parallel violation of the curfew to the Hirabayashi case, the Supreme Court stated that the "appellant's citizenship was not relevant to the issue." Yasui *v.* United States, 320 U.S. 115 (1942). For critical views of the Hirabayashi case, see Jacobus ten Broek, *Japanese American Evacuation and Resettlement: Prejudice, War and the Constitution* (Berkeley and Los Angeles, 1954), pp. 211–233; Morton Grodzins, *Americans Betrayed: Politics and the Japanese Evacuation* (Chicago, 1949), pp. 351–358.

[33] Korematsu *v.* United States, 323 U.S. 214 (1944). See also Bernard Schwartz, *The Supreme Court: Constitutional Revolution in Retrospect* (New York, 1957), pp. 291–292; Carl B. Swisher, *American Constitutional Development* (Boston, 1943) (2nd ed.), p. 1009; Edward S. Corwin, *Total War and the Constitution* (New York, 1947), pp. 97–98.

Court showed more concern for the nation's defense; later, as in the case of *Ex parte Endo,* it drew the line somewhat more in favor of individual rights.[34] In this case, although it did not consider the constitutionality of the legislation and executive orders underlying the relocation program, it made a strict interpretation of them and decided that since they did not specifically mention detention, Miss Mitsuye Endo, a loyal citizen, should be released from the relocation center in which she had been detained.

The relocation program on the West Coast was the most widespread disregard of personal rights in the nation's history since the abolition of slavery. It was based on the military's authority to wage war and its insistence that the evacuation was necessary for the defense of the West Coast, although after the initial round-up of suspected subversives the removal of Japanese and Americans of Japanese ancestry was hardly a military necessity. The Washington government approved the action, and the actual removal was administered by a civilian agency. The Court gave sanction to the military error in the belief that in wartime the military should have requisite authority to wage war. At the same time it set a dangerous precedent for further abridgment of personal rights. As the war progressed and as danger to the nation receded, the Court attempted, as in the case of *Ex parte Endo,* to resuscitate some of the rights of the individual. The Court moved slowly; Miss Endo remained in a relocation center for over two years before the Court found that she should not be detained.[35] Similarly, the Court delayed in reaching a decision on martial law in Hawaii, which had been instituted shortly after the attack on Pearl Harbor. Two persons convicted by military tribunals sought redress in the civilian courts. It was not until February, 1946, after the end of the war, that the Supreme Court decided that martial law, although intended to help the military defend the islands, "was not intended to authorize the supplanting of courts by military tribunals."[36]

The question of civil rights arose in other connections, and since the nation's defense was not so closely related, the courts leaned more heavily toward personal liberties. George Sylvester Viereck, a Nazi propagandist, was brought to trial for concealing information while registered as a foreign agent. He had registered and listed the ac-

[34] Ex parte Endo, 323 U.S. 283 (1944).
[35] Schwartz, *The Supreme Court,* pp. 292–293.
[36] Duncan *v.* Kahanamoku, 327 U.S. 304 (1945).

tivities for which he had received pay as a German agent, but it was charged that he had failed to disclose certain private ventures, and his conviction would stand only if it were proved that his propagandist activities had been made criminal by the registration statute. The Court not only freed Viereck but criticized the highly emotional tone of the prosecution.[37] Criticism of the opinion was sharp, but many considered it a courageous support of civil rights in difficult times.[38] In the case of *Schneiderman* v. *United States,* the Court held that mere membership in the Communist party did not warrant depriving Schneiderman of his citizenship, although three justices, including Stone, bitterly dissented.[39] The Court also set aside denaturalization of a German-American citizen charged with continued allegiance to the German government.[40]

The Court strongly supported free speech in wartime. It refused in a five-to-four decision to halt propaganda to obstruct the draft and stimulate disloyalty among the armed forces and held that unless such action could be found to violate specifically the Espionage Act of 1917 it should not be outlawed.[41] In another five-to-four decision, the Court threw out the government's prosecution of twenty-five German-American Bund leaders on the ground that by counseling refusal to do military service the Bund was simply awaiting the verdict of a test case on the matter.[42] The Court also found that treason was not proved against Anthony Cramer, who had associated with one of the German saboteurs, since two witnesses to the overt act of treason had not been found.[43] Another case, *Yakus* v. *United States,* involved a certain curtailment of the right of judicial review.[44] Presumably in an effort not to impede the administration in wartime, the Supreme Court upheld the law in question.

According to the Selective Service Act of 1940 a person who, "by reason of religious training and belief, is conscientiously opposed to participation in war in any form" in place of induction could be "assigned to work of national importance under civilian direction."[45] A

[37] Viereck *v.* United States, 318 U.S. 236 (1942).
[38] Mason, *Harlan Fiske Stone,* pp. 683–685.
[39] Schneiderman *v.* United States, 320 U.S. 118 (1943).
[40] Baumgartner *v.* United States, 322 U.S. 665 (1943).
[41] Hartzel *v.* United States, 322 U.S. 680 (1943).
[42] Keegan *v.* United States, 325 U.S. 478 (1944).
[43] Cramer *v.* United States, 325 U.S. 1 (1944).
[44] Yakus *v.* United States, 321 U.S. 414 (1943).
[45] *Selective Training and Service Act of 1940,* Section 5 (g) (Pub. L. No.

person who objected only to combatant service was classified I-A-O; if he objected to both combatant and noncombatant service, his classification was IV-E. Local draft boards made these as they did other classifications, and anyone, including conscientious objectors, who disregarded the instructions of the draft board was subject to arrest and imprisonment. The largest number of conscientious objectors who went to prison were Jehovah's Witnesses, who normally requested exemption from military service not as conscientious objectors, I-A-O or IV-E, but as ministers (IV-D), claiming that they were all ministers. When their claims were denied, since most had other employment in addition to their religious work, they refused to comply with regulations imposed on them and went to prison.[46] As a result three times as many conscientious objectors were imprisoned in World War II as in World War I.

Statistically speaking, the conscientious objectors were a small part of the whole; the top estimate of 100,000 comprised only a third of one percent of the 34,000,000 registrants under the Selective Service Act.[47] But involved were matters of the human spirit, and the conscientious objector focused attention on the limits of individual freedom in a democracy at war.

Among several major types of conscientious objectors were the Mennonites, who adhered to the Biblical injunction against violence. Law-abiding, they did not believe in nonresistance as a technique of political pressure. Generally they did not object to civilian service in place of military duty, and they had a strong sense of service for the relief of mankind. Members of the Church of the Brethren also believed in nonviolence, but some felt that the Church might be used as a pressure group to influence legislation. The Friends, or Quakers, had a long record of opposition to war. Their belief in the "Inner Light" or spirit of God working on man through an informed mind and a sensitive conscience, made man's attitude toward war an individual matter; as a result some Quakers entered noncombatant service, others civilian service, and still others refused to comply with

---

783, 76th Cong., 2d Sess.), reprinted in appendix, Mulford Q. Sibley and Philip E. Jacob, *Conscription of Conscience: The American State and the Conscientious Objector, 1940–1947* (Ithaca, N.Y., 1952), p. 487.

[46] For a discussion of Jehovah's Witnesses and the courts, see Hollis W. Barber, "Religious Liberty v. Police Power Jehovah's Witnesses," *The American Political Science Review,* XLI (Apr., 1947), 226–247.

[47] Sibley and Jacob, *Conscription of Conscience,* p. 84.

any Selective Service regulations. Like the Mennonites, the Quakers were greatly interested in relief work. Outside the traditionally pacifist churches, opposition to war on religious grounds was largely a personal rather than a corporate matter. Individual members of a variety of Protestant churches and of the Roman Catholic Church were conscientious objectors.

Draft boards were usually less sympathetic toward those who were conscientious objectors on grounds other than religious. These persons were highly individualistic; the views of some stemmed from socialist doctrine, those of others from the ideas of Henry David Thoreau or of Mohandis K. Gandhi.[48]

Between 25,000 and 50,000 conscientious objectors served in the armed forces in noncombatant roles. The largest single group consisted of Seventh-day Adventists, whose doctrines opposed war but sanctioned noncombatant activities. At first noncombatants were in various branches of the service, and after January, 1943, they were limited to the Medical Corps. Life for most was routine, but a number distinguished themselves on the field of battle by saving, not taking, lives.

Having offered the conscientious objector an alternative to noncombatant duty, the government established camps somewhat on the model and often on the site of Civilian Conservation Corps camps, in which men would work on important but nonmilitary projects. Generally the administration of these camps was delegated to the pacifist churches, mainly the Brethren, Quaker, and Mennonite. During a six-year period some twelve thousand men worked without pay from either church or state, and many of the men paid for their own keep.

General Lewis E. Hershey, Director of Selective Service, described the Civilian Public Service Camps as an experiment "to find out whether our democracy is big enough to preserve minority rights in a time of national emergency."[49] The character of the participants militated strongly against success of the venture, for aside from the single tie of opposition to war service, the conscientious objectors included a heterogeneous assortment of individuals, from college professors to illiterates, from the intensely religious to the atheist, from the law-abiding to the extreme absolutist who refused to comply with any order. The result was discomfort and even injury to some of the con-

[48] For a summary of the different types of conscientious objectors, see *ibid.*, pp. 18–43.

[49] Quoted in *ibid.*, p. 123.

scientious objectors and utter frustration on the part of the authorities when confronted with someone like Corbett Bishop, who conducted fasts to prove his point. In prison he refused to eat, stand up, or dress himself, and finally was fed forcibly. During his imprisonment he fasted a total of 436 days, and finally, after a stretch of 193 days of continuous noncooperation, the authorities released him and made no further attempt to deal with him.

The question of conscientious objectors raised numerous legal problems. The courts upheld the constitutionality of compulsory registration and reaffirmed the Supreme Court's position of World War I that in wartime the government has powers of conscription. The Court did not define clearly "religious training and belief," which was the basis of conscientious objection. It denied the protection of either the First or the Fifth Amendment to conscientious objectors or that there was undue delegation of legislative power to the administrative agencies controlling the Civilian Public Service Camps. Court decisions placed the conscientious objector serving in these camps in a position midway between civilian and soldier; he could be under military control twenty-four hours a day, but if he disobeyed this control he would be tried in a civil rather than military court.[50]

There was no widespread hostility toward conscientious objectors, and Quakers and Mennonites, in particular, had won respect for their humanitarian efforts in war and peace. There were, of course, instances of hostility and of unsympathetic draft boards. The question of the rights of a conscientious objector arose in the Summers case, involving a conscientious objector who, although otherwise fit, was denied admission to the Illinois bar as "morally unfit."[51] Four members of the Supreme Court were convinced by the assertion that Summers' religious freedom was being infringed upon, but the majority upheld the state bar's action. In other cases schoolteachers who were conscientious objectors fared little better than lawyers in defending their right to hold their jobs and their views.[52]

[50] For a discussion of conscientious objectors and the courts, see *ibid.*, pp. 419–458. For cases involving the First Amendment, see Roodenko *et al. v.* U.S., 147 F. 2d 752 (1944); Kramer *et al. v.* U.S., 147 F. 2d 756 (1945). Cases arising from World War I had established that compulsory military service in wartime was not a violation of the Thirteenth Amendment.

[51] *In re Summers,* 325 U.S. 561 (1945).

[52] Sibley and Jacob, *Conscription of Conscience,* pp. 450–451.

Political activity increased during 1944 as the national elections approached. One of the three principal contenders for the Republican presidential nomination was Wendell Willkie, who had polled more than 22 million votes in 1940. An internationalist with considerable opposition within his party, Willkie made an early test of strength in the Wisconsin primaries. Despite an impassioned ten-day speaking tour of the state, he failed to gain a single delegate and ran last in a field of four. He promptly counted himself out of the presidential race, and on October 8, died of a heart attack. Willkie's contribution to his party had been to help it out of isolationism and to restore to it something of the spirit of progressivism and nationalism associated with Theodore Roosevelt.

As early as 1943, Senator Vandenberg of Michigan, General Robert E. Wood of Chicago, the newspaper publisher Frank Gannett, and others began a move to draft General Douglas MacArthur for the Republican nomination, mainly in the conviction that he could defeat Roosevelt. The Wisconsin primary hurt MacArthur badly; Thomas E. Dewey won seventeen delegates, Harold Stassen four, MacArthur three, and Willkie, as we have seen, none. The General had been remaining aloof, but his responses to letters from a strongly anti-New Deal Republican appeared to thrust him into the political controversy. Realizing that MacArthur had virtually eliminated himself as a draft candidate and aware of Dewey's growing strength, Vandenberg through a mutual friend persuaded MacArthur to withdraw his name from the presidential race.[53] This action cleared the road for Thomas E. Dewey, who had jumped into national prominence in 1942 by winning the governorship of New York, a feat which a Republican had failed to accomplish for more than two decades. He was nominated almost unanimously on the first ballot, and as a sop to the conservative wing, Governor John W. Bricker of Ohio became the vice presidential candidate.[54]

Meanwhile, there was no question of the Democratic candidate. Having broken the third term tradition, Roosevelt felt no qualms about a fourth term and shortly before the Democratic convention met in July he wrote the national party chairman that "reluctantly, but as a good

[53] Vandenberg, *Private Papers*, pp. 75–97.

[54] Malcolm Moos, *The Republicans: A History of Their Party* (New York, 1956), pp. 425–426.

soldier" he would serve again if he was "so ordered by the Commander in Chief of us all here—sovereign people of the United States."[55] It was inconceivable that at this time the Democratic party should seek leadership elsewhere. The party in power, especially in the light of Roosevelt's thrice demonstrated strength in presidential elections, could hardly be expected to "swap horses" in the middle of a war.

The selection of a Democratic vice presidential candidate was a more complicated problem. Roosevelt had in effect chosen his previous running mates, and he did the same thing in 1944, but he was so devious in his methods that confusion, misunderstanding, and bitterness resulted. In 1940, Roosevelt had selected Wallace as a sincere liberal devoted to the objectives of the New Deal; however, as Vice President, Wallace had failed to endear himself to the United States Senate over which he perfunctorily presided. Also, he did not have the confidence of many leaders within the party, especially the conservatives, and a number of these men concluded that Wallace should be dropped from the ticket in favor of Senator Truman, and secretly Roosevelt gave evidence of agreement.[56]

On May 20, at the President's request, Vice President Wallace left for a tour of Soviet Russia and the Far East and he did not return until July 10, nine days before the opening of the Democratic convention. He then went to the President and, confident of a wide popular following, said that he would seek renomination unless the President repudiated him. Instead of asking him to retire, Roosevelt promised to write a letter in his behalf and at the end of the conversation, according to Wallace, said, "I hope it's the same team, Henry."[57] The letter which Roosevelt wrote on July 14 stated of Wallace, "I like him and I respect him and he is my personal friend. For these reasons I personally would vote for him for renomination if I were a delegate to the convention." The President then compromised this endorsement by concluding, "At the same time I do not wish to appear in any way as dictating to the convention. Obviously, the convention must do the deciding."[58]

Earlier, on July 11, Roosevelt had met Robert Hannegan, chairman of the National Democratic Committee, and other political advisers

[55] Roosevelt, *Public Papers* (1944–45 ed.) XIII, 198.

[56] George Allen, *Presidents Who Have Known Me* (New York, 1950), pp. 125–126.

[57] John Gunther, *Roosevelt in Retrospect* (New York, 1950), p. 348.

[58] Roosevelt, *Public Papers* (1944–1945 ed.), XIII, 199–200.

who not only opposed Wallace but agreed on his successor. As he listened to the discussion, Roosevelt said, "Bob, I think you and everyone else here want Truman."[59] To place the matter on record, Roosevelt wrote the following letter, which apparently was postdated to July 19: "Dear Bob Hannegan—You have written me about Harry Truman and Bill Douglas. I should of course be very glad to run with either of them and I believe that either of them would bring real strength to the ticket."[60]

Wallace was not the only person who for a time thought he was the President's choice for Vice President. Roosevelt attempted to persuade Cordell Hull to run, but the aging State Department head declined.[61] James F. Byrnes asked Harry S. Truman to place his name in nomination and said that Roosevelt had "decided on him" for his running mate. Truman, at first not considering himself a candidate, agreed to place Byrnes' name in nomination if he was Roosevelt's choice. When the Missouri Senator went to the convention, however, he found strong labor sentiment against Byrnes and pressure from labor and other groups to seek the nomination himself. He doubted Hannegan's statement that Roosevelt favored him until he heard Roosevelt indicate his preference for him over the phone. Grateful for this support, Truman agreed to run, but he said of the President, "Why the hell didn't he tell me in the first place?"[62]

Although Wallace led Truman on the first ballot, the shift came on the second, and Truman won the nomination. Among the numerous factors which may have caused Roosevelt to jettison Wallace and select Truman was the former's failure with the Senate. The President realized that he would need rapport with that body to insure ratification of anticipated postwar treaties, and he knew that Truman had the respect of his fellow Senators.[63]

The campaign started slowly, for during the summer President Roosevelt made a twenty-one-day trip to the West Coast, Hawaii, and Alaska. While as Commander in Chief of the armed forces he was making a nonpolitical inspection of military installations, he was meeting and talking to thousands of voters whom, the Republicans were

[59] Allen, *Presidents Who Have Known Me,* p. 128.

[60] Samuel I. Rosenman, *Working with Roosevelt* (New York, 1952), pp. 446–447; Grace Tully, *FDR, My Boss* (New York, 1949), p. 276.

[61] Cordell Hull, *The Memoirs of Cordell Hull* (New York, 1948), II, 1714.

[62] Truman, *Memoirs,* I, 193.

[63] Rosenman, *Working with Roosevelt,* pp. 439–445.

quick to note, his opponent could not visit.[64] Dewey did not make the war an issue, and throughout the pre-election months Secretary Hull met Dewey's principal adviser on foreign affairs, John Foster Dulles, to inform him of main developments and keep foreign affairs on a bipartisan basis.[65] Inevitably there were minor deviations; Dewey said that the war and not the New Deal had brought jobs and he denounced the Morgenthau Plan for Germany. Roosevelt compared unfavorably the Republican preparedness record with that of the Democrats.[66]

The President's health was only a minor issue in the campaign. The press published widely a photograph of Roosevelt taken in San Diego during his inspection tour, in which he looked worn and ill.[67] On his return to the West Coast from Alaska, at the Bremerton Navy Yard in Washington, Roosevelt made one of the most ineffective public addresses of his career. His enemies insisted that he was failing badly in health, but his friends noted such mitigating circumstances as the wind, the slanting deck of the destroyer from which he spoke, and his consequent difficulty and pain in holding himself up while speaking.[68] After his return to Washington, D.C., Roosevelt began to show his old campaign style. Addressing the Teamsters' Union in Washington on September 23, he delighted his partisans with his resentment at "libelous statements" about his Scottie dog, Fala, for whom, it was asserted, Roosevelt at great expense to the taxpayer had sent a destroyer to the Aleutians.[69] In October, in an effort to counteract rumors of his ill health and Dewey's reference to "tired old men" running the government, Roosevelt on a cold, wet day toured New York City in an open car. There was a good deal of bitterness in the campaign. Roo-

[64] E. E. Robinson, *The Roosevelt Leadership* (Philadelphia and New York, 1955), pp. 335–336; Moos, *The Republicans,* p. 427.

[65] Hull, *Memoirs,* II, 1689–1695.

[66] H. Bradford Westerfield, *Foreign Policy and Party Politics: Pearl Harbor to Korea* (New Haven, 1955), pp. 188–190.

[67] The President's friends insisted that the photograph was more a tribute to an unsympathetic photographer's art than to reality. Rosenman, *Working with Roosevelt,* p. 453; Harold F. Gosnell, *Champion Campaigner Franklin D. Roosevelt* (New York, 1952), p. 206.

[68] For a careful analysis of the question of President Roosevelt's health, see Herman Bateman, "Observations on President Roosevelt's Health During World War II," *The Mississippi Valley Historical Review,* XLIII (June, 1956), 82–102.

[69] Roosevelt, *Public Papers* (1944–1945 ed.), XIII, 290.

sevelt personally disliked Dewey, whom he considered an internationalist through opportunism rather than conviction.[70]

The issue could not seriously have been in doubt, for the nation was still at war and would not change its leadership. In the election the Roosevelt-Truman ticket carried thirty-six states and got 25,602,504 popular votes to 22,006,285 for Dewey; the electoral vote was 432 to 99.[71] Roosevelt polled about a million and a half votes fewer than in 1940, but much of this loss was in the South and immaterial to the outcome of the election.

Roosevelt's death the following year has raised the question whether he should have run for a fourth term. Contemporaries differed on his health, and their comments for the most part have been tinged with partisanship or hindsight. Roosevelt's often demonstrated resiliency after illness or fatigue no doubt influenced his friends, who felt that he still possessed this ability and that basically his health was still sound.[72] Admiral Ross T. McIntire, the President's personal physician, believed that with "proper care and a strict adherence to rule, his chances of winning through to 1948 were *good*."[73] As the campaign progressed, Roosevelt's advisers persuaded him to speak from a sitting position in most of his public addresses to conserve his strength.[74] There is no evidence that Roosevelt seriously thought of Truman as his successor in the White House before the end of his term, but that he thought rather of the Missourian with respect to his influence in the United States Senate.

[70] Robert E. Sherwood, *Roosevelt and Hopkins: An Intimate History* (New York, 1948), p. 828.

[71] Dewey carried Maine, Vermont, Indiana, Iowa, North and South Dakota, Kansas, Nebraska, and Colorado, which Willkie had carried four years before, but, unlike Willkie, lost Michigan. Dewey also carried Ohio, Wisconsin, and Wyoming, which had been won by Roosevelt in the previous election. Eugene H. Roseboom, *A History of Presidential Elections* (New York, 1957), p. 490.

[72] E.g., Sherwood, *Roosevelt and Hopkins,* p. 194.

[73] Ross T. McIntire, *White House Physician* (New York, 1946), p. 194.

[74] Bateman, "Roosevelt's Health," *The Mississippi Valley Historical Review,* pp. 91–92.

CHAPTER 16

Build-up for D-Day

THE idea of invasion of Western Europe entered early into Allied planning and persisted despite differences of opinion over means and competing plans of attack. At the Atlantic Conference in the summer of 1941, Americans learned of the British concept of invasion, one that would come only when Germany was on the verge of collapse as a result of blockade, air bombardment, and internal subversive action. The British Chiefs of Staff at that time reported:

> We do not foresee vast armies of infantry as in 1914–1918. The forces we employ will be armoured divisions with the most modern equipment. To supplement their operations the local patriots must be secretly armed and equipped so that at the right moment they may rise in revolt.[1]

American military planners at about the same time were placing a somewhat different emphasis upon the requirements for victory against Germany. Although they agreed upon the importance of blockade, propaganda, subversion, and air attack, they expressed a conviction that inevitably "we must be prepared to fight Germany by actually coming to grips with and defeating her ground forces and definitely breaking her will to combat."[2] In the Washington meeting of December, 1941—January, 1942, Prime Minister Churchill reiterated a belief

[1] "General Strategy Review by the British Chiefs of Staff," July 31, 1941. Quoted in Maurice Matloff and Edwin M. Snell, *Strategic Planning for Coalition Warfare, 1941–1942 (United States Army in World War II: The War Department)* (Washington, 1953), p. 55.

[2] Quoted in *ibid.,* p. 61.

that ultimately in various parts of Europe armored groups of invading Allies would join rebellious forces to defeat Germany, and he predicted, "It need not be assumed that great numbers of men are required."[3]

No agreement on these concepts was reached in this meeting, and the War Department went ahead with its own planning. On March 6, the Joint U.S. Strategic Committee agreed that the only quick way to use force against Germany was "use of the British Isles as a base area for an offensive to defeat the German armed forces." The planners envisaged a substantial effort, one large enough to cause "a material diversion of German forces from the Russian front." Recognizing that American troops would be slow in reaching England, the group stated that the invasion, consequently, would be largely a British enterprise.[4]

While this study was going on in the Combined Staff, the War Department Operations staff was studying the same problem independently. Shortly after American entry into the war, General Marshall called General Dwight D. Eisenhower to Washington and on March 9, 1942, made him the first head of the new Operations Division of the War Department. In his personal notes, Eisenhower already had indicated his feeling toward the European war when, on January 22, he commented that the Allies were wasting their resources and time in too many areas, and that instead, to keep Russia in the war, the Allies should start air assault and follow it as soon as possible with a land attack.[5] Eisenhower put these ideas in a note dated February 28 which recommended that the United States should begin planning immediately with Britain for invasion of Western Europe.

There was greater solidarity among the British planners than among their American counterparts.[6] Furthermore, the military heads were connected with the Cabinet, and Churchill not only represented their views at high-level conferences but worked more closely than Roose-

[3] Winston Churchill, *The Second World War* (Boston, 1950), III, 657.

[4] Quoted in Matloff and Snell, *Strategic Planning*, pp. 177–178.

[5] Notation by Eisenhower, dated January 22, 1942, quoted in *ibid.*, p. 156.

[6] Marshall and King at times differed on priorities for Europe and the Pacific. For example, see Gordon A. Harrison, *Cross-Channel Attack* (*United States Army in World War II: The European Theater of Operations*) (Washington, 1951), p. 23. King and Marshall agreed, however, that cross-Channel attack was the best means of waging war in Europe. Arthur Bryant, *The Turn of the Tide: A History of the War Years Based on the Diaries of Field Marshal Lord Alanbrooke, Chief of the Imperial General Staff* (New York, 1957), pp. 442–443.

velt with military planners.[7] The Prime Minister's own deep interest in military matters and his enthusiasms, however, at times caused his military advisers no little concern.[8] The British planners, in contrast to the Americans, contemplated invasion in the summer of 1943, not 1942, and then only "under conditions of severe deterioration of German military power." They envisaged a force landing under these circumstances and quickly advancing toward the Ruhr.[9]

The Combined Chiefs of Staff next directed British and American planners to reconcile their differences. Working together, the strategists took into account anticipated shortages of cargo ships and landing craft and concluded that invasion could not come in 1942. They did consider invasion possible in 1943, however, if Soviet Russia still remained in the war and was occupying the attention of most of the German armies.[10] After launching an attack on the Russians in June, 1941, the Germans had made rapid initial advances, featured by air force and armored unit activity. One of three great armored Army Groups, the Northern, pushed through the Baltic areas toward Leningrad. The Center Army Group, in addition to acting as a supporting force for the Northern Group, headed toward Moscow. The Southern Army Group moved south through the Ukraine. Differences between Hitler and his generals led to delays, and then the *Führer* ordered a major thrust south instead of against Moscow. In a wide encircling move, the German armies took Kiev and Kharkov and half a million prisoners. These were indeed impressive advances, but they were not decisive, and when Hitler turned his main effort against Moscow he was a little too late. Although advance German units neared Moscow, the Russians rallied and early in December started a moderately effective counterattack which settled down to a stalemate along the front. Instead of conducting a successful *Blitzkrieg* against the enemy, Hitler found his Eastern armies facing a stubborn foe and a Russian

[7] Field Marshal Sir John Dill sat on the Joint Staff Mission as the representative of the Prime Minister, in his capacity as Minister of Defense. Later, in July 1942, Admiral William D. Leahy became a member of the Joint Chiefs of Staff, as Chief of Staff to President Roosevelt. Harrison, *Cross-Channel Attack,* p. 4.

[8] Brooke wrote that Churchill's "military plans and ideas varied from the most brilliant conceptions at the one end to the wildest and most dangerous ideas at the other." Bryant, *The Turn of the Tide,* p. 355.

[9] British War Cabinet—Joint Planning Staff Study, December 9, 1941, quoted in Matloff and Snell, *Strategic Planning,* pp. 179–180.

[10] *Ibid.,* pp. 180–181.

winter, and it did not alter the situation for Hitler to lay the blame on faulty intelligence regarding the size and fighting ability of the enemy forces.[11] Nevertheless, Germany's difficult position was not generally apparent at the time. Her forces had been checked, but it was a winter stalemate, and a spring offensive could be expected. The Russians had suffered heavy losses of men and serious damage to industry. American military planners, however, who had given the Soviet troops little hope of survival when the campaign started, began to see a chance for a successful stand against the Axis.[12]

While the Joint Staff Mission was considering the possibility of invasion in 1943, General Eisenhower and his staff continued to consider the problem, and on March 25 General Eisenhower presented to General Marshall a memorandum in which he summarized cogently the major reasons for assault from the British Isles on Western Europe. Since under any circumstances the United States had to keep communications open between the United States and the United Kingdom, cross-Channel invasion would not necessitate diversion of forces. Further, the sea route to Britain was the shortest that existed for an invasion force and would make possible maximum shipping. The build-up of forces in the British Isles might cause a diversion of German troops from the Eastern front even before invasion came and would relieve the pressure on the Russians. England already had air bases from which the air assault on Germany could begin. The Allies could stage their invasion without leaving England unprotected, whereas the Germans would have to withstand invasion while facing attacks elsewhere in Europe. In this memorandum Eisenhower stressed the importance of securing joint agreement on cross-Channel invasion as an objective, and he suggested, "Unless this plan is adopted as the eventual aim of all our efforts, we must turn our *backs* upon the Eastern Atlantic and go, full out, as quickly as possible, against Japan!"[13]

On the basis of this and other reports, War Department planners developed an outline for invasion which General Marshall, after mak-

[11] T. L. Jarman, *The Rise and Fall of Nazi Germany* (New York, 1956), p. 228.

[12] Secretary Stimson stated that Army Intelligence at first estimated that the Russians could hold out only from one to three months. Henry L. Stimson and McGeorge Bundy, *On Active Service in Peace and War* (New York, 1947, 1948), p. 383.

[13] Quoted in Matloff and Snell, *Strategic Planning,* p. 182.

ing a few minor changes, presented to Stimson and then to the President. Roosevelt not only approved the memorandum but instructed Marshall and Harry Hopkins to take it to England for the consideration of the Prime Minister and his military advisers.[14] Arriving in London April 8, the Americans met the British Chiefs of Staff and stressed two factors of importance: the Red Army must be kept in the field, and the United States forces, after training, should gain combat experience not only to acquire seasoning but to test and improve their equipment. On April 14, the British Chiefs of Staff endorsed the American plan and agreed that planning should start at once for a main assault in 1943 and if necessary emergency landings in 1942. The "emergency" might consist of either German collapse or threatened downfall of the Russians.[15]

Prime Minister Churchill entertained deep reservations concerning the plan, but he said little against it at the time, since he feared that the Americans might turn their efforts from the Atlantic to the Pacific.[16] In contrast, enthusiastic over the results of the London meeting, American strategists went ahead with planning for Sledgehammer, the contingent operation in 1942, and Roundup, the scheduled invasion in 1943. They began study of some of the critical problems involved in preparation, including schedules of troop movements, shortage of landing craft, and priorities in the different areas of war. Early in June, General Marshall announced the creation of a new theater, the European Theater of Operations for the U.S. Army (ETOUSA), and he designated as its head General Eisenhower, who had demonstrated his ability as a planner for operations in both the Atlantic and the Pacific areas. When, however, Eisenhower arrived in London on June 24, he found that the North African operation had taken priority over the plan for cross-Channel invasion.[17]

When talk of invading North Africa revived in June, 1942, the Combined Chiefs of Staff considered the matter and concluded that

[14] Stimson strongly supported the plan. Stimson and Bundy, *On Active Service,* pp. 417–419.

[15] Matloff and Snell, *Strategic Planning,* pp. 187–188; Robert E. Sherwood, *Roosevelt and Hopkins: An Intimate History* (New York, 1948), pp. 520–544.

[16] Churchill was also interested in other possible military operations, including invasion of Norway and strong defense of India. Churchill, *The Second World War,* IV, 322–325.

[17] Matloff and Snell, *Strategic Planning,* pp. 190–197.

there should be further study of possible points of attack in Western Europe, from the Channel Islands to Norway. Any of these locations, they felt, "would be preferable to undertaking Gymnast [North African invasion], especially from the standpoint of dispersing base organization, lines of sea communication, and air strength."[18] They did not present these conclusions, for the decision came at a higher level. In discussions at Hyde Park, Prime Minister Churchill convinced President Roosevelt of the merits of North African invasion. On June 21, after a conference at the White House, featured by the opposing views of Churchill and Marshall, a new version emerged of the Combined Chiefs of Staff report on operations for 1942–43 in which North African invasion appeared as an alternative to cross-Channel attack in 1942. The British Chiefs of Staff, realizing that the British government did not wish to launch the invasion of France in 1942, on July 8 notified the Joint Staff Mission of the cancellation of the operation and, noting that the Russians would be disappointed at Allied inaction, recommended that the Americans approve the invasion of North Africa as an alternative.[19] Two days later, Marshall presented the President with another alternative, that suggested earlier by Eisenhower, which was to turn American attention to the war in the Pacific. Marshall's real purpose was to force the British to accept fully the principle of "a concentrated effort against Germany," but he was not bluffing and intended to press for war in the Pacific if the British resisted pressure.[20] Roosevelt, however, rejected the suggestion on the ground that defeat of Japan would not insure the downfall of Germany.[21] He then sent Marshall, Hopkins, and King to England to reach an agreement with the British.

In London the Americans made a last futile effort to revive Sledgehammer and then had to face the alternatives, which from the stand-

[18] Quoted in *ibid.*, p. 239.

[19] *Ibid.*, p. 267.

[20] Quoted in *ibid.*, p. 269. There would have been logistical difficulties in the shift. Richard M. Leighton and Robert W. Coakley, *Global Logistics and Strategy, 1940–1943* (*United States Army in World War II: The War Department*) (Washington, 1955), pp. 385–386. Admiral King naturally supported the Pacific alternative. Matloff and Snell, *Strategic Planning*, p. 273.

[21] Harrison, *Cross-Channel Attack*, pp. 28–32. Sherwood quotes Roosevelt's letter and interprets his statement to mean that Roosevelt believed invasion of Japan would be unnecessary after Germany's defeat. Sherwood, *Roosevelt and Hopkins*, p. 605.

point of feasibility had boiled down to two, North Africa or the Middle East, and even Marshall favored the former. On July 25, President Roosevelt assumed leadership again and made the decision to invade North Africa, a decision in which Churchill naturally concurred.

Specially trained British commando forces had made a number of raids on the German-held coast of Western Europe. On August 19, 1942, a force of about five thousand Canadians, a thousand British Commandos, and a token representation of United States Rangers raided Dieppe, on the French coast within range of British fighter planes. The purpose was to test the strength of the enemy and of Allied landing tactics and support. The bulk of the striking force attempted a frontal assault on the beaches of the town, while the remainder made flanking attacks designed to silence the strong defenses on the headlands which dominated the beaches. The planners had decided against preliminary bombardment from either air or sea in favor of a surprise landing. Unfortunately, the element of surprise was lost as the landing forces headed toward shore when a group of landing craft on the eastern flank accidentally encountered an escorted German convoy, and the resultant gunfire alerted the coastal defenses at least on the eastern flank. The main assault troops ran into heavy cross fire which turned landings into carnage and made it impossible to secure the beaches, much less to advance into the town. Half the tanks failed to reach shore and the remainder could not pass roadblocks on the promenade about the beaches. Unaware that the battle was lost beyond recall, the Military Force Commander sent his reserves, the Royal Marine Commando, toward the main beaches. The result was a "sea parallel of the Charge of the Light Brigade," and the Marine commander lost his life signaling the rear landing craft to turn back from the holocaust. Recovering as many men as possible, the expedition, fighting off heavy air attack, made its way back to England.

The Dieppe raid had been costly; 66 percent of the Canadians were casualties, and most Commando units had lost heavily. Other losses included 550 naval casualties, 1 destroyer and 33 landing craft sunk, and 30 tanks destroyed. Enemy losses, in contrast, were about six hundred for all services. Although in most ways the Dieppe raid was an expensive failure, one could take pride in the heroism displayed both in the attack and in the extrication of about a thousand men from the beaches under heavy fire. Dieppe made clear the fact that command of the air, permanent naval assault forces, and adequate preliminary naval gunfire are essential to large-scale amphibious assault. Experiences at Dieppe may well have improved Allied landings in North Africa, Sicily, and Italy.[22]

Assignment of priority to the invasion of North Africa affected other planning and operations. One result was an inevitable delay in preparations for cross-Channel invasion. This delay led to another difference of opinion between British and American leaders. The British strongly favored Bolero, the code name for a build-up of American forces in the United Kingdom, but they were reluctant to commit themselves prematurely to a major cross-Channel assault. The Americans, on the other hand, could see little advantage in a huge concentration of United States forces in the British Isles if there was no definite plan for their use. Consequently, movement to Britain did not proceed so rapidly as anticipated, and a perturbed Churchill protested to Roosevelt and supported cross-Channel invasion. The President responded that the United States had no intention of abandoning the Roundup operation, but he admitted that the North African venture and heavier action in the Southwest Pacific than anticipated had lessened shipments to the United Kingdom. Churchill was reassured, but it became clear to planners that invasion would not come before 1944.[23]

At the Casablanca Conference in January, 1943, a large, well-prepared British military staff met a small, incompletely prepared U.S. military staff whose thinking and action were poorly coordinated with those of the President.[24] Roosevelt, for example, did not discuss in detail with his military staff the "unconditional surrender" statement which he enunciated to the conference and which of course had sig-

[22] S. W. Roskill, *The War at Sea* (*History of the Second World War: United Kingdom Military Series*) (London, 1956), II, 239–253; Hilary St. George Saunders, *The Green Beret: The Story of the Commandos, 1940–1945* (London, 1950), pp. 15–20, 102–114; Great Britain, Combined Operations Command, *Combined Operations, 1940–1942* (London, 1943), pp. 105–137; C. P. Stacey, *Six Years of War: The Army in Canada, Britain and the Pacific* (*Official History of the Canadian Army in the Second World War*) (Ottawa, 1955), I, 325–408.

[23] Matloff and Snell, *Strategic Planning*, pp. 325–327; Churchill, *The Second World War*, IV, 651–653.

[24] Maurice Matloff, *Strategic Planning for Coalition Warfare, 1943–1944* (*United States Army in World War II: The War Department*) (Washington, 1959), p. 21.

nificant military implications.[25] Marshall felt that he was working at a disadvantage and fought against any real changes in military directives. At the conference the Combined Chiefs of Staff refrained from definite commitment on the cross-Channel attack, but they provided for an organization to prepare for possible invasion in 1943 and actual invasion in 1944.[26] Instead of appointing a commander to put into operation a plan that had not yet been formulated, they created the office of "Chief of Staff to the Supreme Allied Commander (designate)," later to be known as Cossac. To this important post of principal planner for cross-Channel invasion, the Combined Chiefs of Staff appointed the British Lieutenant General Sir Frederick Morgan, who drew about him a staff from the American, British, and Canadian armed forces.[27]

The Combined Chiefs of Staff ordered Morgan to prepare not one but three operations plans. One was for a series of diversionary moves in the summer of 1943 to prevent the enemy from taking troops from the west to reinforce armies on either the Eastern or the Italian front. The second plan was premised on the optimistic contingency that Germany might collapse suddenly and was to guide Allied actions in case of such a development. The third, and most important, plan was for a large-scale invasion of the Continent as early as possible in 1944.[28]

The first plan for diversionary action in 1943, Operation Starkey, was partly a dress rehearsal for invasion and partly a huge bluff. The Cossac staff hoped that the deception would work two ways, that the Germans would believe an assault was coming in 1943 and that the attack would be made on a certain part of the French coast, the Pas-de-Calais. Cossac had given a great deal of thought about the best place of attack and had considered the European coastline from Norway to Spain. It wanted not only a shore upon which beachheads

[25] Matloff and Snell, *Strategic Planning,* p. 380; Ray S. Cline, *Washington Command Post* (*United States Army in World War II: The War Department*) (Washington, 1951), p. 217.

[26] Harrison, *Cross-Channel Attack,* p. 44.

[27] *Ibid.,* p. 48; Frederick Morgan, *Overture to Overlord* (New York, 1950), pp. 1–17. Sir Frederick Morgan had commanded an armored group in France in 1940. He was appointed head of a diversionary thrust into North Africa which did not materialize and directed early planning for the invasion of Sicily. Forrest C. Pogue, *The Supreme Command* (*United States Army in World War II: The European Theater of Operations*) (Washington, 1954), p. 15. This volume contains useful brief biographies of leading war figures. *Ibid.,* pp. 1–21.

[28] Morgan, *Overture to Overlord,* p. 57.

could be established, but a lodgment from which continually reinforced invasion forces could emerge and move ultimately into the heart of Germany. Since the need for fighter support eliminated some of the more distant areas, the choice narrowed to two locations, the Pas-de-Calais area, twenty miles from England across the narrowest part of the English Channel, and to the Normandy beaches on the Cotentin Peninsula above Cherbourg. The first, although nearer, was discarded for several reasons. It was more heavily defended, the harbors were not so good, and most important, the hinterland would be more difficult to conquer.[29]

Having made the decision, Cossac naturally hoped that the Germans would expect an attack in the wrong place. Thus the word that slipped out about invasion in 1943 led the enemy to believe that the target would be the Pas-de-Calais. During the summer, things began to happen in southeastern England. Air defense troops moved into the area. Other military personnel prepared for the accommodation of large bodies of troops. Of course, the soldiers were told that this was merely an exercise, but with the rumors flying about, many of them thought it was the real thing.

September 8, 1943, was D-day for Operation Starkey. The Navy was ready with its part of the show, and scattered among the genuine invasion boats were other craft designed by camouflage experts. Made of scantling, sheet iron, and canvas, they were moored in strategic harbors along the southern waterways and were deceptive even at a short distance. Navy minesweepers started the dress rehearsal with a sweep across the channel almost within range of the German guns. British and American fighters flew as if to cover the invaders. Down to the "hards," cement ramps for amphibious embarkation, marched lines of troops, most of whom were turned around and marched away again when they reached the shore.[30]

At the time it was difficult to know whether or not Operation Starkey had been sheer waste of effort. Apparently, the Germans paid little attention, but later it became clear that the enemy was convinced that when invasion did come it would be in the Pas-de-Calais area. The dry run in September, 1943, may have contributed materially to this German miscalculation.

The members of the Cossac staff dutifully worked on the second

[29] *Ibid.*, p. 99.
[30] *Ibid.*, pp. 99–103; Harrison, *Cross-Channel Attack*, pp. 70–71.

task assigned them, but no one for any length of time really expected the Germans to collapse suddenly. To insure readiness for any contingency, however, Cossac developed three phases in this plan. With customary thoroughness, the group considered not only assault but the problems of occupation of Germany and the liberation of conquered peoples.[31]

Cossac's main interest, of course, centered on the master plan, all-out invasion in the face of a powerful, not a disintegrating, foe. As we have seen, Morgan and his staff determined that the attack should be made on Normandy. They did not reach this decision easily, but only slowly after consideration of all possibilities. An example of their care is illustrated in the case of the beaches. Someone asserted that the Normandy beaches had an understratum of mud that would trap mechanized equipment. A British submarine secretly went across the channel, and a British lieutenant casually brought actual borings from Normandy beaches to demonstrate that the story was false and that the shale would support heavy traffic.[32]

Indicating May, 1944, as the date for invasion, Cossac presented its plan to the Quadrant Conference in August, 1943, and that body gave its approval. Operation Overlord was now officially under way. Cossac's function changed from that of formulating a plan to preparing to put that plan in operation. Some of the British leaders still held back from a firm commitment to a definite date for invasion, since they still retained hope of further Mediterranean action.[33] This issue was solved at the Teheran Conference late in November, 1943. At that time Marshal Stalin, brushing the Italian campaign aside as diversionary, insisted that the only real second front must come in a cross-Channel invasion. Thus at Teheran came the final seal of approval.[34]

Cossac had done its work well, but now that the plan was to go into effect, a supreme commander was needed. In the early stages of the planning it was assumed that this individual would be British,[35]

[31] Morgan, *Overture to Overlord,* pp. 104–122.

[32] *Ibid.,* pp. 175–176; Omar N. Bradley, *A Soldier's Story* (New York, 1951), pp. 214–215.

[33] The question of "over-riding priority" for Operation Overlord was sharply debated at Quebec, and the result was a compromise statement. Harrison, *Cross-Channel Attack,* pp. 97–100; Bryant, *The Turn of the Tide,* pp. 575–586.

[34] Harrison, *Cross-Channel Attack,* pp. 123–126.

[35] In July, 1943, Churchill told General Brooke that he should have the post when the time came, but later Churchill agreed that an American should re-

but as the discussions progressed and as the magnitude of potential American military contributions was realized, it began to appear logical that the supreme commander should be an American. Rumors pointed to General George C. Marshall as the probable appointee. General Morgan even visited the United States and discussed matters with the Chief of Staff almost as if he were certain to hold the post.[36] At the Quebec Conference, Churchill indicated that he would accept General Marshall as Supreme Commander, and correspondence as late as September 20 indicates that Roosevelt felt that the post should go to his Chief of Staff. Even Mrs. Marshall quietly began to move some of the family's belongings from Fort Myers to the family home in Leesburg in anticipation of the General's departure. Secretary of War Stimson strongly backed Marshall for the post.[37]

In spite of these things, General Marshall was continued as Chief of Staff and, instead, General Dwight D. Eisenhower became Supreme Commander. The reasons for the decision are debatable and perhaps immaterial, since it seems to be the consensus that Marshall and Eisenhower were each placed in the right post. The Chief of Staff had the experience to allocate men and materials properly to the European and Pacific theaters and the will to resist pressures to change these allocations. General Eisenhower had been battle tested in the Mediterranean area and he possessed the personality to reconcile the British and Americans, sometimes very fractious allies. It is a tribute to General Marshall that although he undoubtedly wished to conclude his distinguished career with a battle command over a major invasion of the European Continent he gave no indication of his interest and accepted the decision with outward equanimity.[38]

General Eisenhower learned of his new assignment in December, 1943, and on January 17 took command. Cossac was replaced by SHAEF (Supreme Headquarters, Allied Expeditionary Force), whose function was not only to continue expanded planning but carry the plan into operation. The post of Deputy Supreme Commander went

---

ceive the appointment. Bryant, *The Turn of the Tide,* pp. 540–541, 578–579; Churchill, *The Second World War* (Boston, 1951), V, 85.

36 Morgan, *Overture to Overlord,* p. 195.

37 Sherwood, *Roosevelt and Hopkins,* pp. 758–760; Stimson and Bundy, *On Active Service,* pp. 436–438.

38 For discussions of the appointment, see *ibid.,* pp. 441–443; Sherwood, *Roosevelt and Hopkins,* pp. 758–768, 787–788, 791, 803; Pogue, *The Supreme Command,* pp. 27–33; S. E. Morison, *History of United States Naval Operations in World War II* (Boston, 1957), XI, 22*n.*

to British Air Chief Marshal Sir Arthur William Tedder, who had served with distinction in the North African campaign. He and Eisenhower had great respect for each other, and like the Supreme Commander he had the ability to work well with both the British and the Americans.

Eisenhower took with him General Walter Bedell Smith as his Chief of Staff. The two men functioned excellently together. Smith could be either rough or suave as the situation dictated, he was experienced in the duties of his office, and performed them well.

The Allied Naval Expeditionary Force under Eisenhower was headed by Admiral Sir Bertram Ramsay. A veteran of over forty years in the British Navy, Ramsay had helped plan the invasion of North Africa, had participated in the assault on Sicily, and had become British naval commander in the Mediterranean.

The command of the air forces for the invasion also went to an Englishman, Air Chief Marshal Sir Trafford Leigh-Mallory, who had won the Distinguished Flying Cross in World War I and had led British fighter groups in World War II.[39]

Nationalistic and personal factors prevented a similar unification of the ground forces for the invasion. Eisenhower had hoped to secure General Sir Harold Alexander as head of the British Twenty-first Army Group, which was scheduled for invasion. He had learned to respect Alexander as a general and as a man in the Tunisian campaign. The choice, however, was not Eisenhower's; Prime Minister Churchill informed the Supreme Commander that Alexander could not be spared from the Italian campaign and designated Field Marshal Sir Bernard Law Montgomery as head of the Twenty-first Army Group.[40] Montgomery had the ability to secure the passionate loyalty of his men and with his beret and baggy uniform he emerged from the war as one of its most colorful figures. Some of the American generals with whom he worked viewed him with less enthusiasm than did his men, although they admitted that he possessed strong qualities as a leader. He was a master of the "set" battle and consequently was an excellent choice for his role in the invasion, which was planned in great detail.

Montgomery participated in the early consideration of Cossac's plan, he outranked the American generals in the area, and if the ground forces were to be unified, he would have been the logical choice as

[39] Pogue, *The Supreme Command,* pp. 41–48.
[40] Dwight D. Eisenhower, *Crusade in Europe* (New York, 1948), p. 211.

head. On the other hand, American participation in the invasion would be very heavy. Instead, therefore, of unifying the ground forces, Eisenhower delegated command to Montgomery only until the landings had been made and lodgments secured. At that time an American Army Group would be formed and would fight in conjunction with the British Twenty-first Army Group and both would be under the command of Eisenhower himself.[41]

In anticipation of these developments, Eisenhower brought from the Mediterranean a man who had been tested in the crucible of war in North Africa and Sicily. General Omar Bradley was not so colorful as the British Montgomery or the American Patton, but he is generally recognized as one of the best military leaders to emerge from World War II. A good strategist, Bradley was also a superb and daring tactician, whose abilities became apparent as the battle on the Continent became more fluid. Bradley became head of the U.S. First Army and was scheduled to hold that post until the formation of the First Army Group. At that time he would advance to its command and in effect become Montgomery's opposite number. Although during the early phases of the invasion, the Americans were under the command of Montgomery, he gave Bradley great latitude and cooperated with him rather than directed him.[42]

As Supreme Commander, Eisenhower was responsible to the Combined Chiefs of Staff, who gave him his basic strategic orders. He was to "enter the continent of Europe and, in conjunction with the other Allied Nations, undertake operations aimed at the heart of Germany and the destruction of her armed forces."[43]

The over-all plans developed by Eisenhower and his staff included the following:

1. Land on the Normandy coast.
2. Build up resources for a decisive battle and break out. The land operations of these first two phases would be under the tactical direction of Marshal Montgomery.
3. Pursue the enemy on a broad front with two army groups, stressing the left to gain necessary ports and threaten the industrialized Ruhr region. The right would join the forces coming up from landings in southern France.

[41] *Ibid.*, p. 223.
[42] Bradley, *A Soldier's Story*, p. 173 and *passim.*
[43] The directive appears in Pogue, *The Supreme Command,* pp. 53–55.

4. Build up the base in western France by securing ports in Belgium and Brittany as well as southern France.
5. At the same time maintain an offensive designed to wear down the enemy.
6. Complete the destruction of the enemy forces west of the Rhine and constantly seek bridgeheads across that river.
7. Launch an attack to envelop the Ruhr, emphasizing the left, and then make a direct thrust into Germany, in a direction to be determined by the situation at that time.
8. Clean out the rest of Germany.[44]

When Eisenhower read the plans prepared by Cossac he raised one strong objection. General Morgan and his staff had been forced to work with the materials judged available, and one of the bottlenecks was considered to be in procurable landing craft. Consequently, Cossac had produced a plan for a three-division invasion. Eisenhower asserted that this was not a large enough force, and in this view he was supported by Montgomery. As Supreme Commander, Eisenhower could exert more pressure than Morgan and he secured approval of expansion of the plan to an invasion by five divisions.[45]

The matter of timing was extremely important. At Teheran, Roosevelt and Churchill had promised Stalin that invasion would come in May. Eisenhower knew that he had a little more leeway than one month, but not much more. The ideal date would have been early in May. Successful landings prior to that date were doubtful because of adverse tides. The first favorable tides and sunrise would come early in May. Requirement of moonlight for airborne drops further limited the choice to three days a month. There were other reasons for speed; the Germans were accelerating development of their coastal defenses which would make landings increasingly difficult. Then Intelligence was bringing word of a new weapon of great power, and scientists were becoming aware of the pilotless missiles to be launched from sites along the coast.

Despite the advantages of a May landing, several factors forced a delay of a month. The most important was the decision to increase the force from three to five divisions. There is some feeling that if Eisenhower had been appointed earlier, he would have won his point and had time to prepare for a May assault. Another important factor for delay, however, would still have remained. The Air Force needed more

[44] Eisenhower, *Crusade in Europe*, p. 229.
[45] Harrison, *Cross-Channel Attack*, p. 166.

time for its preparatory work. Good May weather would give it the opportunity to attack transportation centers and facilities and coastal defenses.[46]

The need for landing craft was met not only by increased production in the United States but by a shift in priorities. One of the controversial Allied moves was the invasion of southern France, Operation Anvil. When it appeared that there would not be sufficient landing craft for both Overlord and Anvil, Marshal Montgomery recommended abandonment of the latter project. Eisenhower, however, insisted that it remain, and the result was a postponement of the date of the landings in southern France to make it possible for landing craft designated for that assault to be used first in the Normandy invasion.[47]

The question of supply was vital to the success of Overlord. France had good ports but they were strongly defended, and even if the Allies could take them it was certain that the Germans would leave them too badly damaged for quick use. To solve this extremely difficult problem, the Allies made the unorthodox decision to create artificial harbors.[48] Operation Mulberry, as it was called, was considered so fantastic that despite the size of the component parts it remained a reasonably well-guarded secret prior to D-day. Two complete harbors, about the size of Dover Harbor, were constructed piecemeal to be taken across the Channel for installation on the Normandy coast on the day after the initial assault. Each harbor would include a breakwater, pier, and bridging leading to the shore. One would be installed in the American sector and the other in the British.

The breakwater was constructed from cellular concrete caissons, known as Phoenix units, varying in length from 176 to 204 feet. It was estimated that forty-seven would be needed to form the breakwater for Mulberry A, the American port. The idea of an artificial breakwater was not new. Churchill had suggested its use in World War I. Both Cherbourg and Dover were man-made ports in which caissons had been used to form a part of the breakwater. The construction of about 150 Phoenix units, however, posed a problem for both industry and security.

[46] Eisenhower, *Crusade in Europe,* pp. 229–231.

[47] *Ibid.,* pp. 231–232; Harrison, *Cross-Channel Attack,* pp. 164–173.

[48] Churchill was an early supporter of the idea if not its originator. Morgan, *Overture to Overlord,* p. 261; Churchill, *The Second World War,* V, 71–74.

A gently sloping beach and twenty-one-foot tides made extremely difficult the problem of constructing a pier that would reach deep water at both low and high tide. Floating bridge units, known as Whales, were built to extend from the shore to the piers. These were eighty-foot steel sections to be towed to the site and linked with telescopic spans to accommodate wave action. One of the most complicated units was the Lobnitz pier. This was a floating steel hull two hundred feet long and sixty feet wide and ten feet high. At each corner was a sixty-foot steel leg, and to meet the problem of tidal changes, the hull could be moved up and down the four legs like an elevator. The legs themselves acted as anchors.

Outside the Phoenix breakwater there was to be a second breakwater. Old merchant vessels, sunk end to end would create a nine-thousand-foot barrier known as Gooseberry. Still a third breakwater was planned; this was constructed of hollow steel structures two hundred feet in lengh, which would float two-thirds submerged. These Bombardons were equipped with steel fins designed to lessen wave action.

The size and ungainly nature of the various Mulberry units posed difficult towing problems for the Navy. A few carefully conducted experiments with tugboats demonstrated that the task was feasible, and Operation Mulberry moved ahead with other projects toward D-day.[49]

Another extremely critical part of the preparations was the development of countermeasures against German beach defenses. Air reconnaissance photographs and other information gave a good idea of the nature of these defenses, and the situation was discouraging. The coasts were heavily mined and studded with logs and steel structures, many of which were mined. Nearer shore were "hedgehogs," triangular steel structures about five feet high, set in rows, and designed to rip holes in landing craft. On shore the defenses included barbed-wire entanglements, mine fields, concrete pillboxes, and huge stone walls.[50]

The British Army took the lead in developing countering devices. On an isolated part of the southern coast of England not far from

[49] For a detailed account of the Mulberry operation by one of its leaders, see Alfred B. Stanford, *Force MULBERRY* (New York, 1951), *passim;* Roland G. Ruppenthal, *Logistical Support of the Armies* (*United States Army in World War II: The European Theater of Operations*) (Washington, 1953), I, 271–282.

[50] Harrison, *Cross-Channel Attack,* pp. 176–179.

Plymouth, they constructed duplicates of the German installations and then devised methods of destroying them.[51] Important in the landing procedure, of course, was the laying down of a heavy air bombardment, including rocket fire, which was intended to detonate many of the enemy mines. The British also made use of a proven antimine device known as the Bangalore torpedo, which was a tube filled with explosives which, when thrust into a mine field, detonated the mines and created a narrow path through which the infantrymen could pass. The British adapted Sherman tanks to use these torpedoes to create an even wider strip through the mined regions.[52] There is some thought that the failure of Americans to make full usc of such special equipment as these "flails" accounted in part for the difficulties encountered on Omaha Beach.[53]

One of the most important special adaptations was the DD, or amphibious tank. Both American and British military leaders recognized its value, and orders went ahead for the necessary conversion of Sherman tanks.

Toward the end of April and early in May, American forces held full dress rehearsals for the Normandy landings. During the last of these a German E-boat, a torpedo patrol craft, attacked and sank two LST's (Landing Ship Tank) with more than seven hundred casualties. Fortunately, the enemy apparently saw no relationship between the exercises and an imminent invasion of Normandy.[54]

Actually, the German military power that stood on the defensive, in spite of its successes and the bristling exterior presented to the English Channel, had serious flaws. One, the weakening of its air power, has already been noted. Then there was the nature of the military command, which while Germany was winning seemed no liability but when the course of victory turned proved a significant disruptive force. At the head, of course, was Adolf Hitler, who was not only the political leader but Commander in Chief of the Army. His qualifications included experience in World War I as a corporal, rather extensive reading of military materials, and a supreme confidence in his military judgment, much of which was based on intuition. Beneath him there was no unified command. Nominally, Field Marshal Gerd

[51] Eisenhower, *Crusade in Europe,* p. 236.
[52] *Ibid.,* pp. 236–237.
[53] Chester Wilmot, *The Struggle for Europe* (New York, 1952), p. 265.
[54] Ruppenthal, *Logistical Support of the Armies,* I, 352.

von Rundstedt was Commander in Chief for the West. Von Rundstedt had shown skill as a leader in the Battle for France, had gone into retirement, and then was recalled to duty. In the summer of 1944, he was old, tired, and no man to stand up against Hitler. Further, important segments of the German fighting force were not under his control. There was little or no coordination with the Navy or the Air Force, and the heads of these forces in the West received their orders from the German Naval Staff or from *Reichsmarschall* Hermann Göring. Göring even had command over some of the ground forces in the West. Although the military governors of France, Belgium, and the Netherlands theoretically were under von Rundstedt for military matters, they reported directly to Heinrich Himmler, head of the German police and *Waffen-SS* (*Schutztaffeln*). The *Organization Todt,* or Labor Corps, was also independent of the Commander in Chief for the West, who could make requests but not issue orders to it.[55]

In the strictly military organization, under von Rundstedt were Army Group B in the Netherlands-Loire section and Army Group G farther south in France. In command of Army Group B after its organization early in 1944 was *Generalfeldmarschall* Erwin Rommel, who had gained the sobriquet of Desert Fox for his brilliant leadership of Nazi forces in North Africa. Rommel's appointment to Army Group B really complicated the problem of German defense. Hitler had envisaged an "Atlantic Wall" of concrete fortifications along the entire coast. The vast project was only partly completed when Rommel arrived. Fortunately for the Allies, Rommel disagreed with von Rundstedt on the nature of the defenses that should be created. In brief, the latter believed that the enemy should be permitted to land, and then the Germans would bring up a strategic reserve of mechanized forces and destroy the invaders. Rommel, on the other hand, believed that without air power such a plan would fail. Instead, he favored having the reserves near the coast to help repel the invader at the shore. Coastal defenses, therefore, should be made as strong as possible to aid in the task. Von Rundstedt not only viewed these proposals as unsound, but like other old-time Regular Army officers looked on Rommel as a political general who had risen rapidly in rank more

[55] Harrison, *Cross-Channel Attack,* pp. 128–140. The *Waffen-SS* were Hitler's black-shirted guards, who were organized with a well-armed special Army formation. Siegfried Westphal, *The German Army in the West* (London, 1951), p. 54*n*.

through influence with Hitler than through real military ability. In essence, Rommel won his point, and the strengthening of coastal defenses continued. The length of shore to be protected and the shortness of time in which Rommel had to work inevitably meant that the line of defense was thin. Uncertainty concerning the point of Allied attack prevented too much concentration in one place. Von Rundstedt believed that the attack would come across the narrowest part of the channel at Pas-de-Calais. Rommel apparently felt that the main blow would be at the mouth of the Somme, but he expected a secondary thrust at Normandy. For once, Hitler's intuition was right; on May 2 he announced his belief that the invasion would be on the Cotentin Peninsula and he issued orders for the strengthening of that area. At this time, however, Hitler was more concerned with the Eastern theater of war than with the threat from England.[56]

When no invasion came in May, German leaders began to think that the attack would not come until after the beginning of a Russian summer offensive, which could not start until after the late thaw in Poland. The tide had already turned against the Germans and they were being forced to retreat. The winter offensive of the Russians had regained the Crimea, but elsewhere by the summer of 1944 the Germans had been reasonably successful in stabilizing the Eastern front. The pressure was still there and was bound to increase with the advent of summer weather.[57]

Meanwhile, Allied preparations continued as two armies made ready to land on three beaches. The British Second Army, under the command of Lieutenant General M. C. Dempsey, on the left of the American forces as they headed toward France, was to land on beaches between Bayeux and Cayenne designated as Gold, Juno, and Sword. The U.S. First Army, under Lieutenant General Omar Bradley, had as its assignment two landings. Under Major General Leonard T. Gerow, the U.S. V Corps was to land on Omaha Beach to the right of the British and the U.S. VII Corps, under Major General J. Lawton Collins, was to effect a landing on the east coast of the Cotentin Peninsula on what was called Utah Beach.[58]

[56] *Ibid.*, pp. 148–157, 231–267; Hans Speidel, *Invasion 1944: Rommel and the Normandy Campaign* (Chicago, 1950), pp. 23–25; Erwin Rommel, *The Rommel Papers*, edited by B. H. Liddell Hart (London, 1953), pp. 465–471.

[57] Harrison, *Cross-Channel Attack*, p. 275; Wilmot, *The Struggle for Europe*, pp. 229–230.

[58] *Ibid.*, p. 213; Bradley, *A Soldier's Story*, pp. 226–229.

As D-day approached, southern England was turned into a huge army camp. Throughout the whole period of preparation the problem of security had been vital because of the desire to inflict as much of a surprise as possible on the enemy. Generally speaking, the attempt to maintain security was successful. There were a few slips. A sergeant through a careless error sent classified documents to his sister in Chicago, but fortunately the envelope came open and postal officials turned the contents over to the proper authorities.[59] A major general of the Air Force over cocktails made an unguarded remark about the date of the invasion. The fact that he had been a classmate of Eisenhower did not help him. He was sent home promptly at his permanent rank of colonel.[60] General Patton, who had caused embarrassment by his treatment of a hospitalized soldier in Italy, made an unfortunate remark in England to the effect that England and the United States would rule the world. This time there was no security leak involved, and Eisenhower, needing Patton as a fighting leader, resisted pressure to remove him.[61]

When the invasion forces moved to southern England, security measures tightened noticeably. Coastal shipping in the area stopped, as did traffic between southern England and the rest of the country. Traffic was checked especially between England and Eire, because of the presence in that neutral country of numerous enemy agents. The British government even stopped diplomatic correspondence and the sending of diplomatic couriers to neutral countries in spite of numerous protests. Air coverage in the area increased and succeeded in preventing the enemy from making significant reconnaissance. Military personnel were kept in quarters for a twenty-four-hour period to facilitate the work of Military Police in rounding up AWOL's.[62]

Final preparations were infinite in variety. Plans were checked and rechecked. Now that the men were isolated, they received a full briefing on what lay ahead. Army publications, in an effort to arouse the will to fight, stressed the worst features of German methods of warfare and to allay fear of personal injury told of recent medical advances in the treatment of wounds. Far more important, however, in prepar-

[59] Pogue, *The Supreme Command,* p. 163.

[60] *Ibid.,* pp. 163–164; Bradley, *A Soldier's Story,* pp. 223–224.

[61] Speaking at the dedication of an Allied service club, Patton said, "The idea of these clubs could not be better because undoubtedly it is our destiny to rule the world." *Ibid.,* p. 230; Pogue, *The Supreme Command,* pp. 164–166.

[62] *Ibid.,* pp. 162–163.

ing the soldier for his great test was the fact that he found out in detail what his own role in the operation would be. In small groups, soldiers received their own assignments, they saw photographs and charts of the beaches to be taken, they learned of the enemy obstacles in the way, and they studied the methods of overcoming them.[63]

The pressure increased on everyone and especially on the Supreme Commander. He was forced to make at least two significant decisions. One was over the objection of the Commander in Chief, Allied Expeditionary Air Force. It had been agreed earlier over Leigh-Mallory's protest that to insure success of the Utah landings two airborne divisions would have to land behind the beach. Late in May, Leigh-Mallory protested once more that these landings would result in excessive casualties. Bradley, on the other hand, insisted that without the aid of airborne troops the losses on Utah Beach would be so high as to threaten the success of the venture. Without the air drop, he argued, there should be no Utah landing. Eisenhower, faced with the project of abandoning a landing that might jeopardize the whole attack, decided against Leigh-Mallory and ordered the air drops to be made. As a slight compromise he agreed to a shift in location of one of the landings. Fortunately, Bradley's prophecy that the landings would not result in excessive casualties proved correct, and Leigh-Mallory promptly admitted that he had been wrong in his judgment.[64]

Eisenhower's other decision was even more critical. The combination of moon, tide, and time of sunrise limited the attack to a period of three days, June 5, 6, or 7. At four o'clock in the morning of June 4, the top leaders met to fix the exact time of assault. To prepare for a possible attack on June 5, some of the more distant units had already started. The report of the meteorologists was most discouraging. Strong winds, low clouds, and high waves would handicap greatly the projected invasion. Reluctantly, and against the counsel of some advisers, including Montgomery, Eisenhower decided to postpone the venture for a day. By three-thirty of the following morning, when the group met again in Portsmouth, a high wind was blowing and it was raining hard. Group Captain J. M. Stagg, head of the Meteorologic Staff, first announced that bad weather had continued in the Channel.

[63] *Ibid.*, pp. 167–168. Part of the force had already been battle-tested, for example, in North Africa, Sicily, and Italy.

[64] Eisenhower, *Crusade in Europe*, pp. 245–247; Pogue, *The Supreme Command*, pp. 118, 120–121; Bradley, *A Soldier's Story*, pp. 232–236.

Eisenhower's decision to postpone was therefore confirmed. More important was Stagg's next statement, which was that he expected the weather to clear and remain clear for the next thirty-six hours. Pressed with questions, Stagg refused to predict beyond that time. The decision was critical and in the last analysis rested with one man, the Supreme Commander. To delay would mean the end of opportunity to surprise and would complicate an already tremendous problem of supply and coordination. Naval vessels might have to refuel, and men could not be kept for an extended period on landing craft. To go ahead with the assault carried with it the risk of bad weather, which might prevent support of the forces that had landed and lead to disaster. After consultation Eisenhower decided to delay no longer and by his order he set into motion the intricate movements that launched D-day, June 6, 1944, on the Normandy coast.[65]

[65] Wilmot, *The Struggle for Europe,* pp. 221–226. This source draws from Dr. Stagg's diary. See also, Eisenhower, *Crusade in Europe,* pp. 249–250; Harrison, *Cross-Channel Attack,* pp. 272–274; Walter Bedell Smith, *Eisenhower's Six Great Decisions* (New York, London, Toronto, 1956), pp. 50–55.

CHAPTER 17

Cross-Channel Assault and the Capture of Cherbourg

H-HOUR for landings on what the world would soon know as Omaha and Utah beaches was set at six-thirty in the morning, June 6, 1944, the most famous of many D-days in World War II.[1] While the vast armada headed for its objective, the Allied air forces continued their work. The R.A.F. and the A.A.F. had already completed the first of their three main duties in the invasion. This was to "establish and maintain control of the air in the critical area for the purpose of eliminating the enemy's capacity to interfere from the air." So effective had been the months of attack on the German Air Force that it was virtually nonexistent in the region and completely impotent on D-day.

Now that H-hour was approaching, the Allied air force turned to its second and third responsibilities, "to isolate the battlefield by interdicting enemy movements of troops and supplies," and "to render immediate support to the ground forces on the battle front."[2] Ready to give this tactical support were two U.S. Army Air Forces, the

[1] Gordon A. Harrison, *Cross-Channel Attack* (*United States Army in World War II: The European Theater of Operations*) (Washington, 1951), p. 300. Each beach had its own H-hour, depending on tides and other circumstances. H-hour on the British beaches came as late as 7:55 A.M. S. E. Morison, *History of United States Naval Operations in World War II* (Boston, 1957), XI, 33.

[2] W. F. Craven and J. L. Cate, *The Army Air Forces in World War II* (Chicago, 1951), III, 186.

Eighth and the Ninth, the R.A.F.'s Bomber Command, and the British Second Tactical Air Force.

While the British Bomber Command began to bomb coastal batteries east from the Cotentin Peninsula, the U.S. Ninth Air Force gave its attention to the project which Leigh-Mallory had opposed so strongly. Late on the night of June 5, the largest airborne invasion yet launched began to leave British fields in huge gliders and planes. Heading south, the air fleet of more than nine hundred planes and one hundred gliders then turned east and crossed the Cotentin Peninsula above the opposite coast from Utah Beach. So far the take-off and trip had gone without incident, but warnings had been flashed to the Germans, and on reaching the coast the invaders ran into heavy and persistent antiaircraft fire. Fog and generally poor visibility made parachute and glider landings difficult, and the *bocage,* or hedgerow, countryside further complicated the problems of landing and assembling. Consequently, landings were scattered and in some instances completely missed vital objectives. These mishaps were partly counterbalanced by confusion created among the Germans by the appearance of paratroopers over a wide area and by the fact that although the divisions as a whole were unable to assemble, smaller groups organized and fought effectively. Furthermore, the drops of the U.S. 82d and 101st Airborne Divisions had not proved excessively costly in lives. In addition, although they had failed to take as many specific objectives as planned, the airborne troops had seized the important exits from Utah Beach and had played an important role in insuring the success of landings on that beach. In addition, they prevented the enemy from flooding lowlands and secured bridges and access roads.[3]

Meanwhile, other units of the Eighth and Ninth Air Forces turned their attention to the softening-up process so essential to the success of beach landings. In the first mission, for example, more than a thousand B-17's and B-24's dropped over 2,900 tons of bombs, with a loss of only one plane to enemy action.[4] In view of the other types of bombardment that went on during this day, it is difficult to isolate

[3] *Ibid.,* III, 186–189; Harrison, *Cross-Channel Attack,* pp. 278–300. For other appraisals of the airborne operation, see Omar N. Bradley, *A Soldier's Story* (New York, 1951), pp. 275–276, 281–282. Rommel had anticipated airborne attack but lacked sufficient time to put his defensive measures fully into effect. Erwin Rommel, *The Rommel Papers,* edited by B. H. Lidell Hart (London, 1953), pp. 459–460, 477–478.

[4] Craven and Cate, *The A.A.F. in World War II,* III, 190.

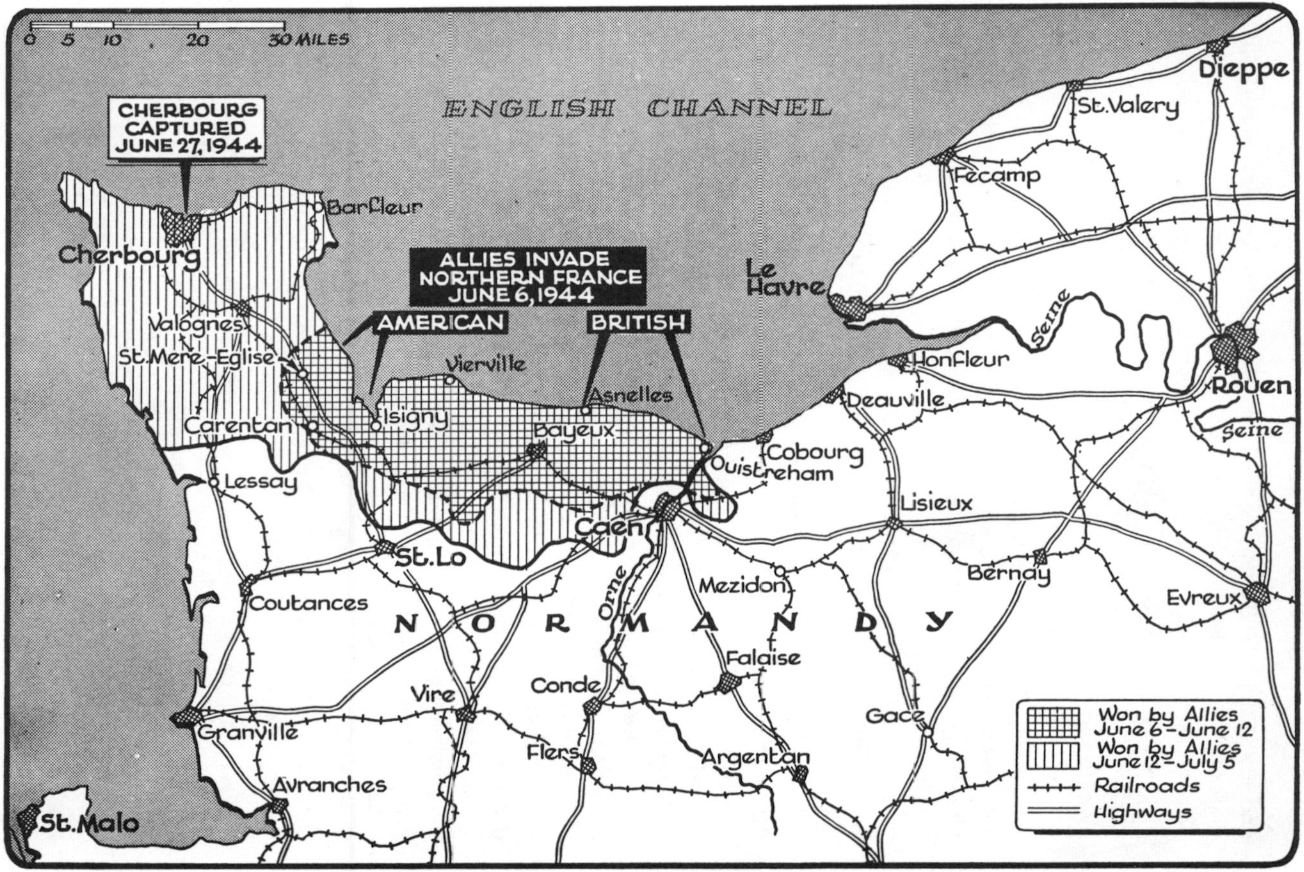

D-DAY AND AFTER

and assess the effectiveness of these air attacks, but certain generalizations appear. Air Force leaders knew that the sky over the beach would be overcast on D-day, and with the agreement of General Eisenhower they ordered crews to delay a few seconds before releasing their bomb-loads, in order to miss the landing forces. This understandable reluctance to bomb "short" led to bombing that fell too far inland, especially at Omaha Beach.[5] Consequently, in that locality the air attack failed in one of its main objectives, to detonate German mines and destroy obstacles on the beaches and in the shallow water offshore. Ultimately, invading troops benefited from some 1,285 tons of bombs which had damaged enemy defenses and destroyed land mines inland from three hundred yards to three miles, but even if he could have known this fact it would have been cold comfort to the soldier pinned down on Omaha Beach.

It was the Allied Navy's task to transport the invading forces, and the armada that headed for France was imposing indeed. Some 1,796 vessels of varying sizes and functions carried the three British forces toward Gold, Juno, and Sword beaches, and 931 vessels escorted the U.S. invasion troops toward Omaha and Utah beaches.[6] British ships were in the majority, but two of the five task forces under Admiral Sir Bertram Ramsay were American, and to them fell the responsibility of carrying the American invasion forces. Rear Admiral Alan G. Kirk, who headed the combined Western Naval Task Force, was experienced in working with the British and had led an amphibious task force in the invasion of Sicily.[7] The cross-Channel undertaking required careful preparation and timing, for vessels had to come together from many different ports in the British Isles.

While Allied aircraft kept guard overhead, the five task forces headed for their objectives along great channels which had been cleared by minesweepers. About midway across the channel each of the five lanes was divided into two parts, one for the combat vessels mov-

[5] *Ibid.*, III, 190–192. Morison implies a lack of communication and asserts that the Air Force did not notify the invading forces of the decision. Morison, *History*, XI, 124. Bradley notes that he did not learn until later of the delayed drop of the bombs. Bradley, *A Soldier's Story*, p. 268.

[6] If one includes landing barges of the ferry service, most of which did not cross the Channel on D-day, and landing craft carried aboard ships, the totals are 2,010 for the Western and 3,323 for the Eastern forces. Morison, *History*, XI, 77*n*.

[7] *Ibid.*, XI, 29–30.

ing swiftly to their appointed positions, the other for slower transport and landing craft carrying the invading force and its mechanized equipment.[8] The actual assault forces for Utah and Omaha were about equally divided and totaled some 60,000 men and 6,800 vehicles. Two other forces were also loaded aboard vessels in the United Kingdom before D-day. Force B, scheduled as reinforcements for Omaha Beach, consisted of 25,600 men and 4,400 vehicles. In addition, 43,500 men and 6,000 vehicles were ready to cross the Channel and land on D plus 1 and 2, according to plan.[9]

After minesweepers cleared the approaches, fire control ships led the convoys toward the beaches. Two U.S. battleships, *Texas* and *Arkansas,* were among the force nearing Omaha. This beach presented serious natural and man-made difficulties for the invader. The French coast in this locality consists of either narrow beaches backed by high cliffs or wide, sandy beaches sloping gently toward sandy bluffs eroded in places by ravines which create possible routes or "exits" to the plateau above. Omaha was such a wide beach, flanked by high cliffs. The task of preinvasion bombardment was to disable or destroy German defenses in the cliffs and bluffs, to detonate mines on the beach, and blast openings in the obstacles with which the Germans had strewn the beach.

About an hour and a half before sunrise, the fire support group took its position, five to ten thousand yards offshore, and began the preliminary bombardment. Principal targets included shore batteries, machine-gun pits and pillboxes in the cliffs, the exit roads, and the towns behind the beach. With mixed feelings, Frenchmen on two renovated French cruisers helped pulverize a portion of their native land. About ten minutes after naval bombardment had started, 480 B-24's arrived and dropped 1,285 tons of bombs, which landed, as we have seen, inland rather than on the beach itself. Preliminary naval bombardment was effective, but not effective enough; the time was too short, for after enduring thirty-five minutes of naval pounding the Germans could still offer bitter resistance. Allied fire support had put the major shore batteries out of action but had been much less success-

[8] *Ibid.,* XI, 78–79, 84–87. For a D-day account which has many details, see Cornelius Ryan, *The Longest Day, June 6, 1944* (New York, 1959).

[9] Roland G. Ruppenthal, *Logistical Support of the Armies* (*United States Army in World War II: The European Theater of Operations*) (Washington, 1953), I, 298.

ful in checking smaller artillery and machine guns which the Germans had placed in strongly protected positions for fire on the beach.[10]

Meanwhile, the invading force made ready to land. Out of respect for the shore battery on Pointe du Hoc, three and one-half miles west of the Omaha beaches, the sixteen transports lined up eleven miles offshore. They were, as a result, in an open roadstead, and assault forces debouched into landing craft which tossed on a choppy sea. All troops were in small craft by four-thirty; the first waves headed for shore, and the others circled to await their turn. Soon the troops were wet, and many became seasick; but as yet only the sea had reacted against them. There was no enemy fire from the shore.[11]

As the landing craft started the long trip toward the beaches, naval and air forces began the preliminary bombardment already noted. The first force scheduled to land consisted of tanks. These were of two types: standard tanks which had to be unloaded directly on shore, and amphibious tanks. The latter were standard tanks designed to stay afloat with the aid of detachable canvas "bloomers," a British device. As the landing craft approached the western sector of the beach, the commander of the LCT's headed for this sector, considering the sea too rough for safety, ran into the beach and unloaded the so-called amphibious tanks directly on shore. Other craft unloaded standard tanks and soon twenty-eight DD's and fourteen standard tanks were on the beach engaged in heavy fire with the enemy. Farther east, an Army captain in charge decided to launch the DD's five thousand yards offshore. The results were tragic. Although the sea was not rough, it was too heavy for the DD's, which were seaworthy only under the most ideal conditions and they began to founder and sink. Of thirty-two tanks headed for the beach, only five reached shore, and three of these were landed directly from one of the LCT's.[12]

Following the tanks came the first wave of assault troops, thirty-six boats, each carrying on the average one officer and thirty-one men. The heavy naval gunfire, the returning fire of the enemy at the ships and at the tanks obscured the air with dust and smoke, and the ad-

[10] Morison estimates that enemy resistance was reduced one-half to three-fourths. Morison, *History,* XI, 124–125. Bradley notes the gratification of V Corps for naval support on D-day. Bradley, *A Soldier's Story,* p. 254.

[11] Morison, *History,* XI, 119–120. For a more detailed account of the Omaha landings, see [Charles H. Taylor], *Omaha Beachhead* (Washington, 1945).

[12] Morison, *History,* XI, 130–134; Harrison, *Cross-Channel Attack,* pp. 305–309. The latter source gives the distance of launching offshore as six thousand feet. The DD's were waterproofed by a process tested in the Italian landings. They had to await removal of waterproofing for use on shore.

vance toward shore at first was a confused mass of men and equipment. The infantrymen had to walk in over one of the most treacherous beaches of the war. Leaving their landing craft in three to five feet of water, they had to wade a distance of fifty to one hundred yards around obstacles and then somehow work their way across two to three hundred yards of sand to the comparative safety of the sea wall, a reassuring ledge of concrete, except for one section which consisted of shale.[13] Carrying heavy equipment, many stumbled and drowned. Those who lingered in the hope of gaining safety behind beach obstacles usually found that they were in direct line of enemy fire, and the rapidly rising tide swept up their bodies. Those who continued straight ahead had the best chance of survival, but many of them fell victims of German bullets.

Subsequent waves of assault troops also came under heavy attack from the German shore defenses. German fire, foundering craft, and a high tide raised casualties on parts of the beach to 66 percent on D-day. A little farther east, troops had greater success reaching the sea wall. Still farther along, the men who reached the shingle sea wall found themselves pinned down behind inadequate protection. The captain and 104 men of Company E of the 116th Infantry died that day around the shingle wall; all but two officers of Company F were killed and of one boatload all but seven of thirty men died.[14]

Underwater demolition teams were among the first to hit the beaches, and they worked courageously but against heavy odds. Enemy fire eliminated one entire team as it landed and all but one member of another just as its members were about to set off their charges. Other demolition teams managed to blow five large channels and part of three more before the incoming tide forced them to stop. There was not sufficient time to mark the channels, however, and coxswains of most landing craft did not know of their existence until low tide hours later.[15]

After the first eight waves of assault troops came Army artillery, but they, too, encountered the greatest difficulty. Germans scored di-

[13] These obstacles included "Element C," steel frames about seven by ten feet, with mines attached. Farther inshore were sharpened wood or concrete poles, pointed toward the sea. Approximately every third pole was mined. Still farther inshore were rows of "hedgehogs" or "horned Scullies," consisting of three six-foot steel bars welded together. Morison, *History,* XI, 114.

[14] *Ibid.,* XI, 137–138.

[15] Underwater Demolition Teams (UDT) consisted of seven sailors and five Army engineers. *Ibid.,* XI, 137–138.

rect hits on numerous craft, and exploding mines added to the death toll and the congestion of foundered craft and equipment. Two hours after the first landings, since no vehicle had worked its way off the beach, the beachmaster temporarily halted further landings.[16]

For a time the men lay pinned down behind the sea wall, isolated and unled. Then, gradually, they began to develop points of strength. Machine guns began to return enemy fire, engineers cut barbed wire that had checked advance, a few patrols pushed inland and returned to attack the Germans from the rear. At about ten-thirty, landings began again as a couple of landing craft beached and with guns firing spearheaded a break in German defenses of one of the exits which led to continuous landings at this portion of the beach.[17] Gradually, beaching and landing craft were directed to this and other relatively easy points of landing.

A spectacular phase of an awesome day was the assault of Pointe du Hoc. As we have seen, the invading forces, out of respect for the battery at the top of this 117-foot cliff, had unloaded their men far offshore. To the invaders' surprise, they saw no enemy fire coming from this point when the battle began, but a specially trained Ranger Force moved toward a daring assault on this important enemy battery. This group went ashore with DUKW's equipped with hook and ladders for the purpose of scaling the cliff, but the steep approach to the base prevented their use. More successful was another innovation; rocket launchers from the landing craft fired not rockets but ropes with grappling hooks to catch at the top of the cliff. These tested devices worked, and under the protection of naval gunfire Rangers worked their way to the top. They found that the Germans had retired underground and, also to their amazement, they discovered that the famous guns of Pointe du Hoc were but wooden dummies, contrived from telephone poles. Gradually, although isolated for two days, the Rangers reduced the Germans on the point and moving inland discovered the real guns, which had been temporarily removed and hidden in anticipation of new casements. The Ranger patrol quickly spiked the guns with thermite grenades.[18]

Throughout the desperate landing operations on the main Omaha

[16] *Ibid.*, XI, 140.

[17] A destroyer supported the action with gunfire. *Ibid.*, XI, 141; Harrison, *Cross-Channel Attack*, p. 325.

[18] Morison, *History*, XI, 125–129; Harrison, *Cross-Channel Attack*, pp. 322–324. Hoc is also spelled Hoe in some sources.

beaches, naval vessels gave gunfire support. When connections were maintained with shore fire control parties or when naval personnel could see German targets, the fire was most helpful. In other instances, vessels which could have helped, particularly destroyers, held their fire for lack of knowledge of enemy positions.[19]

Omaha Beach was one of the most strongly prepared defenses along the French coast; in fact, the complicated system of beach barricades and defensive positions which Rommel placed on this beach and hoped to place all along the coast surpassed in effectiveness anything which the Japanese devised in the Pacific.[20] In addition, German manpower was unexpectedly strong behind Omaha Beach. In one of its relatively few lapses, Allied Intelligence failed to locate in the area the German 352d Infantry Division, and reported the presence of only one division, the static 716th, which lacked armor and wheeled transport. Thus, without advance knowledge, the Americans landed against two well-equipped German divisions.[21] During D-day, however, the German general in the area canceled out some of his advantage. Thinking that his forces were stopping the Americans on Omaha Beach, he became concerned over reports of rapid advances of the British inland from their beaches and dispatched his reserve regiment to attack the British. Later he learned that his information had been incorrect and he recalled the regiment, but it was absent at a critical point in the fighting and tired from long marching when it returned.[22]

The attack went more smoothly at Utah Beach. This strip of coastline, like Omaha, is a series of connected beaches, but behind it lies low pastureland instead of cliffs. For protection the Germans relied heavily on some twenty-eight German batteries in coastal fortifications, eighteen inland batteries which ranged on the beaches, and on numbers of mobile 88-mm. guns. They had protected the beach but lightly in contrast to Omaha; there were some beach obstacles, but they were not mined.[23]

Eleven and one-half miles offshore, assault troops shortly after four in the morning went over the sides of transports and down landing

[19] Morison, *History,* XI, 142–149.

[20] *Ibid.,* XI, 115.

[21] *Ibid.,* XI, 113–115; Harrison, *Cross-Channel Attack,* p. 319. There is apparently no basis for the story that a German division just happened to be on maneuvers behind Omaha Beach as the invasion began.

[22] Harrison, *Cross-Channel Attack,* p. 321.

[23] Morison, *History,* XI, 94–97, 101. For another description of Utah beach, see Ruppenthal, *Logistical Support,* I, 384–386.

nets to landing craft. Four hours earlier, British and American minesweepers had started their work on the approach channels and fire support areas. As they neared the coast, they and the destroyers escorting them drew the fire of coastal batteries. To protect these vessels Rear Admiral M. L. Deyo ordered an early start of preliminary bombardment. The minesweepers continued their activity but missed numbers of a delayed action type mine which came to life only after several sweeps and which subsequently caused heavy damage to the invading forces. Firing from eleven thousand yards offshore, Allied battleships and cruisers sought out the German batteries. Shortly before H-hour the supporting vessels turned their fire on the beaches themselves and on flanking positions. LCT's fired five-inch rockets into the beaches ahead of the first assault wave.[24]

In order to secure air spotting for naval gunfire, the Navy, instead of using slow, ship-borne Kingfishers and Seagulls, borrowed fast R.A.F. Spitfires and Mustangs and Royal Navy Spitfires. Leaving an English air base, the planes had time for only forty-five minutes over the target, but acting in relays they gave a creditable performance. Shore fire control parties were also useful in calling on the warships for fire at specific targets. One destroyer sank as a result of enemy fire, but in return naval bombardment pounded heavily and effectively shore batteries and other German defenses.

The first assault wave, as at Omaha, was of amphibious tanks. When mines destroyed a P-C boat guiding the tank carriers and one of the carriers themselves, the control officer decided to launch the "bloomered" DD's a mile from the beach. Fortunately, the sea was calm, and all twenty-eight tanks reached shore and went into action.

Brigadier General Theodore Roosevelt landed with the first wave of assault troops, which had to wade through a hundred yards of water but drew no enemy fire. Pleased but perplexed, Roosevelt consulted his maps and discovered the landing force had missed the intended spot by some two thousand yards. It was just as well, for the enemy was waiting to pour enfilading fire on the place originally intended for a landing. The U.S. forces quickly set up a new sector and began bringing troops into two adjacent sections of the beach. Underwater teams arriving with the second wave cleaned out the beach obstructions with a minimum of time and loss of life. Engineers moved ahead to blast openings in the concrete sea wall which the Germans

[24] Morison, *History,* XI, 93–98.

had constructed. Within three hours landings were almost normal, although occasional enemy fire hit the beach, and landing craft commanders encountered difficulty with the rapidly incoming tide.[25]

Not only were coastal defenses less difficult to counter at Utah than at Omaha, but the German forces behind the former were less numerous and aggressive. The German 709th Regiment which defended Utah consisted of reservists and foreign volunteers who displayed neither the vigor nor the ability of the troops behind Omaha Beach. Communications were inadequate; General Friedrich Dollman, commanding the German Seventh Army, did not hear until late in the day of the attack on Utah Beach.[26]

By noon some of the forces which had landed on Utah Beach had joined members of the hard-pressed 101st Airborne Division and before the end of the night had established contact with the 82d Airborne Division. The VII Corps had not reached all its planned objectives, but it had established a beachhead and was moving toward the forces on Omaha Beach.[27]

East of the American landings, the British launched their operations. Their three beaches actually constituted one sand strip about eight miles in length, but offshore reefs and obstructions broke it into three parts when approached from the sea. The Eastern Naval Task Force encountered the only German surface opposition of D-day. Three enemy torpedo boats sighted the convoy and, launching eighteen torpedoes, made a single hit, which sank a Norwegian destroyer. The pattern of amphibious assault resembled that of the Americans, and the accomplishment approximated Utah rather than Omaha. British, French, and Canadian troops landed against opposition that ranged from light to moderately severe. The sea was rough, but the British started their landing runs far nearer shore than did the Americans, and they launched their amphibious tanks only in smooth water. Like the Americans they sent an airborne unit inland, and in addition they had special commando teams designed to seize specific objectives.

[25] For accounts of the Utah landings, see *ibid.*, XI, 97–107; [R. G. Ruppenthal] *Utah Beach to Cherbourg* (6 June to 27 June 1944) (Washington, 1947); Harrison, *Cross-Channel Attack*, pp. 304–305; Bradley, *A Soldier's Story*, pp. 274–275. General Roosevelt, son of President Theodore Roosevelt, died later in the campaign as a result of a heart attack. The planes over the Salerno landings had only twenty minutes. Clearing beaches of obstacles was of course a part of assault landings on any defended beach.

[26] Morison, *History*, XI, 103.

[27] Bradley, *A Soldier's Story*, pp. 276–278.

By the end of the day, the British had established their beachheads but they had not advanced as far inland as they had hoped to go.[28]

The first day of the Normandy invasion must be counted a success. Only at Omaha had the issue been in doubt, and even there by afternoon it was clear that the Americans were establishing a foothold. A good basic plan, the air drop behind Utah, naval gunfire, seamanship on the beaches, demolition teams, men who left the sea wall at Omaha to continue the fight, and courageous G.I.'s and junior officers everywhere are a few of the factors that account for success.

An appraisal of D-day also includes criticism. The preliminary bombardment at Omaha was too short; extended bombing, however, might have alerted the enemy. The Allies could not engage in the softening-up process possible in some of the Pacific assaults, for the Germans could have brought tremendous force to bear on the coast if they had known precisely where the attack would be. Even after the Normandy invasions began, the Germans held reserves for three weeks in anticipation of a major thrust in the Pas-de-Calais area. At Omaha, therefore, the Allies had to sacrifice a certain amount of preliminary bombardment in favor of surprise.[29]

The transport area was too far at sea off the American sectors, but although this fact made life most uncomfortable for many soldiers, one cannot be sure how seriously it affected the course of the landing operations. Admittedly, the failure of Army Air Force bombers to blast the beaches was costly, yet later the A.A.F. received sharp criticism when it did bomb short. Intelligence made a serious mistake when it overlooked the 352d Division, but one wonders what else the invader could have done if he had known of this division's presence behind Omaha Beach.

Although there had been severe losses, especially on Omaha Beach, there was ground for restrained optimism. Perhaps the invasion was not going quite on schedule, but it was going. The enemy had mis-

[28] For accounts of the British landings, see Chester Wilmot, *The Struggle for Europe* (New York, 1952), pp. 267–280; Bernard L. Montgomery, *Normandy to the Baltic* (Boston, 1948), pp. 60–72; Bernard L. Montgomery, *The Memoirs of Field-Marshal the Viscount Montgomery of Alamein, K. G.* (Cleveland and New York, 1958), pp. 225–227. An account of commando activity is in Hilary St. George Saunders, *The Green Beret: The Story of the Commandos, 1940–1945* (London, 1949), pp. 264–272.

[29] Morison, *History,* XI, 152–153.

judged the place of attack and had met the invaders with no overwhelming concentration of men or mechanized equipment. Rommel's main tactical mistake was to send the mobile reserve into battle piecemeal. The German Air Force had been helpless, and the German Navy ineffectual in a few minor thrusts.

The so-called "Battle of the Beachhead" extended from D-day to July 25. Even before the beaches were well secured, the first units for the artificial harbors appeared. On the afternoon following D-day on Omaha Beach, Mulberry units began sinking the old freighters that were to constitute one of the breakwaters. A little later a similar procedure commenced at Utah Beach. There were complications, for these men were conducting an unprecedented operation, sometimes under fire, in waters not completely cleared of mines, delayed by having their tugs frequently called to temporary duty elsewhere. It took until the fifth day after D-day to complete the sinking of the block ships. Slowly the Phoenix units, the Whales, the Lobnitz piers, and the other component parts were towed to Omaha and Utah beaches and at great effort and with occasional mishaps sunk or established in place. At four-thirty of the tenth day after D-day, the first roadway was completed on Omaha Beach. LST 342, aided by a tug, nosed alongside two Lobnitz piers at the end of the center Whale roadway. The doors of the LST opened, and in a moment the first vehicle emerged on the ramp and went along the steel runway to the beach. Within thirty-eight minutes, seventy-eight vehicles had unloaded themselves from the LST. The artificial harbor, with its unloading facilities, had become a reality. Mulberry A meant doubling the lift from England to the beach, and during June 16 and 17, eleven LST's were unloaded. The average time of unloading was sixty-four minutes as contrasted with twelve to fourteen hours of drying out on the beach waiting for the tide. Mulberry B was not yet completed, but it was expected that it would soon be in operation for the British forces.[30]

Jubilation was short-lived. On June 20 the worst summer storm in forty years hit the French coast. By the time it blew itself out on the twenty-third, the Mulberry installations were a shambles. Landing craft out of gas had crashed into the Whale roadways, the backs of

[30] Ruppenthal, *Logistical Support,* I, 271–282, 402–406; Alfred B. Stanford, *Force MULBERRY* (New York, 1951), pp. 137–176.

sunken vessels had been broken, Lobnitz piers had been wrecked, and the huge steel Bombardons had broken loose to create havoc among craft in the area. After a somber survey of the damage, authorities decided that they could cannibalize enough equipment from the American installations to complete Mulberry B, which had not been so hard hit. The Phoenix and Gooseberry breakwaters of Mulberry A, however, had offered a measure of protection even during the storm and were repaired. While there is a tendency to consider the costly Mulberry operation a failure, although it worked well until the storm came, in one important regard it was a success. The very belief that they could create artificial harbors gave the Allies confidence in their decision to invade the Normandy coast, and the Germans' lack of knowledge of such plans contributed to their disbelief that a major invasion would take place in that area.[31]

The Allies, of course, did not await completion of the Mulberries to start unloading operations but began landing their supplies and equipment on the beaches. One of the most effective methods was so-called "drying-out," in which vessels beached at high tide and unloaded directly on the beach during low tide. The Navy started drying out small landing craft immediately but feared that the larger LST's would break apart in the process.[32] When several LST's showed no ill effects from drying out, however, the practice became common, and during the first two weeks at Omaha alone more than two hundred LST's discharged their cargoes in this fashion.[33]

For a brief period the Army insisted that vessels be unloaded in accordance with priority listing. The plan quickly proved unworkable, for priority lists were drawn late, frequently changed, and often unavailable on the French beaches. As a result Transportation Corps and Navy personnel had the thankless and difficult task of seeking out each ship to find its priority rating. When the backlog of vessels threatened insoluble congestion, the Army yielded to the importunings of other services and agreed to the unloading of vessels as they arrived.

[31] *Ibid.*, pp. 177–200; Ruppenthal, *Logistical Support,* I, 406–415.

[32] Joseph Bykofsky and Harold Larson, *The Transportation Corps: Operations Overseas* (*United States Army in World War II: The Technical Services*) (Washington, 1957), p. 273. Morison asserts that the Americans had early recommended drying out LST's, but that Admiral Ramsay objected. Morison, *History,* XI, 165*n*. Bradley criticized naval reluctance to beach LST's. Bradley, *A Soldier's Story,* p. 305.

[33] Ruppenthal, *Logistical Support,* I, 392.

During the confusion of the first few days at least, it was far easier to establish priorities on the beach than on the sea.[34]

Larger vessels unsuited for the drying-out technique discharged their cargo on a variety of smaller craft. The DUKW's which reached shore were valuable in this work, and the Rhino barges or ferries, which had proved themselves in the Mediterranean, were also most serviceable in the days following the Normandy landings.[35]

Although German air and naval forces had been ineffectual on D-day, they made desperate attempts in the ensuing days and weeks to check the tremendous flow of men and materials across the Channel. The *Luftwaffe* rushed about a thousand planes from Germany and Italy and launched nightly strafing and bombing attacks on the beaches. In striking at surface craft, a glide-bombing attack sank the destroyer *Meredith,* but the German Air Force was even more successful in mine-laying operations. On June 8, the destroyer *Glennon* suffered serious damage on hitting a mine off Omaha Beach, and the destroyer-escort *Rich* became another mine victim as it rushed to the *Glennon's* aid. The Germans began laying a pressure-type mine, designed to explode from the pressure caused by vessels passing over it. As soon as Allied minesweepers discovered these mines, orders went to surface craft to lower their speed to four knots, and this practice prevented the rise of pressure necessary to detonate such mines.[36]

Meanwhile, German E-boats made night raids on Allied shipping. Air reconnaissance located four German destroyers, and a British destroyer flotilla attempted to intercept and destroy them. The attack sank two of the German vessels and forced the other two, one badly damaged, to leave the area. Although the E-boats exacted some toll from Allied convoys, they, like the German Air Force, failed materially to affect the heavy flow of men and equipment to France.[37]

Having made successful landings, the U.S. forces moved next to strengthen and then expand their beachheads. One of the first objectives was to unite the two American sectors. The Germans had been surprised by the location of the D-day landings; they were much

[34] *Ibid.,* I, 392–393; Morison, *History,* XI, 164–165. For a somewhat different view, see Bradley, *A Soldier's Story,* pp. 304–305. Bradley is critical of both Army and Navy service commands.

[35] Rhino ferries were pontoon barges, propelled by outboard motors. Morison, *History,* XI, 86*n.*

[36] Morison, *History,* XI, 170–174.

[37] *Ibid.,* XI, 174–176.

better informed about American operational plans after the invasion started for they secured a copy of the orders of the VII Field Corps from a boat which drifted ashore and a copy of V Corps orders from the body of an American officer killed in action.[38]

Stubborn German resistance, aided by these lucky discoveries of American plans, checked for a time the union of the American beachheads. After visiting the assault area General Eisenhower ordered both corps to start a concerted drive toward Carentan and eliminate the gap between them.[39] A tank battalion spearheaded the thrust of the 175th Infantry and succeeded in penetrating the left flank of the enemy. Pushing ahead the V Corps seized Isigny and by carrying out this assignment thwarted the German effort to prevent consolidation of the beachheads, although the enemy did not yet give up the effort. The U.S. 101st Airborne Division, assigned VII Corps' role in the action, encountered more difficulty than did the forces from V Corps. Repulsed in its first thrust on June 7, the division made a heavier attack on the following day and pushed the enemy back toward the key city, Carentan. The Germans vigorously contested advance along an extended causeway leading to the city, and Rommel, realizing the significance of Carentan, decided to send air reinforcements to the area, but U.S. forces also increased their numbers in an enveloping advance on the city. When air reinforcements failed to arrive, the Germans realized the futility of trying to hold out, and most of them managed to withdraw before the Americans took Carentan on June 12.[40]

In addition to attempting to strengthen and extend the consolidated beachhead, the American forces started the next important operation, which was to cut across the Cotentin Peninsula, isolate the Germans in the area, and seize the port of Cherbourg. As a preliminary move, after hard fighting the VII Corps strengthened its north flank above Utah Beach and in the process reduced some of the coastal batteries which threatened that segment of the beachhead.[41]

On June 8, General Bradley ordered General Joseph Lawton Collins to head the Cotentin operation. "Lightning Joe," as he was called,

[38] Harrison, *Cross-Channel Attack,* p. 350.

[39] *Ibid.,* p. 352; *Utah Beach to Cherbourg* (Washington, 1947), p. 77.

[40] It took until the fifteenth to secure Carentan. *Ibid.,* pp. 77–93; Harrison, *Cross-Channel Attack,* pp. 352–365.

[41] *Ibid.,* pp. 386–396.

was aggressive and had gained rugged fighting experience on Guadalcanal. He assigned the principal task of cutting across the peninsula to the veteran 9th Infantry Division, effectively led by General Manton Sprague Eddy.[42]

Despite his eagerness to isolate the Germans and attack Cherbourg, Collins carefully protected his flank against counterattack before moving ahead. Eddy then successfully cut across the peninsula and in a surprise move directed by Bradley turned his forces north to join others converging on Cherbourg. The fighting was hard, for the *bocage* countryside presented obstacles fully as difficult in Collins' opinion as the jungles of Guadalcanal.[43] The peninsula also had much marshland and lowland protected by dikes.

Instead of accepting the fact that the peninsula was lost and withdrawing quickly to fight another day, the German forces remained to make a last-ditch struggle. This decision was not theirs, nor for that matter their commanders', but Hitler's. On June 12, the German leader ordered the Army in the West to fight to the last bullet. He instructed reinforcements to move to the area, but it was apparent to Rommel and von Rundstedt that a reappraisal of strategy was in order. Hitler decided to confer with the commanders in the field and on June 17 left Berchtesgaden and met Rundstedt and Rommel near Soissons. In the discussions Hitler was adamant; not only did he prohibit retreat, but he considered any withdrawal to be retreat even if it was designed to regroup and mass strength against the enemy. Furthermore, Hitler was inconsistent and in the following days issued orders and counterorders which contributed materially to the isolation and loss of much of the 77th Division.[44]

The Germans had prepared Cherbourg carefully for defense by ringing it with concrete and field fortifications well located in hilly positions which controlled every entrance to the city. Under pressure of advancing U.S. forces, the Germans on the Cotentin Peninsula

[42] Bradley, *A Soldier's Story,* pp. 295–298; Harrison, *Cross-Channel Attack,* pp. 402–403.

[43] Bradley, *A Soldier's Story,* pp. 296–301.

[44] Harrison, *Cross-Channel Attack,* pp. 412–415; *The Rommel Papers,* pp. 478–479; Hans Speidel, *Invasion 1944: Rommel and the Normandy Campaign* (Chicago. 1950), pp. 92–99. Hitler was unimpressed by Rommel's prediction of the fall of Cherbourg and instead predicted that the V-1, just released for the first time against Britain only the day before, would bring the Germans victory.

pulled back to defend the city. The units by this time, however, were reduced in numbers and strength by the hard fighting they had just experienced.[45]

The Americans knew the nature of the Cherbourg defenses, and by June 21 three divisions of the VII Corps were ready to launch the assault on the city. The storm which had shattered the Allied artificial beaches emphasized the need for securing the port. That night General Collins in a multilingual broadcast urged the enemy to surrender, but there was no response.[46] On the following morning the assault began with a heavy air attack designed to complete the demoralization of a weakened and beleaguered foe. Several hundred fighters strafed the area for about twenty minutes, and 375 bombers followed with an hour of bombing runs. There was no enemy air opposition; the antiaircraft batteries shot down twenty-four fighters but found themselves the targets for Collins' artillery.[47]

U.S. ground forces then began their attacks, but in spite of the terrific pounding they had been receiving the Germans held tenaciously to their strong points and prevented significant advance on the twenty-second. When the Americans pushed through the outer defense ring the following day, General Karl-Wilhelm von Schlieben, who headed the German ground forces, knew that defeat was certain. Nevertheless, he ordered his men to fight as long as ammunition remained. Hoping to speed up the conquest, General Collins requested naval bombardment. The advance on land continued, but the Germans fought desperately and exacted heavy toll for almost every position which the Americans took. On the morning of the twenty-fifth, von Schlieben radioed a report to Rommel that the city's capture was inevitable and he asked if the loss of the remaining troops was really necessary. Rommel replied, "You will continue to fight until the last cartridge in accordance with the order from the Fuehrer."[48]

On the twenty-fifth, a naval bombardment force arrived in response

[45] Harrison, *Cross-Channel Attack,* pp. 420, 421.

[46] The broadcast was given in German, Russian, Polish, and French. *Ibid.,* p. 428.

[47] The figures are those cited in *ibid.,* pp. 428–429. The Army Air Force account states that 557 fighter-bombers and 396 mediums of the Ninth Air Force and 118 aircraft of Second Tactical Air Force (R.A.F.) participated. Craven and Cate, *The A.A.F. in World War II,* III, 200.

[48] Quoted in Harrison, *Cross-Channel Attack,* p. 434.

to General Collins' request. Operating in two groups, the vessels, including the battleships *Nevada, Arkansas,* and *Texas,* began a duel with the shore batteries. The coastal defenses were among the best in existence, and the warships were forced to expend some of their fire on the enemy shore batteries on Cap de la Hague instead of concentrating exclusively on the Cherbourg defenses. On the other hand, the naval bombardment caused some damage and at least kept the shore batteries busy firing out to sea rather than inland.[49]

As the end of the fighting in Cherbourg neared, small groups of Germans began to surrender. On the twenty-sixth, tank destroyers flushed about eight hundred Germans from a tunnel entrance. Included in the haul were Admiral Walther Hennecke, Naval Commander Normandy, and General von Schlieben.[50] Officially the battle for Cherbourg ended with the capture of von Schlieben, but a difficult "mopping-up" procedure continued until June 30. Some groups of Germans responded to the urging of psychological warfare officers and surrendered, but others resisted bitterly to the end.[51]

The Germans realized full well the potential value of Cherbourg to the Allies and, failing in their attempt to hold the port, they sought to render it useless to its captors. In the original engineering plan for rehabilitation of the port is the following tribute to German efforts: "The demolition of the port of Cherbourg is a masterful job, beyond a doubt the most complete, intensive, and best planned demolition in history."[52] Hitler bestowed the Knight's Cross upon Admiral Hennecke for his leadership in this destruction. When the Allies reached the port they found sunken ships, sometimes piled on top of each other, blocking the various basins. They discovered twenty thousand cubic yards of masonry blown into the basin used in peacetime for transatlantic liners, installations demolished, breakwaters breached, and the lighting and heating system destroyed. In addition, the Germans had heavily and ingeniously mined the port and environs.[53] Basing their predictions on experiences in Italy, the Allies had hoped to start using Cherbourg within three days after its cap-

[49] Morison, *History,* XI, 195–212; Harrison, *Cross-Channel Attack,* p. 434.

[50] Von Schlieben refused to make a general surrender of German forces. *Ibid.,* p. 438; *Utah Beach to Cherbourg,* p. 194.

[51] *Ibid.,* pp. 195–199.

[52] Quoted in Harrison, *Cross-Channel Attack,* p. 441.

[53] *Ibid.,* pp. 441–442. For another description of the destruction, see Morison, *History,* XI, 216–217.

ture, and in view of its strategic location they had plans for Cherbourg far greater than its peacetime role, which as a naval base and passenger port had made it only twenty-second among French ports in tonnage handled.[54] The thoroughness of German destruction far exceeded Allied expectations, and it was three weeks before the port began limited operations, and even by July 25, instead of receiving an anticipated 150,000 tons of supplies, the shattered port had discharged a total of less than 18,000 tons.[55] Progress of reconstruction was steady, if slow. Engineers utilized some of the debris in constructing landing ramps, and the first unloadings were by DUKW's and barges in much the same manner as on the beaches. Although the Allies used prisoners of war and French civilians, the thorough devastation, inclement weather, and poor lighting facilities for night operations conspired to prolong delays in reconstruction.[56] On September 7, the first troop convoy arrived at Cherbourg direct from the United States. Former convoys had transshipped through England.

By the middle of September, the port was considered 75 percent rehabilitated, but the figure was misleading for much of the unloading still went on with lighters and barges and the remaining reconstruction was of dock facilities which would make possible a greater proportion of direct unloading from vessels on the dock. By October, there appeared another bottleneck, inability to move forward cargo that was ashore; although by this date the port could unload twenty thousand tons of goods daily, the cargo piled up in the port. Additional rail facilities gradually eased the situation. Cherbourg reached the peak of its operations in December and declined thereafter as other ports came into use.[57]

[54] Ruppenthal, *Logistical Support,* I, 290–291.
[55] *Ibid.,* I, 464.
[56] Bykofsky and Larson, *The Transportation Corps,* pp. 280–282.
[57] *Ibid.,* pp. 313–315.

CHAPTER 18

Breakout and Advance to the Seine

WHILE American forces moved to the capture of Cherbourg, other Allied troops continued the struggle to strengthen and extend the beachhead. One of the early disappointments had been Montgomery's failure to seize Caen shortly after the landings. Overlord planners had stressed the importance of this city and also of the surrounding countryside for the development of airfields. Considering Caen to be a crucial city in the way of Allied armored advance toward Paris, the Germans poured in reinforcements. Faced with increased armored resistance, Montgomery on June 13 stated that he intended to take Caen, and on June 18 he issued orders to the U.S. First Army to cut off the Cotentin Peninsula and to the British Second Army to seize Caen.[1] Heavy storms delayed the projected British offensive and for a time reduced materially the arrival of supplies from England. Nevertheless, by June 25, seven German divisions, four of which were armored, opposed twelve British divisions, most of which were stronger than the enemy's. Both Rommel and von Rundstedt wanted to withdraw from Caen to a line out of range of naval guns to reorganize an armored force for counterattack. After listening to their arguments in person at Berchtesgaden, Hitler rejected them; rather, he ordered German troops to hold fast everywhere on the Western front and on July 3 he replaced von Rundstedt with Field

[1] Forrest C. Pogue, *The Supreme Command* (*United States Army in World War II: The European Theater of Operations*) (Washington, 1954), pp. 181–182.

Marshal Günther von Kluge.[2] On June 30, Montgomery issued orders to the British Second Army to continue its offensive tactics "and develop operations for the capture of CAEN as opportunity offers—and the sooner the better." At the same time Montgomery told the Army that its main mission was to "hold the main enemy forces in the area between CAEN and VILLIERS BOCAGE" and "to have no set-backs."[3] In his memoirs, General Bradley later explained, "For another four weeks it fell to the British to pin down superior enemy forces in that sector [Caen] while we maneuvered into position for the U.S. breakout."[4]

In June, the Germans began to put into operation one of their new weapons. The V-1 was a small, pilotless plane which flew at a high speed on a predetermined course and by means of mechanical settings crashed with its explosive charge. It was 25.4 feet long and, with a wingspread of 17.67 feet, carried a warhead holding 2,200 pounds of high explosives. A projection device operated by decomposition of hydrogen peroxide launched the flying bomb from a ramp, and a propulsive duct, or pulse jet, increased the speed to about 360 miles per hour.[5] The Germans had been working on the project for some time at Peenemünde, on the Baltic, when the British, becoming aware of developments taking place, on August 17, 1943, bombed Peenemünde and on another occasion plastered a huge bunker being constructed at Watten.[6] The Germans continued their efforts in spite of these setbacks and early in 1944 began to build launching sites along the coast opposite England. Discovering these ramps, the British tried to bomb them out of existence, but they wasted their efforts on large "ski sites" which the Germans had discarded in favor of more

[2] Hans Speidel, *Invasion 1944: Rommel and the Normandy Campaign* (Chicago, 1950), pp. 92–96, 108–109; Erwin Rommel, *The Rommel Papers,* ed. by B. H. Liddell Hart (London, 1953), pp. 478–480; Gordon A. Harrison, *Cross-Channel Attack* (*United States Army in World War II: The European Theater of Operations*) (Washington, 1951), pp. 445–447.

[3] Quoted in *ibid.,* p. 445.

[4] Omar N. Bradley, *A Soldier's Story* (New York, 1951), p. 326.

[5] Willy Ley, *Rockets, Missiles, and Space Travel* (revised and enlarged edition) (New York, 1958), pp. 225–226. This source states that Dr. Joseph Goebbels' Propaganda Ministry said that V stood for *Vergeltung,* meaning "vengeance."

[6] *Royal Air Force, 1939–1945,* Volume III, *The Fight Is Won,* by Hilary St. George Saunders (London, 1954), pp. 143–145, 163–164; W. F. Craven and J. L. Cate, *The Army Air Forces in World War II* (Chicago, 1949), II, 687. Watten is near Calais.

easily concealed mobile sites and supply tunnels.[7]

On June 13, 1944, the Germans launched their first salvo of V-1's against England. After a number of delays, they dispatched ten flying bombs; five crashed, a sixth disappeared, four reached England, and of these only one inflicted casualties, six people dead and nine badly wounded. On the fifteenth, the enemy made a more substantial effort, as they sent 244 V-1's toward London. Some 143 reached the English coast and 73 reached greater London. To strengthen their defenses, the British brought in barrage balloons, attempted to improve anti-aircraft operations, and sent pilots in swift planes against the pilotless intruders. Some pilots became so adept that they could parallel a V-1 in flight and cause it to crash by moving in to use a wing to tilt the V-1.[8] Despite all efforts, the flying bombs continued to penetrate Allied defenses and inflict heavy destruction. On June 18, a V-1 hit a chapel at Wellington barracks and killed 121 persons. Three other bombs reportedly killed more than a hundred persons each; the heaviest loss came August 13, when a bomb landing at East Barnet killed 211 persons. Of about ten thousand V-1's launched toward London, less than one-fourth reached the target area.[9]

The Germans had also been working at Peenemünde on their A-4, later known as V-2, which was not a plane but a rocket, sent to a very high elevation and then back to earth at a tremendous speed. With a range of a little over two hundred miles, the forty-six-foot rocket carried a one-ton warhead.[10] Unlike the V-1, the rocket could not be heard as it approached, and if it hit a building created terrific destruction. Starting in August, 1944, the Germans directed 1,403 V-2 bombs by the end of the campaign, and of these about 517 reached the London area. Although terrifying in the implication of things to come, the V-2 dealt out less punishment than the V-1, which in turn was much less destructive than conventional bombing from air attacks.[11]

Nevertheless, these new weapons were hard on the morale of the

[7] Basil Collier, *The Defence of the United Kingdom* (London, 1957), p. 360.

[8] *Ibid.*, pp. 369–376.

[9] *Ibid.*, pp. 377–378, 396, 523. The flying-bomb offensive consisted of 8,892 launched from ramps and 1,600 from aircraft; 2,419 reached the London Civil Defence Region.

[10] *Ibid.*, p. 521.

[11] *Ibid.*, pp. 527, 528. Figures of persons killed or seriously injured are as follows: bombing, 112,932; flying bombs, 24,165; rockets, 9,277; cross-Channel guns, 403.

British, who hoped that once landings had been made in France they would be free from direct attack. There was a temptation on the part of invasion leaders to turn aside to attack the launching sites, but they realized that such a move would be a costly diversion from the main plan.[12] General Carl A. Spaatz of the Army Air Force also felt that bombing raids against the launching sites would not only be largely ineffectual because of the heavy concrete construction, but would weaken the more important strategic bombing of Germany.[13] The R.A.F., however, with a certain amount of assistance from the U.S. Eighth Air Force, dropped some seventy thousand tons of bombs on launching sites in Belgium and France with about the result that Spaatz had anticipated. Altogether, in the counteroffensive against flying bombs and rockets, the Allied Air Forces dropped about 118,000 pounds of explosives, lost almost 450 planes and 2,900 pilots and crew members, yet the enemy moved away from its launching sites only as the Allied ground advance gradually menaced them. The Germans then turned with some success to launching flying bombs from Heinkel aircraft.[14]

The battle between the British and the Germans around Caen continued. By the end of June, Rommel had concentrated seven Panzer (tank) divisions against the British sector in contrast to but one such division against the U.S. forces.[15] Another factor kept the Germans to the eastern end of the beachhead. Until late in June Nazi leaders still believed that the Allies planned to open a second front in the Pas-de-Calais area.[16] They were even sure that they knew who would lead this invasion. The Germans were convinced that Patton would attempt to open the new beachhead, and the Allies attempted to mislead the enemy by giving the impression that Patton headed an Army Group in England, although in actuality he commanded the Third Army, which was waiting to join the other forces fighting in Normandy. The First Army Group had been commanded by General Bradley since October, 1943. After the invasion and after the Third

[12] Dwight D. Eisenhower, *Crusade in Europe* (New York, 1948), pp. 259–260.

[13] Spaatz suggested the possibility of sending remotely controlled bombers with excess bombloads against some of the concrete establishments. The experiment was tried several times but not followed up. Craven and Cate, *The A.A.F. in World War II,* III, 531.

[14] Collier, *The Defence of the United Kingdom,* pp. 388–389.

[15] Pogue, *The Supreme Command,* p. 182.

[16] *Ibid.,* pp. 182–183.

Army had joined the rest of the group fighting in France, the First Army Group was reconstituted as the Twelfth Army Group in order to confuse the enemy. The First Army Group remained in England, but only on paper. To add to the illusion, this mythical army group was commanded by a real general, Lieutenant General Lesley J. McNair, brought from his training duties in the United States to assume his new post in England. After McNair's death in late July, the paper organization received another three-star general, John L. De Witt, former commander of the Western Defense Command. Before the attempted break-through was made in Normandy, the Allies developed a cover plan designed to hold substantial enemy forces in the Pas-de-Calais area. By using a mock-up invasion fleet, spurious radio nets, and other devices, they attempted with no little success to convince the Germans that a second major cross-Channel assault soon would come at Pas-de-Calais.[17]

The Allied forces in Normandy were growing rapidly in numbers. At the end of the third week after D-day, the U.S. First Army alone was larger than the Allied force that had taken Sicily, and had thirteen divisions, composed of nine infantry, two airborne, and two armored divisions. These men occupied a forty-mile front extending from the point of juncture with the British to the west channel shore across the Cherbourg peninsula. The British beachhead extended about forty miles in the other direction. In these cramped quarters were sixteen divisions, of which five were armored. As the pressure on the British increased, U.S. forces took over a small portion of the British sector. Since it was a quiet part, a "rubber division" took its place in the line. Composed of inflated rubber tanks and a communications section to simulate the radio activity of a real tank division, this unit apparently performed its defensive function adequately until more aggressive replacements arrived.[18]

The enthusiasm that had been engendered by the successful establishment of a beachhead began to dim in some quarters as the Allied forces failed to make headway against the Germans. Montgomery became the particular target for criticism. He had failed to secure Caen after predicting that he would, while the Americans had cut off the Cherbourg peninsula and captured its port. Most of the critics

[17] Pogue, *The Supreme Command,* pp. 199, 261*n;* Bradley, *A Soldier's Story,* pp. 344–345. For German views, see Hans Speidel, *Invasion 1944,* pp. 83–84; *The Rommel Papers,* p. 478.

[18] Bradley, *A Soldier's Story,* pp. 315–316, 328.

could not know that Montgomery by his engagement of the enemy had helped make possible the capture of Cherbourg, and Eisenhower could not tell them without also telling the enemy.[19]

Although Eisenhower appreciated what Montgomery was doing, he, like others, wished that Montgomery would do it faster and harder. Finally on July 7, he gave Montgomery a broad hint to accelerate his movements.[20] Whether spurred by this reminder or ready on his own account, the British Marshal on the following day began a serious attack on Caen, following a heavy preliminary bombardment. By July 10, the British Second Army had taken most of the city, with the exception of suburbs across the river. The Air Force felt that the Second Army had not fully exploited the opportunity created by the advance bombing, but it appears that the Army found it difficult to work its way through the rubble and extensive cratering left by the bombing attack.[21]

On July 18, Montgomery began a major offensive, known as Goodwood, which like the earlier move against Caen was preceded by an air attack. With Eisenhower's support, Montgomery had secured the diversion of strategic air bombers to assist the ground forces. The result was the heaviest air support yet given to ground troops. At a quarter to six in the morning the heavy bombers began to lay down a carpet of bombs south and east of Caen and before the attack was over 7,700 tons of explosives had been dropped. The result was no break-through and the advance was limited to about ten thousand yards.[22] Montgomery, however, felt that the damage done the enemy forces constituted a successful operation. Unfortunately, Montgomery had been rather optimistic in his prebattle statements and had given the impression that more was in the offing than an attrition of German armor. Allied airmen were annoyed and of the belief that they had wasted their efforts. Pressure came from various quarters on the Supreme Commander to relieve the British leader. Eisenhower had been somewhat misled by Montgomery's earlier statements, but he defended him, even to the point of making a statement drawing at-

[19] Eisenhower, *Crusade in Europe*, p. 267; Pogue, *The Supreme Command*, p. 183.

[20] *Ibid.*, pp. 184–185.

[21] *Ibid.*, pp. 185–187.

[22] Craven and Cate, *The A.A.F. in World War II*, III, 208–209; Pogue, *The Supreme Command*, pp. 188–189.

tention to his own personal responsibility for the conduct of the war on the front.[23]

In addition to the general objective of defeating the German military power, certain more specific objectives seemed necessary as preparation. One was to extend the lodgment to make possible freer use of mechanized equipment. Another was to seize Brittany. The anticipated September storms would check the unloading of supplies on the beaches, and although Cherbourg was a valuable prize, even when in good working order, it could handle supplies for only fourteen divisions.[24] Brittany with its good harbors offered the answer.

When they saw that the enemy was resisting so stubbornly the advance of the British forces, the Allied leaders, Eisenhower, Montgomery, and Bradley, agreed that the general plan of attack should be a great wheeling movement with Montgomery's forces acting as the "pivot." Eisenhower would have preferred a general advance forward, but this seemed impossible in view of the German defenses around Caen. Bradley, while concurring in the general plan, believed that the best method of putting it into effect was by a break through the German lines. This move would enable armored and other mechanized units to carry on a swift war of movement against the rear of the enemy.[25]

Accordingly, the commander of the U.S. First Army began to develop a plan. There were natural obstacles. The hedgerows or *bocage* not only provided excellent defenses for German infantry but greatly impeded the progress of mechanized equipment. Sherman tanks running against a hedgerow, instead of pushing through "bellied" upward and presented a vulnerable target. At the neck of the Cotentin Peninsula, also, the Carentan marshes threatened to mire mechanized forces that attempted to cross them. There appeared to be two possible points for a breakout attempt. One was at Saint-Lô, south of the American beachhead. At first Bradley felt that this place

[23] *Ibid.*, pp. 189–191. Montgomery asserts that he never had any intention of breaking out on the eastern flank, and that Eisenhower and other officers at Supreme Headquarters did not understand his plan. Montgomery admits that he was too optimistic in the press conference that he gave during the operation. Bernard L. Montgomery, *The Memoirs of Field-Marshal the Viscount Montgomery of Alamein, K. G.* (Cleveland and New York, 1958), pp. 229–231.

[24] Bradley, *A Soldier's Story*, p. 317.

[25] "Pivot" was Bradley's term. *Ibid.*, pp. 317–318; Pogue, *The Supreme Command*, p. 197; Montgomery, *Memoirs*, p. 231.

would be too strongly defended and he discarded it in favor of a thrust down the west coast of the Cherbourg peninsula. He hoped that the Germans would not send too many reinforcements that far west in fear of a second Allied attack at Saint-Lô which might isolate the western units.[26]

Since Montgomery was still in command of the Allied forces in France, Bradley presented his plan to him. Montgomery, as he did throughout the fighting, gave Bradley a free hand to go ahead. The latter gave the assignment to the victor of Cherbourg, and on July 3 General Collins began the attack on the western end of the American lines, and sought to move toward Coutances. His men encountered heavy resistance and found the terrain to be extensively mined. After Collins' forces had fought for twelve days with a gain of only twelve thousand yards, Bradley called off the attack. One explanation for Collins' failure to break through was that his armored units were too closely confined to operate effectively.[27]

Having failed to penetrate the line in the Coutances thrust, Bradley sought an alternative. By July 10, he had decided that under certain circumstances a breakout at Saint-Lô was feasible. From the old fortress town there was a road running west through the town of Périer, twenty miles away. Extensive preliminary bombing constituted an important part of plan Cobra. Bradley reasoned that the old road running parallel to American lines would be an excellent marker for bombers flying along it and would eliminate fear of "short" bombs falling on U.S. troops. Cobra provided that after the bomb carpet had been laid two infantry divisions would attack to create a hole through which tanks and mobilized infantry could pour. Still having confidence in Collins as a fighting leader, Bradley selected him to head the new venture.[28]

Before they could put Cobra into operation the U.S. forces had to push their way slowly through the Carentan marshes. Cobra involved the use of two types of air support. One was the laying down of the bomb carpet. The other was support of the actual attack. Bradley was fortunate in having assigned to him as leader of the IX Tactical Air Command, Major General Elwood R. Queseda, a vigorous young officer who with Bradley worked out an ingenious system of fire control parties which operated not in jeeps but in Sherman

[26] Bradley, *A Soldier's Story,* pp. 318–319.
[27] *Ibid.,* pp. 319–321.
[28] *Ibid.,* p. 332.

tanks and thereby could give more effective instructions to the supporting planes. The carpet bombing was a different matter and, as was the case with Montgomery's Goodwood operation, Cobra required the help of the Strategic Bomber Command. Clearing with Montgomery, Bradley flew to England and conferred with the Allied leaders of this command, who agreed to provide the necessary air force. Wishing to avoid extensive cratering by large bombs, Bradley insisted on the use of hundred-pound fragmentation bombs. Agreement on this point meant that U.S. bombers would conduct the attack, since R.A.F. bombers were not equipped to handle this type of bomb. Bradley also thought that there was clear understanding that the planes would fly along the Saint-Lô-Périer road and he arranged as an added precaution to have the U.S. forces pull back fifteen hundred yards from this road.

The air support promised was indeed impressive. Fifteen hundred heavy bombers, each carrying forty hundred-pound bombs would be accompanied by 396 medium bombers and 350 fighter bombers. In other words, more than two thousand bombers would lay down a bomb carpet on five square miles of Normandy hedgerow country.[29]

About this time Bradley received another stroke of good fortune. A tank sergeant, Curtis J. Culin, had been experimenting with four steel prongs attached to a Sherman tank. Thus equipped, the tank moved up to a hedgerow and instead of "bellying" dug into the bank and crashed through the obstacle, creating an opening. Culin's idea reached Bradley, who hastily ordered the adaptation of other tanks. By the time of the assault 60 percent had been provided with spikes, the steel for most of which came from the obstacles the Germans had placed on the beaches.[30]

On the German side the total strength had increased from fifty-eight to sixty-five divisions, but fundamentally the enemy situation was serious. The German Seventh Army opposing the U.S. forces was battle-weary and had asked for replacements which were not forthcoming, although behind the Pas-de-Calais the Fifteenth Army still awaited the expected attack by Patton's Army. The problem of command was becoming exceedingly critical. The failure of the German defenses to prevent the establishment of an Allied beachhead de-

[29] *Ibid.*, pp. 337–341.

[30] Eisenhower, *Crusade in Europe*, pp. 268–269; Bradley, *A Soldier's Story*, p. 342. Although Bradley describes the devices as "tusklike prongs," they were like scythes and could cut through the hedge growth.

manded a scapegoat. Von Rundstedt had too much popularity to be fired outright, but he was retired for reasons of his health.[31]

Many persons felt that Marshal Rommel would succeed von Rundstedt, but instead Hitler appointed Marshal Günther von Kluge, a Prussian who had won his reputation especially on the Eastern front. On July 5, von Kluge arrived to take over his new post and held a tense meeting with Rommel. The new Commander in Chief berated Rommel for the failures in the West and Rommel angrily recommended that von Kluge look at the conditions on the front before criticizing. After this bitter interview, von Kluge went to see the front and when he saw what the actual situation was he apologized to Rommel and like the latter took a pessimistic view of the future course of events.[32]

Now that his forces had secured lodgment in France, Eisenhower, as he had planned, announced the creation of the U.S. Twelfth Army Group, headed by Bradley, who turned the First Army over to the capable direction of General Courtney Hicks Hodges. General Patton arrived in France in August as head of the Third Army. It was further expected that as soon as Eisenhower could establish his headquarters in France rather than in England, he would assume command of the Allied forces in the field. Until the Supreme Commander was able to make this move, he continued to delegate his authority to General Montgomery even after the creation of the U.S. Twelfth Army Group. Bradley made no objection to this arrangement since Montgomery had always given the Americans a free hand.

The shifting of command organization did not delay the plans for attack. Bradley determined to make the first thrust with the First Army and hold the Third Army for later action. Before launching the Cobra operation, he sent the XIX Corps against Saint-Lô, which U.S. forces had been struggling to seize since shortly after establishing the beachhead. Realizing the significance of this hill town, the Germans had reinforced it so strongly that heavy American casualties counterbalanced the immediate need for capture of the town. The conquest of the Cotentin Peninsula and of Cherbourg took priority over Saint-Lô, and around that region fighting for a time reached a stalemate. Now, however, Saint-Lô was needed, and on July 11, the XIX Corps, under command of Major General Charles Harrison

[31] Speidel, *Invasion 1944*, p. 108.
[32] *Ibid.*, pp. 109–111; *The Rommel Papers,* pp. 480–485.

Corlett, began an assault. The advance was slow and costly through the hedgerow country in the face of strong resistance featured by counterattacks, but it was an advance, beating its way along both sides of the Vire River. On the seventeenth, the 35th Division penetrated enemy defenses on the right flank of the corps, and during the next two days of fighting Saint-Lô passed into the possession of the Americans.[33]

The launching date for Cobra was set at July 24, and early that morning the first bombers started on their way from England. Since the weather continued to be poor, the command reconsidered and postponed the attack. The leading planes did not receive the order in time; they had already crossed the coast and soon afterward dropped bombloads through the overcast. More unfortunately still, some of the bombs fell short and landed on the U.S. 30th Division more than a mile behind the carpet. When Bradley heard the bad news, he realized that the bombing attack had been vertical to the Saint-Lô-Périer road instead of parallel to it. He immediately protested, but he was informed that the intricate planning for such a tremendous air attack made it impossible to change the direction.[34]

The following day clearing weather enabled the Strategic Air Command to conduct its full assault. The previous day's mishap led to precautionary measures to prevent a repetition. American forces were to be identified with cerise and yellow panels. Red smoke shells fired at two-minute intervals or less at the boundaries were to guide the bombardiers, and the heavy bombers were to bomb visually, since it was hoped that preliminary Army counterbattery fire would reduce enemy flak.

Following an intricate time schedule the planes carried out their attack from 9:38 in the morning until 12:23 P.M. One thousand, five hundred and seven heavy bombers, more than 380 medium bombers, and 559 fighter bombers dropped 4,790 tons of bombs. Enemy fighter planes were practically nonexistent and completely ineffective. The only losses were four heavy bombers and one medium bomber to ground fire.[35]

[33] For a convenient chronological summary of the war, see Mary H. Williams, *Chronology 1941–1945 (United States Army in World War II: Special Studies)* (Washington, 1960).

[34] Bradley, *A Soldier's Story,* pp. 346–347; Craven and Cate, *The A.A.F. in World War II,* III, 230.

[35] According to Air Chief Marshal Leigh-Mallory, the bombing at Saint-Lô

Despite the precautions, perhaps because of the size of the operation, there were bombing errors, some bombs fell short, and the 30th Division again was the hardest hit. More than a hundred men were killed, and among them was General McNair, head of the fictitious army group, who had gone to the front lines to observe the effectiveness of training in the United States. About 380 men were wounded.[36] In addition to inflicting these casualties, the short bombing had thrown the Collins' attack off stride; consequently, when the first day ended Bradley did not know whether Cobra would succeed or fail. Eisenhower, who had been with Bradley, left for England saying that it was the last time he would use heavy bombers as ground support. Preliminary bombing was a task for artillery, not bombers.[37]

The American leaders soon saw that their pessimism was unwarranted, for United States forces were on the edge of winning one of their most significant battles of the war. While the bomb carpet had not been so successful as some had hoped and there had been regrettable casualties among the Americans, the damage inflicted on the enemy was great. Restricted by Bradley's request from using large bombs, the attacking air force had failed to destroy heavier equipment and emplacements of the Germans or kill the enemy hiding in protected places. Even the small bombs resulted in some cratering, but the engineers were prepared for this contingency and set to work creating passable routes for mechanized equipment. Statements made subsequent to the war by Germans who were subjected to the bombardment attest to its tremendous impact. One of the most important effects was on morale. The awesome size of the air armada and the literal blanket of bombs stunned many who were not physically injured. The commander of a Panzer division, rapidly changing his vantage point from a motorcycle to a thick stone tower, compared the cratered landscape to the surface of the moon and stated that 70 percent of his men were killed, wounded, or incapacitated by shock. The air attack had a devastating effect on exposed personnel, light tanks, antiaircraft guns, and other smaller equipment. One of the

---

was the third largest in Normandy in number of tons dropped. On July 18, at Caen 1,676 heavy and 343 medium bombers dropped 7,700 tons. On the night of August 7–8 and the succeeding day, 1,450 bombers of the Eighth Air Force and Bomber Command dropped more than 5,200 tons of bombs. Pogue, *The Supreme Command,* p. 199*n*.

[36] Craven and Cate, *The A.A.F. in World War II,* III, 231–234.

[37] Bradley, *A Soldier's Story,* pp. 348–349.

most important contributions was a widespread destruction and disruption of communications.[38]

After the bombardment was over the ground forces began their advance. Although thrown off stride by the short bombing, they had not been knocked out and, reorganizing, they joined the attack. They did not find the way uncontested. Germans, recovering from the shock of the air assault, fought back, but they did so at a disadvantage because of that assault. A combination of infantry and tanks broke through the German lines. Tactical air support was especially effective as planes and tanks, working as a team, ranged ahead to strike the enemy.[39] Moving quickly, the First Army exploited the breakthrough by pursuing and surrounding units of the temporarily disorganized enemy and advancing toward Coutances, which it took on the twenty-eighth of July. Next it headed toward Avranches, on the coast at the base of the Cotentin Peninsula. Armored divisons, followed closely by motorized combat teams of infantry, spearheaded the advance. They captured the bridges over the See River and seized Avranches on July 30; on the following day other units took nearby Granville. On August 1, the Third Army became operational, with four American corps and Forces Françaises de l'Intérieur (F.F.I.), and was assigned the task of securing Brittany Peninsula and its ports.

When the Americans started their break-through effort on the right flank of the Allied lodgment, British and Canadian forces launched an offensive on the left. On the twenty-fifth, the latter encountered heavy armored resistance and suffered severe casualties. Notwithstanding, Eisenhower urged Montgomery to increase the pressure to hold enemy forces around Caen, and he stated, "Never was time more vital to us, and we should not wait on weather or on perfection of detail of preparations." In turn, Montgomery pressed General Henry D. G. Crerar, commander of the newly activated Canadian First Army, to continue the offensive regardless of casualties.[40]

After the breakout, the U.S. First Army's task was to hold its line and then move east to attack the rear of the German forces. The favorable course of the attack to date and the knowledge that German reserves in Brittany were not too numerous caused a shift in the

[38] Craven and Cate, *The A.A.F. in World War II,* III, 234–236.
[39] *Ibid.,* III, 238–243.
[40] Pogue, *The Supreme Command,* pp. 200–201.

Third Army's orders. A single corps, Major General Troy H. Middleton's VIII, advanced on Brittany. The remainder of the Third Army headed farther south to turn left and then, like the First Army, approach the rear of the German forces.[41]

Instead of contesting Middleton's advance, the garrison troops on the Brittany Peninsula barricaded themselves in such fortified seaports as Saint-Mâlo and Brest. Rather than attempt to take all these fortresses, Allied troops simply isolated two of the least dangerous, in which the Germans held out until the end of the war. Since Saint-Mâlo and especially Brest would have required too large a force to hold the Germans from raids on communications, U.S. forces took these strongholds after a costly siege. Although a prime motive in invading Brittany had been to secure ports, none of them was actually used for the landing of Allied supplies. The shifting of the war east and the possibility of securing Antwerp eliminated the need for the more distant Brittany ports.[42]

The successful advance of the Americans in the days following July 25 forced Marshal von Kluge to consider his next action. Not only had the American move to the right taken Avranches and threatened Brittany, but the thrust south had exposed the left flank of the German forces. Von Kluge was faced with two hard choices. He could retreat to the Seine. While the withdrawal would be difficult in view of wrecked roads and bridges, lack of organic transport, and continued Allied control of the air, he would be retreating to a strong position and could gain reinforcements from the Pas-de-Calais area. The other possibility was to attempt what the Americans had just accomplished, a breakout. If the Germans could push through the American lines and retake Avranches, they could seal off the Brittany Peninsula and isolate the American forces to the left in the interior of France. The German commander really had no choice. It was one of Hitler's fetishes to have his men stand and fight and he ordered von Kluge to attack the American line. General Bradley later expressed the opinion that this order, more than anything else, cost the Germans the Battle for France, since tactically they did not have the facilities for success in the venture.[43]

[41] Eisenhower, *Crusade in Europe,* pp. 272–274; Bradley, *A Soldier's Story,* pp. 358, 362–363.

[42] *Ibid.,* pp. 365–367. It took an entire U.S. infantry division and seventeen French battalions of infantry to contain the two ports of Lorient and Saint-Nazaire.

[43] *Ibid.,* p. 371.

At one o'clock in the morning, August 7, the Germans launched their counterattack toward their first objective, Mortain, some distance east of Avranches. Five Panzer and SS divisions headed the assault, which was initially successful. The 2d Battalion of the 120th Regiment was isolated and held out desperately for six days until relieved. United States forces rushed to the rescue, however, and prevented a break through the line.[44]

It was now Bradley's turn to make a critical strategic decision. He could call back the four divisions that had gone through into the interior of France and use them to resist the assault of the enemy. His other choice was to hope that the American forces presently engaged could hold the line and turn the four divisions farther east against the open flank of the Germans. Informed that he could count on at least two thousand tons of supplies daily by air, Bradley took the risk that the Mortain line could hold in an endeavor to knock out an entire army. As a safety measure, Bradley held the four divisions in reserve for twenty-four hours to guard against a sudden break-through and then ordered them eastward against the German flank.[45]

The American forces at Mortain held, and instead of succeeding in its counterattack, the German Seventh Army found itself confronted on three sides by Allied forces. In addition, it was being mercilessly attacked from above.[46] Engineer battalions with the American forces constructed airfields to meet the needs of the tactical air force. By August 5, they had surfaced seventeen fighter-bomber and two medium-bomber fields in Normandy with several types of prefabricated surfacing, including square mesh track and pierced-steel plank. They continued their work of construction and repair throughout the advance across Western Europe until by V-E day there were 182 operational American fields in Western Europe.[47] Based within striking distance, the tactical air force made the most of its opportunity. Rocket-firing Typhoons were especially successful against tanks and mechanized equipment, and their strikes helped prevent a break-through at Mortain and continued to harass the enemy.

[44] Eisenhower, *Crusade in Europe,* pp. 274–275; Pogue, *The Supreme Command,* pp. 206–208.

[45] Eisenhower, *Crusade in Europe,* p. 275; Bradley, *A Soldier's Story,* pp. 371–374. The 2d Battalion of the 120th Regiment earned a presidential unit citation for holding out for six days until relieved although completely surrounded by Germans.

[46] Craven and Cate, *The A.A.F. in World War II,* III, 243–253.

[47] *Ibid.,* III, 562–573.

The next Allied move was inevitable. This was an effort to close the German Seventh and Fifth Panzer Armies in a trap. Patton was to come up from the south as one part of the pincers, and Montgomery would move south as the other part to close the trap near Falaise. General Walter Bedell Smith, Eisenhower's Chief of Staff, later wrote: "To a staff officer, seeing it all in the red, blue, and black symbols on the map, it was almost unbelievable that the German High Command could have let the bulk of its forces in France be maneuvered into such a desperate situation."[48] Von Kluge knew how critical the situation was, but Hitler refused to see it until too late. At one time he ordered a renewed attack on Avranches and he delayed overlong even limited retreat. He was suspicious of von Kluge and once, when communications had been knocked out temporarily, thought that the Field Marshal had gone over to the enemy.[49]

Fortunately for the Germans, the Allies failed to close the trap in time to isolate all the enemy. Patton finished his assignment by reaching Argentan and asked for permission to push into the region reserved for British seizure, but Bradley refused the request. He feared the complications and possible casualties of Allied armies meeting head on, since communications were hard to establish on such a fluid front. Further, while Patton might be able to close the gap, his line would be too attenuated to withstand the force of nineteen divisions madly trying to get out of a trap. Eisenhower endorsed Bradley's decision as sound.[50]

On the other side of the gap British and Canadian troops encountered heavy resistance and moved slowly. The enemy held Falaise until August 16; meanwhile, thousands of Nazi soldiers slipped through to safety. Montgomery ordered forces on both sides of the gap to move northeast and make another effort to seal off the Germans, and on August 19 the trap closed as elements of the Canadian II Corps and the U.S. V Corps met at Chambois.[51]

The encirclement of the German forces was disastrous for von Kluge. He had been unable to convince Hitler that the armies must

[48] Walter Bedell Smith, *Eisenhower's Six Great Decisions: Europe 1944–1945* (New York, London, Toronto, 1956), p. 63.

[49] Pogue, *The Supreme Command*, pp. 210–213; Speidel, *Invasion 1944*, pp. 133–134.

[50] Bradley, *A Soldier's Story*, pp. 376–377; Eisenhower, *Crusade in Europe*, pp. 278–279.

[51] Pogue, *The Supreme Command*, pp. 214–215.

retreat to save themselves, and instead on August 16 the *Führer* ordered the forces in the pocket to fight to the end. Von Kluge apparently decided to order the withdrawal himself, but the next day before he could take action Hitler replaced him with Field Marshal Walter Model. Knowing that he undoubtedly faced court-martial and hanging, von Kluge two days later committed suicide by taking poison while in a car headed for Germany.[52]

By the time the gap was closed Bradley had permitted Patton to send some of his forces after the Germans who had escaped from the trap and were retreating north, and after completing the encirclement Montgomery's forces joined in the pursuit toward the Seine River. The situation became somewhat confused, but still dangerous for the enemy. Meanwhile, Hodge's First Army ground relentlessly against the Germans in the trap. The Third Army in a spectacular manner and with few casualties had moved swiftly and far against the flank of the German forces. The First Army in a less spectacular way and with heavy losses had advanced slowly and directly against a pocket of desperately fighting, cornered German troops. The sledge hammer blows of the First Army not only helped create the pocket but did much to smash it. Then it, too, was ready to push toward the Seine. Hoping to trap more Germans east of the Seine, Bradley sent U.S. troops of the First Army diagonally across the British Second Army. He secured permission for the difficult maneuver when General Sir Miles Christopher Dempsey stated that he could not spare men for the task.[53]

In breaking through the German lines at Saint-Lô, encircling the Germans, and advancing toward the Seine, the Allies had inflicted a major defeat on the Germans. They had caught about ninety thousand men and the equipment of two German armies in the trap. While they had not captured every German in the road, those who did escape across the Seine took little of their equipment with them. Five regiments were so badly cut to pieces that they were sent to Germany. From eleven infantry regiments only sufficient men remained to reconstitute four, and they had little material. The eleven Panzer divisions were reduced to an equal number of combat teams.[54]

[52] Speidel, *Invasion 1944,* p. 137.

[53] Bradley, *A Soldier's Story,* pp. 380–383.

[54] There were about 125,000 men in the trap and from 30,000 to 35,000 escaped. Pogue, *The Supreme Command,* p. 215.

In the midst of the heavy fighting in Western Europe came news of an attempt on the life of Adolf Hitler. A group of Germans, mainly Army officers, had long been plotting the death of Hitler. Stemming originally from conflict between members of the German General Staff and high Nazi party members, the movement gained impetus as men came to feel that Hitler's policies were leading Germany to destruction. In 1944, a group of men made careful plans for a *coup d'état* which included assassination of Hitler, seizure of the government and the military forces, and peace negotiations with the enemy. There were ramifications of the plan. The leading conspirator in the west was General Heinrich von Stülpnagel, Military Governor of France, who had concluded that Germany's cause in France was lost. He began to intrigue for the detachment of the German forces in the West from Germany in a separate peace.

Stülpnagel was one of those who approached Rommel. The Desert Fox was probably the one man who could gain popular support if Hitler should be killed, and the conspirators offered Rommel the possibility of playing a role similar to that of von Hindenburg after World War I. Rommel was intrigued and gave qualified approval. He was not directly involved in the assassination plot and at first opposed the idea on the ground that such an act would make a martyr of Hitler. Instead, he felt that Hitler should be arrested and brought to trial.[55]

From July 12 to 15, Rommel was at the front. Talking to his field commanders he concluded that they also felt the necessity for independent action by the Western armies when the time came. Marshal von Kluge also apparently was in sympathy with the idea of a separate peace, but he indicated that he would participate only after Hitler's death.[56]

This unusual attitude of the high military officers in the West undoubtedly came in part from Hitler's attitude toward the war on the Western front. The *Führer* had failed to realize the seriousness of the situation, he counted heavily on winning the war with such new weapons as the V-1, and he failed to give the forces in Belgium and France the supplies they needed so desperately. No arguments, no matter how vigorously written or spoken by Rommel in occasional

[55] John W. Wheeler-Bennett, *The Nemesis of Power: The German Army in Politics, 1918–1945* (New York, 1954), pp. 604–605. For a background study of Hitler and his generals, see Telford Taylor, *Swords and Swastika: Generals and Nazis in the Third Reich* (New York, 1952).

[56] Wheeler-Bennett, *The Nemesis of Power,* p. 630.

conferences in Germany with Hitler, changed his views. On July 15, in a last desperate effort to get help, Rommel sent a pointed and prophetic memorandum to the *Führer*.

In this document he noted that the situation in Normandy daily was becoming more critical and that a serious crisis was near. The armored might of the Allies, their artillery, and their air power were depleting the German divisions. Rommel drew attention to the utterly inadequate replacements from Germany and the disastrous effect on transportation of the enemy's air interdiction program. In contrast, he reported, the Allied armies were steadily increasing in size and strength. Concluding, the Field Marshal predicted that within two or three weeks the enemy would succeed in breaking through the lines especially of the Seventh Army and would penetrate to the interior of France. Von Kluge forwarded the document with an endorsement of its opinions and demands.[57]

Two days later Rommel again went to the front. When he was returning to his headquarters in an unescorted staff car, British fighter aircraft spotted and attacked the vehicle. The driver was killed, and the Marshal was seriously wounded. If Rommel had planned independent action, the accident terminated the plot. Instead of appointing a replacement, on July 19 von Kluge himself assumed the command of the Army Group in addition to his other duties.[58]

On July 20, the assassination plan came to a climax. The message sent to leaders throughout Germany that Hitler was dead was to be the signal for a revolution that would sweep the Nazis out of power and lead to peace. Colonel Count Klaus von Stauffenberg, a wounded veteran of the North African campaign, and a leader in the plot with General Ludwig Beck, former Chief of the German General Staff, attended the conference in which Hitler was present. Leaving a briefcase containing a bomb, Stauffenberg on a pretext departed from the room. When he was a short distance from the building he heard a terrific explosion, and thinking that he had succeeded put the revolution in motion by sending the message that Hitler was dead.

Unfortunately for the conspirators, although there were four dead men in the small room, Hitler was not one of them. Evidently two factors largely explain the *Führer's* escape from almost certain death. Since Hitler's bunker was being reinforced with concrete, the meeting took place in a small structure with wooden walls and windows opened

[57] Speidel, *Invasion 1944,* pp. 115–117; *The Rommel Papers,* pp. 486–487.
[58] Wheeler-Bennett, *The Nemesis of Power,* pp. 632, 665.

wide. Had the explosion occurred in a concrete bunker, probably all present would have been killed. In addition, an unusually heavy wooden table seems to have taken the brunt of the explosion. As a result, through rare luck Hitler was only slightly wounded and later in the day met Mussolini and reviewed some Italian troops headed for the Eastern front.[59]

The revolution still might have succeeded, but some persons who were to put the plan in effect moved too slowly, others hesitated, and then when the news came through about an hour later that Hitler had escaped they gave up the venture.

In the West, it happened that von Kluge was temporarily absent when the news arrived that Hitler was dead. The second message came before the Commander had decided to move, and upon hearing that Hitler was alive von Kluge decided to do nothing about an independent movement by the armies in the West.[60]

The failure of the assassination attempt made the situation even worse than it had been. Himmler's Secret Police rounded up the ringleaders, and instead of revolution there was a vicious purge in which Hitler exacted retribution from those who had worked against him. Even persons not implicated in the plot suffered.[61] Von Kluge had not been aware of the plot, yet Hitler suspected him and hampered his activities as commander in the West. Rommel, who had taken no part in the plot to assassinate Hitler, soon found that its failure sealed his own fate. Recuperating from his wounds in his own home near Ulm, Rommel was given the choice of suicide or arrest with its inevitable consequences not only to him but to his family. He chose the former, and Nazi leaders wept false tears over the nation's hero whom they reported as dying of his wounds.[62] The physical injuries to Hitler in the assassination attempt had been slight; the psychological effects were considerable and colored his subsequent dealings with Army officers.

[59] *Ibid.*, pp. 635–645. For extended treatments of the assassination attempt and its aftermath, see Constantine FitzGibbon, *20 July* (New York, 1956), *passim;* Ritter Wilhelm von Schramm, *Conspiracy Among Generals* (London [1956]), *passim.*

[60] Speidel, *Invasion 1944,* pp. 121–122.

[61] Wheeler-Bennett, *The Nemesis of Power,* pp. 657–689.

[62] For an account of Rommel's death written by his son, see *The Rommel Papers,* pp. 499–506.

CHAPTER 19

Advance Across France

AS THE trap closed on the German armies between Mortain and Falaise, Allied forces moved quickly toward their next objective, the Seine. The Germans were having difficulty crossing the river, since all bridges between Paris and the sea had long since been destroyed, Allied planes relentlessly patrolled the river, and Allied artillery bombarded key crossings. While many Germans made their escape across the river, they found it difficult to use the stream as a barrier, for Allied forces were hot in pursuit. Elements of the Third Army established bridgeheads by August 24, and shortly afterward the British pushed across in several places farther downstream. These Allied advances were part of the plan to take Paris by siege instead of a frontal assault which might decimate the city's population and reduce the famed city to rubble. The Third Army's advance was so fast that a planned air drop proved unnecessary.[1]

Gratifying though the rapid advance was, the problem of logistical supply was becoming critical, for the devastation of transportation facilities which had hampered the enemy now impeded the supplying of American forces. About 140 miles of railroad had been built out of Cherbourg, but the shortage of engineers delayed repair of bombed bridges. Consequently, the Americans resorted to air and truck transport to supply the swiftly moving forces.[2]

[1] Omar N. Bradley, *A Soldier's Story* (New York, 1951), p. 385. For an account of German confusion at this time, see Milton Shulman, *Defeat in the West* (New York, 1948), pp. 162–177.

[2] Bradley, *A Soldier's Story,* p. 386; Roland G. Ruppenthal, *Logistical Sup-*

This supply problem affected Bradley's view toward Paris, since were the city taken, humanitarian factors would render it necessary to feed the four million residents, and diversion of supplies for this purpose might seriously affect the movement of troops after the Germans. Bradley, therefore, having isolated Paris, was in no hurry to take it.[3] Loyal Parisians, however, wanted foreign domination ended as soon as possible. Hectic political bargaining went on inside Paris,[4] as a result of which General Dietrich von Choltitz, commandant of the German garrison, ignored Hitler's orders to withdraw and destroy the Seine bridges and agreed to surrender to regular Allied troops. On August 25, he surrendered to a French divison under General Jacques Le Clerc, aided by the U.S. 4th Division.[5] Liberation set off a celebration such as could take place only in Paris. General Eisenhower already had advised General de Gaulle, leader of the Free French, to set up his headquarters in Paris, and the day after liberation he and Bradley paid the French leader a call. De Gaulle suggested that U.S. troops march through Paris as a sign of Allied strength. Bradley complied, but for practical reasons; he wanted to send his troops east and the most direct route was through the city. Consequently, what Parisians saw as a parade was a tactical march toward a military objective. Unaware of this fact at first and also not knowing that Montgomery had rejected an invitation to enter Paris, British newspapermen criticized the American love of parades.[6]

Ten days before the fall of Paris, an Allied force invaded the southern shores of France. This operation came at the insistence of U.S. military leaders and only after vigorous British opposition had changed to grudging consent. British and American military leaders had approved the plan (Anvil) at Quebec in August, 1943, and at

port of the Armies (*United States Army in World War II: The European Theater of Operations*) (Washington, 1953), I, 544–550.

[3] Bradley, *A Soldier's Story,* pp. 386–387.

[4] *Ibid.,* pp. 387–390; Arnold Toynbee and Veronica Toynbee (ed.), *Hitler's Europe* (*Survey of International Affairs, 1939–1946*) (London, 1954), pp. 425–426.

[5] Hans Speidel, *Invasion 1944: Rommel and the Normandy Campaign* (Chicago, 1950), pp. 143–144. For a time there was fear that underground French resistance might force von Choltitz to follow Hitler's orders to destroy the city. Bradley, *A Soldier's Story,* p. 389.

[6] *Ibid.,* pp. 394–396; Dwight D. Eisenhower, *Crusade in Europe* (New York, 1948), p. 297; Forrest C. Pogue, *The Supreme Command* (*United States Army in World War II: The European Theater of Operations*) (Washington, 1954), pp. 241–243.

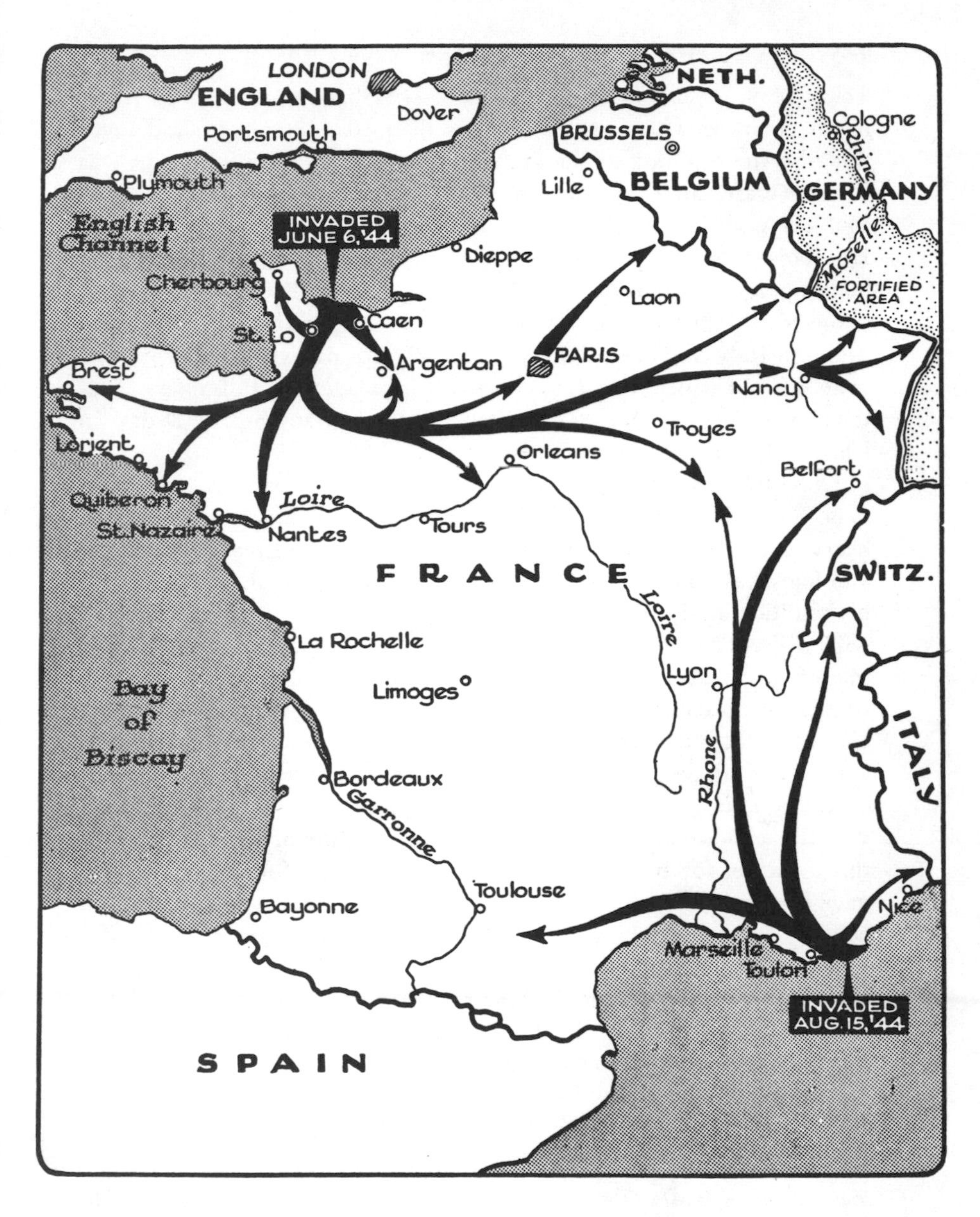

THE BATTLE OF FRANCE

Teheran in December, 1943.[7] Early in 1944, it appeared that Anvil might compete with Overlord rather than complement it, and there was also the question of the Italian campaign. The critical point was landing craft, for there were not enough to go around. The British, cool to Anvil, wanted more support for the Italian campaign, and Eisenhower, though a supporter of Anvil, did not want to compromise build-up for Overlord. General Montgomery on February 21, 1944, wrote to Eisenhower: "Let us have two really good major campaigns—one in Italy and one in OVERLORD."[8] Eisenhower agreed to postpone but not cancel Anvil, and plans went ahead for full-scale operations in Italy. An offensive started, and two days before D-day in Normandy, the Allies took Rome.

These two events marked a significant shift in Allied strategic planning. The Allies had put into action their basic plan to strike at the heart of Germany, and the war in Europe became primarily a tactical and logistical endeavor left largely to the guidance of Eisenhower and his coalition staff, Supreme Headquarters, Allied Expeditionary Force (SHAEF). The time had also come for a final decision for the future role of Mediterranean forces in the war. One possibility was to move from Italy to capture Istria and Trieste and to advance through the Ljubljana Gap toward Hungary and eventually Vienna. Such an advance would have political as well as military implications. The other choice was to continue the strategy of Overlord, which was to strike directly at Germany. Anvil, in Eisenhower's opinion, was necessary to this advance, for it would free a satisfactory port for the delivery of men and supplies for the main effort. Allied forces would engage in holding action elsewhere in the Mediterranean, except that the Air Force based in Italy would continue to participate in strategic air war on Germany.[9] General Marshall flew to Italy and convinced General Sir Henry Maitland Wilson, Allied Commander in Chief, Mediterranean, of the necessity of obtaining a port through which

[7] Maurice Matloff, *Strategic Planning for Coalition Warfare, 1943–1944* (*United States Army in World War II: The War Department*) (Washington, 1959), pp. 288, 365–366; Gordon A. Harrison, *Cross-Channel Attack* (*United States Army in World War II: The European Theater of Operations*) (Washington, 1951), pp. 123–125.

[8] Montgomery to Eisenhower, Feb. 21, 1944, quoted in Matloff, *Strategic Planning,* p. 420.

[9] *Ibid.,* pp. 466–467.

forty to fifty divisions from the United States could be taken to join Eisenhower's forces.[10]

The British, notably Churchill, fought vigorously against Anvil in favor of advance from Italy. They argued that a major port was not necessary, since smaller Normandy ports could be developed. Churchill felt that political and military strategy should combine to win the war, and it seems clear that his earlier policy of encirclement of Germany was beginning to give way to a new concept of containment of Soviet Russia.[11] Roosevelt disagreed and urged that the primary operations should be "striking at the heart of Germany."[12] When the President and the U.S. Chiefs of Staff stood firmly behind Eisenhower, the British Chiefs of Staff reluctantly agreed, and Churchill outwardly acquiesced.[13] On the next day, July 2, the Combined Chiefs of Staff issued orders to General Wilson to launch Anvil on a three-division basis by August 14, and General Eisenhower listed the objectives: to contain and destroy forces that might otherwise oppose Overlord, to secure a major port in southern France, and then advance north to threaten the enemy's flank and communications. Wilson would remain in command until SHAEF took over. Wilson agreed but stated that he would have to have help to move more than 225 miles inland.[14] Ultimately, seven divisions were withdrawn from the Italian front to aid Wilson.

Although they had agreed to the operation, the British Chiefs of Staff were still unhappy, and Churchill had not given up hope. After the breakout at Saint-Lô, he suggested dropping Anvil in favor of landing troops on Brittany beaches already captured, and then on August 5 and 9 he made a final effort to have Anvil, now designated as Dragoon for security purposes, shifted from southern France to the

[10] Pogue, *The Supreme Command,* p. 220.

[11] Note by the Prime Minister and Minister of Defence, June 28, 1944, in Winston Churchill, *The Second World War* (Boston, 1953), VI, 716–721.

[12] President Roosevelt to Prime Minister, June 29, 1944, in *ibid.,* VI, 721.

[13] For discussions of this controversy, see *ibid.,* VI, 57–71; Eisenhower, *Crusade in Europe,* pp. 281–284; Pogue, *The Supreme Command,* pp. 218–226; John Ehrman, *Grand Strategy* (*History of the Second World War: United Kingdom Military Series*) (London, 1956), V, 345–367; Herbert Feis, *Churchill, Roosevelt, Stalin: The War They Waged and the Peace They Sought* (Princeton, 1957), pp. 344–349. S. E. Morison, *History of United States Naval Operations in World War II* (Boston, 1957), XI, 221–232; Matloff, *Strategic* Planning, pp. 466–475.

[14] Pogue, *The Supreme Command,* pp. 223–224.

Bay of Biscay. Eisenhower refused to agree, and even Wilson said it was too late for a change.[15] Eisenhower suggested that Churchill must have political reasons for his desire to push against the enemy from Italy, and he declared that if the decision were to be made on military grounds he would not back down but that he was willing to change if political considerations were paramount and if the Prime Minister wished to prolong the war to gain these political objectives.[16] Seeing that the U.S. Chiefs of Staff still stood firmly behind Eisenhower, the British Chiefs of Staff once more decided in favor of the invasion of southern France, and on August 10 General Wilson received the final signal to go ahead. This directive was issued only four days before the landings.[17]

Both Eisenhower and Churchill helped terminate what might have become a serious breach of rapport. The Supreme Commander wrote a complimentary letter to the Prime Minister and received a cordial reply.[18] The inimitable Churchill flew to Corsica, boarded a British destroyer and observed the landings, irritated that the ship had orders to stay seven thousand yards offshore.[19]

The invasion consisted of three U.S. and seven French divisions, including three arriving later as reinforcements, which embarked from Italian and North African ports, under Lieutenant General Alexander M. Patch, commander of the U.S. Seventh Army. The American forces landed first, on beaches east of Toulon, and encountered light opposition on all but one, which they later took by a land attack. On the next day, French divisions, under General Jean de Lattre de Tassigny, commander of French Army B, landed and started a drive toward Toulon and Marseille. About 25,000 armed members of the French resistance were eagerly awaiting the invasion and assisted the Allied forces.[20]

[15] *Ibid.,* p. 225.

[16] Eisenhower, *Crusade in Europe,* p. 284.

[17] Pogue, *The Supreme Command,* pp. 225–226.

[18] Quoted in *ibid.,* pp. 226–227.

[19] Churchill, *The Second World War,* VI, pp. 94–95.

[20] For accounts of the invasion, see Morison, *History,* XI, 233–292; W. F. Craven and J. L. Cate, *The Army Air Forces in World War II* (Chicago, 1951), III, 420–438; J. F. C. Fuller, *The Second World War: A Strategical and Tactical History* (New York, 1949), pp. 322–324; Jean de Lattre de Tassigny, *The History of the French First Army* (London, 1952), pp. 63–121; Guy Salisbury-Jones, *So Full a Glory: A Biography of Marshal de Lattre de Tassigny* (London, 1954), pp. 128–154. This last account is an uncritical eulogy

Generaloberst Johannes Blaskowitz, commander of German Army Group G, had eleven divisions with which to attempt to hold France south of the Loire River, and he received orders to move inland but to hold fortresses and ports. The first two weeks of the invasion exceeded expectations. Toulon and Marseille fell and their ports were soon put in operation. About 57,000 Germans surrendered at a cost of some 4,000 French and 2,700 American casualties.[21] Dragoon strengthened Eisenhower's position and provided a new major port.[22] Churchill sent his congratulations, although in his memoirs he subsequently questioned that the gains were worth the cost of foregoing a thrust north from Italy.[23]

The advance continued until on September 11 advance French forces near Châtillon-sur-Seine effected a juncture with parts of the U.S. Third Army which had turned east to meet them. This union meant the defeat of the remaining forces west of Dijon and they capitulated formally on September 16. The day before, the command had shifted to SHAEF, and Lieutenant General Jacob L. Devers became the head of the newly created Sixth Army Group. Skillful leadership by General Blaskowitz had enabled about half his men to elude the trap.[24]

Rapid advances in northern France matched those of Dragoon troops. Making little effort at defense, the Germans retreated toward the Siegfried Line, or West Wall, along the German border. This line of fortifications built up in the late 1930's had points of strength and had been at least a psychological barrier to the Allies in the early years of the war. After the Battle of France, it seemed to have lost its purpose, and its weapons and other military equipment were taken to boster the Atlantic Wall along the seacoast. Now the Germans hurriedly tried to reinforce the West Wall.[25]

In pursuit, British and American advance units covered as many as fifty to seventy-five miles a day and the former took Antwerp on

---

and should be counterbalanced by L. K. Truscott, Jr., *Command Missions* (New York, 1954), pp. 381–433.

[21] Pogue, *The Supreme Command,* pp. 227–228.

[22] Morison, *History,* XI, 291. Between November 1, 1944, and April 1, 1945, Marseille received an average of half a million tons of cargo and 54,000 troops monthly.

[23] Churchill, *The Second World War,* VI, p. 100.

[24] Pogue, *The Supreme Command,* pp. 228–230.

[25] Siegfried Westphal, *The German Army in the West* (London, 1951), pp. 43, 73–74, 170, 174.

September 4, in a move so rapid that the Germans did not have time to damage the port severely. On the next day Patton's forces crossed the Moselle River near Nancy.

As the Germans reached the Siegfried Line, they tightened their defenses and thereby forced Eisenhower to reappraise the situation. The fluid war which had resulted in such phenomenal gains for the Allies at the same time had taxed logistics to the utmost, and the Supreme Commander, consequently, had both to solve the problem of supply and to determine the next offensive moves.

Antwerp, which the British had just seized, was one of the finest harbors in Europe, but it was an inland port on the Scheldt Estuary, the banks of which the Germans still menaced from island strongholds which it would be hard to capture. In addition to clearing the approach to Antwerp, Eisenhower had another immediate objective in mind, driving beyond Antwerp and if possible establishing a bridgehead on the Rhine. General Montgomery unexpectedly made another suggestion; fired by the amazing gains already made, he said that if Eisenhower would turn over all available supplies to the Twenty-first Army Group, Montgomery would take it straight to Berlin.[26] At about the same time, on the right flank, another military leader was expressing a similar idea except that it was he, Patton, who would take the U.S. Third Army to victory. Eisenhower did not share the optimism of either of his subordinates. He feared the effect of lack of supplies on the remainder of the line if any part, at this time, should get full logistical support. He also anticipated serious injury to the Allied cause if the major thrust failed.[27]

The Supreme Commander therefore rejected the proposals and told Montgomery that the Allies needed use of Antwerp as a port for supply operations to make possible a major blow against the enemy. He also expressed the belief that an operation to secure a bridgehead on the Rhine would also protect Montgomery's flank on Walcheren Island near the Scheldt Estuary. In addition, Eisenhower was interested in making use of the First Airborne Army, which was ready in England.[28] The debate over strategic as opposed to tactical use of air power extended to the employment of airborne troops. Air Force

[26] Eisenhower, *Crusade in Europe,* p. 305; Bernard L. Montgomery, *The Memoirs of Field-Marshal the Viscount Montgomery of Alamein, K. G.* (Cleveland and New York, 1958), pp. 244–256.

[27] Eisenhower, *Crusade in Europe,* p. 306.

[28] *Ibid.,* pp. 306–307.

leaders, such as General H. H. Arnold, wanted to make a large enough drop to affect the course of the war, as, for example, landing large bodies of troops far behind German lines toward Berlin, but they were unable to secure authorization for the attempt.[29]

After abandoning an earlier plan, General Montgomery planned a joint air drop (Market) and a ground thrust (Garden) in the vicinity of Arnhem. The only American contingents were two U.S. Airborne Divisions, the 82d and the 101st. There were known risks involved. The ground forces had to make a sixty-mile advance along a narrow front, and air operations needed several days of good weather at a time when bad weather was normal. However, SHAEF was optimistic about the disorganized nature of the German forces and thought one thrust was worth trying. Just before the attack, news that two Panzer divisions had moved into the Arnhem area made Montgomery want to delay because of lack of supplies. Eisenhower assured him that Allied planes and U.S. trucks would provide a thousand tons of supplies daily, and Montgomery set the date for attack at September 17.[30]

The operations started with generally successful airborne drops near Arnhem, but the troops began to encounter serious difficulty as they endeavored to secure bridges that would help the ground attack. *Generaloberst* Karl Student, although initially surprised, regrouped his First Parachute Army north of Arnhem and was aided by a captured copy of the Allied attack order. A German infantry regiment on its way to the area was detrained and put into the fight against the 101st Airborne Division. Next, bad weather turned against the Allied attack and prevented or delayed landing reinforcements and supplies for the beleaguered forces. Meanwhile, the British ground attack had started, but it moved ahead much more slowly than had been planned, as restricted roadways and determined opposition checked its advance. Finally, the British 1st Airborne Division, which had been isolated, received orders to retreat; only about a fourth of the nine or ten thousand men made their way to safety.[31]

The Arnhem offensive had failed to secure the desired bridgehead on the Rhine; General Montgomery felt that the advance of fifty miles accomplished made the venture successful, and he blamed the weather

[29] E.g., Pogue, *The Supreme Command,* pp. 119, 280.
[30] *Ibid.,* pp. 283–284.
[31] Bradley, *A Soldier's Story,* p. 418; Bernard L. Montgomery, *Normandy to the Baltic* (Boston, 1948), p. 240. For an account by the 1st Airborne Division's leader, see R. E. Urquhart, *Arnhem* (London, 1958), *passim.*

for lack of greater gains.[32] There were other factors, a breakdown of communications at a critical point, underrating of the enemy, and perhaps too obvious a plan. German views were that not enough airborne troops landed the first day and that the ground attack should have started before and not after the air drops were made to cut down opposition to the air drops.[33]

The breakout and resultant evacuation of occupied France and Belgium left planning for supplies far behind. As a result the Allied armies resorted to improvisation, which was justified in a great gamble to bring the war rapidly to a close. When the Germans did not collapse, but along the Siegfried Line stood again on a determined defensive, the attacking armies had to wait for more effective methods of supply to develop.

Furnishing one of the most important types of supply, gasoline and other petroleum products, fell into two main categories, delivery to the Continent and distribution to the armies in the field. Overlord planners devised three principal ways of transporting gasoline and other POL (petrol, oil, and lubricants) to the French coast. For the first three weeks after D-day, the armies would be supplied by packages or tins of gas and oil. It was hoped that by that time the so-called Minor System would be in use; motor and aviation gasoline would be delivered to British-controlled ports east of Omaha Beach by tankers, which would discharge their gas through six-inch pipes to hastily installed tanks a short distance inland. Next, Major System would be ready to function. Basic to this system was an untried venture, a cross-Channel underwater pipeline. Pluto (pipeline under the ocean) consisted of ten three-inch flexible cables from the Isle of Wight to Cherbourg, sixty miles away, and had a theoretic capacity of three hundred tons of gasoline daily. Expecting that the Germans would destroy the extensive tank facilities of Cherbourg, the Allies prepared to construct new tanks.[34]

[32] Montgomery, *Memoirs,* pp. 266–267.

[33] For discussions and analyses of the Arnhem operation, see Chester Wilmot, *The Struggle for Europe* (New York, 1952), pp. 498–522; *Royal Air Force, 1939–1945,* Vol. III, *The Fight Is Won,* by Hilary St. George Saunders (London, 1954), pp. 192–195; Pogue, *The Supreme Command,* pp. 284–288; Craven and Cate, *The A.A.F. in World War II,* III, 598–611; Ehrman, *Grand Strategy,* V, 527–529; Matthew B. Ridgway, *Soldier: The Memoirs of Matthew B. Ridgway* (New York, 1956), pp. 105–111.

[34] Ruppenthal, *Logistical Support,* I, 319–326. After considerable experi-

When actual invasion came, efforts to put these systems into operation succeeded, but somewhat more slowly than expected. It took longer than anticipated to clear out Cherbourg's harbor; in contrast, the Allies found the Cherbourg tank farms undestroyed, quickly cleaned them out, and made available a storage capacity of almost 500,000 barrels.[35] The delay in putting the Major System into use did not impede the progress of the armies; packaged gasoline landed on the beaches at first provided an adequate supply since the hard task of securing a lodgment restricted the demand for petroleum products.

The gasoline shortage that developed was not one of delivery to the Continent but of transportation to the armies in the field. Engineers began building pipelines inland from Cherbourg. The lines were plagued with breaks and leaks, sometimes the result of inexperienced workmen. Some of the leaks were deliberate, and a few came from sabotage efforts. The number of breaks, for example, was large enough on August 29 to force trucks to travel an additional 160 miles for their loads. At the height of the gas crisis, some of the armies were 250 miles from the end of the pipeline. The situation improved, and by the middle of September the pipeline from Cherbourg was dispensing gas at Chartres. Early in October, the line reached Coubert, about ten miles beyond the Seine, and since the advance had moderated, it was decided not to extend the line farther. Thoughout much of its route the line really consisted of three pipes, two for gasoline for ground vehicles and one for aviation gasoline, which at the peak of operation supplied about one-third of the armies' needs.[36]

Motor transport, railroads, and airplanes also carried gasoline as well as other supplies to the rapidly expanding front. In motor transport critical shortages developed after the breakout, and until the slowdown at the border hectic improvisation usually replaced careful planning. The most highly publicized system, the so-called Red Ball Express, was such a development, coming into being suddenly and reaching the height of its performance only five days after it started to operate. On August 29, 132 truck companies with 5,958 vehicles delivered 12,342 tons of supplies forward, and by September 5 had delivered about 89,000 tons.[37]

---

mentation the British developed cables that could be laid underwater and carry petroleum products under high pressure.

[35] *Ibid.*, I, 500.

[36] *Ibid.*, I, 510–514.

[37] Joseph Bykofsky and Harold Larson, *The Transportation Corps: Opera-*

At the start, the Red Ball Express ran on two parallel highways from Saint-Lô to Chartres. According to the rules, all traffic was one-way, and one highway was restricted to inbound trucks and the other to those outbound. No other vehicles could use these highways over which a stream of traffic flowed twenty-four hours a day. Allied control of the air was such that trucks could use their lights. They were supposed to travel in convoy at a maximum of twenty-five miles per hour and take a ten-minute rest break every even hour. The system did not function without mishaps. There were not enough military police to enforce the rules in the face of competing units trying to be the first after the Germans. Unauthorized vehicles got on the roads, even going the wrong way. Truck drivers, especially if they fell behind in schedule, ignored the speed limit. Mechanical failures were inevitable, and by the middle of September forty thousand tires needed repair or replacement.[38] A limited amount of trading on the black market occurred,[39] but the major leaks came through "losing" a load by diversion to other units than those officially designated as its recipients. The Third Army gained a reputation for skill in hijacking supplies to aid its advance, and Patton was not one to bear down on such offenses.[40]

Although by September 5 it had completed its assignment of delivering goods to Chartres, the Red Ball Express continued functioning and by the middle of the month had delivered 135,000 tons of supplies to the armies. It was a hastily contrived and costly operation which could be justified primarily as a part of a great gamble to bring the war quickly to a close. When the Allied attack slowed down, the wasteful methods exacted their toll on transportation efficiency in the months that lay ahead.[41]

The use of air power for supply was also a matter of improvisation, for it was established air policy that air supply of ground units would be an emergency procedure only, to be decided upon by the Supreme Commander. After the storm that wrecked Mulberry installations, aircraft was used extensively for transport. Another valuable function

tions Overseas (*United States Army in World War II: The Technical Services*) (Washington, 1957), pp. 330–334.

[38] Ruppenthal, *Logistical Support*, I, 565–571.

[39] Bykofsky and Larson, *The Transportation Corps*, p. 335; Ruppenthal, *Logistical Support*, I, 571.

[40] *Ibid.*, I, 499–565.

[41] *Ibid.*, I, 571; Bykofsky and Larson, *The Transportation Corps*, p. 335.

was the removal to British hospitals of about a fifth of the U.S. war casualties.[42]

After the breakout Eisenhower and SHAEF determined to make heavy use of air to supply ground forces. Deliveries began, but for various reasons did not reach the quotas set. There was a lack of Continental airfields, the heavy transport planes were hard on hurriedly constructed runways, and toward the end of August there developed a shortage of planes. The need for planes was so great that bombers were converted into cargo carriers, although their use necessitated enlargement of numerous airfields. There was a three-way pull on aircraft. The Strategic Bombing Command wanted to return to its primary function, strategic bombing of the enemy, the Arnhem venture drafted cargo planes as troop carriers, and the needs of the population in Paris and the ground forces demanded air transport of supplies.[43]

Added to the shortage of planes were operational difficulties, including shortage of trucks in England to carry supplies to airports, too few airfields where needed in France, inadequate provisions for unloading planes, and lack of coordination throughout. Consequently, deliveries ran far short of orders, and by the end of the month, realizing that for some time logistics would dominate military action, the Army Group leaders began to dole out supplies on a priority basis.[44] During the first half of September planes had raised their daily average of deliveries to one thousand tons.

Overlord planning for transportation naturally included reconditioning French railroads badly damaged by the widespread Allied air interdiction program before D-day. As a part of invasion activities, the Allies began to transport to France rolling stock that had been specially constructed in the United States for use on the French rail lines, a practice first developed for North Africa. The first diesel engine and flatcars arrived on the Continent by way of an LST and across the beaches. Sea trains began carrying railroad heavy equipment to Cherbourg even before the dock facilities had been repaired and unloading it with cranes from barges. Reconstruction of roads and bridges began, and only four days after the liberation of Paris a

[42] Ruppenthal, *Logistical Support,* I, 572–574. There were about 20,000 casualties evacuated by the end of July.

[43] *Ibid.,* I, 575–579; Craven and Cate, *The A.A.F. in World War II,* III, 555–561.

[44] Ruppenthal, *Logistical Support,* I, 581–582.

line was completed to it from Cherbourg. It was a tenuous thread, however, and for some time little went through but engineer's supplies, hospital equipment, and civil affairs relief. Air damage beyond the Seine was less, and reconstruction correspondingly faster. By August 1, cumulative rail shipments totaled one million ton-miles; a month and a half later the railroads were averaging almost two million ton-miles a day. The battle of transportation had not yet been won; Paris was still a bottleneck and shortages remained in rolling stock.[45]

The demand for food remained relatively constant, but the nature of the war affected the type of food the armies received. For the first weeks the invading forces subsisted on packaged C and K rations, and a packaged ration known as 10-in-1, which was somewhat more popular. In the second week of July, there began a shift to the bulk-type B ration. The breakout prevented expanding this to an A ration by adding perishable items, and instead took the forces back on packaged rations.[46] Although on a couple of occasions armies got

[45] For accounts of railway reconstruction in France, see *ibid.*, I, 544–553; Bykofsky and Larson, *The Transportation Corps*, pp. 285–289.

[46] The C ration was designed for the combat soldier who could carry a day's supply of food, but who could be resupplied daily. It consisted of six twelve-ounce cans, three of which contained certain combinations of meat and vegetables. The remainder held biscuits, cigarettes, and soluble coffee, lemon powder, and cocoa. Designed to withstand changes in temperature, the C ration could be eaten hot or cold. The soldier disliked certain features of the C ration, including monotony, bulkiness of the round cans, and lemon powder. As a result of experimentation, the C ration improved with the addition of variations in the diet.

The K ration was designed for the fighter in a period of actual assault, and the basic idea was derived from the American Indian's concentrated venison, or pemmican. Undergoing numerous changes during the war, this ration included biscuits, a meat preparation, coffee, cigarettes, chewing gum, candy.

The D ration was not a meal, but a bar, designed at first as a survival ration. This Logan bar, as it was called, consisted of chocolate, dried skim milk, oatmeal, and sugar, and three bars, totaling twelve ounces, provided 1,800 calories. Later, the D ration was used primarily to supplement other rations. It produced nausea in some soldiers and since it made most soldiers thirsty was not satisfactory in combat conditions in which water was scarce.

The 10-in-1 ration was a packaged ration for feeding of small groups, and was modeled on a British Composite Pack used successfully in North Africa.

A rations were used in most posts and other Army stations in the United States, and included fresh fruits and vegetables when available.

B rations were like A rations, except that nonperishable foods replaced perishable items. The Army attempted to improve techniques of preservation and packaging foods. For accounts of development and delivery of food to the armies in the field, see Erna Risch, *The Quartermaster Corps: Organization,*

U.S. Army Photo

1. Allied Conference in Quebec, August, 1943. Seated (left to right) Prime Minister Mackenzie King, President Roosevelt and Prime Minister Winston Churchill. Standing, Gen. H. H. Arnold, Sir Charles Portal, Gen. Sir Alan Brooke, Admiral E. J. King, Field Marshal Sir John Dill, Gen. George C. Marshall, Admiral Sir Dudley Pound, and Admiral W. D. Leahy

U.S. Army Photo

2. Thanksgiving Day meeting, 1943, in Cairo. Front row, left to right, Generalissimo Chiang Kai-shek, President Roosevelt, Prime Minister Churchill and Madame Chiang Kai-shek. Among others in the picture (back row) Sir Alexander Cadogan (extreme left), Anthony Eden, John G. Winant (at Eden's left), Dr. Wang Chang-hui (wearing glasses), R. C. Casey (at Dr. Wang's left), Lord Killearn (at Mr. Casey's left), Averell Harriman, Lewis Douglas, and Harry Hopkins (extreme right)

U.S. Navy Photo

3. Aircraft carrier loaded with fighters and torpedo bombers operating against German submarines in the Atlantic

4. Grumman Hellcats (F6F) fighter planes on deck of aircraft carrier

U.S. Navy Photo

U.S. Army Photo

5. Marshal Joseph Stalin with President Roosevelt and Prime Minister Winston Churchill at Teheran, November 28, 1943—the first three-power meeting in which Stalin took a personal part

6. General Eisenhower giving the order of the day to paratroopers somewhere in England before they board their airplanes to take part in the invasion of the continent, June 6, 1944

Wide World Photos

U.S. Coast Guard Photo

7. D-Day landings in Normandy

8. Wreckage of artificial harbor at Omaha Beach after the storm, June 21, 1944

U.S. Army Photo

U.S. Army Photo

9. American infantrymen in the rubble of a French town—Domfront

10. Lüdendorf bridge at Remagen after its collapse

U.S. Army Photo

11. M.P. waves on a motor convoy rushing matériel to the forward areas in France

U.S. Army Photo

12. Rocket launchers in the Hürtgen Forest

U.S. Army Photo

13. General Dwight D. Eisenhower

Wide World Photos

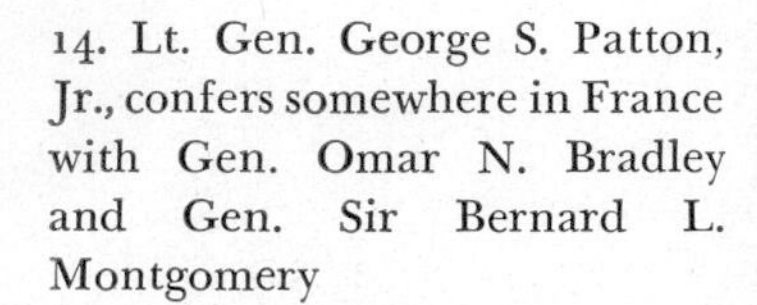

14. Lt. Gen. George S. Patton, Jr., confers somewhere in France with Gen. Omar N. Bradley and Gen. Sir Bernard L. Montgomery

Wide World Photos

Wide World Photos

15. American soldiers, thousands strong, march along the Champs Elysées during liberation celebration, August 26, 1944

U.S. Army Photo

16. Bazooka being fired into cave on Saipan

17. Marines pinned down on Pelelieu

Defense Department Photo (Marine Corps)

Wide World Photos

18. Gen. Douglas MacArthur returns to the Philippines, October 20, 1944

19. Coast Guard beach party seeks cover from Japanese fire at Lingayan Gulf, Luzon, January, 1945

U.S. Coast Guard Photo

Wide World Photos

20. President Roosevelt at Yalta, February, 1945, shows the effects of ill health. Winston Churchill and V. M. Molotov stand nearby

Associated Press Photo

21. Marines raise the American flag on Mount Suribachi, Iwo Jima

U.S. Army Photo

22. The "Big Three" meeting in Berlin, July, 1945. President Truman faces the camera from the far side, flanked by Secretary of State James F. Byrnes and Charles Bohlen. Generalissimo Joseph Stalin is seated on the far left and Prime Minister Winston Churchill is in the right foreground

Wide World Photos

23. An Allied correspondent stares at the mass of rubble after the atom bomb fell on Hiroshima, August 6, 1945

24. Nagasaki, where the atomic explosion on August 9 wrecked 18,000 buildings and killed, 26,000 people

Wide World Photos

U.S. Army Photo

25. Japanese surrender signatories arrive aboard the U.S.S. *Missouri* in Tokyo Bay for the ceremonies, September 2, 1945

26. General of the Army Douglas MacArthur signs as Supreme Allied Commander. Behind him (left) is Lt. Gen. Jonathan Wainwright, who surrendered to the Japanese after Bataan and Corregidor

U.S. Army Photo

down to one day's reserves, there was never a shortage of food. Captured food sometimes varied the monotony, if it did not improve the quality of the diet.[47]

The demand for ammunition varied somewhat in inverse proportion to the need for gasoline. During the dash across France ammunition needs slackened and then increased as the requirement for gasoline lessened when the armies neared the Siegfried Line. Ammunition always had to be rationed, and occasionally there were local shortages; on the Brittany Peninsula limitations on ammunition rather than gasoline delayed the taking of Saint-Mâlo and Brest.[48]

Another shortage developed in mechanized warfare. Higher losses than anticipated resulted in an insufficiency of medium tanks, which was relieved by a number of devices, including shipment of tanks directly to France instead of to England first. Also, American tanks proved inferior to the German Panther and Tiger tanks in both armament and defensive armor.[49] Belatedly, the Americans sought modifications at least to reduce the inferiority.[50] Later in the campaign, armored units began to receive a new high-velocity round (HVAP) that could pierce all but the front of the German Panther. The supply, however, was limited and could be used only in emergency situations.

Medical supplies in the main kept pace with demands during the race across France. Refrigerated whole blood, a new feature in World War II, was distributed by a theater blood bank through base and advance depots. Early in August, the supply became critical and had to be allocated by the Army Group surgeon. By the beginning of the month, the flow of blood from America took this commodity off the critical list.[51]

A serious shortage developed in one area of manpower, as a result

---

Supply and Services (*The United States Army in World War II: The Technical Services*) (Washington, 1953), pp. 174–207; Ruppenthal, *Logistical Support,* I, 439–441.

[47] *Ibid.,* I, 517–518.

[48] *Ibid.,* I, 525–543.

[49] C. M. Green, H. C. Thompson, and P. C. Roots, *The Ordnance Department: Planning Munitions for War* (*United States Army in World War II: The Technical Services*) (Washington, 1955), p. 13.

[50] For an account of developments in tank production during the war, see *ibid.,* pp. 274–310. See, also, Ruppenthal, *Logistical Supply,* I, 523–525.

[51] *Ibid.,* I, 519. Regular flights of blood-bank planes had begun in Italy in 1943.

of an important miscalculation in estimating casualties. Despite the mechanized nature of warfare, the infantryman was still an important individual, and among the infantrymen the rifleman was a key figure. It was among this type of soldier that the casualties ran the highest and the replacements the fewest. During June and July, there were a little over 100,000 casualties (85,000 battle and 16,000 nonbattle). Eighty-five percent of these had been infantry losses and of these 63 percent had been riflemen. As a result there was a shortage of replacements for riflemen in contrast to an oversupply of other categories of soldiers, even other infantrymen. At one time, July 23, there were only 12,985 trained riflemen in the Ground Force Replacement System (GFRS) in the United Kingdom and actually only 750 available in France for replacement. Efforts had been made in the preparations for Overlord to reclassify individuals but the results were not wholly satisfactory. Fortunately, the flight of the enemy after the failure at Mortain gave the United States a chance to catch up on replacements.[52]

[52] *Ibid.*, I, 458–463. For losses in rifle platoons, see Bradley, *A Soldier's Story*, pp. 445–446.

CHAPTER 20

Fall Deadlock and the Battle of the Bulge

WHILE the Allied forces were struggling with the problems of supply, the debate over military strategy continued. Early in September, 1944, Eisenhower's idea was the rejection of a single major attack by Montgomery or Patton in favor of a general advance of all Allied armies toward the Rhine. The Supreme Commander was influenced in his thinking by the capture of Antwerp on September 4 and by a belief that this port would soon be handling great quantities of supplies. It became quickly apparent, however, that Antwerp was useless until the Scheldt Estuary could be cleared.[1]

Consequently, in a conference held September 10 Eisenhower gave priority to the attack on German forces that were preventing the use of Antwerp. Since the work that followed was that of British and Canadian forces, it is sufficient for this narrative to note that amphibious assaults, air bombardment of dikes to flood out a German garrison, and commando tactics combined after heavy fighting to eliminate a stubborn foe. On November 28, the first Allied vessels began to unload at Antwerp.[2]

While Montgomery's forces were headed toward fierce resistance along the Scheldt Estuary and reverses at Arnhem, the other Allied

[1] Forrest C. Pogue, *The Supreme Command* (*United States Army in World War II: The European Theater of Operations*) (Washington, 1954), pp. 250–256.

[2] For descriptions of this operation, see Winston Churchill, *The Second World War* (Boston, 1953), VI, 200–205; Chester Wilmot, *The Struggle for Europe* (New York, 1952), pp. 544–548.

troops in Western Europe were slowing down in their impetuous rush after the enemy. In approaching Antwerp, the two armies of the Twenty-first Army Group under Montgomery had pushed ahead along the coast on a fifty-eight-mile front. The Canadians on September 1 had seized Dieppe, scene of the spectacular but unsuccessful Anglo-Canadian raid earlier in the war, and on the following day Canadian tanks crossed the Somme River.[3]

Some distance to the east, the U.S. First Army was moving ahead on a sixty-five-mile front, which was spearheaded by armored columns. Realizing that German forces would be attempting to escape the British and Canadian advance, General Hodges sent General Collins and the VII Corps north in an effort to catch the enemy in a trap. The result was one of the spectacular episodes of the war; the two forces ran into each other near Mons before either was aware of what was happening. The VII Corps recovered first from the shock and struck so swiftly and effectively that when the engagement was over, about two thousand Germans were dead, and some thirty thousand were taken prisoner. It is a commentary on both the general success of the Allied forces at this time and the resultant optimism of Allied people and leaders that this astonishing victory elicited relatively little notice from the press of the day. The victory deprived the Germans of needed reserves and enabled the First Army to break through the Siegfried Line and take Aachen six weeks later.[4]

Farther to the north and east, Patton's Third Army advanced along a ninety-mile front. Two of Patton's corps were driving toward Metz and Nancy as a supporting move for a major thrust of the Third Army to the northeast. In addition, this Army had an extended flank along the Loire River, which gave it a combined front and flank of about 450 miles. Approximately 175 miles south of the Third Army, the forces under Lieutenant General Alexander M. Patch had penetrated north from their Mediterranean landings to the industrial city of Lyons. These Dragoon forces consisted of the U.S. Seventh Army

[3] H. M. Cole, *The Lorraine Campaign* (*United States Army in World War II: The European Theater of Operations*) (Washington, 1950), p. 4. The Anglo-Canadian raid on Dieppe took place in August, 1942. While the costs were heavy, the Allies learned a number of lessons from the operations. See S. W. Roskill, *The War At Sea, 1939–1945* (London, 1956), II, 239–252.

[4] Cole, *The Lorraine Campaign,* p. 5; Omar N. Bradley, *A Soldier's Story* (New York, 1951), pp. 407–408; Dwight D. Eisenhower, *Crusade in Europe* (New York, 1948), p. 294.

and French Army "B," under General Jean de Lattre de Tassigny.[5]

On paper, the forces which faced each other in Western Europe early in September, 1944, were roughly equal in size; confronting Eisenhower's thirty-eight divisions were forty-one German divisions. Five of the latter were isolated in coastal forts or on the Channel Islands, but five additional divisions were on their way as reinforcements. In reality, the Allies had a preponderance of strength on the ground and virtually complete superiority in the air. Most German divisions were far below complement, and many of the replacements were inferior either in ability or training. These additions, thrust into the front lines to bolster German defenses, included war workers formerly exempted from conscription, sailors turned into infantrymen, young men just arriving at military age, and soldiers returning to duty after hospitalization. The Allies also held the advantage in armament and mechanized equipment; they had, for example, two and a half times as many guns and twenty times the number of tanks.[6]

While in Western Europe the Germans were retreating to the West Wall, on the Eastern front heavy fighting was going badly for the Nazi forces. In the south, the Russians broke through the German defense and occupied all of Rumania and Bulgaria and parts of Hungary. In October, the Russians took Belgrade; in Yugoslavia the activities of guerrilla forces complicated Hitler's efforts to withdraw some twelve divisions from the Balkans to help hold back the enemy in Hungary. Relentlessly, the Russians pushed ahead against a bitterly contesting foe and by Christmas they had encircled Budapest. Farther north another Russian Army Group had reached the Vistula, near Warsaw, in a summer offensive but had been checked in the Carpathian Mountain passes to the south. Still farther north, Russian forces advanced northeast as far as the Narev River and launched an attack on East Prussia which with only the greatest effort the Germans were able to halt. The Baltic front, on the other hand, was relatively static. In the fall, the Germans endeavored to establish a line of defenses from the Carpathians to the Baltic and to withdraw Panzer and Panzergrenadier divisions to form a mobile reserve. The

[5] Cole, *The Lorraine Campaign,* pp. 5–6; Jean de Lattre de Tassigny, *The History of the French First Army* (London, 1952), pp. 121–133.

[6] Cole, *The Lorraine Campaign,* p. 32. The forces included *"Volksgrenadier"* divisions, Germany's last reserves, who, with little training, were sent into battle. F. W. von Mellenthin, *Panzer Battles, 1939–1945* (London, 1956) (2nd ed.), p. 306; Milton Shulman, *Defeat in the West* (New York, 1948), pp. 206–219.

front was over seven hundred miles long, and the twelve divisions gathered in reserve seemed pitifully small to the German military leaders and their line of defense depressingly thin. Other Nazi forces were tied down elsewhere in Europe; some twenty-four divisions opposed the Allies in Italy, ten more were in Yugoslavia, and seventeen guarded Scandinavia.[7]

On September 1, General Eisenhower made a significant change in command organization. As he had planned, he moved his headquarters, SHAEF, to France and assumed operational control of the Allied armies. Under his command were the Twenty-first Army Group, headed by Montgomery, and the Twelfth Army Group under Bradley, which recently had been augmented by the U.S. Ninth Army, headed by Lieutenant General William H. Simpson, who also took command of forces in Brittany formerly under Patton. Under Eisenhower, also, was a new Army Group, the Sixth, which became active September 15. Commanded by General Jacob L. Devers, this Army Group controlled the Anvil-Dragoon forces and civil affairs in southern France. Toward the end of the year, another U.S. Army, the Fifteenth, under Lieutenant General Leonard T. Gerow, began to move into France.[8]

SHAEF first moved to Jullouville, on the Cotentin Peninsula, but it soon became apparent that this was too far from the front, and on September 15 the Allied command transferred to Versailles. A few days later Eisenhower opened advance headquarters at Gueux, near Rheims.[9] In the organizational shifting that took place, the Supreme Commander lost direct control of the Strategic Air Forces, but he was not disturbed since he knew that with such airmen as General Spaatz and Air Chief Marshal Sir Arthur T. Harris in command he would receive all possible cooperation.[10]

While the Allies were engaged in reorganization and the problems of supply, the opposing forces were regrouping desperately to with-

[7] Heinz Guderian, *Panzer Leader* (London, 1952), pp. 373–379.

[8] The Twelfth Army Group became active August 1, 1944, but Bradley acted under the control of Montgomery until September 1. Pogue, *The Supreme Command,* pp. 261–263. Bernard L. Montgomery, *The Memoirs of Field-Marshal the Viscount Montgomery of Alamein, K. G.* (Cleveland and New York, 1958), pp. 240–241.

[9] Pogue, *The Supreme Command,* pp. 275–278.

[10] Eisenhower, *Crusade in Europe,* pp. 307–308; Pogue, *The Supreme Command,* pp. 273–274; W. F. Craven and J. L. Cate, *The Army Air Forces in World War II* (Chicago, 1951), III, 320–322.

stand the assault on the Siegfried Line. On September 5, Hitler once again placed Field Marshal von Rundstedt in command on the Western front. Two other military leaders, von Kluge and Rommel, who had gone into retirement, were dead by their own hand, both indirect victims of the abortive July attempt on Hitler's life. Marshal Model was more fortunate, at least for a time, for when von Rundstedt returned to the command, Model remained as head of Army Group B. As commander in the West, Model had been remarkably effective in pulling together the shattered remnants of the retreating German forces and instilling in the new and scarcely trained units the will to resist.[11] The presence of the Siegfried Line aided the armies in their efforts to reform. The Germans had started construction of the Siegfried Line, West Wall, in 1936, after the remilitarization of the Rhineland and had continued work on the fortifications until the collapse of France in 1940. The line followed the German border from its junction with the Dutch and Belgian borders at München-Gladbach to the Swiss border about 350 miles away. Some portions were weak; from Karlsruhe to Basel the line was relatively thin with but two rows of forts. Near Aachen, the line again was weak, but in the vicinity of the industrialized Saar, the line was almost three miles deep and it consisted of about forty forts per thousand square yards. The forts varied considerably in size, averaging thirty-five by forty-five feet and generally their roofs and walls were of concrete five feet thick.[12] Since little work had been done on the forts since 1940, they were classed by some observers as World War I models. American soldiers, however, would soon find some of these defenses formidable indeed.

Although the Germans had repulsed the Allied thrust toward Arnhem, they were badly extended. When von Rundstedt resumed command he realized that the Germans had no chance of winning, but he hoped to make the victory costly for the Allies by standing on the defensive.[13] His plans soon received severe shocks, the first of which was news that an armored division of the U.S. First Army had cracked the West Wall above Trier, just north of the Saar. Von Rundstedt

[11] Bradley pays tribute to Model's ability. See Bradley, *A Soldier's Story,* pp. 415–416. For other appraisals of Model, see Mellenthin, *Panzer Battles,* p. 304; Hans Speidel, *Invasion 1944: Rommel and the Normandy Campaign* (Chicago, 1950), pp. 139–140.

[12] Shulman, *Defeat in the West,* pp. 204–205.

[13] See von Rundstedt's postwar statements, quoted in *ibid.,* pp. 205–206.

immediately sent in reinforcements, even to the extent of weakening the line elsewhere, and forced the American spearhead back from its advanced position. Fortunately for the Germans, the American command did not throw its strength behind the First Army's thrust.[14]

The second blow to von Rundstedt's defensive plans came from Hitler. Seeking to bolster German defenses, the Army commander requested replacements, and Hitler announced that he was sending additional men to the Western front. Instead of utilizing them for defensive purposes, however, von Rundstedt was to launch an attack. Hitler's immediate object was to prevent the U.S. Third Army from effecting a juncture with the U.S. Seventh Army. Once again Hitler was acting on intuition and without counsel of his military leaders in the field. Looking ahead, Hitler sought a second objective; by striking at the Third Army's south flank he could drive across to Antwerp, the major Allied supply base, and attack the Allied forces from the rear. Hitler not only conceived this ambitious plan but he selected the Panzer units that were to put it into operation. Some of these units were already engaged along the front, one had been reduced badly in strength, and of the three new Panzer brigades only one had reached the front.[15] Instead of withdrawing experienced units and replacing them with raw recruits or partly disabled forces, von Rundstedt desperately needed competent troops to prevent a break through the Siegfried Line, along which the major Allied forces were aligning themselves.[16] But after July 20, generals did not argue with Hitler, and von Rundstedt and General Johannes Blaskowitz, who headed the projected attack, moved ahead with their preparations.

So intent was Hitler upon launching his campaign that he issued an order that the Fifth Panzer Army should not make frontal attacks on the advancing Americans but should hold itself in reserve for its

[14] Siegfried Westphal, *The German Army in the West* (London, 1951), pp. 174–175. Westphal, Chief of General Staff under von Rundstedt when the latter returned to command, asserts that until the middle of October the Allies could have pushed through the West Wall at almost any point, crossed the Rhine, and penetrated into Germany. *Ibid.,* p. 174. On September 28, the First Army sent General Bradley a captured bronze bust of Hitler and offered to seize the original within thirty days if given seven units of fire and an additional division. Bradley was in no position to comply with their request. Bradley, *A Soldier's Story,* p. 426.

[15] Cole, *The Lorraine Campaign,* pp. 190–192.

[16] One division, for example, consisted of men with ulcers and other stomach disorders, and became known as the Stomach Division, or "White Bread Division." Shulman, *Defeat in the West,* pp. 209–210.

role in the new operation. The U.S. Third Army made it impossible for Blaskowitz to adhere literally to this order, for the American force began a drive along a forty-mile front toward the Moselle River. Disturbed by American gains, Blaskowitz issued orders for a limited Panzer counteroffensive. The 112th Panzer Brigade, which got the assignment, had a full complement of new tanks: a battalion of forty-eight Mark IV's and one of forty-eight Mark V's. Moving to the south, the brigade spent the night in and near the little town of Dompaire. French civilians notified the Allies of its presence, and a French armored division moved quickly. One column advanced to cut off the main road leading out of the town, and the other column attacked the tanks at Dompaire. The Germans had selected a poor spot, for the town was in a low region easily covered by elevations which the French quickly occupied. The 406th Group of the XIX Tactical Air Command cooperated closely with the French and made four attacks with bombs and rockets. The combined French ground and U.S. air assault cost the Germans sixty tanks in one day and eliminated the 112th Panzer Brigade as an effective participant in Hitler's contemplated counteroffensive.[17]

In the meantime, caught between the U.S. Third and Seventh Armies as they pressed toward each other, the German 16th Division fell apart as individuals and groups sought to escape the trap. By the middle of September, the two American armies had eliminated the pocket between them.[18]

The defeat of the 112th Panzer Brigade not only had been a victory in the war of attrition, but it had so restricted the area for armored movement that the Fifth Panzer Army, of which the 112th Panzer Brigade was a part, could not launch a counterattack west of the Moselle and the Vosges. Instead, Blaskowitz recommended a limited attack east of the Moselle. Von Rundstedt passed the request on to Hitler, who approved, without abandoning his larger plan of attack. General Hasso von Manteuffel, who headed this venture, received promises of artillery and air support. The failure of these to materialize and the German piecemeal use of tanks contributed to an American victory in a running tank battle at Arracourt from September 19 to 22. Losing three tank destroyers and five M-4 tanks, and with casualties of but six men killed and thirteen wounded, the Americans

[17] Cole, *The Lorraine Campaign,* pp. 195–201.
[18] *Ibid.,* pp. 203–204.

destroyed forty-three German tanks, most of which were new Panthers. Other Panzer units during the same period also suffered heavily and received orders to continue fighting long after chances of success had faded. Here as elsewhere Hitler's policy of "no withdrawal" led to an unnecessary waste of life and matériel. When the attack failed, Hitler found a convenient scapegoat in General Blaskowitz and replaced him with General Hermann Balck.[19]

Balck found the going no easier than had Blaskowitz, for the American forces were still pressing against the Fifth Panzer Army and despite the change in German leadership had crushed it by the end of September. Once more U.S. air power, artillery, and aggressive ground tactics had defeated German Panzer units, which still committed themselves piecemeal to battle. The weather, too, in September favored the Allies, for sunny days made it possible for them to exploit their control of the air in relentless assaults on the enemy. The faster and more maneuverable American tanks also benefited from the drier terrain to engage in successful tactical operations against the harder-hitting but slower-turreted Panthers.[20]

Although they had suffered a reversal in their counterattack, the Germans were still dangerous, as the 35th Infantry Division of the Third Army soon discovered. Elements of this division held a bridgehead extending into the Forêt de Grémecey north and east of the Seille River. Toward the end of September, the Germans made a concerted drive to eliminate this salient. After heavy fighting the Germans forced their way into this forest and exerted tremendous pressure on U.S. infantry units. The fighting was intense and confused within the forest, but gradually the American battalions appeared to be gaining, while artillery and fighter bombers prevented enemy reinforcements from entering the battle area. Inexperience of some of the German troops aided the Americans, who in places fought from trenches dug in World War I. The American line of defense, however, was thin, and by noon on September 30, Major General Paul W. Baade ordered his last reserves into action. At a conference held later

[19] *Ibid.,* pp. 215–230. Hitler disliked Blaskowitz, who, like von Rundstedt, was in the tradition of East Prussian Army officers, nonpolitical and devoted to their profession. *Ibid.,* p. 46. Balck, on the other hand, was strongly pro-Nazi. He had gained experience and a reputation for personal bravery on the Eastern front. For differing views of Balck, see *ibid.,* p. 230; Mellenthin, *Panzer Battles,* pp. 304–305.

[20] Cole, *The Lorraine Campaign,* pp. 242–243.

in the afternoon, the top military leaders in the sector, including Major General Hugh J. Gaffey, Patton's Chief of Staff, decided to withdraw from the Forêt de Grémecey and make a stand behind the Seille River. When Patton was told of this plan, however, he reacted vigorously and declared that the American forces should not give ground to the Germans. Accordingly, Baade, who had called off his reserves, sent them back into action, and with their support the defense held and then slowly began to turn against the Germans. The German commander, *Generalleutnant der Waffen-SS* Herman Priess, had already received orders to withdraw, and in the face of increased resistance brought to an end the four-day battle.[21]

By this time the Third Army was feeling very definitely the shortage of supplies. General Eisenhower, as we have seen, believed that the Allies could break the logistical bottleneck only by clearing the way to Antwerp and in order to concentrate on this objective had ordered other forces on the line to cease their offensive operations. General Patton was unhappy at receiving such orders and persuaded General Bradley to allow him to continue limited operations in order to effect "minor adjustments" in his lines.[22] Making the most of this relaxation of the rule, Patton sent his forces into action in several sectors, one of which was in the vicinity of the fortress city of Metz. The first step in the effort to take the city was a coordinated air and ground assault on the key stronghold, Fort Driant, which guarded approaches from the south or southwest. In addition, from this fort, which was on a dominant elevation, the Germans could direct fire from other batteries in the area.

Located in the outer ring of the city's defenses, Fort Driant had been built in 1902 and later modernized and strengthened by both the French and the Germans. Four casements set into the ground with concrete walls seven feet thick were connected by underground tunnels with a pentagonal central fort. A wide, dry moat surrounded the elevation, and the Germans had emplaced great quantities of barbed wire as added protection. The defenders had ample supplies of food

[21] *Ibid.*, pp. 244–255.

[22] *Ibid.*, p. 259. Eisenhower did not feel that the lines should be completely static. Eisenhower, *Crusade in Europe*, p. 325. Bradley professes to have been irritated by Patton's actions, but noted that he would not object to battalion action. Bradley, *A Soldier's Story*, p. 427. Montgomery feels that the logistical support which Patton secured weakened the priority given the Allied attack on the northern flank. Montgomery, *Memoirs*, pp. 265–266.

and water, in addition to a system of artificial ventilation. Allied Intelligence officers finally located engraving plates showing ground plans in 1940, but these were not available in time for adequate briefing of the first assault troops, who consequently acted without sufficient knowledge of the details of the fortification.[23]

On September 27, P-47's from the XIX Tactical Air Command started the attack, but their thousand-pound bombs and napalms had little effect on the fort, nor was succeeding artillery bombardment, howitzer, or tank-destroyer fire any more effective. As a result, when ground forces of the XX Corps started their attack, the enemy opened fire with small arms, machine guns, and mortars. Two American platoons worked their way to the west side of the fort, where small-arms fire checked further progress. The entanglements and vigorous enemy fire forced the assault troops to retire in the afternoon. Losses had been slight, but progress had been nil.

On the insistence of Major General Walton Walker, in command of the XX Corps, elements of his corps made a second attempt on October 3 and immediately ran into trouble. Tankdozers, which were to fill in the moat, broke down, and snakes designed to clear routes through barbed wire failed to perform their function. Artillery fires helped break some of the wire barrier, and parts of the attacking force got into a segment of the fort. They failed, however, to dislodge the Germans from their main defenses, and after heavy fighting in tunnels were forced out of the fort into a nearby concrete barracks.

Top U.S. generals met again to discuss the situation at noon, October 9. Reasoning that they would need four additional divisions to take the fort and that these would make the venture too costly, they called off the attack. The failure to take Fort Driant was the first reversal of consequence for the Third Army, and it came at the start of a period of relative quiet which did not permit the Army to attempt another offensive immediately. Nevertheless, the Third Army had learned some hard lessons, from which it profited when the offensive was resumed in November.[24] Other elements of the Third

[23] Cole, *The Lorraine Campaign,* pp. 259–265.

[24] *Ibid.,* pp. 266–275. The tankdozer was a tank equipped with a blade and was designed to remove dirt and other obstructions under battle conditions. After experiments in Florida, the tankdozer was introduced in Italy and used in subsequent campaigns. It was much less vulnerable than a bulldozer, but less maneuverable and subject to mechanical breakdowns. The snake was a Canadian mine-clearing device adapted by U.S. Engineers. The American snake

Army also engaged in hard fighting to make "minor adjustments" in the line. There were pitched battles for some of the towns in the area, and the U.S. forces developed the technique of employing heavy artillery and antitank fire to level buildings which the enemy occupied. Patton also used the period to test his new replacements. The 26th Infantry Division, a National Guard division, reached the front without a full complement of men or equipment, but Patton sent it into action after a limited objective, and in its first battle experience the division gave a good account of itself.[25]

Meanwhile, the Third Army as a whole entered what an Army historian calls the "October pause." Most of the rest consisted of preparing for action, but in some ways life was a little easier. The food became somewhat better as fresh bread and captured beef gave variation to the K rations. Marlene Dietrich's USO show provided a morale lift, as Bing Crosby's tour had done in September. Always, however, it seemed, there was rain, and everywhere there was mud. Patton increased his discipline in such matters as uniform regulations, while men worked on mechanized equipment, making repairs and installing metal grousers, or "duck bills" which would help tanks traverse mud when the time came to resume the attack.[26] As a part of the "October pause," P-47's breached a dam to prevent later flooding of the Seille River area, which the Third Army would have to cross.[27]

The First Army, like the Third Army and for similar reasons, slowed to a halt during the fall. Like the Third Army, too, it engaged in a number of actions in the process. Early in October it began the most significant of these operations, the assault on Aachen. As usual, the Army Air Forces cooperated in the venture, but the 9th Bombardment Division was relatively unsuccessful, largely as a result of in-

---

was a pipe made of corrugated sheets and loaded with explosives which was shoved forward by a tank. B. D. Coll, J. E. Keith, and H. H. Rosenthal, *The Corps of Engineers: Troops and Equipment* (*United States Army in World War II: The Technical Services*) (Washington, 1958), pp. 470–475.

[25] Cole, *The Lorraine Campaign,* pp. 290–291.

[26] *Ibid.,* pp. 291–295. General Patton believed firmly in discipline as a means of promoting alertness. In his instructions to his corps, division, and separate unit commanders, March 6, 1944, he stated: "There is only one kind of discipline—PERFECT DISCIPLINE. If you do not enforce and maintain discipline, you are potential murderers. You must set the example." George S. Patton, Jr., *War As I Knew It* (Boston, 1947), p. 402.

[27] Craven and Cate, *The A.A.F. in World War II,* III, 617.

clement weather. On the first day of the attack, 363 medium bombers left to participate, but only sixty reached the targets. Weak preliminary planning by the ground forces led to bombing over too large an area for effectiveness, and some plane crews made incorrect identifications. The worst instance occurred when, through error, a plane bombed and badly damaged a small Belgian town. The fighter bombers of IX TAC, on the other hand, coordinated their attacks very effectively with advancing ground forces. They destroyed vital enemy pillboxes and helped break up an enemy counterattack.[28]

In the meantime, two corps of the First Army assaulted the city, into which the Germans had poured reinforcements from the Arnhem region. The U.S. forces gradually encircled the city and called on the Germans to surrender. When the besieged troops declined, American ground and air forces began a systematic and heavy bombardment of the city, lasting from October 11 to 13. On the fourteenth, American troops pushed into a section of the city and began a house-to-house battle for its control.[29] Using tactics which the Third Army employed on villages, the First Army brought up 155-m. rifles and other heavy artillery to blast buildings apart.[30] The Germans held out against this terrific pounding for about a week, but on October 21 were forced to surrender. Aachen was the first German city of importance to fall into American hands.[31] Further, the Americans not only had breached the West Wall at Aachen, but they had also broken through it near Rötgen and were in a position to launch a flanking attack from this location.

Having taken Aachen, the First Army settled down to defensive operations, with exceptions similar to those experienced by the Third Army. The period of pause was also one of preparation for the First Army, as, for example, its V Corps made ready for a thrust through the Hürtgen Forest to take Schmidt. This town was not only at a vital crossroads, but it was on an elevation overlooking one of the important Roer dams, which the Germans might destroy to flood terrain over which advancing Allies must pass.[32]

[28] *Ibid.*, III, 614–616.

[29] Pogue, *The Supreme Command,* pp. 304–305.

[30] Eisenhower, *Crusade in Europe,* p. 312.

[31] Shulman, *Defeat in the West*, pp. 219–220.

[32] C. B. MacDonald and S. T. Mathews, *Three Battles: Arnaville, Altuzzo, and Schmidt* (*United States Army in World War II*) (Washington, 1952), p. 251.

On the right of the Allied line, the Sixth Army Group, like the other groups, continued to have supply problems. General de Lattre de Tassigny, whose French Army "B" had become the French First Army, chafed under the role assigned to his Army as a covering force for the U.S. Seventh Army on his left. He protested at the lack of supplies and requested a more active assignment for his forces. General Jacob L. Devers, commanding the Sixth Army Group, was sympathetic, but the logistical requirements of the war in the north limited the support he could give de Lattre de Tassigny. Handicapped by lack of supplies, in October the French First Army attempted to move north of the Vosges toward Colmar. The enemy bitterly resisted advance, and the French were forced to call off the attack.[33] General Patch's Seventh Army was a little more successful, taking some six thousand prisoners as it seized high ground above the Meurthe Valley.[34]

Late in October, the Combined Chiefs of Staff met in Washington to consider the possibility of winning the war by the end of the year. They recommended use of the proximity fuze, hitherto unavailable on land for fear of loss to the enemy, to aid in the great assault. General Marshall informed Eisenhower of the Combined Chiefs' considerations and asked his opinion. Eisenhower replied that he was as anxious as anyone to end the war, but he insisted that full use of Antwerp was a prime requisite for a major assault. The Strategic Air Command objected to diversion from its main task of bombing Germany's oil industry to support of a land attack. It agreed, however, to a secondary strategic bombing of transportation, but bad weather nullified much of its effort.[35]

The extended struggle necessary to clear the approaches to Antwerp killed hopes of ending the war quickly. Instead, Allied leaders turned to more limited objectives. Even before he heard of the optimistic plan of the Combined Chiefs of Staff to terminate the war, Eisenhower conferred with the Twelfth and Twenty-first Army Group heads on operational plans for November and December. He decided that since the Twenty-first Army Group was still trying to clear the Scheldt Estuary the First and Ninth Armies should begin limited

[33] De Lattre de Tassigny, *The History of the French First Army,* pp. 181–207; Guy Salisbury-Jones, *So Full a Glory: A Biography of Marshal de Lattre de Tassigny* (London, 1954), pp. 160–162.

[34] Pogue, *The Supreme Command,* p. 305.

[35] *Ibid.,* pp. 307–309.

thrusts aimed at securing bridgeheads on the Rhine. In preparation, the Allies launched two subsidiary attacks. On November 12, the British First Army began a movement which netted some gains along the west bank of the Maas River opposite Roermond.[36] Ten days earlier, on November 2, the U.S. First Army launched an attack designed to seize the Schmidt area north of important dams on the Urft and Roer rivers.

The V Corps, which made the attack, had several objectives in mind: to clear supply routes for anticipated VII Corps operations to the north, to protect that corps' right flank, to prepare for an attempt to seize the Roer dams and to draw Germans away from the VII Corps in order to facilitate its advance.[37] The hilly, woody terrain was part of a general region which the Americans called the Hürtgen Forest. The V Corps had among its specific objectives the towns of Schmidt and Kommerscheidt. One of the principal problems was access, for the attackers had to cross the small, but swiftly running Kall River and ascend a narrow mountain trail. The corps hoped that the Army Air Force could isolate the region to prevent the Germans from taking in heavy armored reinforcements and that artillery could keep the enemy from making use of a nearby elevation. Unfortunately, bad weather made it impossible for the Tactical Air Command to accomplish its mission successfully, and the invaders found themselves fighting against a not only determined but reinforced foe.[38]

A battalion managed to seize Schmidt without too much difficulty, but the poor condition of the trail made it impossible to bring up armored support to defend the town from counterassault, and German tanks spearheaded its recapture. Heavy fighting went on around Kommerscheidt as well. Engineers worked feverishly to widen the forest trail, but mechanical difficulties, rain and later snow, and enemy action turned the battle into a confused melee. When weather permitted, fighter bombers aided the ground forces, but as the action continued, battle fatigue affected troops so that in one instance men broke and ran from a fancied German counterattack. Other U.S. soldiers in and near the towns and on Vossenack Ridge endured days of enemy shelling. By the eighth it was apparent that the operation had failed, and orders went out for withdrawal. Before the surviving

[36] *Ibid.*, p. 311.
[37] MacDonald and Mathews, *Three Battles,* pp. 251–252.
[38] *Ibid.*, pp. 272–274.

members of the 28th Division had pulled out this unit had taken one of the worst beatings of the war. Hardest hit were the three infantry regiments that had made the main assault, and the casualties of the division as a whole totaled 6,184 persons. Material losses were also high and included sixteen out of twenty-four M-10 tank destroyers and thirty-one out of fifty medium tanks.[39]

The V Corps had failed in all but one of its objectives; it had drawn off German reserves, but in the process had incurred about three thousand more casualties than the enemy. The Army historian who made a special study of this operation has concluded that this was a gamble that lost as a result of a number of factors, including bad weather and resultant inability to use air power as expected, an inadequate supply route, and insufficient reserves.[40]

On November 16, the First and Ninth Armies started their major attacks. Unusually effective ground-air cooperation enabled the Ninth Army to make satisfactory initial advances. The First Army, however, found impenetrable obstacles in the German West Wall and in the Hürtgen Forest, which thwarted operations of armored forces. A few gains toward the end of the month varied what was otherwise a stalemate.[41] General Patton, instead of continuing the effort to batter down the Metz fortresses, surrounded the city and took it November 19. His forces then gradually reduced the outlying fortifications.[42]

On the extreme right, the French and American armies of the Sixth Army Group, although cast in a minor role, actually made some of the most successful advances of the period. On November 23, the 2d French Armored Division took Strasbourg near the Rhine. The II French Corps of the French First Army inflicted a sharp defeat on the enemy in Alsace.[43] The Sixth Army group forced the Germans out of strong places in the Vosges Mountains and was in a position to threaten the Saar.

The failure of the First and Ninth Armies to make significant gains prompted Montgomery to request a re-examination of objectives. Re-

[39] *Ibid.,* p. 415.

[40] *Ibid.,* p. 416.

[41] Pogue, *The Supreme Command,* p. 311.

[42] Cole, *The Lorraine Campaign,* pp. 372–449. See pp. 590–607 for a good summary of the Third Army's campaign in Lorraine.

[43] Pogue, *The Supreme Command,* pp. 311–312; Eisenhower, *Crusade in Europe,* pp. 330–331; de Lattre de Tassigny, *The History of the French First Army,* pp. 213–284.

minding Eisenhower of the October directive that the main thrust should be in the north, the British leader made a new appeal for a single major blow at the enemy rather than a series of attacks along the frontier. Eisenhower challenged Montgomery's contention that departing from a concentration of effort in the north was a "strategic reverse." He reminded Montgomery of the significance of Bradley's breakout at Saint-Lô, and he stated that he would not stop the operations of either Patton or Devers so long as they were making it possible to concentrate in that area, although he assured Montgomery that he would not encourage them to needless attacks.[44]

By early December, Eisenhower was convinced that the rebuilding of German forces in the West would prevent a rapid conclusion of the war. Allied air commanders were also beginning to fear a revival of the German *Luftwaffe,* and it looked as if the Germans might beat the Allies to operational use of jet aircraft. Nevertheless, Allied air leaders decided to hold to the German oil industry as the primary target.[45]

On December 7, Eisenhower met again with Montgomery, Bradley, and Air Chief Marshal Tedder and encountered the same strong differences of opinion. This time Eisenhower decided that there should be a major thrust in the north and a minor attack farther south.[46] In an effort to straighten lines north of the Ardennes Forest in preparation for the major assault planned for January, 1945, British and American troops engaged in heavy fighting and suffered severe casualties in and near the Hürtgen Forest.[47]

Feeling that forces south of the Ardennes would not be needed for the main northern thrust, Eisenhower authorized the Third Army, with the support of the Seventh Army, to launch an attack on the Saar December 19. By the middle of December not two but several sectors were ready to take the offensive. On the extreme left, Montgomery's Twenty-first Army Group, supported by the U.S. Ninth Army, planned to make the major assault which was designed to cross the Rhine north of the Ruhr. The Ninth Army, in turn, although a part of the major thrust, looked to the Roer and then to the Rhine, which it hoped to reach with the support of the U.S. First Army. To

[44] Pogue, *The Supreme Command,* pp. 312–314.
[45] *Ibid.,* pp. 315–316.
[46] *Ibid.,* p. 316; Montgomery, *Memoirs,* pp. 270–274.
[47] Pogue, *The Supreme Command,* p. 317.

the south, on the other side of the Ardennes, the U.S. Third Army was ready to attack toward the Rhine, and to its right the U.S. Seventh also had the Rhine as an objective, as well as the West Wall. The Allied forces farther south, as we have seen, had reached the Rhine.

There was only one significant sector of the Allied front that was not prepared for offense. This was the narrow line of men and equipment that guarded the Ardennes Forest region between the U.S. First and Third Armies.[48] Four divisions only were assigned to protect this wooded stretch of seventy-five miles. The Germans were aware of this weakness and out of that knowledge came the plan for the last great German offensive on the Western front. Although this assault sometimes is called the Rundstedt offensive, the idea was not von Rundstedt's but Hitler's.

As early as September 13, the *Führer* secretly ordered the constitution of a new Panzer Army, the Sixth, whose mission, as we have seen, would be to conduct a counteroffensive. Hitler's aim was to drive through to Antwerp, isolate the British and perhaps create another Dunkirk. He did not seek the advice of the field commanders but ordered his staff under *Generaloberst* Alfred Jodl to develop a detailed plan from his idea. Toward the end of October, he told von Rundstedt and Model of the plan. He explained the objective and stated that he was attacking the Ardennes because of the weakness of the U.S. forces in that region. Optimistically, he promised supplies and air support, including jet aircraft.

Although they made no vigorous protest at the time, von Rundstedt and Model were not sanguine of success. Von Rundstedt's chief of staff expressed the prevailing view when he said that the plan was too ambitious. It would be most difficult to protect the flanks if the Germans moved ahead too rapidly, in spite of a secondary thrust included in the plan as a protection to the south flank. Then, even if they could secure Antwerp, they did not have enough strength to hold it and would have to withdraw.

Urged to protest in person to Hitler, von Rundstedt declined the suggestion as futile. Model, on the other hand, several times attempted to persuade Hitler to modify the plan in favor of a more limited objective which would kill large numbers of Allied soldiers but not involve so much risk. Hitler, however, remained obdurate and had his

[48] *Ibid.*, p. 318.

way. In November, he shifted his headquarters to a spot in Hesse to be nearer the Western front.[49] At this time he visited Berlin, and for the first time he saw the devastation inflicted by strategic air bombardment. Throughout the war he had sedulously avoided visiting bombed cities as he had kept himself far removed from the battlefields, usually at his heavily guarded "Wolf's Lair" near Rastenburg in East Prussia.

Although they were convinced that the attack was too great a risk and would probably fail, the generals obeyed their orders and prepared for the venture. Hitler insisted on the greatest secrecy; only officers who had to know were told of the plans and they had to take an oath that they would pay with their lives for slips.[50] Troops began to move quietly into the region. Their shift to the west weakened the Polish and Hungarian fronts. Twenty-four divisions, ten of which were armored, prepared to participate. Armor was expected to play an important part in the attack, and in the initial stages German officers and men dressed in American uniforms would attempt to add to the confusion of the forces attacked.[51]

The early success of the operation made the Germans feel that their efforts to maintain secrecy had resulted in a completely surprised foe, but the matter is somewhat more complicated than that interpretation. The Allied leaders, of course, knew that the Ardennes defenses were weak. Intelligence officers found that there were unusual developments across the line and reported that information. Just how strongly they made their points and how accurately they predicted an attack are questions upon which the experts do not agree. Their warnings would have had to be very strong to effect a change in plans. In thinning out the Ardennes line Bradley was taking a calculated risk. If an attack came, it would probably be in the vicinity of the Roer, and in that sector there would be strength to meet it. Bradley would have had to weaken plans for a January offensive to bolster the Ardennes, and rather than jeopardize the projected attack

[49] *Ibid.*, pp. 359–360; Westphal, *The German Army in the West,* pp. 178–183.

[50] Mellenthin, *Panzer Battles,* p. 329.

[51] The head of the planned operation was SS Leader Otto Skorzeny, who had rescued Mussolini from the Allies. Westphal asserts that the operation was canceled and denies the truth of the rumor that Skorzeny's orders were to attempt to assassinate Eisenhower. Westphal, *The German Army in the West,* p. 184. When the attack started, Germans in American uniform were seized. Bradley, *A Soldier's Story,* pp. 467–469; Shulman, *Defeat in the West,* pp. 238–242.

he was willing to take a risk in the Ardennes. Neither Eisenhower nor Montgomery felt that the Germans would make an all-out assault at this time. In discussing with Eisenhower the possibility of attack through the Ardennes, Bradley expressed the opinion that even if the Germans broke through they would extend themselves beyond their fuel supply. Intelligence gave quite accurate reports of German concentrations, but Allied leaders thought the Germans were massing for defense against an Allied attack.

Clearly, the Allied leaders were surprised by the German attack and had made some errors of interpretation. They underestimated the weight of the blow and believed that it would be no worse than a spoiling attack which they could contain. Receiving Intelligence reports of German conservation of oil, they reasoned that the enemy was running short, not saving it for an attempted breakout. They also felt that von Rundstedt, known to be conservative, would not attempt such a reckless thrust. What they did not realize was that Hitler, not von Rundstedt or any other responsible military leader, had originated the plan and was insisting on its execution. In other words, the top military leaders on both sides looked on the operation as unwise.[52]

Hitler originally planned the attack for the middle of November, but bad weather and the difficulty of assembling the new units caused a month's delay. Once the attacking force was ready to move, Hitler looked on poor weather as an asset, since it would reduce Allied air effectiveness. In mid-December, units of the VIII Corps holding the Ardennes front included two divisions which recently had seen heavy action; the 4th Infantry Division had fought in the Hürtgen Forest, and the 28th Infantry Division had incurred many casualties in the First Army's drive to the Roer. In addition to these weary divisions there was the 106th Infantry Division, just arrived on the Continent and new to battle. Rounding out the defenses were the 14th Cavalry Group consisting of the 18th and 32d Cavalry Squadrons, and the 9th Armored Division, minus Combat Command B, which was with V Corps.[53]

Facing the VIII Corps were four German divisions and behind them, as we have seen, a great concentration of armor and manpower.

[52] Pogue, *The Supreme Command,* pp. 361–372; Bradley, *A Soldier's Story,* pp. 457–464; Eisenhower, *Crusade in Europe,* pp. 338–341.

[53] For a detailed account, see S. L. A. Marshall, *Bastogne: The Story of the First Eight Days . . .* (Washington, 1946), *passim.*

At eight in the morning of December 16, the enemy launched an infantry tank attack on the north flank and moved ahead about four and one-half miles before the 14th Cavalry Group and the 106th Division, aided by committed reserves, were able to slow down the advance. Against the 28th Division the enemy leaders sent two Panzer divisions, three infantry divisions, and one parachute division in an assault which in some places netted a gain of some four and one-half miles. The Germans also struck diversionary blows at the 9th Armored and the 4th Infantry Divisions in the south to prevent the sending of reinforcements north to the scene of the principal attack.

The VIII Corps reserve consisted of an armored combat command and four battalions of combat engineers, but as soon as the seriousness of the situation was realized, other troops were made available. A combat command of the 9th Armored Division and the 7th Armored Division headed for an assembly center near Saint-Vith, which was seen as an enemy objective. The 10th Armored Division was sent to assemble near the city of Luxembourg in the south, and the 101st and 82d Airborne Divisions received orders to the general area.

On the seventeenth, the enemy increased pressure along the whole front, and by nine in the morning had cut off two regiments of the 106th Division. The 168th Engineer Combat Team fought desperately to hold Saint-Vith, as armored units were committed piecemeal in an effort to bolster defenses. In the center, the Germans made heavy gains against the 28th Division; in places they penetrated as far as eight miles, and came within eleven miles of Bastogne. In the south, enemy attacks were weaker and American defenses correspondingly stronger.

On the following day, the Germans increased their drive at the center. Reserves enabled the corps' north flank to hold, but the Germans broke through the defenses of the 28th Division and their armored thrusts isolated and captured or destroyed large segments of the disintegrating division. Behind the 28th Division the Combat Command Reserve of the 9th Armored Division had established roadblocks; on the night of December 18–19, the Germans overran one of these and approached within three kilometers of Bastogne. Already recognizing the importance of this town as a highway center in a hilly region in which roads were essential to armored travel, Allied leaders had dispatched three experienced units to its defense. Combat Command B, 10th Armored Division, left a rest area at Remeling, France, the 101st Airborne Division departed from Camp Mourmelon, a training center area near Rheims where it had been refitting, and the 705th Tank Destroyer Battalion, at Kohlscheid, Germany, sixty miles north of Bastogne, received orders from the Ninth Army to report to VIII Corps. In sending Combat Command B into action, Lieutenant General Troy H. Middleton, commanding VIII Corps, ordered, "Move with the utmost speed. Hold these positions at all cost."[54] The commander of the XVIII Airborne Corps, Major General Matthew B. Ridgway, was at rear headquarters in England, the division commander was in the United States, and numerous other divisional officers were in England. The senior division officer present, Brigadier General Anthony C. McAuliffe, called the staff together and said, "All I know of the situation is that there has been a break and we have got to get up there."[55] Without waiting for men to return from leave, the 101st Airborne Division started on its way, not even knowing at the outset that its destination was Bastogne. During the day of December 18, 380 trucks needed for the movement of eleven thousand men were commandeered from Rouen and Paris, and that night they headed for Bastogne, lights blazing as far as Bouillon, Belgium, in defiance of a *Luftwaffe* which fortunately did not appear. By the time the various reinforcements reached Bastogne, it was apparent to the Allied leaders that the town might be encircled by the enemy before relief could be supplied again.

The enemy spent the next two days trying to break through Bastogne. The Americans, with massed artillery fire, tanks, tank destroyers, and infantry, fought stubbornly to hold their outposts. There were heavy casualties on both sides as the opponents slugged it out, sometimes in fog so thick that visibility was restricted to yards. On the night of December 20, the road to Neufchâteau was cut by the Germans, and Bastogne was isolated. Instead of producing defeatism, the encirclement brought the defenders closer together. The Armored Combat Command and the 101st Airborne Division, which to this point had been fighting separate wars, became knit into a cohesive, confident unit, notwithstanding the siege. Fortunately, after completing the encirclement, the enemy paused to make ready for the next blow and gave the besieged forces time to gather their own strength. At eleven-thirty on the night of December 22, four Germans,

[54] Quoted in *ibid.,* p. 13.
[55] Quoted in *ibid.,* p. 10.

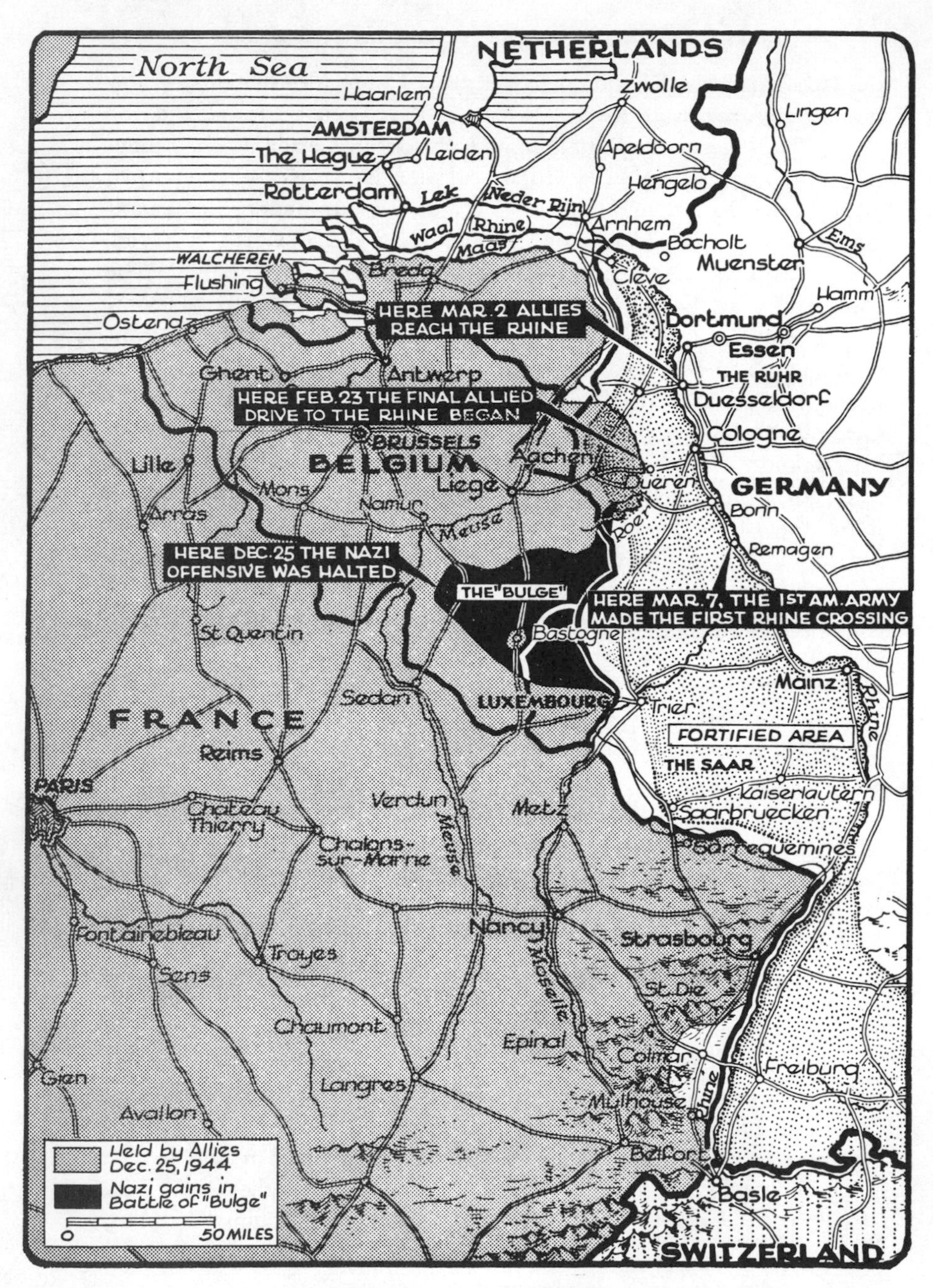

BATTLE OF THE RHINE

bearing a white flag, approached Bastogne with surrender terms for the Americans. Confident that his men could hold out until relief came, the General had no intention of surrendering and was persuaded by his staff to respond with one word, "Nuts." When the German emissary had difficulty understanding this colloquialism, an American colonel supplied another, "If you don't understand what 'Nuts' means, in plain English it is the same as 'Go to hell.' "[56] That night the *Luftwaffe* began a bombardment which continued for four nights.

Bold though McAuliffe was in his reply to the German demand for surrender, he was in desperate need of supplies for his beleaguered forces. Artillery ammunition was so low that McAuliffe was on the verge of rationing his guns to ten rounds a day. Small-arms ammunition was also running short. On the twenty-third, air supply began arriving; by four in the afternoon 241 planes had dropped 144 tons of equipment by parachute into a mile-square drop zone, and 95 percent was recovered. There were still many shortages, however, and Christmas dinners that year in Bastogne featured K rations. Fog, meanwhile, had given way to snow, which in general aided the defenders, for in the crisp air they could distinguish the enemy even in snowsuit camouflage. The Germans continued to make their fundamental error of committing their forces piecemeal to run into massed artillery fire. German artillery, on the other hand, proved generally ineffective and failed to subject Bastogne to continuous shelling. On the morning of the twenty-third, Allied planes entered the battle and in careful coordination with the beleaguered forces began a systematic bombardment of the Germans. In the next four days they made more than 250 sorties daily with such effectiveness that the commander of the Armored Combat Command asserted that they were worth two or three infantry divisions. The enemy sent over two air attacks Christmas Eve and on Christmas Day made a series of sharp attacks which the defenders stubbornly resisted. On the following day, a narrow column from the U.S. Third Army knifed its way into Bastogne, and the German encirclement came to an end.

In their initial blow at the Ardennes sector, the Germans had surprised and driven back the American defenders. So badly disrupted were communications that Twelfth Army Group Headquarters did not hear of the attack until more than four hours after its start. As

[56] Quoted in *ibid.*, p. 117.

late as nine-fifteen in the morning the briefing at headquarters noted no change in the front line situation. By afternoon news of the attack but not the extent of it began to reach Eisenhower's headquarters at Versailles, to which, as it happened, Bradley had gone for a conference. Eisenhower and he soon concluded that this was a major attack and, although surprised at the strength the Germans had amassed, made ready to meet the emergency. An immediate halting of enemy progress was out of the question. Instead, the U.S. leaders determined to strengthen the shoulders on each side of the break-through, rush assistance to Middleton's forces which were taking the brunt of the blow, and bring up reserves, not to throw them in piecemeal, but to prepare for counterthrusts at the bulge the Germans were creating.[57] Defense of the shoulders, at the outset, was especially critical, and it was when Bradley saw that they were holding that he decided to try to hold Bastogne.

Since this was a major break-through, Eisenhower began extensive shifts to meet the emergency. He temporarily dropped preparations for offensive operations, ordered the forces along most of the line to stand on the defensive, and shortened the line so that he could withdraw units for the projected flanking attacks.

One of the most important moves was that made by the Third Army. In an outstanding maneuver of the war, General Patton extricated his Army from fighting toward the Saar and executed a swing to the left to attack the enemy in the Ardennes some fifty to seventy-five miles away.[58] One objective, as we have noted, came to be the relief of the forces at Bastogne.

The German thrust had separated the First Army from Twelfth Army Group headquarters in Luxembourg. Fearing that this communication break might keep Bradley from effective control of this Army, Eisenhower decided to turn over temporary control of all Allied forces north of the Ardennes to Montgomery, who placed British troops in support of Hodges and ordered the U.S. Ninth Army to take over part of the First Army's zone.[59] Thus strengthened, Hodges reorganized the First Army to make a successful stand against

[57] Pogue, *The Supreme Command,* pp. 381–382.

[58] Bradley, *A Soldier's Story,* pp. 472–473; James Wellard, *General George S. Patton, Jr.: Man Under Mars* (New York, 1946), pp. 235–237; Charles R. Codman, *Drive* (Boston, 1957), pp. 231–238.

[59] Pogue, *The Supreme Command,* p. 378; Eisenhower, *Crusade in Europe,* p. 355.

the enemy. Meanwhile, SHAEF hastened to secure reserves from England and from reassignment of French troops behind the Meuse River.[60]

Of great assistance to the Allied defense was the clearing weather. On December 23, the fog on which the Germans had counted so heavily and which had aided their initial advance dissipated, and for several days Allied air power asserted itself not only at Bastogne but elsewhere on the front through tactical air support, interdiction campaigns on transportation, and elimination once again of the *Luftwaffe* as an important force in the area.[61]

Unquestionably, the German attack on the Ardennes was a surprise to the Allies and without doubt it inflicted heavy destruction of men and materials of war. It delayed the projected Allied attack for six weeks and diverted the Allied air forces from their strategic warfare for about a month. However, the Battle of the Bulge was a part of the war of attrition which the Germans could ill afford to lose. German manpower and supplies were running low; it was easier for the United States to replace casualties of 76,890 and losses of 733 tanks and tank destroyers than for Germany to make up its losses of 81,834 men and three or four hundred tanks. American ground forces after the initial shock, in which for a time nearly all was confusion, fought back with initiative, valor, and strength. While the Germans were losing their battle of supplies and communications, the Americans were holding and coming on again with tremendous troop and supply movements. In the first week, the First Army transported 248,000 men and 48,711 vehicles, and on one day, December 17, 11,000 vehicles moved 60,000 men into position. Supplies were moved into the Bulge for the fighting troops, while tons of other supplies, especially gasoline, were moved out to keep them from falling into the hands of the Germans. Allied air power, once the weather cleared, greatly aided the ground forces in their determined stand. Allied planes dealt a crippling blow to an already weakened *Luftwaffe,* blasted such crucial road centers as Saint-Vith and Laroche, gave tactical support to the ground forces, and struck at the area behind the Germans in an effort to isolate

[60] Pogue, *The Supreme Command,* pp. 381–382. Bradley agreed to the shift, but feared that it might cast discredit on the American command. Bradley, *A Soldier's Story,* p. 476.

[61] Pogue, *The Supreme Command,* p. 384. For air operations during the Battle of the Bulge, see Craven and Cate, *The A.A.F. in World War II,* III, 672–701.

the attackers. Although, as we have seen, the Battle of the Bulge forced the Allies to delay their own assault, when they did launch their offensive they encountered a foe which had been seriously weakened by its own desperate gamble. When, in addition, the great Soviet offensive began on January 12, 1945, the Germans found it difficult to send reserves from the West to the Eastern front.[62]

[62] Westphal, *The German Army in the West,* pp. 186–187. For a good summary of the Battle of the Bulge, see Robert E. Merriam, *Dark December: The Full Account of the Battle of the Bulge* (Chicago, New York, 1947), *passim.*

CHAPTER 21

The Collapse of Germany

EISENHOWER had shifted control of the First Army from Bradley to Montgomery purely as a temporary military measure. After the check in the German advance, this transfer became the cause of Anglo-American bitterness. British newspapers implied that Montgomery had rescued a weak American command, and the British Marshal's air of apparent condescension toward his American allies and his revived pressure for a unified command, presumably under his leadership, added to the friction.[1] While Bradley had agreed to the military logic behind the shift, he believed that it should last only as long as the Bulge existed and he was of course angered by the reflections cast on the Americans. Furthermore, he was irritated by what he considered to be Montgomery's delay in assuming the offensive.[2]

[1] Montgomery's statement to the press from group headquarters January 7 especially incensed Bradley and other American leaders, for in it Montgomery gave his role a dominant position in explaining the repulse of the enemy. Omar N. Bradley, *A Soldier's Story* (New York, 1951), pp. 484–485. Montgomery states that the Germans intercepted the statement and slanted it to give it an anti-American bias, but in his memoirs he states his belief that it was an error to hold a press conference at that time. Bernard L. Montgomery, *The Memoirs of Field-Marshal the Viscount Montgomery of Alamein, K. G.* (Cleveland and New York, 1958), pp. 278–282. Montgomery asserts that the Battle of the Bulge would not have occurred if the Allies had followed proper strategy earlier on the Western front. *Ibid.*, p. 282. For a careful account, see Forrest C. Pogue, *The Supreme Command* (*United States Army in World War II: The European Theater of Operations*) (Washington, 1954), pp. 378–380.

[2] Bradley, *A Soldier's Story,* pp. 480–482. Citing postwar German sources

Disturbed by the recriminations, Eisenhower, Churchill, and others sought to alleviate the situation with statements designed to heal the breach between the Allies. The possibility of replacing Deputy Supreme Commander Tedder by Field Marshal Alexander helped induce Montgomery to drop his recommendation for a unified ground command. The air officer, Tedder, had posed no problem, but a ground officer of Alexander's caliber between Eisenhower and the group commanders was apparently a development Montgomery did not favor. Tedder remained as Deputy Supreme Commander, and Eisenhower continued to head the forces in the field as well as at SHAEF. On January 17, the First Army returned to Bradley's command. The Ninth Army, however, remained with the Twenty-first Army Group.[3]

Having checked the enemy and prevented his reaching the Meuse, the Allied leaders planned a counteroffensive. Bradley and Montgomery issued orders January 10, 1945, for a concerted attack to start three days later. This assault came as no surprise to the Germans, who became aware of the preparations as early as December 28. Foreknowledge did not ease the situation for them. As had been the case at Mortain, the German forces found themselves confronted on three sides by the enemy. Once again, the leaders in the field knew that they had lost, but Hitler refused until too late to authorize a withdrawal. The situation was even more serious than it had been at Mortain, for Russian armies were ready to launch an offensive on the Eastern front.[4]

General Heinz Guderian, Acting Chief of the German Army General Staff (*Oberkommando des Heeres*) since the assassination attempt on Hitler the preceding summer, was keenly aware of the Soviet threat and after a tour of the Eastern defenses strongly urged Hitler to transfer armored divisions from the West to strengthen the Eastern lines.[5] Instead, Hitler ordered a second offensive in the West, on the

---

Bradley insists that instead of saving the Americans, Montgomery assumed his temporary control after the Germans knew that they had lost the offensive. *Ibid.*, p. 487.

[3] Forrest C. Pogue, *The Supreme Command*, pp. 385–391. Montgomery states that he abandoned the attempt to secure operational control when he learned of a message from General Marshall to Eisenhower expressing confidence in the Supreme Commander and saying that it would be unacceptable to place Bradley under control of a British officer. Montgomery, *Memoirs*, p. 286.

[4] The Russians started an offensive January 12, 1945. Siegfried Westphal, *The German Army in the West* (London, 1951), p. 186.

[5] Heinz Guderian, *Panzer Leader* (London, 1952), pp. 382–383.

Alsatian front. The U.S. Seventh and the French First Armies withstood the assault, although it appeared for a time that Strasbourg might have to be evacuated.[6] Aiding the Allies was the fact that for a time the German commander on the upper Rhine was Heinrich Himmler, who although powerful politically was utterly inept as a military leader.[7]

The second phase of the Battle of the Ardennes started late in December and continued through January. In flanking attacks the First and Second Armies struck at the Bulge. They were unable to surround the Germans in a pocket, but they forced them back. Once Hitler authorized the Germans to withdraw they did so with considerable skill. Their leaders rationalized the Ardennes offensive as a successful delaying action, but from the longer view it was a catastrophe. Both sides lost heavily and about equally in the sanguinary struggle, but it was the Germans and not the Allies who could least afford the attrition.[8]

Eisenhower's next objective after the removal of the Ardennes bulge was to force the Germans across the Rhine along the entire front.[9] This move not only would give the Allies a strong defensive position on the river but would continue the attrition of the enemy forces and reduce their ability to resist a subsequent break-through. The Supreme Commander met opposition to this plan from the British, who stressed again the advisability of a single great thrust to the north over dissipation of Allied power by a series of actions along the line.

Refusing to be dissuaded by the British, Eisenhower developed plans for three assaults, one in the north by the Twenty-first Army Group, one by the Twelfth Army Group in the center, and a combined attack

[6] Pogue, *The Supreme Command,* pp. 397–404; Jean de Lattre de Tassigny, *The History of the French First Army* (London, 1952), pp. 285–333.

[7] Westphal, *The German Army in the West,* pp. 187–189. Himmler was in command of all the defenses on the eastern bank of the upper Rhine from late November, 1944, to late January, 1945.

[8] U.S. casualties are given as 75,482 (8,407 killed, 46,170 wounded, and 20,905 missing) and enemy losses were roughly the same. Pogue, *The Supreme Command,* p. 396.

[9] Since the Germans had been shifting forces from the Eastern to the Western front, Eisenhower was interested in knowing Russian plans for resuming the offensive. Marshal Stalin agreed to talk with SHAEF representatives. Air Chief Marshal Tedder and two other members of Eisenhower's staff flew to Moscow and learned on January 14, 1945, that the Russian offensive had started earlier. Stalin would not promise a full-scale operation but he indicated that he would harass the Germans in the East to enable the Allies to mount an offensive in the West. *Ibid.,* pp. 405–407.

by the Twelfth and Sixth Army Groups against the Saar Basin.[10] In addition, far to the right the Germans long had been maintaining a pocket around Colmar. Eisenhower directed part of Devers' Sixth Army Group to aid French forces, and by early February they had eliminated this German advanced position.[11]

The campaign started in the north with an attack by the Canadian Army. It made satisfactory initial headway but soon bogged down in water and mud and met increasingly heavy resistance as German reinforcements shifted over in its path. Montgomery had insisted on the U.S. Ninth Army as a support to the Canadians and had requested cancellation of the proposed attacks of the U.S. First and Third Armies to make available more supplies for his own thrust. Eisenhower had acceded to the use of the Ninth Army, but he declined to curb Bradley's offensive plans.[12]

Simpson followed the Canadian move by directing his Ninth Army to attack across the Roer toward the Rhine. First Army's orders were to await Ninth Army's start before launching its own attack in the direction of Cologne. Patton, in turn, received orders to delay action until the First Army had begun its offensive.

While the Ninth Army waited to attack, Hodges sent the V Corps of the First Army to seize the dams on the Roer River. The attacking force succeeded by February 10, but before leaving, the Germans dynamited floodgates which inundated lands farther down the Roer and held up the advance of both the Ninth and the First Armies. Consequently, it was not until two weeks after the Canadians had started their campaign that the Ninth Army was able to bridge the swollen stream and begin its attack. Earlier transfer of German troops from this sector to the Canadian front naturally helped the Ninth Army, but although aided by heavy bombardment the Americans still encountered strong opposition.[13]

Bradley followed with the projected advances to the right. The First Army began crossing the Roer on the same day as the Ninth Army, February 23. Its plan was to advance toward the Rhine, acting as a cover to the Ninth Army's flank, and then turn southeast to

[10] *Ibid.*, pp. 407–413.

[11] De Lattre de Tassigny, *The History of the French First Army,* pp. 334–401; Dwight D. Eisenhower, *Crusade in Europe* (New York, 1948), p. 374.

[12] Bradley, *A Soldier's Story,* pp. 492, 497. Montgomery always displayed a predilection for building up a huge supply.

[13] *Ibid.*, pp. 499–506.

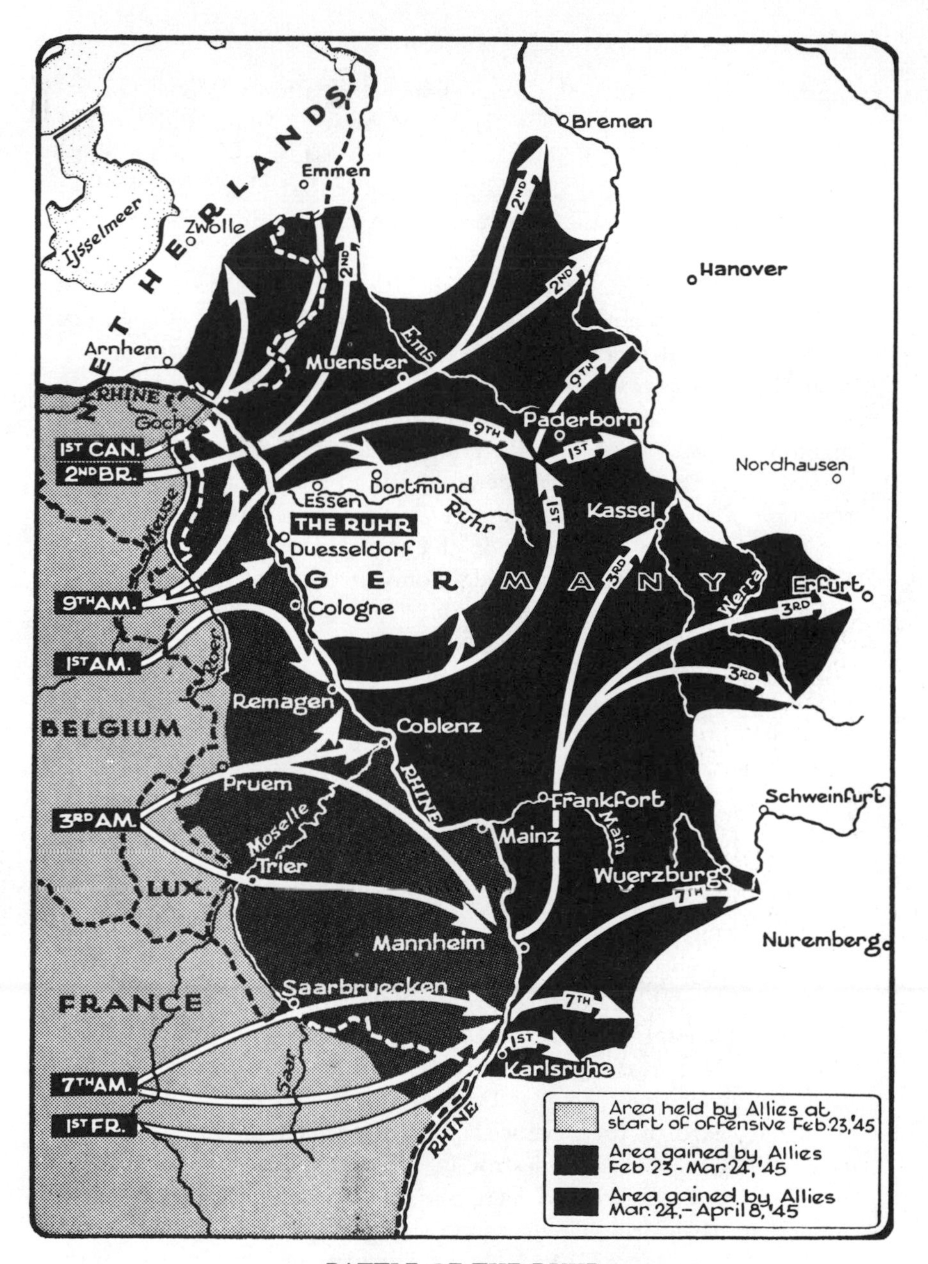

BATTLE OF THE RUHR

capture Cologne and make connection with Patton's forces. The attack proceeded with precision, and by March 7 Collins and the VII Corps took Cologne.[14] Failure of the Germans to make a determined stand in the city placed the Americans somewhat ahead of schedule. On the same day another segment of the First Army made an even more unexpected gain.

As the Allies advanced toward the Rhine, the railroad bridge at Remagen had become one of the targets of the Allied Air Forces. Damaged several times, the bridge was out of commission for several weeks but was restored to use and became one of the funnels through which Germans flowed in retreat. Confused and shifting German command and a conviction that the Allies would strike elsewhere resulted in a weakening of the forces defending the bridge, and after the destruction of the Mülheim Bridge at Cologne by a fortunate hit of an American bomb on the demolition chamber, Hitler ordered that demolition charges be attached to bridges only at the last minute.

On the morning of March 7, Able Company of the 9th Armored Division and a platoon of tanks were ordered to advance from their position about ten miles from Remagen toward the town. The company had lost two commanders in as many days and Lieutenant Karl Timmermann, a veteran of the fighting in the Battle of the Bulge around Saint-Vith, was experiencing his first company command. Going through the intervening towns with little difficulty and taking a number of prisoners, Timmermann and his men late in the morning reached the heights overlooking the Rhine and to their amazement saw the railroad bridge still standing. By two in the afternoon, the U.S. forces secured enough control of the town of Remagen to turn their rifles on the bridge, and they could see Germans on the opposite side making frenzied preparations to blow up the structure. Brigadier General William M. Hoge, in command of Combat Command B, who had directed construction of the Alaskan Highway and later led an engineer combat brigade on the beaches of Normandy, when he heard of the advance, ordered his men to take the bridge before the Germans could destroy it. The task fell to Lieutenant Timmermann and a few of his men, and the officer who gave the order treated as rhetorical Timmermann's question, "What if the bridge blows up in my face?" And blow up it very nearly did, for as the Americans were about to start, the Germans detonated a charge two-

[14] *Ibid.*, pp. 509–510.

thirds of the way across. The bridge lifted under the impact, but when the air cleared the Americans could see that although battered, the structure still stood. Supported by tank fire the men inched their way across; a few paused to subdue Germans in the bridge tower with the help of tank fire. Under the American fire most of the German soldiers and many of the townspeople had retired to a nearby railroad tunnel. More Americans crossed and established a shaky beachhead, while others worked to repair the bridge, and just before midnight nine tanks crossed to the other side of the river. These tanks and infantrymen had to spread themselves thin along a 3,500-yard perimeter and hold off enemy attacks which kept coming during the night. Movement continued across the river, however, and within twenty-four hours after taking the bridge the Americans had poured almost eight thousand men into the little beachhead on the east bank of the Rhine.[15]

Hitler, furious at the loss of the bridge, soon relieved von Rundstedt of his command and demanded punishment for those responsible for the loss. Four men died before firing squads for their alleged share in the responsibility, and a fifth escaped only because he was already a prisoner of the Americans. Not expecting to lose the bridge, the Germans had no plans for its recapture. Command difficulties, action elsewhere on the front, shortages of supplies hampered their efforts. In addition to assaulting the beachhead with ground forces, the Germans tried air attack. The *Luftwaffe,* near its collapse, was ineffective; on March 15, fifteen of twenty-one fast bombers fell victims to Allied antiaircraft fire. Skilled swimmers, with rubber suits and flippers, attempted to swim downstream to bomb the bridge. Failure of the effort came in large part from American use of a new, powerful type of armor-protected searchlight mounted on a medium tank. The blinding light and frequent dropping of depth charges in the river near the bridge kept the swimmers away. In an attempt to dislodge the Americans, Hitler even ordered use of V-2 bombs, and the Germans from launching locations in Holland fired eleven rounds, one of which landed near the bridge but did not destroy it. On March 17, however, the bridge suddenly collapsed, not from any one cause but from the general pounding it had been taking, including the damage done when the retreating Germans attempted to demolish it, from the

[15] For a detailed account of the taking of the Remagen bridge, see Ken Hechler, *The Bridge at Remagen* (New York, 1957), *passim.*

heavy traffic over it, and even from the construction work going on in the effort to save it. The Remagen Bridge, however, had served its purpose, for General Hodges already had moved four divisions across the river and had constructed subsidiary pontoon bridges.[16] Furthermore, the event was hailed by the Allied world, and dampened the spirits of the Germans. The possibility of securing a bridge had seemed so remote that the Allied leaders had made no specific plans to exploit the opportunity. There were generals, however, who were quite willing to improvise. Receiving the information in a phone call from Hodges, Bradley ordered the establishment of a bridgehead.

While the First Army was making its advances, the Third Army engaged in action in preparation for its main assault. Several corps removed enemy resistance in the Saar-Moselle triangle, penetrated the Siegfried Line, and secured beachheads across the Saar and Kyll rivers. The main advance then began as segments of the Third Army advanced to the Rhine and juncture with the First Army on the left. Other corps made a similar advance, not only reaching the Rhine but encircling and capturing thousands of German prisoners. Much of the enemy's difficulty had resulted from Hitler's insistence past the point of common sense that the Germans should stand their ground and not retreat.

The Seventh Army, while on the defensive, except for elimination of the Colmar pocket, had been building up its strength. On March 15, it began an assault toward Worms. Concentration on the attempt to withstand this attack left the Germans unprepared for the second phase of the American assault, an encircling movement to the left by the flank of the Third Army. The enveloping procedure succeeded, and by March 23 the Americans had cleared the Saar of enemy forces, and in so doing deprived the Germans of one of their most important industrial areas.[17]

Air power played an important part in the increasing success of the ground forces. Strategic air bombing of Germany continued, although the fierce counteroffensive in the Ardennes had shaken the optimism of airmen as well as others regarding a rapid termination of the war. Bad flying conditions during January limited the number of raids,

[16] Bradley, *A Soldier's Story,* pp. 510–515; Eisenhower, *Crusade in Europe,* pp. 378–381.

[17] Pogue, *The Supreme Command,* pp. 422–427; de Lattre de Tassigny, *The History of the French First Army,* pp. 407–437.

which still gave highest priority to the oil industry. Although radar-equipped bombers were beginning to come into use, they were disappointingly inaccurate at first and, in fact, they did not reach a high level of accuracy before the war's end in Europe.

The tightening of the bonds around Germany made it possible for the air command to carry on strategic bombing which hurt the enemy on both Western and Eastern fronts. Realizing this fact, the air leaders meeting at Malta in preparation for the subsequent Yalta Conference issued a revised directive for strategic air war against Germany. The German oil industry continued to hold top priority. Second were attacks on such cities as Berlin, Leipzig, and Dresden in order to create confusion among civilian evacuees from the East and to limit reinforcements reaching front-line soldiers. The third priority went to communications behind the Western front to prevent the shuttling of troops east.[18]

A few days later, on February 3, 1945, the Air Force made one of its largest raids on Berlin. Almost one thousand Fortresses bombed Berlin while four hundred Liberators raided rail and oil targets around Magdeburg. Escort planes warded off the *Luftwaffe,* but twenty-one heavy bombers fell from antiaircraft fire. The attack inflicted heavy damage on transportation facilities and government buildings, and in the process about 25,000 civilians lost their lives. Answering widespread protests, air leaders insisted that they were not conducting terror warfare, but striking such legitimate military objectives as rail centers. One reason for this particular Berlin raid had been the understanding that the German Sixth Panzer Army was moving through on its way from the Western to the Eastern front.[19]

During February, the Air Force persisted in its devastating raids despite generally adverse weather conditions. As the advancing Russians captured many of the German-controlled oil lands, the Strategic Air Force blasted much of the synthetic oil industry out of operation and by repeated blows prevented its restoration. One purpose of the attack on oil was to hinder the appearance in strength of new German jet aircraft, and for the same reason airfields were bombed repeatedly.

Among the more controversial efforts of the Strategic Air Forces were their so-called Clarion operations late in February, in which

[18] W. F. Craven and J. L. Cate, *The Army Air Forces in World War II* (Chicago, 1951), III, 715–725.
[19] *Ibid.,* III, 725–727.

heavy bombers sought to drop a wide blanket of bombs on smaller transportation centers throughout Germany. German air resistance was negligible, and bomber losses light. Later investigations indicated, however, that important military equipment still managed to pass through the bombed area.[20] On several occasions bombing errors produced considerable embarrassment and unintentional damage. Allied bombs fell on neutral Swiss cities, including Basel and Zurich, instead of German targets for which they were intended twenty-four to forty miles away. At General Marshall's suggestion, General Spaatz made a special trip to Switzerland to apologize for the errors.[21]

During March, a few jets appeared to challenge Allied air dominance. They showed their superiority as interceptor aircraft, but there were too few of them and not enough trained pilots to fly them. In answer, the Allies increased the number of escort aircraft and sought with considerable success to destroy the jets in the factory and on the ground. Germany's new aircraft, consequently, furnished a portent of air operations to come but did not check materially Allied air victory over Germany in World War II.[22]

As Eastern and Western fronts drew nearer, the problems of air coordination became increasingly vexatious. The Americans tried unsuccessfully to arrange for airfields in Hungary and near Vienna for the use of the Fifteenth Air Force and in April, 1945, finally gave up the effort. Another frustration was the attempt to agree upon a satisfactory bomb line to prevent casualties among friendly ground troops. Early in February the Russians seemed to agree on such a line, and British and American air leaders said they would give the Russians twenty-four hours' notice if they planned to bomb east of the line. They rejected as unworkable the Russian request that such missions await Russian approval, and the bombing missions in these regions continued throughout the war on the basis of a day's advance notice to the Russians.

The Russians showed a distinct unwillingness to welcome foreigners to their airports. The failure to install Micro-H stations in Russia to aid in bombing accuracy apparently stemmed from this suspicion of the Western Allies. The Russians also refused to designate special airfields to which crippled Allied planes could go and stated that such

[20] *Ibid.*, III, 728–735.
[21] *Ibid.*, III, 735–736.
[22] *Ibid.*, III, 743–745.

planes could go to any Soviet field. Unfortunately, it proved difficult to locate the personnel of these planes, and the planes themselves more often than not became additions to the Russian Air Force.[23]

By early April, the Strategic Air Command was beginning to run out of suitable targets. Western German ports, especially Hamburg, and their surrounding industries had received terrific and repeated beatings. Berlin had taken an almost daily pounding, and throughout Germany the Air Force had blasted industries, transportation, airfields, and port facilities along the Baltic. The German Air Force was no longer a menace, much of Germany had ceased to be enemy territory, and the need for further destruction had passed. On April 16, 1945, General Spaatz terminated the strategic air war against Germany.[24] Only tactical air support of the ground armies remained for the Allied air forces in Europe.

By the end of March the German cause was hopeless, but the war continued. The Western Allies had pushed the enemy to the Rhine and in the process had killed, wounded, or captured the equivalent of twelve divisions. Only about sixty German divisions, many of them weakened and undermanned, faced eighty-five Allied divisions with superior equipment and almost unchallenged air support.[25] The situation was fully as black on the Eastern front, for at the start of 1945 about three hundred Soviet divisions and twenty-five tank armies, in addition to numerous Cossack formations, confronted barely one hundred partially depleted Nazi divisions. On January 17, the Russians occupied Warsaw and shortly afterward they took other important Polish cities; the road to Berlin lay ahead, blocked principally by fortifications along the Oder River. Two other Soviet Army Groups had smashed through to the Baltic and isolated East Prussia. From the southeast, the Russians had advanced toward Budapest and by mid-February had taken this city astride the Danube. From this point the road was open to Vienna. The Germans conducted a counterattack and were fairly successful until they ran out of fuel. The Rus-

[23] *Ibid.*, III, 747–751. General John R. Deane arrived in Moscow in October, 1943, as head of a military mission and worked with some success to secure bases for shuttle missions to and from Russia. John R. Deane, *The Strange Alliance: The Story of Our Wartime Cooperation with Russia* (New York, 1947), pp. 107–125.

[24] Craven and Cate, *The A.A.F. in World War II,* III, 754.

[25] Pogue, *The Supreme Command,* p. 427. The Allied armies took more than 250,000 prisoners in the Rhineland battles.

sians forged back to regain the land lost and cross the Austrian border on March 29; about two weeks later, on April 13, they marched into Vienna. By this time the Germans had lost out in the Balkans and elsewhere in Southeastern Europe, partly as a result of political intrigues but mainly as a consequence of Russian military advances which made these intrigues possible. Russian forces combined with Tito's Partisans to drive the Germans from Belgrade in October, 1944. When the Red Army advanced into Rumania and the Allies moved north in Italy, the Nazi positions in Greece and adjoining areas became untenable, and German forces pulled north in an effort to hold Hungary.[26] All around Germany the cordon drew tighter. But as long as Hitler willed it and the German forces obeyed, the Allies had to continue to seek their basic objective, the destruction of German armed might.

After the loss of the Remagen Bridge, von Rundstedt went into his last retirement. Field Marshal Albert Kesselring, who had led the effective delaying action of the Germans in Italy, became the next Commander in Chief in the West and carried on the hopeless task of directing the defense against the Allies, who were moving ahead. Their Air Force gave cover and naval landing craft aided the ground forces in crossing the Rhine.[27]

When his armies had established strong positions across the river, Eisenhower considered the next moves. The first of these was obvious, the encirclement of the Ruhr, which although hard hit by air bombardment was still a valuable prize. Earlier it had been felt that Montgomery's Twenty-first Army Group would conduct the major assault, but Bradley's remarkable brilliance as a tactician, and the successful execution of his plans by the Twelfth Army Group, caused Eisenhower to give Bradley's forces an increased share in the invasion of the Ruhr. As a result, the attack became one of encirclement, in which the U.S. Ninth Army advanced around the northern and the U.S. First Army around the southern edge of the Ruhr. Moving more

[26] For brief accounts of developments in Eastern and Southeastern Europe, see Guderian, *Panzer Leader,* pp. 373–424; Arnold Toynbee and Veronica M. Toynbee (ed.), *Hitler's Europe* (*Survey of International Affairs, 1939–1946*) (London, New York, Toronto, 1954), pp. 585–604, 619–631, 655–690.

[27] Craven and Cate, *The A.A.F. in World War II,* III, 769–775. Four Navy task units of 24 boats, 13 officers, and 205 men each assisted the Allied armies in crossing the Rhine. Two types of landing craft were taken overland to the Rhine. S. E. Morison, *History of United States Naval Operations in World War II* (Boston, 1957), XI, 317–323.

rapidly, the latter forged ahead and by April 1 at Paderborn completed the encirclement, which closed almost a third of a million men in the trap.[28]

Within the Ruhr, Marshal Model knew his predicament but he hoped by delaying to prevent the engagement elsewhere of large bodies of the enemy. From the German government came orders to institute a scorched-earth policy, but Model apparently ignored these instructions.[29] Albert Speer, who had directed Germany's war production, tried to persuade Hitler to change his policy so that Germans would have the economic means for survival after the war, but Hitler refused. Secretary of War Stimson, trying to save as much of German industry as possible for postwar European recovery, asked Marshall if further destruction was necessary. The Chief of Staff unofficially passed the question on to Eisenhower, who replied that although he was willing if possible to avoid destroying industrial centers he insisted on the rapid conquest of the Ruhr as a military necessity. He noted, however, that heavy bombing of the area had already ceased.[30]

Having closed the Ruhr, the bulk of the Ninth and First Armies advanced toward the Elbe. Several corps remained to reduce the pocket, and they began to close in on forces whose supplies were rapidly dwindling. Faced with disaster and ignoring orders from the German government to counterattack and break through, the German leaders in the trap chose a curious alternative to surrender. On April 17, they announced the dissolution of Army Group B, dismissed the young and very old from the service, and in effect told the others to get out of the situation as best they could.[31] Model himself disappeared and, according to some contemporaries, committed suicide.[32] Organized resistance ended April 18. Within three weeks the Allies had captured not only the Ruhr but over 300,000 Germans, including two dozen generals and an admiral.[33]

After the successful conquest of the Ruhr, the problem became one of direction, and Eisenhower at this time made a decision that pro-

[28] Pogue, *The Supreme Command,* pp. 434–438.

[29] F. W. Mellenthin, *Panzer Battles, 1939–1945* (London, 1956), pp. 340–341; H. R. Trevor-Roper, *The Last Days of Hitler* (New York, 1947), p. 113.

[30] Pogue, *The Supreme Command,* p. 439.

[31] *Ibid.,* p. 440.

[32] No trace of his body was found, but Westphal asserts that Model shot himself. Westphal, *The German Army in the West,* p. 196.

[33] Pogue, *The Supreme Command,* p. 440.

duced sharp controversy. Originally it was planned that the major thrust would be on the northern side of the Allied lines with Berlin as the ultimate goal. By the end of March, however, the Supreme Commander believed that there were more important objectives than Berlin. Furthermore, over two hundred miles and the Elbe River lay between the Western armies and Berlin in contrast to thirty-five miles between the advance Russian forces and the German capital. Instead of competing in a race, Eisenhower felt it more advisable to continue the destruction of German power. Accordingly, he decided to turn the armies toward Leipzig rather than Berlin. Planning to make connections with the Russians and cut Germany in half, Eisenhower requested the Allied military mission in Moscow to inform Stalin of his intentions.[34]

This action provoked resentment and protest from the British Chiefs of Staff. Charging that Eisenhower had exceeded his authority by dealing directly with Stalin, they clearly showed resentment that Montgomery and the British forces, which they had hoped would lead the march into Berlin, were to be relegated to a secondary and perhaps even static role. Churchill took up the matter in correspondence with Roosevelt since he was concerned by the political implications of Eisenhower's shift in plans. Again, as in the case of the invasion of southern France, Eisenhower and Churchill clashed on a matter of principle. The Prime Minister feared the postwar results with Russians in both Vienna and Berlin. Eisenhower felt bound to seek a military objective, which was by the most direct means possible to effect the destruction of German military power. He was not trying to cast discredit on the British forces, he would take Berlin if it could be done easily, and British and American troops would share in the capture. More important, however, was the isolation and defeat of the German armies and the seizure of Lübeck and other ports on the Baltic as a blow at the German naval forces and German forces in the Scandinavian countries. Eisenhower defended his direct approach to Stalin as a communication from one military commander to another; he had found attempts to deal with lesser Soviet officials ineffective.

The debate continued for several days as the U.S. Chiefs of Staff and Roosevelt supported the Supreme Commander.[35] Churchill, ap-

[34] *Ibid.*, p. 441.

[35] *Ibid.*, pp. 442–443: Eisenhower, *Crusade in Europe,* p. 399. Eisenhower insisted that the Combined Chiefs of Staff had authorized him to communicate

preciating the need for seizure of the U-boat bases on the Baltic and aware that only about a fourth of the forces in the Western armies were British, gave up the struggle to give priority to the advance of the Twenty-first Army Group. He felt and continued to believe that Berlin was a political objective of strategic importance. The Yalta meeting with the Russians had taken place, and the Prime Minister already had seen the rising intransigence of Soviet Russia and its threat to Western Europe. Roosevelt, on the other hand, sensitive to the war that still had to be won in the Pacific, apparently continued to regard the Russians as staunch and necessary allies. Furthermore, the President was at Warm Springs when the controversy arose. Churchill is undoubtedly right in stating that at this critical period of decision political leadership was temporarily lacking in the United States. Roosevelt died April 12, and Harry S. Truman was not yet well informed concerning the issues involved. Whether either would have denied Eisenhower the right to determine his strategy in the conclusion of a successful land campaign is another question.

The Supreme Commander had considered carefully with Bradley and the SHAEF staff the problem of an attempt to reach Berlin. Two hundred miles lay before the Western armies to the Elbe, and beyond the river were fifty miles of lowlands interlaced with streams and canals. They estimated that determined German resistance might cost 100,000 Allied casualties, and this expense in their opinion was too high for the prestige to be gained by entry into Berlin.[36]

The British abandoned their arguments, and the Combined Chiefs of Staff gave Eisenhower no instructions. Some time later, when General Simpson reached the Elbe, he asked for permission to continue to Berlin. Eisenhower declined the request and stated that such a move would be inadvisable in view of relations with the Russians. The key to his refusal lay in his belief that Simpson did not have the strength to seize the capital since only his advance forces had reached the Elbe.[37]

The elimination of the Ruhr pocket ended significant fighting by large bodies of German troops, but isolated and occasionally hard struggles still occurred as SS or other die-hard Nazi forces made a last

directly with Stalin on purely military matters. *Ibid.*, p. 367. For Churchill's views and some of the correspondence, see Winston Churchill, *The Second World War* (Boston, 1953), VI, 458–468.

[36] Pogue, *The Supreme Command,* p. 445.

[37] *Ibid.*, pp. 446–447.

stand. The Twenty-first Army Group under Montgomery accepted its new assignment and headed for the Elbe. Informed by the German High Commissioner for the Netherlands that he would not flood the region if the Allies would not invade it, Montgomery by-passed the area temporarily in the interests of the Dutch inhabitants, and in fact even before the Germans surrendered made arrangements to provide American food for the destitute civilian population. Reaching the Elbe, his forces turned north toward the Baltic. They took Lübeck on May 2, and the surrender of Hamburg the next day signalized the end of the war in this region.[38]

Some of Bradley's forces delayed to clean out the Ruhr pocket and others spent a week quelling resistance in the Hartz Mountains. His main forces advanced toward the Elbe and encountered more problems of supply than of fighting. On April 25, advance units established contact with Russian troops on the Elbe and one of its tributaries, the Mulde. The divisional commanders of the two Allied forces met formally the following day at Torgau, east of Leipzig.[39]

Farther to the right the Third Army encountered little opposition. On April 11, Bradley drew a restraining line for Patton's men just west of the Czechoslovak border. On the fourteenth, the Third Army reached this line and regrouped for a move into Czechoslovakia and south to Bavaria and Austria. In preparation, elements of the First Army moved over into Third Army positions. On April 22, the latter force started its move into Czechoslovakia and encountering little opposition by May 4 reached Austria and occupied Lenz. The Third Army then took over a portion of the First Army's sector, since Hodges was taking his Army back to the United States in anticipation of further duty in the Pacific. Patton's forces also began to follow orders to advance to a predetermined line and make contact with the Russians. They had not completed this movement by the end of hostilities, although they had reached Russian units by May 8.[40]

The Sixth Army Group, to Patton's right, made a similar advance. Its Seventh Army ran into determined resistance at Nuremberg but after a nine-day battle took the city. A combination of American and French forces attacked Stuttgart, and the French took possession

[38] Bernard L. Montgomery, *Normandy to the Baltic* (Boston, 1948), pp. 340–345; Eisenhower, *Crusade in Europe*, pp. 424–425.

[39] Bradley, *A Soldier's Story*, pp. 546, 551.

[40] Pogue, *The Supreme Command*, pp. 453–454.

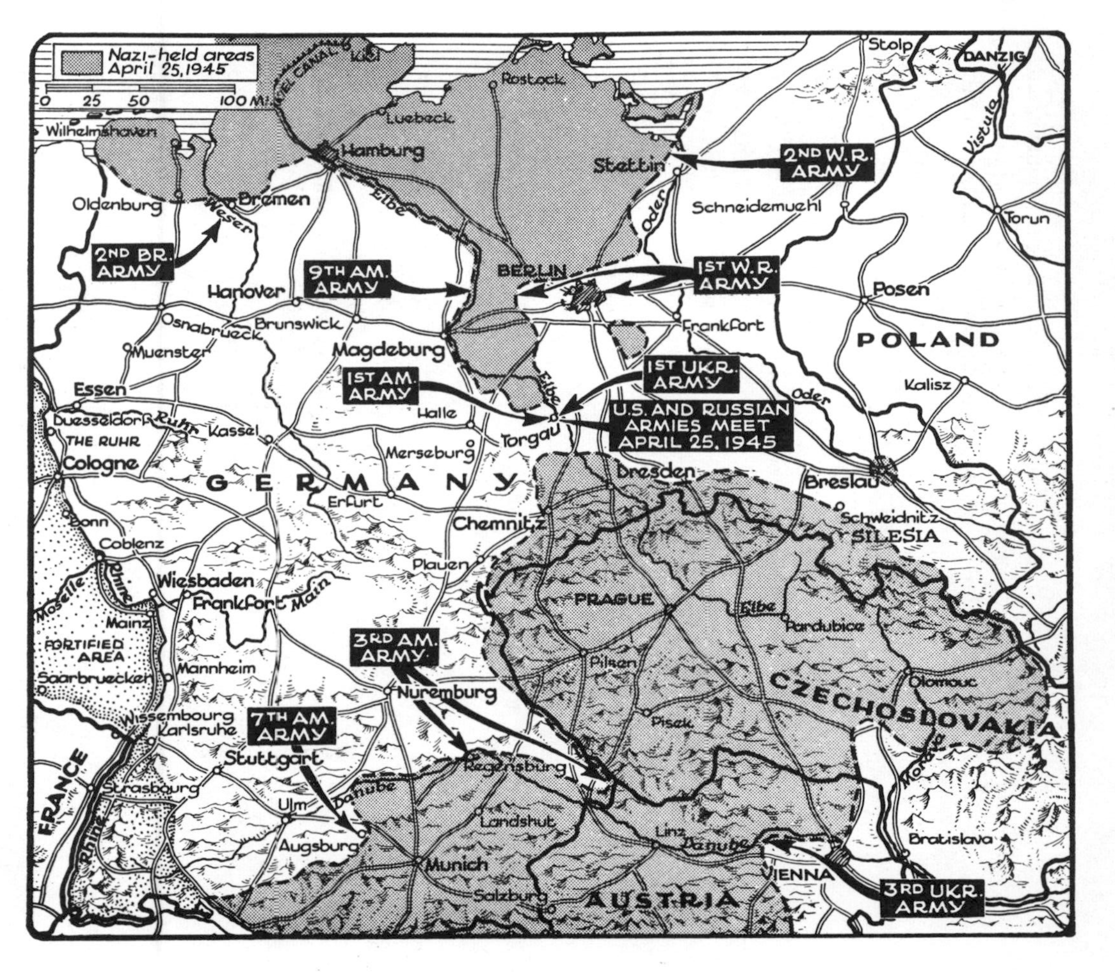

GERMANY'S COLLAPSE

April 22. Other action by the Sixth Army Group demonstrated that one of the objectives of the Allied armies was largely nonexistent. Eisenhower and others, including those around the *Führer,* believed that if Hitler lost Berlin he would retire to fortified positions in the mountains to the south and stand on the defensive. One of the Supreme Commander's purposes in making contact with the Russians near Leipzig was to cut Germany in half and prevent a German move to such a "National Redoubt." Devers' assignment included destruction of these defenses. In Bavaria he received some help from the German citizens, who at last turned against the Nazis and aided in the capture of Munich on April 30. The taking of Berchtesgaden May 4 ended any hope that might have existed for a National Redoubt.[41]

As the Eastern and Western fronts came together, military and political considerations complicated each other. The major Allied powers had long considered the problem of occupying conquered territories and at Yalta had agreed upon zones of occupation for Germany. Eisenhower and the U.S. Chiefs of Staff determined to conclude the war by adhering strictly to military objectives. Eisenhower had declined to take Berlin for political reasons, and he informed Marshall that he would not make any move he considered "militarily unwise" unless he received "specific orders from the Combined Chiefs of Staff."[42] They issued no such orders, and Eisenhower conducted the closing operations in Europe according to this principle.

The successful advances of the Eastern and Western Allies brought to an end Nazi control of Germany, but Hitler was among the last to recognize or admit defeat. By the middle of April even he realized that he could not hold Berlin indefinitely and he began to send members of his government elsewhere. Hermann Göring left for Berchtesgaden April 20 and two days later Admiral Karl Doenitz, who had become one of the most important figures around Hitler, went north to command defenses in that area. Hitler remained in Berlin, at first hoping to save the capital and then determining to commit suicide if he failed. Military leaders, such as Keitel and Jodl, moved out of Berlin by the end of the month.

Hearing that the *Führer* had decided to remain in the capital and die, Göring radioed Berlin and indicated that if he received no reply he would assume control of the German government. When Hitler

[41] *Ibid.,* pp. 454–456; Eisenhower, *Crusade in Europe,* pp. 415, 418.
[42] Quoted in Pogue, *The Supreme Command,* p. 468.

learned of Göring's action he denounced him as a traitor, ordered his arrest, and dismissed him from command of the Air Force. In the meantime, Jodl and Keitel gave military orders which in effect told the remaining forces that the Western enemy was incidental and that they should concentrate on resisting the Russians. They also made efforts to secure troops for the relief of Berlin, but by April 30 it was obvious that the capital was doomed. These efforts came from outside the city and without orders from Hitler, who was isolated within Berlin.

On April 28, the *Führer* had reached his decision. Drawing his political testament, he disinherited Göring and Himmler, cast them from the party, and disavowed any claim they might have had for the succession. Instead, he appointed Admiral Karl Doenitz head of the German State and Supreme Commander of the Armed Forces. Then on April 30, after marrying Eva Braun, who unlike most of his political sycophants had remained with him, Adolf Hitler committed suicide.[43]

The Nazi leader was dead and the German armies beaten, yet there still remained the complicated and at times chaotic problem of reaching a formal conclusion of hostilities. Although Hitler and some of the extreme Nazis had clung to hopes of victory until the last, other Germans had made overtures to the Allies for peace. The failure of the attempt to assassinate Hitler in July, 1944, and the resultant purge deprived Germany of potential leaders who might have paved the way toward an earlier peace and intimidated many others who might have been inclined toward intrigue with the enemy.

About the middle of January, 1945, Foreign Minister Joachim von Ribbentrop secretly endeavored to establish contacts with the Allies which might lead to a negotiated peace. News of the venture leaked out, and his representatives failed to make the connections they sought.

Early in February, the German military command in northern Italy tried to make a separate peace. This time German delegates met Allied agents in Switzerland, but the most significant immediate result was an exchange of bitter correspondence among the leaders of the three major powers. Allied authorities in Italy had informed the Rus-

[43] *Ibid.*, pp. 469–474; Trevor-Roper, *The Last Days of Hitler, passim.* Joseph Goebbels chose to remain with his family. His six children were poisoned, and then he and his wife deliberately went to their own deaths. *Ibid.*, p. 213.

sians of the meetings with the Germans and invited them to send representatives. Stalin chose to charge that the British and Americans were negotiating a separate peace which would enable the Germans to continue fighting Russia. In the acrimonious dispute which followed Stalin showed that an ally was not necessarily a friend. Churchill's reactions to Stalin's insulting bluntness help explain his interest in taking Berlin. Roosevelt, nearing his death, sent Stalin a strong note, probably drafted by Marshall, but he was inclined to disregard Stalin's charges in the interest of Allied harmony.

In northern Germany early in April, Walter Schellenberg, a member of Heinrich Himmler's Intelligence Staff, apparently on his own initiative made overtures to Count Folke Bernadotte, head of the Swedish Red Cross, who was in Germany endeavoring to secure the release of Danish and Norwegian prisoners to Sweden's custody. Schellenberg asked the Count to approach Eisenhower with suggestions of peace, but Bernadotte laid down certain requirements which had to be met first. These included an announcement that Himmler had been chosen as Hitler's successor, dissolution of the Nazi party, and return of Danish and Norwegian prisoners to Sweden. Since Schellenberg was unable to meet the conditions Bernadotte declined to approach Eisenhower.

About the middle of April feelers came from Denmark of the possible surrender of some of the German forces in that country. These and other rumors indicated that widespread unconditional surrender was an increasing probability. Consequently, the Combined Chiefs of Staff suggested that accredited representatives of the three major Allies be available at headquarters on both fronts. The Soviet high command agreed to this procedure.

Schellenberg had not given up his efforts. Now working with Himmler, he arranged a meeting of the latter with Bernadotte. Stating that Hitler soon would be dead and that he would succeed him, Himmler suggested a surrender on the Western front. Bernadotte doubted that a capitulation on one front only would be acceptable, but since Himmler also promised to surrender forces in Norway and Denmark, the Count agreed to act as an intermediary. He transmitted the offer to the British and U.S. Ministers to Sweden, and they forwarded it to their governments. The news reached Churchill, who relayed it to Roosevelt by transatlantic telephone.

Roosevelt replied that he wanted peace, but he asserted that he could accept only unconditional surrender on all fronts in agreement with the Russians. Information of the German proposal went to Stalin. Eisenhower, when he was told of the proposition, looked on it as a scheme to divide the Allies.[44]

Any hopes that the Germans may have had to continue the war were killed by the surrender of the German forces in Italy, May 2, after hectic changes in the German military command in the area. Hitler's death had been kept secret from Doenitz until May 1. Then assuming control he announced the *Führer's* death and conferred with the leaders who were left. They reached the same decision as that of Himmler, to attempt to make a separate peace with the Western enemy. Unable to accomplish this objective, Doenitz began what was in effect a piecemeal surrender. The Combined Chiefs of Staff had laid down the bases for surrender of German forces through their commanders. All surrenders had to be unconditional, without commitment to the enemy, and would be superseded by general surrender terms which might be imposed later by the United Kingdom, the United States, and the USSR.

When Montgomery informed Eisenhower of the possibility of German surrender in Denmark, the Netherlands, Helgoland, the Frisian Islands, and Schleswig-Holstein, the Supreme Commander made the rather broad interpretation that these were tactical problems and capitulation could be accepted. He stated, however, that the surrender of Norway and of troops from another front would have to be dealt with at Supreme Headquarters and discussed with the Russians.

Montgomery proceeded along the lines set by Eisenhower and said that he would not accept surrender of German forces in the Soviet Zone. He did indicate that Germans could give themselves up as individuals and that he would not transfer them to Russian control. On May 4, under orders of Doenitz widespread capitulations to Montgomery began, under the specifications set by Eisenhower.[45]

Along the Elbe, Germans in danger of being overrun by the advancing Russians sought to surrender to the Americans. Ninth Army officials said that they could not accept mass capitulation without discussions with the Russians but they agreed to individual surrenders. As a result, German soldiers and women and children fleeing from the Eastern enemy made their way as best they could across the river. By

[44] Pogue, *The Supreme Command,* pp. 475–477.
[45] *Ibid.,* pp. 480–481.

the end of formal hostilities between 75,000 and 100,000 German soldiers had surrendered in this fashion.

When troops in southern Germany and Austria tried to surrender, SHAEF directed them to the Sixth Army Group since not all the units in the area wanted to capitulate. A few SS troops held out, and in one instance the former German garrison helped the Allies retake a castle from the extremists. Generally, in the south as well as elsewhere on the front, the Germans showed a strong preference for surrender to the Western armies rather than to the Soviet forces.

While these separate capitulations were taking place, Eisenhower moved toward a general surrender of the Germans. By arrangement, Admiral Hans Georg von Friedeburg was to go to SHAEF in Rheims, May 5, to begin negotiations for surrender of the troops on the Western front. It became apparent that the Germans were delaying in the hope of withdrawing as many men as possible from the Eastern front to surrender to the Western forces. Eisenhower, therefore, called Moscow that he planned to have all Germans opposing the Russians surrender to them. Still viewing the war as a military and not a political problem, he wished to end the conflict simultaneously on both fronts.

When the Russians were informed of the proposed surrender at Rheims, they raised no objection provided Doenitz agreed to simultaneous surrender on other fronts. In anticipation of victory, the British, Americans, and Russians in July, 1944, had agreed upon the surrender document to be used. The leaders at the Yalta Conference changed this instrument to include dismemberment of Germany in addition to complete disarmament and demobilization as a method of pacification, but they had failed to inform France of this change. Then on May 1, 1945, the European Advisory Commission, organized by the three major Allies in 1943 to draft terms of peace, altered the protocol to include France as a signatory power but did not make it clear whether the original or amended document was to be used.

Faced with this problem, SHAEF chose neither document but announced that it would use a shorter instrument which it had prepared. SHAEF accepted certain modifications suggested by Ambassador John G. Winant and noted that its document could be superseded by later surrender terms.

Eisenhower kept Moscow informed of the steps being taken and gave instructions that Russian military representatives be called to

Supreme Headquarters before the Germans arrived. He also asked the Moscow government if it wished to participate in a more formal ratification of the surrender at a later date. No answer came from Russia prior to the meeting with the German representatives.

After a delay occasioned by bad weather, Admiral Friedeburg arrived at Rheims late in the afternoon, May 5. Presented with the surrender document, he asserted that he did not have authority to capitulate on both fronts. When he wired Admiral Doenitz for such authorization, the latter, instead of complying, sent General Jodl to Rheims to explain why the Germans could not agree to surrender on all fronts. Jodl arrived in Rheims Sunday evening, May 6, and it soon became evident to those with whom he conferred that he was deliberately procrastinating. When informed of this fact, Eisenhower threatened to break off discussions and prevent further Western surrender of German troops. Jodl, who formerly had opposed simultaneous surrender, felt that nothing further could be done and wired Doenitz to accept the Allied demands. Under protest, but hopeful of saving many German troops from surrender to the Russians during the forty-eight-hour period that would elapse before the terms went into effect, Doenitz gave Jodl authorization to sign in accordance with the capitulation terms.

At 2:41 in the morning, May 7, General Jodl signed the two documents presented to him. The first was the surrender document; the second, an agreement that the commanders of the main branches of the German military services would meet later for a formal ratification of the capitulation.[46]

The Russian answer to Eisenhower's request for approval of the preliminary surrender at Rheims did not reach American hands until after the ceremony had taken place. It disapproved the two signings and requested a single ceremony at Berlin. Eisenhower had not waited for this reply, since a Russian representative was present at Rheims, and it had been agreed that the document signed there could be superseded. In accordance with Russia's demand, Allied representatives met in Berlin and called in Marshal Wilhelm Keitel, head of the German representatives, who signed the formal surrender at about 11:45 at night, May 8.

[46] *Ibid.*, pp. 482–490. For an interpretation of the German surrender and other surrenders in World War II, see Paul Kecskemeti, *Strategic Surrender: The Politics of Victory and Defeat* (Stanford, Calif., 1958), pp. 118–154 and *passim.*

The announcement of the final surrender was almost as confused as the events leading up to it. The Germans released the first news of the surrender, and on hearing this one of the accredited American correspondents at SHAEF violated censorship and forwarded the information.[47] Efforts to get a simultaneous announcement by the three major powers failed. The British and United States governments made their announcements May 8, but the Russians withheld their statement until after the conclusion of the Berlin ceremony.[48]

Military actions in Germany after the surrender fall more appropriately into a study of postwar reconstruction than in an account of the war itself. It may be noted briefly that the first phase consisted of bringing to a close the various military commands. This period ended with a meeting in Berlin, June 5, in which representatives of the United States, the United Kingdom, France, and the Soviet Union met to assume control of assigned zones in Germany.[49]

At first Eisenhower attempted to work with the Doenitz government in the hope that it might be able to accelerate rapid demobilization, especially of the naval forces. The Admiral and those about him decided to keep their government in existence for a time in case the British and Americans should decide to recreate a strong Germany. Soon, however, there arose vigorous criticism of the Doenitz government and Allied support of it, and a principal charge was that the victors were imposing a "soft" peace. By May 17, as a result of incidents and observations, SHAEF political officers advised Eisenhower to disband the Doenitz government and arrest its leaders. On May 19, the Supreme Commander issued such an order, temporarily exempting some high-level naval officers. Two days later, General Lowell W. Rooks, Eisenhower's deputy, placed Doenitz, Jodl, and Friedeburg under guard. Doenitz and Jodl were taken to a German prison camp, but Friedeburg avoided observation long enough to commit suicide. Other SHAEF representatives dissolved German command units in southern Germany.[50]

On Eisenhower's orders, Doenitz issued instructions to naval personnel not to scuttle or damage naval vessels or aircraft. Allied naval parties began to seize records that might aid in the war against

[47] Eisenhower, *Crusade in Europe,* p. 427.
[48] Pogue, *The Supreme Command,* p. 494.
[49] *Ibid.,* p. 495.
[50] *Ibid.,* pp. 497–500.

Japan; others started to clear entrances to Baltic ports to facilitate the return and surrender of German vessels. Isolated German forces in Western Europe surrendered after they heard of the collapse of Germany. These included units in the Channel Islands, Dunkerque, and western Netherlands.

The problem of surrender in Czechoslovakia was especially acute, since the Germans in this country were intent on capitulation to the Western Allies instead of Russia. Eisenhower resisted pressure to challenge the Russian Army's desire to occupy Prague, and directed Doenitz to issue a radio order to German troops in the region to stop fighting and lay down their arms. Unfortunately, Doenitz earlier had told the Germans to try to reach Western lines, and it was not easy to convince them that he had changed his mind. After the Germans surrendered, United States and Soviet troops remained in Czechoslovakia. The United States feared that if they left, the country might lose its independence, for the removal of certain Czechs from office indicated a shift to the Soviet orbit.[51]

There were complicating factors in the dissolution of German forces in Denmark and Norway. Enemy troops in these areas had not been defeated in battle, and the units sent to disband them were fewer in number than they were. The Russians added to the problem in Denmark by invading the island of Bornholm to disarm a German force that already thought it had surrendered to Montgomery. There was still further friction when Germans objected to yielding their arms to Danish resistance forces. However, a large percentage of the Germans had marched out of Denmark by the time SHAEF dissolved, and a British commander was assigned the task of completing the removal.

In Norway there were about 400,000 Germans, 90,000 Russian prisoners and displaced persons, and 30,000 displaced persons of other nationalities. Fewer than 40,000 Allied troops, aided by aircraft and naval vessels, carried out the demobilization. The main problems included evacuation of displaced persons, persuading the Russians to accept back in their zone Germans from that region, and incurring Norwegian resentment at the destruction of enemy armament they would like to have kept for themselves. After the dissolution of SHAEF, separate British and American agencies concluded the work.[52]

[51] *Ibid.*, pp. 500–508.

[52] *Ibid.*, pp. 508–510. For a study of American Military Government in Germany, see Carl J. Friedrich and Associates, *American Experiences in Military Government in World War II* (New York, 1948), pp. 197–291.

Earlier expressions of the Combined Chiefs of Staff made it clear that SHAEF would cease to exist after the war in Europe had been won. Eisenhower had recommended that the organization continue until national controls were established in the zones of occupation. Briefly it may be noted of this early postwar reconstruction that SHAEF began the preparations for the military governments that later controlled occupied Germany. As part of its work, Supreme Headquarters set up military governments, suspended Nazi forms of government and seized Nazi leaders, attended to civilian relief, and restored communications.

Relieved on June 5 from the task of further disbanding and disarming the Germans, Eisenhower made ready for the shift to separate national controls. Also, already among his forces redeployment was under way. Some were to remain in Europe, but many others could look forward to participation in the Pacific war.[53]

Although Japan still was an active and dangerous foe, there was cause for satisfaction and even restrained rejoicing. The Allies had completed their first and most important objective. Superior manpower on land, sea, and in the air, backed by the incomparable American arsenal of democracy, and led by able and imaginative military commanders, had effected the destruction of Germany's armed might.

[53] Eisenhower, *Crusade in Europe,* p. 435; Pogue, *The Supreme Command,* pp. 511–515.

CHAPTER 22

China, Burma, India

ONE possible approach to Japan lay across the vast expanse of China, but formidable obstacles blocked the way. Since northern China and the entire coastline had fallen to the Japanese, aid to Nationalist China had to go from India through Burma along routes made inhospitable by terrain, climate, and Japanese forces farther south in Burma.

The United States was interested in China not only as a potential base for assault on Japan but also as a state whose political independence was essential to the equilibrium of the Far East, and, as we have seen, American refusal to acquiesce in Japanese expansion on the Asian Continent had been a major cause of war. Loans to Generalissimo Chiang Kai-shek's government gave early evidence of American sympathy. In November, 1940, the Chinese government sent a mission to the United States in search of another type of aid, an air force of five hundred planes with American pilots and crews, since trained Chinese personnel was lacking.[1] The driving power behind this proposal was an American Army Air Force officer, Captain Claire L. Chennault, who after retirement for defective hearing in 1937 had gone to China to become technical adviser and colonel in the Chinese Air Force.

From the original request, which was denied, came Chinese par-

[1] Charles F. Romanus and Riley Sunderland, *Stilwell's Mission to China* (*United States Army in World War II: China-Burma-India Theater*) (Washington, 1953), pp. 10–11; W. F. Craven and J. L. Cate, *The Army Air Forces in World War II* (Chicago, 1948), I, 487.

ticipation in Lend-Lease and the formation of the American Volunteer Group (AVG) in China, an initial group of about a hundred volunteer pilots who signed a one-year contract to fly for the Chinese Nationalist government. Escorted by U.S. warships, the first contingent of pilots in the summer of 1941 traveled on a Dutch vessel to Burma and began training in tactics prepared by Colonel Chennault on the basis of his knowledge of Japanese planes and methods of operation.[2] Chennault's forces began operations on December 20, 1941, and with meager resources soon demonstrated a phenomenal ability to inflict sharp losses on Japanese air power in China and Burma. When conditions became untenable in Burma, the AVG retired to Kunming and continued their combat operations.[3]

Complications soon affected the Lend-Lease program for China. Mr. T. V. Soong, American-trained brother-in-law of the Generalissimo, came to the United States with requests for aid in developing a thirty-division army. The United States government was sympathetic, but had other commitments, and furthermore Chinese demands were often unrealistic and sometimes vague. The numerous problems of Lend-Lease led to the appointment of Brigadier General John Magruder, who on October 10, 1941, arrived in Chungking as head of an American Military Mission to China.[4] He found a Chinese Army that was a coalition of war lords holding positions through loyalty to Chiang Kai-shek rather than military ability. They received a lump sum from which they paid their men and were little interested in fighting, for the lighter the division strength, the more money could the war lord retain, but he could not afford to lose any divisions in battle, since his revenue might decrease accordingly. Magruder knew China and was not shocked, but other members of the mission were and wrote home that the Chinese did not anticipate fighting the Japanese but expected to win through diplomacy. They wanted arms for the preservation of order in China itself after the end of the war. The mission also found that there was so much graft in the administration of traffic over the Burma Road that much of Lend-Lease equipment was being lost in transit.

The entrance of the United States into the war prompted Chiang Kai-shek to seek an agreement among the major belligerents. The

[2] Romanus and Sunderland, *Stilwell's Mission to China,* pp. 18–19.

[3] Craven and Cate, *The A.A.F. in World War II,* I, 490.

[4] The work of the Magruder mission is described in Romanus and Sunderland, *Stilwell's Mission to China,* pp. 28–49.

Russians, not at war with Japan, declined the overture, but American and British representatives met the Generalissimo at Chungking on December 22, 1941. The American representative was an air officer, Major General George H. Brett, whom the War Department was sending to China to investigate possible use of heavy bombers in the area. Field Marshal Sir Archibald P. Wavell, apparently convinced that the Japanese were overextending themselves, offended the Chinese by giving only qualified acceptance of Chiang Kai-shek's offer of military aid to Burma.[5]

Meanwhile, in their first wartime meeting, the Arcadia Conference, American and British leaders followed the principle of unified command by appointing Wavell to command the area of Southeast Asia, including northern Burma, and asked Chiang Kai-shek to be Supreme Commander, China Theater. President Roosevelt, in particular, wanted to maintain the Generalissimo's prestige as part of a policy to establish China as a great power, and Chiang Kai-shek differed from supreme commanders of other military theaters in that he was responsible only to himself.[6] Accepting the position, the Generalissimo requested that Washington send a high-ranking U.S. officer to become his chief of staff. Secretary of War Henry L. Stimson and General Marshall tentatively selected General Hugh A. Drum; when he seemed uninterested, they turned to Major General Joseph W. Stilwell, who possessed some remarkable talents and one undeniable liability for the assignment. He had been military attaché in China, spoke Chinese, knew the Chinese Army, and had a keen mind, but able soldier though he was, he was no diplomat. His nickname, "Vinegar Joe," indicated a nature that came not from sourness of temper but impatience with inefficiency, procrastination, and corruption.[7]

General Stilwell went to the Far East to assume several difficult responsibilities. His orders made him Commanding General of the United States Army Forces in the Chinese Theater of Operations, Burma, and India, and they also designated him Chief of Staff to the Supreme Commander, Chiang Kai-shek, who also had a Chinese Chief of Staff of his Chinese armies. If Stilwell's forces operated in

[5] *Ibid.*, pp. 55–56; S. Woodburn Kirby, *The War Against Japan* (*History of the Second World War: United Kingdom Military Series*) (London, 1958), II, 16–19.

[6] Romanus and Sunderland, *Stilwell's Mission to China*, pp. 61–63; Robert E. Sherwood, *Roosevelt and Hopkins: An Intimate History* (New York, 1948), p. 458.

[7] Joseph W. Stilwell, *The Stilwell Papers* (New York, 1948), *passim.*

Burma, they would come under control of General Wavell. Not the least of Stilwell's duties was to act as liaison between Chiang Kai-shek and Wavell, and he was also in charge of Lend-Lease. Among Stilwell's objectives were the maintenance, improvement, and defense of the Burma Road and the establishment of an air supply line from India "over the Hump" of the Himalayas to China.[8]

On January 10, 1942, a force of about eighteen thousand Japanese struck Burma from Thailand, cut successfully through the country to force the evacuation of Rangoon.[9] Indian forces were able to move up the Irrawaddy River Valley and, although irritated by Wavell's qualified rejection of their earlier offer of help, the Chinese sent several divisions of the Sixth Army into Burma to bolster defenses. Arriving in Karachi, India, February 24, 1942, Stilwell soon became aware of the desperate situation in Burma, which was complicated by mutual Anglo-Chinese suspicions. Chiang Kai-shek placed Stilwell in command of the Chinese forces in Burma but hamstrung him with restrictions on his authority. Colonel Chennault agreed to absorb the AVG into the U.S. armed forces, and briefly that group gave air assistance until lack of reinforcements and exhaustion of pilots terminated their efforts in the area and led to loss of air cover for the ground forces.[10]

By May, 1942, the cause was hopeless, and the Allies were forced to withdraw. Although planes from India evacuated as many as possible, Stilwell chose to walk out of Burma to India with his men. He shook off efforts to lionize him for courageous leadership of a successful withdrawal by saying, "We got a hell of a beating."[11] Privately, he castigated numerous conditions which had led to defeat, including apathy, interference by Chiang Kai-shek, inadequate supply and communications, "stupid, gutless command," and a vulnerable tactical situation.[12] By conquering Burma and closing the Burma Road, the Japanese completed their blockade of China. The only communication left was by air over some of the highest mountains in the world.

The defeat in Burma convinced Stilwell of the prime necessity of reforming the Chinese Army. His recommendation, however, met a

[8] Romanus and Sunderland, *Stilwell's Mission to China,* pp. 73–76.

[9] For an account of the early war in Burma, see Kirby, *The War Against Japan,* II, 1–104.

[10] Craven and Cate, *The A.A.F. in World War II,* I, 502–505; Romanus and Sunderland, *Stilwell's Mission to China,* pp. 81–117.

[11] Quoted in *ibid.,* p. 143.

[12] Quoted in *ibid.,* p. 148.

rebuff from the Generalissimo, who for political reasons declined to remove incompetent military leaders and who further was angered by the departure of Allied air forces from India to meet the threat of General Rommel's armies in the Middle East. Consequently, Chiang Kai-shek demanded of the Allies minimum requirements for the maintenance of the Chinese Theater and he implied the possibility of a separate peace. He requested three American divisions to help restore communications through Burma with China, maintenanace of five hundred planes for the Chinese front, and a monthly air shipment to China of five thousand tons. Under pressure he reduced his demand by two American divisions but continued to push for his other points. Stilwell's relations with the Generalissimo reached a low point, and the Supreme Commander's entourage made the American General the scapegoat for its difficulties.[13]

Meanwhile, General Stilwell established a China-Burma-India (CBI) Theater of operations with headquarers at Chungking, branch office headquarters at New Delhi, and the Tenth Air Force with a branch office at Kunming, the Chinese terminal point of the air ferry. The office at New Delhi outstripped the others and by November, 1942, received a more appropriate title, Headquarters, Rear Echelon, United States Army (CBI). At first the only actual combat troops in this huge area were the Tenth Air Force and its subordinate China Air Task Force.[14] By October, Stilwell added an India Air Task Force for the India end of the air ferry and gave greater freedom to the newly activated India-China Ferry Command. He then established a training command at Karachi to prepare crews for combat and transport duty. All these developments naturally required expansion of the services of supply. In April, 1942, with Chiang Kai-shek's approval of the principle of a Chinese Army trained in India, Stilwell created a training center at Ramgarh in Bihar Province for the Chinese soldiers who had retreated from Burma. Despite initial opposition, the project got under way, and some 45,000 Chinese troops began training.[15]

[13] *Ibid.*, pp. 152–190; Sherwood, *Roosevelt and Hopkins*, pp. 598–599; William D. Leahy, *I Was There: The Personal Story of the Chief of Staff to Presidents Roosevelt and Truman Based on His Notes and Diaries Made at the Time* (New York, London, Toronto, 1950), p. 111.

[14] Romanus and Sunderland, *Stilwell's Mission to China*, pp. 191–205; Craven and Cate, *The A.A.F. in World War II*, I, 492–510.

[15] Romanus and Sunderland, *Stilwell's Mission to China*, pp. 204–221; Kirby, *The War Against Japan*, II, 196, 390–391.

Plans moved ahead for a spring offensive against Burma in 1943. Roosevelt finally told Chiang Kai-shek that he could not furnish an American division and suggested the use of American air forces and Chinese troops in India. It became apparent that the Generalissimo did not wish to risk failure and that the British were not enthusiastic about the campaign. Instead, General Chennault began to make headway with a counterproposal that with a force of 105 fighters, 30 medium bombers, and 12 heavy bombers he could defeat Japan.[16] In October, Wendell Willkie visited China as Roosevelt's representative and became an enthusiastic supporter of Chennault's plan to attack military objectives in Japanese-held China, destroy the defending aircraft, and then launch an attack on Japan itself.[17]

Stilwell's plan was to persuade the Chinese to reorganize their armies and in Yunnan assemble twenty divisions, which would join the Ramgarh corps in an attack on Burma. General Marshall favored Stilwell's arguments, but Chiang Kai-shek was won over to Chennault's program, urged its acceptance by President Roosevelt, and ended the possibility of a spring offensive by declining to move his troops across the Salween River.

Meanwhile, Allied leaders considered top strategy at Casablanca. Impressed by the strategic location of China, they pressed for a Burma campaign to open a route for supplies to China.[18] China was not represented, and at the close of the conference a special mission went to Chungking and secured the Generalissimo's promise of cooperation. However, Chennault had powerful friends, including Harry Hopkins, who continued to urge an enlargement of the Air Force, and on March 8, 1943, Roosevelt rejected the proposal of Marshall and Stilwell in favor of the Chennault plan. Vainly, Marshall argued that a premature air attack would provoke not only Japanese air resistance, but a ground attack on as yet inadequately defended Chinese and American bases.[19]

By Roosevelt's decision, Stilwell in effect had been rebuked but

[16] Romanus and Sunderland, *Stilwell's Mission to China,* pp. 250–251.

[17] Claire Lee Chennault, *Way of a Fighter: The Memoirs of Claire Lee Chennault* (New York, 1949), pp. 212–216.

[18] Richard M. Leighton and Robert W. Coakley, *Global Logistics and Strategy, 1940–1943* (*United States Army in World War II: The War Department*) (Washington, 1955), p. 542.

[19] See memorandum, Marshall to Roosevelt, Mar. 16, 1943, quoted extensively in Romanus and Sunderland, *Stilwell's Mission to China,* pp. 280–282; Chennault, *Way of a Fighter,* pp. 220–227.

not recalled, and his influence with the Generalissimo reached a low ebb for the ensuing year. Meanwhile, Chennault's prestige increased, and on March 11, 1943, he became a major general in charge of the newly activated Fourteenth Air Force. Nevertheless, since priorities on Hump deliveries remained unchanged, he made little immediate progress toward his goal.[20]

Early in 1941, the British had started constructing a road from Ledo toward Burma which would meet the Burma Road and once again provide a land route to China. In December, 1942, U.S. engineers assumed the task of building this road and by February, 1943, had reached the border of Burma, but lack of supplies and the May monsoon halted work. Although this phase of Allied activity came to a stop, the Tenth Air Force became better supplied and launched a harassing campaign against the Japanese in Burma.[21]

Stilwell's relations with Chiang Kai-shek became more strained as the latter threw his support behind Chennault. In conferences with the Chinese leader Stilwell was correct and courteous, but in his own headquarters he was more outspoken, and one suspects that his references to Chiang Kai-shek by his code name "Peanut" reflected more than a mere security precaution. Late in April, both Stilwell and Chennault were called to Washington, to express their views, and Roosevelt decided to continue support of the Chennault plan.[22] Shortly thereafter, in the Washington (Trident) Conference, Churchill recommended by-passing much of Burma and striking at Sumatra instead. Rejecting this proposal, the conference agreed on a counterproposal which involved increasing air forces in China, continuing the air assault on Burma, and launching a land attack on northern Burma to make possible completion of the Ledo Road.[23]

During the summer of 1943, Chennault began an air attack on Japanese shipping which prompted a strong Japanese air counterattack that in a few weeks caused the outnumbered American fliers to seek help. In India work shifted to construction of air bases to strengthen support of the Hump transport. A major obstacle to im-

[20] Romanus and Sunderland, *Stilwell's Mission to China,* pp. 284–292.

[21] Craven and Cate, *The A.A.F. in World War II* (1950), IV, 415–416.

[22] Romanus and Sunderland, *Stilwell's Mission to China,* pp. 320–327; Stilwell, *The Stilwell Papers,* pp. 203–206.

[23] For Trident discussions on the Pacific and Far East, see Maurice Matloff, *Strategic Planning for Coalition Warfare, 1943–1944* (*United States Army in World War II: The War Department*) (Washington, 1959), pp. 135–143.

plementation of the Trident decisions was Chiang Kai-shek's reluctance to take the offensive with his troops, and Roosevelt's support of the air plan strengthened the Generalissimo's decision not to act.

The Quadrant Conference at Quebec in August, 1943, made no significant changes in strategic planning but did create a new Southeast Asia Command under Lord Louis Mountbatten as Supreme Commander and it authorized increased logistical support. Stilwell's relations with Mountbatten were cordial from the start and he began to receive more cooperation from Chiang Kai-shek, but the American General finally decided that he could do no more in the effort to reorganize and strengthen the Chinese armies and thereafter he turned his major attention to his duties as a theater commander.[24]

There were several significant developments in the fall of 1943. In the midst of terrific famine conditions in India which cost the lives of more than a million persons, the Allies began construction of a pipeline to parallel the Ledo Road. The thin-walled four-inch pipe could be carried in by air, but its flimsy nature led to later maintenance problems.[25] Although lack of supplies placed the Chennault program behind schedule, as the situation improved the Air Force began to extend its blows farther into Japanese-held territory. Late in October, Chennault asked for permission to bomb Japanese islands, but the request was denied on the ground that premature attack might give a warning which might later hurt projected B-29 raids, and Chennault's forces struck Formosa instead. Japanese Air Forces responded, but a counter ground offensive did not materialize, in part as a result of withdrawal of Japanese troops to fight in the Pacific. Encouraged, Chennault requested authorization for expanded air activity; however, headquarters, because of logistical shortages, in effect relegated the Fourteenth Air Force to a position secondary to the B-29's.[26]

In the meantime, the Allies prepared to invade northern Burma as soon as the monsoons subsided. Their first objective was the Hukawng

[24] Romanus and Sunderland, *Stilwell's Mission to China,* pp. 355–389. For a critical British view of Stilwell, see John Ehrman, *Grand Strategy* (*History of the Second World War: United Kingdom Military Series*) (London, 1956), V, 141–143.

[25] Charles F. Romanus and Riley Sunderland, *Stilwell's Command Problems* (*United States Army in World War II: China-Burma-India Theater*) (Washington, 1956), pp. 11–15.

[26] *Ibid.,* pp. 18–25; Craven and Cate, *The A.A.F. in World War II,* IV, 529–532.

Valley, a pestilential jungle through which flows the Chindwin River. To the south lay narrow Mogaung Valley, which opens into the valley of the great Irrawaddy River. It was through these regions that the American and Chinese forces planned to advance from India. The basic fighting units were the Chinese regiments trained by Americans in India. In addition, an American force of some three thousand volunteers had been trained in jungle warfare in a manner similar to that conducted by British forces known as Chindits, who specialized in long-range guerrilla penetration of Burma. In October, a Chinese force moving into position for a December attack unexpectedly encountered large bodies of Japanese, and the campaign got under way prematurely.[27]

While the opposing forces were locking in northern Burma, high American strategists, preparing for the Cairo conferences, looked once again at the whole question of the war in China. By this time planners were convinced that the successful route to Japan would lie through the Pacific and not across the mainland of China. Consequently, the Joint Chiefs of Staff and other strategists no longer believed that a Chinese Army was essential to victory and they felt no particular obligation to the Generalissimo since he had failed to develop the forces which Stilwell long had urged.[28]

At Cairo and in subsequent conferences President Roosevelt showed a definite shift in interest. Earlier he had tried to build China into one of the great powers and he had yielded to the Generalissimo's requests without the bargaining that Stilwell thought essential. Also, he had gone against military advice in supporting Chennault's proposal. But the situation had changed, and Roosevelt was willing to curtail plans for action in China to concentrate on the European Theater and to gain full Russian support. He therefore canceled an amphibious invasion of Burma promised Chiang Kai-shek and, instead, pledged support of operations to open a land route to China. The Generalissimo responded with a report of the low state of morale in China and a request for a loan of a million dollars in gold. Roosevelt answered that the loan request was being considered and he urged the Chinese leader to begin land operations.[29]

[27] For a description of the preparation and early conduct of this campaign, see Romanus and Sunderland, *Stilwell's Command Problems,* pp. 26–48.

[28] *Ibid.,* pp. 49–59.

[29] *Ibid.,* pp. 59–82; Ray S. Cline, *Washington Command Post: The Opera-*

General Stilwell, meanwhile, put on another of his hats and went to north Burma to assume command of the Chinese forces there engaged with the enemy. The situation was quite different than when he had left Burma in March, 1942. Anglo-American air power, based in India, could deliver supplies to the ground troops and even make mass transfers of troops, while denying use of the air to the enemy. Close Allied air-ground cooperation increased steadily in effectiveness, and air evacuation removed more than 100,000 casualties in sixteen months, eliminating tortuous travel over jungle trails. Less effective was strategic air bombardment, which though damaging was not a determining factor in producing victory.[30] Planes were delivering supplies by parachute drops, "free drops" in sacks or baskets, or landings on airstrips. Some casualties occurred in free drops, particularly among Chinese soldiers, who failed to realize that a sack of rice hurtling through the air could be a lethal weapon.[31]

Stilwell's troops constituted but one of four Allied threats to the Japanese in Burma. Some two hundred miles south of Stilwell, along the India-Burma border Indian troops were ready to launch an attack. On the border along the Bay of Bengal the British XV Corps had been pushing ahead since November, and on the east, along the Salween River, were eleven divisions of the Chinese Expeditionary Force, which so far had failed to open an attack.

In northern Burma, the Chinese troops advanced under the relentless prodding of their leaders by Stilwell and accomplished the conquest of the Taro Plain by taking Taro January 30, 1944. The opposing general later stated that loss of this plain was decisive in producing defeat of his forces all along the line. Next, Chinese forces, American tanks, a regiment of jungle fighters, now commanded by Brigadier General Frank D. Merrill and to be known as Merrill's Marauders, secured Hukawng Valley by March 8, but in the confused fighting the Japanese escaped from the trap planned by Stilwell's enveloping movements.[32]

Lord Mountbatten and other British leaders, intent on retaking Singapore, wanted to abandon the Burma campaign. Stilwell strongly

---

tions Division (*United States Army in World War II: The War Department*) (Washington, 1951), pp. 226–232.

[30] Romanus and Sunderland, *Stilwell's Command Problems,* pp. 83–95.

[31] Craven and Cate, *The A.A.F. in World War II,* IV, 502–510.

[32] For a description of this campaign, see Romanus and Sunderland, *Stilwell's Command Problems,* pp. 119–159; Stilwell, *The Stilwell Papers,* pp. 261–284.

advocated continuing it, and unknown to him, President Roosevelt pushed for the same objective. In March, the Joint Chiefs of Staff endorsed the Burma campaign and rejected the plan to attack Singapore.[33]

Stilwell began a slow and costly struggle which eliminated a Japanese force that had attempted to cut off extension of the Ledo Road.[34] Stilwell's securing of Mogaung Valley by taking the town of Myitkyina on August 3 stood in sharp contrast to Chiang Kai-shek's virtual demand of a million dollars in gold to launch a drive of his twelve divisions across the Salween River against a single Japanese division. While Roosevelt became increasingly critical in pressing the Generalissimo to attack, Chinese forces began to experience Japanese pressure from the east, and consequently two attacks began at roughly the same time. Chiang Kai-shek finally ordered his troops across the Salween River, and the Japanese launched an attack from the east on Chinese nationalist forces. The Japanese plan *Ichigo* sought to seize East China airfields and railways primarily to protect Japanese shipping on the Yangtze River and was weak in that there was no coordination with Japanese movements in Burma.

Starting in mid-April, Chiang Kai-shek had wasted several months of good fighting weather and had only a little more than a month before the start of the monsoon season. Aided by American counsel and logistical support, Chinese troops began their attack in incredibly rough terrain. They made unopposed river crossings, but against American advice slowed down to reduce all opposition instead of bypassing points to effect deeper penetration. Toward the middle of May, although monsoon weather was setting in, the Chinese decided to strike directly along the Burma Road, and a Japanese counterattack definitely ended hope of a break-through.[35]

The Japanese *Ichigo* was essentially a ground operation which was contested by Chennault's Air Force since East Chinese ground troops at this time proved ineffective. Chennault's forces struck sharply at the Japanese but were unable to check advances and called for help. Stilwell, who had been ordered back to China, although highly critical

[33] Romanus and Sunderland, *Stilwell's Command Problems,* pp. 171–172; Matloff, *Strategic Planning,* pp. 437–442.

[34] This phase of the campaign in Burma is described in Romanus and Sunderland, *Stilwell's Command Problems,* pp. 200–256.

[35] For descriptions of the *Ichigo* operations and Allied responses to it, see *ibid.,* pp. 316–374.

of Chennault, sought to increase his allotment of Hump tonnage. Higher command, however, rejected efforts to divert B-29 allocations to the Fourteenth Air Force on the ground that strategic air warfare against Japan was more significant than Chennault's tactical operations against the advancing forces in China.

The command situation next became critical. In June Vice President Henry A. Wallace arrived in Chungking and, becoming well impressed by the Chennault view, recommended to Roosevelt Stilwell's recall from China.[36] General Marshall, on the other hand, had concluded that Chennault's air offensive and the huge air transport service to support it had been a waste of effort. The Joint Chiefs of Staff agreed and on July 4, 1944, recommended that, instead of removing Stilwell, Roosevelt should promote him to the temporary rank of general, relieve him from his position as Deputy Commander of the Southeast Asia Command, and recommend to Chiang Kai-shek Stilwell's appointment to command all Chinese armies. Their conviction was that Stilwell was the only man who had "been able to get Chinese forces to fight against the Japanese in an effective way."[37] Having swung from his earlier criticism of Stilwell, Roosevelt acted on the recommendation of the Joint Chiefs of Staff. When first approached, Chiang Kai-shek agreed "in principle" but suggested a delay during which an influential American might be sent to China to "adjust" relations between the Generalissimo and Stilwell. Primarily concerned with other matters, Roosevelt accepted the suggestions and departed for a tour of the West Coast, Hawaii, and Alaska.

Meanwhile, the China Theater declined in relative significance, and the Ledo Road, instead of becoming an important artery to China, developed primarily into a supply route for the north Burma campaign. The situation on the eastern China front remained critical as the Japanese took Changsha with little difficulty but were checked for a time by the heroic Chinese stand in Heng-yang. One result of the fall of Heng-yang was dissatisfaction among the Chinese, and some of the war lords made overtures to Stilwell for cooperation in a move against Chiang Kai-shek, but he refused to become involved.[38]

In response to Chiang Kai-shek's request for an "important Amer-

[36] Craven and Cate, *The A.A.F. in World War II,* V, 227.
[37] "Memorandum for the President from the U.S. Chiefs of Staff," a copy of which is in Romanus and Sunderland, *Stilwell's Command Problems,* p. 382.
[38] *Ibid.,* pp. 405–413.

ican," President Roosevelt selected Major General Patrick J. Hurley, Secretary of War in President Hoover's Cabinet and a diplomatic emissary for President Roosevelt on a number of missions, including arrangement of Generalissimo Chiang Kai-shek's presence at the Cairo Conference in 1943. Arriving in Chungking early in September, 1944, Hurley began discussions with Chiang Kai-shek and Stilwell.[39] Among the difficult problems were Stilwell's power in the new command, Chiang Kai-shek's demand for Chinese control of Lend-Lease in China, and his apparent desire to withdraw his troops from Burma to a defensive position behind the Salween River. Stilwell became convinced that all Chiang Kai-shek wanted was "an overall stooge, apparently foisted on him by the U.S., with a deputy commander for the Chinese Army,"[40] and Stilwell was not interested in responsibility without authority. A message from President Roosevelt issued a virtual ultimatum to Chiang Kai-shek to continue fighting in northern Burma and place General Stilwell in "unrestricted command" of all Chinese forces or "be prepared to accept the consequences and assume the personal responsibility."[41] Unfortunately, Roosevelt had directed Stilwell to deliver the message in person to the Generalissimo, who not only was angered by the President's letter but believed that Stilwell had inspired it. Even General Hurley, who had received no advance warning of the message, reached the same incorrect conclusion. The ensuing deadlock tightened when Chiang Kai-shek reversed himself and instead of accepting General Stilwell accused him of lack of cooperation and refused to assent to his appointment. Roosevelt responded with compromise suggestions, to which the Generalissimo retorted with a denunciation of Stilwell which could also be interpreted as criticism of Roosevelt. Throughout, intrigue, pressure, and suspicions mounted in Chungking.

On October 18, Roosevelt ended the deadlock by yielding to Chiang Kai-shek's demand for Stilwell's recall, but he declined to name another officer for the post in question. Instead, he separated the China-Burma-India Theater into two parts, Burma-India and China, and he announced the appointment of Major General Albert C. Wedemeyer as Commander of U.S. forces in China and recommended him as Chiang Kai-shek's chief of staff. The Generalissimo had won his

[39] Stilwell, *The Stilwell Papers,* pp. 324–325.
[40] Quoted in Romanus and Sunderland, *Stilwell's Command Problems,* p. 437.
[41] *Ibid.,* pp. 445–446; Stilwell, *The Stilwell Papers,* pp. 333–334.

point at Stilwell's expense, but he had lost heavily in American friendship, for his victory produced a distinct chill in subsequent relations with Washington.[42]

By October, 1944, Chinese bases were no longer considered essential in the war against Japan; U.S. naval forces had defeated the Japanese in the Battle for Leyte Gulf, and General MacArthur's forces were on their way toward reconquest of the Philippines. Furthermore, the Russians had said they would enter the war against Japan after the collapse of Germany. However, the Allies could not drop the Chinese, for if China signed a separate peace or Chiang Kai-shek fell to a pro-Japanese coup, Japanese military forces might leave the Asiatic mainland to buttress the home defenses. The political situation in China complicated matters; Chinese Communists in the north had set up a state that controlled its own territory and hired its own forces. Its boundaries were unclear, and it partly supported itself by taxes on trade with the enemy. Chinese Nationalists not only feared the Chinese Communists, but were divided among themselves. Out of the welter of circumstances came the charge that Chiang Kai-shek had reached an understanding with the Japanese that they would leave him alone in Southwest China if he would not interfere with their capture of airfields in East China which threatened Japan. While there is no direct evidence of the Generalissimo's complicity, it does seem that Chiang Kai-shek did not exert himself to defend recalcitrant local commanders although valuable airfields lay in their domains.[43] Terrific economic distress also complicated the Chinese scene; as a result of depreciation the Chinese government in 1944 was buying only a third of the goods and services purchased in 1937. The U.S. money supply in China resulted in further inflation of Chinese money and not in the production of more goods.

On the positive side in China when General Wedemeyer arrived was the fact that the flow of supplies into the country had increased greatly; 35,131 tons were flown into China in October, 1944, four times the amount entering the previous October.[44] In October, 1944,

[42] Romanus and Sunderland, *Stilwell's Command Problems,* pp. 468–471; Stilwell, *The Stilwell Papers,* pp. 338–349. For a somewhat different appraisal, see Chennault, *Way of a Fighter,* p. 309.

[43] For an analysis of this question, see Charles F. Romanus and Riley Sunderland, *Time Runs Out in CBI* (*United States Army in World War II: China-Burma-India Theater*) (Washington, 1959), pp. 8–9.

[44] Chart in *ibid.,* p. 14.

also, one of half a dozen Chinese divisions which had opened an offensive in northern Burma had made significant advances, and the Japanese hold on north Burma seemed doomed.

Stilwell's orders had been to create conditions for maximum use of U.S. resources and to induce the Chinese to "play an active role in the war." Wedemeyer's orders, issued by the Joint Chiefs of Staff on October 24, 1944, and which remained the same to the end of the war, were as follows:

> Your primary mission with respect to the Chinese Forces is to advise and assist the Generalissimo in the conduct of military operations against the Japanese.
>
> Your primary mission as to U. S. combat forces under your command is to carry out air operations from China. In addition, you will continue to assist the Chinese air and ground forces in operations, training, and logistical support.
>
> You will not employ United States resources for suppression of civil strife except insofar as necessary to protect United States lives and property.[45]

The Joint Chiefs of Staff appointed Wedemeyer Commanding General, United States Forces, China Theater, and authorized him to accept the position of Chief of Staff to the Generalissimo. This authorization was more broadly worded than that given Stilwell and made it possible for Wedemeyer to advise the Chinese leader on a wide range of matters. The General's orders alone did not make this close association possible; his personality, tact, and ways of conducting himself help explain his success with the Generalissimo.

To carry out his mission, Wedemeyer had some 27,739 military personnel distributed among Army Air Forces, Air Transport Command, theater troops, and Services of Supply.[46] There were no ground combat troops, for the War Department had always believed that Chinese troops should do the fighting, and the U.S. forces would provide technical and air support and advice. The XX Bomber Command,[47] which with its B-29's made a heavy drain on the logistics of the China Theater, was not under Wedemeyer's command, and the China Wing of the India-China Division was not under Wedemeyer, although it flew missions to support him when requested. Among the projects undertaken was the continued flying of supplies over the

[45] Albert C. Wedemeyer, *Wedemeyer Reports!* (New York, 1958), p. 271.

[46] Romanus and Sunderland, *Time Runs Out in CBI,* p. 19.

[47] For an account of the XX Bomber Command, see Craven and Cate, *The A.A.F. in World War II,* V, 58–175.

Hump. Small American liaison groups with the Chinese forces engaged in activities which varied from supervising demolitions to setting up field hospitals.

To head the India-Burma Theater, the Joint Chiefs of Staff selected Lieutenant General Daniel I. Sultan, who had been Stilwell's deputy theater commander, and informed him that his primary mission was to support the China Theater.[48] Sultan had under his command a U.S. force of 183,920 in contrast to Wedemeyer's 27,739, and the main task of his Services of Supply was to provide ground facilities for the line of communications from the docks in Calcutta to unloading stands in China.[49] Railroad traffic increased markedly in 1944; new ferries, double tracking, American engineers, and more efficient railroad yards were among the reasons for the rise.[50]

After arriving in Chungking, General Wedemeyer conferred with senior Chinese military officials and his own subordinates. Although he favored the replacement of Chennault as he had of other American officers in China, he met with the Air Force General and quickly established a good working relationship with him.[51] From his conferences Wedemeyer made a series of recommendations to Chiang Kai-shek. One set dealt with strengthening the Chinese Army through reorganization, training, and food for the badly undernourished Chinese soldier. Another was a plan, which he called Alpha, for more effective defense.[52] He had difficulty persuading the Chinese to accept the plan and put it into operation. Throughout, he was uncertain as to whether the Chinese would actually fight when attacked. The Generalissimo resisted all American efforts to make use of Chinese Communists against the enemy.

While General Wedemeyer was attempting to better the situation in China, in Burma Allied forces were waiting for the end of the fall monsoon season to start an offensive against the Japanese.[53] The British planned advances along the coast and on the central front; in

[48] The directive of the Joint Chiefs of Staff is quoted in Romanus and Sunderland, *Time Runs Out in CBI,* p. 32.

[49] *Ibid.,* p. 33.

[50] See table in *ibid.,* p. 40.

[51] See favorable appraisal of Wedemeyer by Chennault in his *Way of a Fighter,* pp. 309–310.

[52] For a description of plan Alpha and Wedemeyer's efforts to put it into effect, see Romanus and Sunderland, *Time Runs Out in CBI,* pp. 57–75.

[53] For this phase of the campaign in Burma, see *ibid.,* pp. 77–141; Craven and Cate, *The A.A.F. in World War II,* V, 233–251.

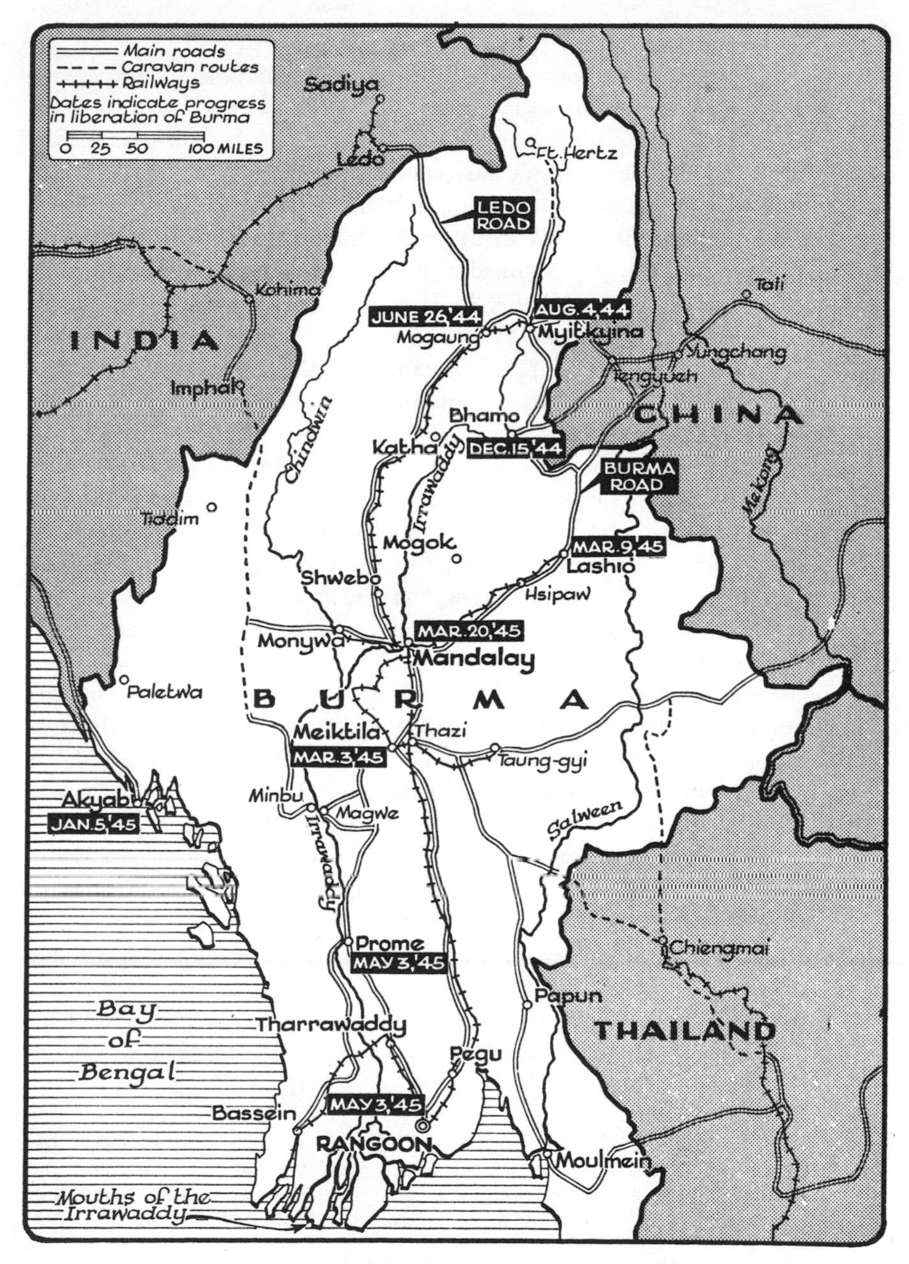

BATTLE OF BURMA

north Burma, forces opposing the Japanese Thirty-third Army were commanded by Americans through a headquarters with a Chinese name and a nominal Chinese head. By this time the Allies in Burma had complete control of the air, which gave them a tremendous edge in mobility and freedom of lines of communication.

To carry out the attack in the exceedingly rugged terrain of northern Burma, a new force trained in long-range penetration tactics came into being. This was the 5332d Brigade (Provisional), later known as the Mars Task Force, including two American and one Chinese regiments. Before and during the campaign the Tenth Air Force provided effective support; its air-ground liaison was reportedly superior to that on the European front at the same time.

The attack in north Burma got under way in October, 1944, and by the middle of December Chinese forces seized the important city of Bhamo. By early 1945, a land blockade of China seemed less significant to the Japanese and they thought more of making their main stand around Mandalay. Meeting less resistance, Allied forces reached the China-Burma border and later in January linked the Ledo Road with the Burma Road.[54]

In China, confronted by the possibility of an attack on Kunming, General Wedemeyer secured the transfer of two divisions from Burma, over Mountbatten's protests. Air transport of the 14th and 22d Divisions to China was a remarkable feat; 25,105 Chinese soldiers, 249 American liaison personnel and the equipment, including trucks, howitzers, mortars, antitank guns, and 1,596 horses and mules, were flown to their new location.[55] On the ground that they were not needed in China and that their supply demands handicapped other operations, the B-29's were removed to India by the end of January and made ready to leave for Pacific bases.[56]

On December 16, 1944, General Wedemeyer sent General Marshall a long report on the Chinese which, though devoid of the pungent phraseology which Stilwell had used, was sharply critical of the Chi-

[54] The official convoy had been preceded by two trucks and an eleven-ton wrecker which had taken a different route from Myitkyina to Kunming and had arrived on January 20, 1945. The route taken, however, was too precipitous to be practical. Romanus and Sunderland, *Time Runs Out in CBI,* pp. 140–141.

[55] *Ibid.,* p. 150.

[56] For withdrawal of B-29's, see Craven and Cate, *The A.A.F. and World War II,* V, 131–152.

nese neglect of their own armed forces. He stated that Chiang Kai-shek was trying to run the war from Chungking and would not decentralize his power, although "the management of affairs of state in itself would require a Disraeli, Churchill, and Machiavelli all combined in one." Noting that his relations with the Generalissimo were good, Wedemeyer asserted, "It is the influence and chicanery of his advisers, who have selfish, mercurial motives and persuade him when I am not present to take action which conflicts with agreed plans. . . ."[57]

In January, 1945, the Japanese moved swiftly and successfully against airfields in South China which the Fourteenth Air Force had been using.[58] The victory, however, was slight, for the American forces moved elsewhere to continue the fight and left little behind. In Burma, fighting in the north was indecisive; on March 28, 1945, the British Fourteenth Army conquered Meiktila and by this victory determined control of central Burma.[59] The Japanese began to retreat south and west, and the Mars Force and Chinese divisions in north Burma were released for duty in China.

On January 29, 1945, General Wedemeyer moved ahead to reorganize the air forces in China as part of a larger plan to strike through the Japanese defenses to a seaport in southern China. This plan, called Beta, was based on several assumptions, including the following: that the European war would end May 15, 1945, that continued Allied advances in the Pacific would compel the Japanese to move their forces northward, that a four-inch pipeline would be completed to Kunming from Burma, and that the Hump and the Stilwell Road (the new name for the road) could deliver sixty thousand tons a month.[60]

Logistical difficulties soon developed which made any real Chinese offensive unlikely. Fortunately, the Japanese, having troubles elsewhere, began to retreat in order to provide troops for defense of the

[57] The letter is quoted extensively in Romanus and Sunderland, *Time Runs Out in CBI,* pp. 165–166. General Marshall forwarded the letter to President Roosevelt.

[58] The Japanese offensive is described in *ibid.,* pp. 169–179.

[59] For a description of the American role in the conclusion of the Burma campaign, see *ibid.,* pp. 183–230. For a British account, see Ehrman, *Grand Strategy,* VI (1956), 193–201.

[60] For details of plan Beta and the attempt to put it into operation, see Romanus and Sunderland, *Time Runs Out in CBI,* pp. 330–396; Wedemeyer, *Wedemeyer Reports!,* pp. 321–343.

homeland, and the Chinese advanced in their wake. There was a shift of command in the Army Air Forces, and in effect General Chennault found himself eased out of the scene in China.[61] Although bitter at the turn of events, Chennault could well be proud of the role he and the Fourteenth Air Force had played in the war in China.

In June, plans got under way to open the port at Fort Bayard in southern China, in the hope that some 25,000 tons a month might be supplied through this route.[62] The problem of Chinese Communists arose again in the summer of 1945. Wedemeyer was interested in having liaison teams work with the Communists as well as Nationalists in an effort to prevent postwar clashes between the two elements.[63] The war's termination prevented development of this proposal. As the end approached, Wedemeyer's problem became increasingly one of preparing for peace rather than conducting a war. Hearing of the atomic bomb and the news that Soviet Russia was entering the war, Wedemeyer held up the attack on Fort Bayard. Shortly after the news of Japan's surrender arrived, he issued his first postwar orders. World War II was over, but for Wedemeyer and China there were new problems.

[61] Chennault, *Way of a Fighter,* pp. 346–355; Craven and Cate, *The A.A.F. in World War II,* V, 270–271.

[62] Romanus and Sunderland, *Time Runs Out in CBI,* p. 362.

[63] *Ibid.,* p. 385.

CHAPTER 23

The Statesmen Face the Peace

THE Normandy invasion and subsequent breakout changed the atmosphere, and optimistically plans progressed for another international conference in order to discuss problems attendant upon victory in Germany and a redeployment of forces against Japan. Since Stalin declined to leave Russia, Roosevelt and Churchill decided to meet, although some of the President's political advisers feared the effect of too close Anglo-American cooperation upon the coming election. The meeting, first scheduled for Scotland, was changed and began in Quebec, September 11, 1944.[1]

Meanwhile, since victory seemed to be in sight economic problems increased in significance. The United States was demonstrating its tremendous productive capacity in supplying its own forces and through Lend-Lease those of its allies. The British also had exerted great effort in the massive preparations for D-day. But what was to happen when the war ended, and this great production no longer was needed for the war effort? United States leaders began to think of reconversion to peacetime activities, and a bitter difference of opinion developed between military heads, who opposed any diminution of

[1] Robert E. Sherwood, *Roosevelt and Hopkins: An Intimate History* (New York, 1948), p. 813. American military leaders felt that since the war in Europe was practically won (Intelligence estimates placed Germany's collapse at December 1) and since the American Joint Chiefs of Staff were largely directing the war in the Pacific, there was no need of a conference, and they consented to it reluctantly. Maurice Matloff, *Strategic Planning for Coalition Warfare, 1943–1944* (Washington, 1959), pp. 508–509.

war production until victory was actually achieved, and business leaders, who wished to take steps immediately toward postwar readjustment.[2] In England the situation was even more serious, for the United Kingdom had dug deeply into its capital resources, had lost much of its normal international trade, and had accumulated heavy indebtedness with such countries as Egypt and India. Anxious to avoid postwar catastrophe, the British wished to utilize Lend-Lease materials to enable her to regain a footing in foreign trade. American leaders, however, looked upon this move as a use of the American taxpayer's money to compete with American trade, and this interpretation carried particular weight during an election year.[3]

Unable to reach any long-range economic solutions, the British and Americans turned to more specific solutions in a conference held at Bretton Woods, New Hampshire, July 1–22, 1944. This conference saw Henry Morgenthau, Jr., Secretary of the Treasury, enter the temporary void in American diplomatic leadership, when he became chairman of this meeting, which devoted itself to monetary matters and recommended the establishment of an International Monetary Fund and an International Bank for Reconstruction and Development. The purpose of the Fund was to prevent the recurrence of the international fiscal warfare of the 1930's, and the Bank was designed to finance long-range capital improvements of backward and devastated countries after conclusion of the war. American thought largely created the Fund and Bank, and to the United States went the major financial responsibility for underwriting the programs. Later in the summer, the United States also initiated an Interim Commission of Food and Agriculture, whose function was to establish a permanent international agency to aid governments in solving technical agricultural problems. An attempt to reach international agreement on oil failed of accomplishment.[4]

The Quebec Conference of September, 1944, met in an atmosphere of imminent victory. No significant differences developed on military matters. American military planners encountered no opposition when

[2] William Hardy McNeill, *America, Britain, and Russia: Their Cooperation and Conflict, 1941–1946* (*Survey of International Affairs, 1939–1946*) (London, 1953), pp. 434–437.

[3] W. K. Hancock and M. M. Gowing, *British War Economy* (*History of the Second World War: United Kingdom Civil Series*) (London, 1949), pp. 520–524.

[4] McNeill, *America, Britain, and Russia,* pp. 449–453.

they insisted on the continuance of war plans already agreed upon, and they had no objection to a British push into Istria if it did not interfere with these plans. In the European Theater, air power gained in stature by the transfer of strategic air command from Eisenhower's control, but the shift made no difference in the conduct of the war. Churchill, continuing to assent to American dominance in the Pacific war, at Quebec offered the services of the British Fleet and Air Forces in the war against Japan. The Prime Minister had publicly pledged Britain's intention to continue in the war after the collapse of Germany; furthermore, with her own interests in the Far East Britain needed to bolster her postwar position in that area by active military participation against Japan. Roosevelt accepted the offer of British support against the recommendation of Admiral King and other military advisers. So far the American Joint Chiefs of Staff had had a fairly free hand in directing the Pacific war; introducing the British would force solutions at a higher level, and the Americans would have to cope with Churchill's concept of strategy for the Far East. In the Pacific as well as in Europe, American military leaders were concerned with winning the military war and were reluctant to deviate from this aim for political objectives.

At Quebec the President, who hitherto had rejected compromise on proposed zones of occupation for Germany, suddenly agreed to the suggestion, first made by Cossac, which gave the northwestern zone to the British, southwestern Germany to the United States, and the east to Soviet Russia. To facilitate supply and administration of the United States Zone, the city of Bremen and its port Bremerhaven were to be under American control.[5]

To help him, Roosevelt summoned Morgenthau to Quebec, and the Secretary was able to present a plan to the conference which he had discussed a few days earlier with other members of the President's Cabinet. In August, 1944, while on a plane bound for Europe, Morgenthau had read a State Department memorandum on Germany which he felt suggested overly lenient treatment of the enemy after the end of the war.[6] In conversations with General Eisenhower in

[5] Matloff, *Strategic Planning,* p. 511.

[6] Henry Morgenthau, Jr., "Postwar Treatment of Germany," American Academy of Political and Social Science, *Annals,* Vol. 246 (July, 1946), 125–126. The document was prepared for General Eisenhower and reached Morgenthau "without going through Army channels." See James Forrestal, *The Forrestal Diaries,* edited by Walter Millis (New York, 1951), p. 10.

England a few days later, the Secretary gained the impression, whether rightly or wrongly, that the Supreme Commander also opposed a "soft peace"[7] and on his return to the United States he discussed the problem with President Roosevelt, who said, "We have got to be tough with the German people, not just the Nazis. . . . They have been tough with us." The President also, a few days later, expressed dissatisfaction with a SHAEF Military Government Handbook which indicated that Germany should be restored approximately to her pre-war condition, and he wrote the Secretary of War that all Germans should understand that their nation had been defeated. "I do not want them to starve to death," he stated, "but, as an example, if they need food to keep body and soul together beyond what they have, they should be fed three times a day with soup from Army soup kitchens." They would thus keep healthy but they would remember the experience as long as they lived and would be so impressed with defeat that they would "hesitate to start any new war."[8]

Roosevelt then appointed a committee of the Secretaries of State, Treasury, and War to prepare a report for him on the postwar treatment of Germany. When this committee met with the President September 6, a critical difference developed over Secretary Morgenthau's proposal to remove all industrial plants and destroy all mines in the Ruhr. Secretary Stimson protested vigorously that such action would endanger the economy of much of Europe and he declared that reducing the Germans to a subsistence level would breed not prevent war. Secretary Hull shifted ground on the industrial issue and stood with Stimson, although earlier he apparently had inclined toward a harsh peace.[9]

The matter remained undecided, however, as President Roosevelt left for the Quebec conference. Meanwhile, Morgenthau had progressed to a belief that Germany should be turned from a highly industrialized nation to one of farmers. Informed that the major points to be discussed at Quebec would be military, Secretary Hull

[7] Dwight D. Eisenhower, *Crusade in Europe* (New York, 1948), p. 287.

[8] Quoted in John L. Chase, "The Development of the Morgenthau Plan Through the Quebec Conference," *Journal of Politics,* XVI (May, 1954), 334–336. For bibliographical references on the Morgenthau Plan, see John L. Snell, *et al., The Meaning of Yalta: Big Three Diplomacy and the New Balance of Power* (Baton Rouge, La.), p. 42*n*.

[9] Henry L. Stimson and McGeorge Bundy, *On Active Service in Peace and War* (New York, 1948), pp. 570–573; Cordell Hull, *The Memoirs of Cordell Hull* (New York, 1948), II, 1605–1606.

stated that he was tired and wished to be excused.[10] The President did not ask Harry Hopkins to attend.[11] Morgenthau, however, accompanied Roosevelt as far as Hyde Park, and after the President arrived in Quebec he directed the Secretary of the Treasury to join him.[12]

At dinner with Roosevelt, Churchill, and Eden, Morgenthau was asked to explain his plan, and, to quote Morgenthau himself, Churchill reacted violently to the deindustrialization scheme and declared that he looked on the Treasury plan "as he would on chaining himself to a dead German."[13] On the following day the Prime Minister reversed himself and drafted a slight revision of the Morgenthau proposal which ended as follows: "This programme for eliminating the war-making industries in the Ruhr and in the Saar is looking forward to converting Germany into a country primarily agricultural and pastoral in its character."[14]

Both Churchill and Roosevelt initialed this document, and Morgenthau had won a victory. Some persons have suggested that the other principal nonmilitary agreement of the conference, the question of Lend-Lease, was not dissociated with the Morgenthau Plan in that it may have had some bearing on Churchill's reversal. Secretary Morgenthau recommended that Britain should receive $3.5 billion of Lend-Lease between the end of the war with Germany and the collapse of Japan and he further proposed an additional $3 billion for nonmilitary Lend-Lease materials. His recommendations went to an Anglo-American Committee of Experts for detailed study, but at least the principle was established of continued Lend-Lease after Germany's defeat.[15]

Morgenthau returned to Washington and recounted his success to Hull and Stimson. The latter, unwilling to let the matter rest, continued to fight the proposal in both writing and personal interview with the President. This time he argued primarily on the level of the economic welfare of Europe, the starvation that would be forced upon the Germans, and the vengeful spirit that would be engendered in

[10] *Ibid.*, II, 1602.
[11] Sherwood, *Roosevelt and Hopkins*, p. 814.
[12] Chase, "Development of the Morgenthau Plan," p. 355.
[13] Quoted in *ibid.*, p. 356.
[14] Quoted in Morgenthau, "Postwar Treatment of Germany," p. 126.
[15] Hull, *Memoirs*, II, 1614–1617; Chase, "Development of the Morgenthau Plan," pp. 353–354.

them. By this time President Roosevelt evidently had reconsidered the problem, for he indicated that he had initialed the statement at Quebec without much thought and he assured Stimson that he had no intention of turning Germany into an agrarian community.[16] Despite Roosevelt's reversal, the Morgenthau Plan had some impact on the early postwar military government of Germany.[17] A partial explanation of Roosevelt's shift no doubt stemmed from strong public criticism of the Morgenthau Plan, news of which had "leaked" to the press.[18]

In early October, Harry Hopkins prevented the President from making another serious diplomatic blunder. After his return from Quebec, Churchill sought a conference of the Big Three to discuss problems arising from the Russian Army's rapid advance into the Balkans. Roosevelt's determination to remain in the United States until after the presidential election and Stalin's refusal to leave Russia led to Churchill's decision to go to Moscow. Roosevelt drafted a cable to the Prime Minister indicating lack of interest in the Balkans and implying that at Moscow Churchill could speak for the Americans as well as the British. When he heard of the message, Hopkins realized the danger of such a carte blanche and without authority he stopped the cable from being sent. He then explained his action to Roosevelt and persuaded him instead to request of Stalin that Ambassador Averell Harriman attend the conference between Churchill and Stalin as an observer and that the meeting be viewed as preliminary to a later conference of the Big Three.[19]

Shortly afterward, Cordell Hull left the State Department because of illness, although he was persuaded to withhold his formal resignation until after the election.[20] James F. Byrnes, whose high standing in the U.S. Senate would be valuable when the time came to vote on the United Nations, was a logical choice as successor, but Harry Hopkins, who had no affection for Byrnes, felt that the South

[16] Stimson and Bundy, *On Active Service,* p. 580. For reactions in the State Department, see memorandum by N. Freeman Matthews, Sept. 20, 1944, *Foreign Relations of the United States: Diplomatic Papers: The Conferences at Malta and Yalta 1945* (84th Cong., 1st Sess., House Document 154) (Washington, 1955), pp. 134–135.

[17] Carl J. Friedrich and Associates, *American Experiences in Military Government in World War II* (New York, 1948), pp. 224–228.

[18] Stimson and Bundy, *On Active Service,* p. 580.

[19] Sherwood, *Roosevelt and Hopkins,* pp. 832–834.

[20] Hull, *Memoirs,* II, 1715–1716.

Carolinian was too strong a personality for a President who wished to be his own Secretary of State in dealings with Stalin and Churchill and he persuaded Roosevelt to appoint the more pliable Under Secretary Edward R. Stettinius, Jr., as Hull's replacement.[21]

During the summer and early fall of 1944, the United States and its allies made measurable strides toward world organization. Committed by the Four-Power Declaration of the previous year, they began to draft tentative plans for such a body. American diplomats, remembering postwar rejection of the League of Nations by the United States, were especially eager to establish a legal international organization before the close of World War II. Once again the fact that Soviet Russia was not at war with Japan caused complications, and the conference which met at Dumbarton Oaks had two parts. In the first and most significant meeting on the estate in Georgetown the Americans, British, and Russians conferred, and later the Americans and British went over the same matters with the Chinese.

The conference resulted in substantial agreement that a new international body to be known as the United Nations should consist basically of four elements: (1) a General Assembly of representatives from all the member states; (2) a Security Council on which the great powers, the United States, the United Kingdom, Soviet Russia, China, and France, would have permanent seats and the smaller powers representatives elected by the General Assembly; (3) a secretariat; and (4) an International Court of Justice.[22]

The Dumbarton Oaks Conference failed to solve some of its most important problems, but instead of becoming mired in indecision its delegates did what they could and placed to one side the difficult questions for a later meeting of the Big Three, who were not in attendance. Among the unsolved matters were those of veto power and membership. The attempt by the United States to secure membership for six Latin-American nations not at war with the Axis led the Soviet government to advocate the admission of the sixteen Soviet Republics for separate representation. After exchange of telegrams, Stalin and Roosevelt agreed to defer this problem until they met.[23] Other unsolved problems included voting procedures, the nature and jurisdiction of the Permanent Court, and trusteeship of dependent

[21] Sherwood, *Roosevelt and Hopkins,* p. 835.
[22] McNeill, *America, Britain, and Russia,* p. 504.
[23] Hull, *Memoirs,* II, 1678–1680.

territories which undoubtedly would be wrested from the defeated enemy.[24]

Several factors dictated another meeting of the Big Three: the unresolved questions of the Dumbarton Oaks Conference, the problems attendant upon the anticipated collapse of Germany, and the determination of Soviet Russia's role in the war against Japan. There was a repetition of the dickering over a meeting place which had preceded the Teheran Conference. This time Stalin pleaded ill health and resisted all suggestions that he leave Russia. Finally, Roosevelt and Churchill consented to go to Yalta in the Crimea, although Churchill was said by Hopkins to have grumbled that a worse spot could not have been selected.[25]

The President made the first leg of the journey by sea and arrived at Malta February 2, 1945, on the last day of a military conference which had started on that island January 30. This was a meeting of the Combined Chiefs of Staff to plan the forthcoming conversations with the Russians and to attempt to resolve some of their own difficulties. The British and Americans, in an atmosphere which became somewhat heated, presented different strategic plans for the last assault on Germany, and the Combined Chiefs endorsed General Eisenhower's plan, which was ably defended at Malta by General Walter Bedell Smith. There was little disagreement over the war in the Pacific, and the Combined Chiefs approved the proposed attacks on Iwo Jima and Okinawa. On one point the British emerged successfully, for the Americans accepted the British definition of American rights of access through Bremen and Bremerhaven to the United States zone of occupation in southern Germany. Final approval of the zones, themselves, did not come until the Yalta meeting. Roosevelt and Churchill arrived at Malta in time to endorse the actions of the Combined Chiefs of Staff.[26]

Late on the night of February 2, leaving at ten-minute intervals, planes began the task of ferrying more than seven hundred persons from Malta to Yalta, the winter resort on the wooded coast of the Black Sea, to begin one of the most significant and certainly the most

[24] *Yalta Papers,* pp. 48–93.

[25] Snell, *The Meaning of Yalta,* pp. 34–36; Sherwood, *Roosevelt and Hopkins,* p. 847; *Yalta Papers,* pp. 3–28; Winston Churchill, *The Second World War* (Boston, 1953), VI, 342.

[26] Minutes and other documents of the conference are in *Yalta Papers,* pp. 459–546.

controversial of the wartime conferences.[27] It was a wearing round of meetings at various levels, banquets, and informal discussions.

One of the most important questions discussed by the Big Three was that of Russian entry into the war against Japan. At Teheran Stalin had promised such action when the German war ended; Roosevelt's purpose at Yalta was to formalize and fix this promise and to reach an agreement on the benefits the Russians would derive from such aid. The President went to Yalta with the conviction that the Japanese should lose their earlier continental conquests and he accepted Russian demands for a return of properties which they had lost in the Russo-Japanese War of 1904–5. More critical, however, were Stalin's demands for concessions which infringed upon Chinese sovereign rights, for he sought outright control rather than internationalization of Port Arthur and dominance of the Manchurian railways instead of joint Russo-Chinese management. He further asked for international guarantees that would maintain the autonomy of Outer Mongolia. Acting in utmost secrecy, President Roosevelt acceded to the Russian demands, and Churchill, who entered the discussions late, added his signature. Possibly the President felt protected by the statement relating to Russian control of the Manchurian railways, which promised, "It being understood that the preeminent interests of the Soviet Union shall be safeguarded and that China shall retain full sovereignty in Manchuria," and by the Soviet pledge to negotiate a treaty with the Nationalist government of China "in order to render assistance to China with its armed forces for the purpose of liberating China from the Japanese yoke." Unfortunately, the President also agreed to the following statement: "The Heads of the Three Great Powers have agreed that these claims of the Soviet Union shall unquestionably be fulfilled after Japan has been defeated."[28]

There are several observations possible on the President's action. In the first place, he faced an important military problem without the

[27] "President's Log," Feb. 2 [1945], in *Yalta Papers,* p. 462.

[28] *Ibid.,* p. 984. For discussions of this problem, see Snell, *The Meaning of Yalta,* pp. 144–152; Herbert Feis, *Churchill, Roosevelt, Stalin: The War They Waged and the Peace They Sought* (Princeton, 1957), pp. 505–517; Edward R. Stettinius, *Roosevelt and the Russians: the Yalta Conference* (New York, 1949), pp. 91–98. Churchill states that the British considered the matter "as an American affair and . . . certainly of prime interest to their military operations." Churchill, *The Second World War,* VI, 390.

hindsight available to his subsequent critics. This was to defeat the Japanese enemy with as much economy of American lives as consistent with victory. Although Roosevelt was aware of progress being made on the atomic bomb, it had not yet been tested, and even high-ranking military officials were skeptical of its potentialities. The B-29's to date had not demonstrated their terrific striking power, and the Iwo Jima and Okinawa campaigns were in the future. Furthermore, military advisers strongly urged the entry of Soviet Russia into the war against Japan. Roosevelt apparently felt confident of his ability to explain the situation to Chiang Kai-shek, whom, incidentally, he was regarding less highly as the war progressed. Secrecy seemed essential to protect military movements preparatory to the Russian attack in the Far East, particularly since Chungking had become notorious for the leakage of confidential information. One wonders, however, why Roosevelt considered it necessary to keep his Secretary of State uninformed of the agreement.[29]

Other important discussions centered around the defeat and occupation of Germany. The conference ratified a protocol which defined three zones of occupation, established an Allied Control Council, and designated Berlin as a special zone controlled by the three great powers. The Big Three reached easy accord on such matters as destruction of the Nazi party, laws, and institutions, as well as of German militarism. The question of permanent dismemberment was referred to the three ministers, Anthony Eden, Edward R. Stettinius, Jr., and Vyacheslav Molotov, who agreed that mention of dismemberment should be written into the terms of the peace with Germany and that a special commission composed of Eden and the American and Russian ambassadors in London should work out details on the manner in which dismemberment should be effected. The three ministers also helped pave the way for an agreement by the Big Three that France should share on an equal basis in control of Germany.[30]

The Russians went to Yalta interested in securing tangible repara-

[29] At Yalta President Roosevelt told his Secretary of State, Edward R. Stettinius, that negotiations on the Far East should remain "on a purely military level." The secret agreement was taken to Washington and placed in the President's personal safe and was there at the time of his death. Stettinius wrote: "I had not actually seen it, nor to the best of my belief, had President Truman when he moved into the White House." Stettinius, *Roosevelt and the Russians,* pp. 92, 96.

[30] Snell, *The Meaning of Yalta,* pp. 53–56; Stettinius, *Roosevelt and the Russians,* pp. 117–129; Feis, *Churchill, Roosevelt, Stalin,* pp. 530–534.

tions from Germany. Their demand for reduction of Germany's capital plant of heavy industry by about 80 percent was less drastic than the Morgenthau Plan which Roosevelt and Churchill had initialed at Quebec the preceding September, but these leaders had reversed their opinions. While Roosevelt indicated that the United States was not interested in securing reparations, Churchill and Stalin could reach no accord on this problem.[31] The Big Three, however, did agree on certain principles, one of which was a most disturbing concession by a democratic President. These were that German reparations should be of three types: capital equipment, current production, and "use of German labour."[32]

Roosevelt was intent on forwarding the move for an international organization and sought at Yalta to settle the issues left unsolved by the Dumbarton Oaks Conference. The leaders at Yalta decided that the first meeting of the United Nations organization would be at San Francisco, April 25, 1945. The British and the Americans had agreed on the principle of a veto in July, 1944.[33] Russia had assented but at Dumbarton Oaks raised the question of the formula concerning the right of a member to a veto vote in a dispute in which it was a participant. On December 5, 1944, the State Department had prepared a document suggesting solutions for the impasse on the voting formula which gave a major nation a veto on sanctions or war against itself. Stettinius presented this at Yalta, and after some delay Stalin agreed, but then he demanded that the Ukraine and White Russia (Byelorussia) be admitted as voting members of the Assembly. This request was more modest than the earlier Russian proposal of sixteen votes but it would give Soviet Russia three votes to one for the United States. The British representatives, anxious to secure membership for their dominions and even India, were willing to agree.[34] Roosevelt, on the other hand, was reluctant until James F. Byrnes suggested that he seek a promise of British and Russian support if necessary for three votes for the United States in the Assembly.[35] Churchill and Stalin acquiesced, and then to his subsequent discomfiture Roosevelt requested that the whole matter be kept secret.[36] Another proposal of the Americans

[31] Snell, *The Meaning of Yalta,* pp. 57–74.
[32] Protocol on German Reparation, Feb. 11, 1945, *Yalta Papers,* p. 983.
[33] Sherwood, *Roosevelt and Hopkins,* p. 854.
[34] Stettinius, *Roosevelt and the Russians,* pp. 135–150.
[35] J. F. Byrnes, *Speaking Frankly* (New York, 1947), p. 40.
[36] Snell, *The Meaning of Yalta,* pp. 185–186; Sherwood, *Roosevelt and Hop-*

aroused temporary opposition by the British, for when Stettinius urged that the five permanent members of the Security Council prior to the San Francisco meeting prepare a recommendation for dealing with "dependent nations," Churchill viewed the move as an attack on the British Empire. He subsided when the Secretary of State made it clear that dependent nations referred only to former League of Nations mandates, lands taken from the enemy, or colonies voluntarily released by a ruling power.[37]

The question of Poland occupied much of the conference's time, for what the Americans considered a secondary issue was a primary one for the Russians. In the end the agreement was mainly a Russian victory, since the eastern boundary was roughly the old Curzon Line and the western boundary remained unfixed. Roosevelt and a more reluctant Churchill yielded to continuance of the Russian-sponsored provisional government in Poland. Political bargaining and wishful thinking entered into Roosevelt's action; a retreat on the Polish issue would insure success in the establishment of a United Nations organization, and furthermore, the solution was only temporary since Polish elections in the near future would create a new Polish government responsible to the will of the people. Possibly these were rationalizations in the face of the blunt fact that Soviet forces occupied most of Poland. Stalin added to Roosevelt's optimistic view of the future by subscribing to a Declaration of Liberated Europe, prepared by the State Department, which looked forward to processes which would enable the liberated peoples of Europe to "create democratic institutions of their own choice."[38] At the conclusion of the conference the participants issued a communiqué which described part but not all of the agreements reached. The public did not hear at this time of such matters as dismemberment of Germany, bargains with Stalin concerning the Pacific war, or the voting formula and multiple Russian representation in the United Nations.[39]

The only real force holding the United States, the United Kingdom, and Soviet Russia together was the war against Germany, and as that conflict neared its end, frictions of various sorts frayed the bonds. The

---

kins, p. 875. For a bitter attack on Roosevelt's actions at Yalta, see George N. Crocker, *Roosevelt's Road to Russia* (Chicago, 1959), pp. 241–280.

[37] McNeill, *America, Britain, and Russia,* p. 554.

[38] Snell, *The Meaning of Yalta,* pp. 94–126; Feis, *Churchill, Roosevelt, Stalin,* pp. 518–529; *Yalta Papers,* p. 972.

[39] *Ibid.,* pp. 968–975.

Russians became suspicious that Britain and the United States were seeking a separate peace, and German peace overtures through Swiss channels intensified these suspicions.[40] The British became annoyed at the United States when General Eisenhower dealt directly with Stalin to arrange details of the merging of the Eastern and Western fronts, although such dealings were tactically necessary to keep the Allied armies from shooting at each other.[41] Both the British and the Americans viewed with concern Soviet Russia's political actions as its armies moved farther into Europe, for within a month after the close of the Yalta Conference the Russians had forced a Communist-dominated government on Rumania. It soon became apparent that the Russians and their Western allies interpreted differently the Yalta agreement on Poland, and by the end of March the two sides were deadlocked on the issue of representation in the Polish government.[42]

Toward the end of the month, a security leak divulged to the American public the secret of the agreement to give the Soviets three votes in the United Nations Assembly. The issue itself was not particularly important, and there was little pressure for an equal number of votes for the United States, but the effect of the revelation and the government's admission of its truth made the Yalta agreement suspect. How many other secret deals had been made?[43]

Other developments reduced the optimism people felt toward the approaching United Nations conference in San Francisco. On March 29, the Russians stated that Foreign Minister Molotov would not attend the meetings, and the tendency was to view this announcement as indicating lack of interest if not of sympathy with the aims of the meeting. Then on April 12 came President Roosevelt's death at Warm Springs, Georgia.[44] The new President quickly announced that American participation in the conference would continue as planned.[45]

One of President Roosevelt's most serious acts of omission was his failure to keep his Vice President informed of significant international developments. Neither precedent nor law dictated that he take the Vice President into his confidence, but the importance of the

[40] McNeill, *America, Britain, and Russia,* pp. 569–570.

[41] Eisenhower, *Crusade in Europe,* pp. 399–403.

[42] McNeill, *America, Britain, and Russia,* pp. 574–578.

[43] Sherwood, *Roosevelt and Hopkins,* p. 876.

[44] Ross T. McIntire, *White House Physician* (New York, 1946), pp. 242–243.

[45] Harry S. Truman, *Memoirs by Harry S. Truman* (New York, 1955), I, 9.

war to the American people, the highly personal nature of Rooseveltian diplomacy, and the state of Roosevelt's health in this his fourth term made it a matter of utmost urgency to prepare fully the man who at any time might have to take command. Truman had not been told of the atomic bomb, nor had he even been in the secret White House map room.[46]

Shortly after Truman took office, others in the government sought to inform him on many matters. Secretary Stimson told him of the atomic bomb project, and Secretary Stettinius continued to provide the Chief Executive with a daily summary of diplomatic developments and furnished other information which Truman requested.[47] Truman quickly and conscientiously began to prepare himself for the terrific task that lay ahead. He called James F. Byrnes to Washington and received from him a detailed account of the Yalta Conference, which Byrnes had attended and from which he had brought extensive stenographic notes. Truman also told Byrnes that he wanted him to become Secretary of State, but it was decided to postpone the shift until after the San Francisco Conference. An important factor behind the removal of Stettinius, who became American representative on the United Nations's Security Council, was that the Secretary of State at that time was next in line for the presidency. Since Stettinius had not held an elective office, Truman felt that he should be replaced by one who had.[48] Stettinius was not a professional politician and had gone into government administration from business.

After Roosevelt's death, on the advice of Ambassador Harriman, Stalin reversed his earlier decision and sent Molotov to the San Francisco Conference, which began April 25, 1945.[49] Four nations, the United States, the United Kingdom, the USSR, and China, sponsored the gathering; the French attended, but de Gaulle, piqued by earlier treatment of his government, had declined an invitation to become a sponsor. Forty-six nations had qualified for membership by declaring war on Germany prior to March 1, 1945. Since the deadlock over the Polish government had not been resolved, that country was not represented.[50] Molotov, who had come to the conference as a gesture

[46] *Ibid.*, I, 10, 50; Jonathan Daniels, *The Man of Independence* (Philadelphia, 1950), pp. 262–265.

[47] Truman, *Memoirs*, I, 10, 14–27.

[48] *Ibid.*, I, 22.

[49] Sherwood, *Roosevelt and Hopkins*, pp. 883–884.

[50] McNeill, *America, Britain, and Russia*, pp. 591–592; Ruth B. Russell, *A*

of goodwill, failed to live up to his role and instead gave early evidence of the truculence which would characterize much of Soviet action in the United Nations.

The first important debates centered about the admission of new members. Molotov, without waiting for agreement on a new Polish government, sought the admission of the pro-Communist provisional government. Russia earlier had attempted to bargain with the United States for admission of this government in return for Russian support of Argentina's effort toward membership, and when the United States refused to deal, Molotov took the Polish case to the floor of the General Assembly. He lost, but he took so much time that when Stettinius next sought the admission of Argentina he employed steamroller tactics in order to save time. He was successful in gaining membership for Argentina, but his heavy-handed measures caused widespread resentment. Russia was mollified somewhat by the redemption of a Yalta pledge as the Ukraine and White Russia were admitted to the United Nations. Denmark was liberated from the Germans at about this time and brought the number of United Nations to an even fifty.[51]

After its votes on membership the General Assembly really decided little. The United States, with its influence over the Latin-American states, Liberia, and the Philippines, had in effect a veto power in the Assembly, but it could not turn this into a positive force lest the Soviet Union withdraw from the conference.[52] The result was that major decisions were reached in behind the scenes discussions by representatives of the Big Three. The Chinese and French often participated in such meetings, but neither had a significant influence. In essence the pattern of control was as simple as the issues were complicated; an impasse continued until the three major powers reached

History of the United Nations Charter: The Role of the United States, 1940–1945 (Washington, 1958), p. 630.

[51] Argentina had remained neutral throughout most of the war, and its government was accused of being pro-Nazi. Under pressure by the United States and other Latin-American states, Argentina declared war on Germany and Japan on March 27, 1945. In the interest of pan-American solidarity United States representatives sought Argentina's admission to the United Nations. In the opinion of one of these, Senator Arthur H. Vandenberg, by opposing admission, Molotov "has done more in four days to solidify Pan-America against Russia than anything that has ever happened." Arthur H. Vandenberg, *The Private Papers of Senator Vandenberg,* edited by Arthur H. Vandenberg, Jr. (Boston, 1952), p. 182.

[52] McNeill, *America, Britain, and Russia,* pp. 595–596.

agreement, and then, although smaller powers might speak, they could not prevent approval by the Assembly.

Possibly the most serious deadlock developed over the voting formula prepared at Yalta and over the question of veto power. On May 27, Andrei Gromyko, who had succeeded Molotov as the senior Russian delegate, shocked the conference by insisting that the Security Council, dominated by the veto, could even decide whether a particular dispute could be discussed. This challenge of the right to a hearing aroused strong opposition and brought to a halt the work of the meeting.[53]

President Truman had already become perturbed over the Polish matter and other points at issue with the Russians and, acting on Ambassador Harriman's recommendation, sent Harry Hopkins to Moscow in the hope that he, who had been such an important adviser of Roosevelt in earlier conferences, might have some influence on Stalin. Hopkins, who had been seriously ill, performed the last of a series of valuable services for the United States. Arriving in Moscow on May 25, he held several conferences with Stalin on a number of important issues. He explained American support of Argentina, assured Stalin that Lend-Lease to Russia would continue despite earlier stoppage of the flow by subordinate officials, and discussed at length the Polish question. Stalin admitted high-handed Russian action in Poland but declined to release Polish underground leaders who had been seized; on the other hand, he agreed to the inclusion of certain Polish leaders in the government, and a list of such individuals was agreed on by British, Russian, and American authorities.[54]

The impasse on veto procedure in the United Nations developed while Hopkins was in Russia, and Truman cabled his emissary to attempt to solve this matter. Hopkins explained the situation to Stalin, who unexpectedly assented, and shortly afterward the Soviet delegates in San Francisco abandoned their stand. Stalin also informed Hopkins that he intended to invade Manchuria August 8, 1945. Hopkins, in addition, reached agreement for a meeting of Truman, Churchill, and Stalin to be held in Berlin about the middle of July.[55]

Stalin's action made it possible for the San Francisco Conference to continue its work. Inevitably, most agreements were compromises;

[53] *Ibid.*, p. 601; Vandenberg, *Private Papers*, pp. 199–204.
[54] Sherwood, *Roosevelt and Hopkins*, pp. 887–910.
[55] *Ibid.*, pp. 909, 911.

a trusteeship principle emerged with a rather vague promise of freedom for dependent peoples which did not in itself threaten existing empires or prevent the United States from securing strategic bases in the Pacific, and a formula was agreed on which permitted regional organizations, as, for example, of American states, to exist and work for peace within their own areas. The smaller powers, which had fought Russia's effort to stifle the right to a hearing, were also able to gain increased flexibility in the amending process. Finally, the delegates finished their work and on June 26, 1945, signed the United Nations Charter.[56] On July 2, President Truman, who had gone to San Francisco to help close the conference officially, was back in Washington and presented the Charter to the United States Senate for ratification.[57]

In his appointment of delegates to the San Francisco Conference, Roosevelt showed his clear appreciation of Wilson's blunders of omission in selecting his delegates for the Versailles Conference, and Truman made no changes. Heading the delegation was Secretary of State Stettinius; former Secretary Hull was also a delegate but because of illness did not attend. Other members were Commander Harold E. Stassen, liberal Republican and former Governor of Minnesota; two prominent members of the Senate Foreign Relations Committee, Democratic Senator Tom Connally of Texas and Republican Senator Arthur H. Vandenberg of Michigan; two members of the House Foreign Affairs Committee, Democratic Congressman Sol Bloom of New York and Republican Representative Charles A. Eaton of New Jersey; and Dean Virginia C. Gildersleeve, independent Democrat, of Barnard College, whose appointment indicated women's increasing role in public affairs. Later, because of pressure from Stettinius and Vandenberg, Roosevelt added John Foster Dulles as a principal adviser to the delegation.[58]

The work of these individuals and the earlier resolutions of both houses of Congress made it clear that the Senate would not reject the Charter. It went first to the Senate Committee, which held hearings and returned it without suggested reservations or amendments. The only dissenting committee vote came from bedridden Hiram W.

[56] Ruhl J. Bartlett, *The Record of American Diplomacy: Documents and Readings in the History of American Foreign Relations* (New York, 1947), pp. 676–696.

[57] Truman, *Memoirs,* I, 293.

[58] *Ibid.,* I, 46; Vandenberg, *Private Papers,* pp. 155–171.

Johnson. The Senate then ratified the document with dissenting votes from only two of its members, Republican Senators William Langer of North Dakota and Henrik Shipstead of Minnesota, although Johnson indicated that if he had been able to be present he would have voted in the negative as well.[59] By this overwhelming vote, the Senate showed its understanding that world power carried with it not only leadership but a responsibility which included participation in the affairs of the nations of the world.

While the Senate discussed the Charter of the United Nations, President Truman was in attendance at the last great wartime conference. The President was inexperienced in international dealings, and his new Secretary of State, James F. Byrnes, aside from his presence at Yalta, had a record which, although distinguished, was almost exclusively in the domestic field. They had the services, however, of State Department men who long had been working on the problems to be considered in the conference and of Admiral Leahy, who had attended the major conferences of the war.

The Potsdam meeting began July 17 and lasted intermittently until August 2, 1945. Military problems, which had been dominant in the earlier conferences, had become secondary since only the war against Japan remained. The United States Joint Chiefs of Staff recommended to Truman that he encourage Soviet Russia to enter the war, although there is evidence that some military leaders were becoming less interested in Russian participation.[60] In fact, they were becoming convinced that they could defeat Japan without any outside help. A difference developed when the British sought to shift strategic control in the Pacific from the United States Joint Chiefs of Staff to the Combined Chiefs of Staff. They based their arguments on the fact that since March, 1945, a British naval force had been operating under United States command while in contrast Lord Mountbatten in his South-East Asia Command had Americans on his staff. The United States Joint Chiefs of Staff had no intention of relinquishing

[59] H. Bradford Westerfield, *Foreign Policy and Party Politics: Pearl Harbor to Korea* (New Haven, 1955), pp. 181–182; Vandenberg, *Private Papers,* pp. 216–219.

[60] Truman, *Memoirs,* I, 314–315, 387; Ray S. Cline, *Washington Command Post: The Operations Division* (*United States Army in World War II: The War Department*) (Washington, 1951), p. 346; John R. Deane, *The Strange Alliance: The Story of Our Efforts at Wartime Cooperation with Russia* (New York, 1947), p. 267; W. F. Craven and J. L. Cate, *The Army Air Forces in World War II* (Chicago, 1953), V, 711.

their guidance of the war at this late date; they suggested disbanding the Combined Chiefs of Staff and, further, refused to agree to continuance of Lend-Lease for British occupation troops in Europe. In the end, the Americans retained control of the Pacific war, although they agreed to consult with the British Chiefs of Staff and to accept British troops as part of a land assault on Japan if that became necessary. President Truman overrode the Joint Chiefs of Staff on the matter of Lend-Lease and ordered its continuance as long as the war with Japan lasted. Military conversations with the Russians were friendly but inconclusive. The United States declined to promise naval action to open and protect sea lanes north of Japan, and in effect the three Allies agreed to fight their own separate wars in the Pacific.[61]

Truman and Byrnes went to Potsdam hoping that the United States could help Europe reconstitute itself along the lines of the Yalta Declaration on Liberated Europe and then withdraw as soon as possible.[62] The British were concerned with some of the economic problems of German occupation; they sought to secure American Lend-Lease and also to effect an arrangement with Soviet Russia whereby food from the rural parts of Germany occupied by Russians could be used to feed people of the highly industrialized parts of the British zone of occupation. The British election, occurring while the conference was in session, undoubtedly hampered British action, for Churchill, who attended the first meetings, was defeated. As a result Prime Minister Clement R. Attlee and Foreign Minister Ernest Bevin replaced Churchill and Eden. They attempted to continue the same policies, but although Bevin, in particular, was aggressive, neither had had extensive experience in foreign affairs.[63]

The leaders reached an early agreement on a new Council of Foreign Ministers which replaced the European Advisory Commission and became the agency to prepare drafts of treaties with the defeated powers.[64] After a heated discussion on the Polish issue, the Big Three by-passed the problem by turning it over to the Foreign Ministers.[65] To them also went the task of preparing instructions for political conduct of occupation forces. This was one problem for

[61] McNeill, *America, Britain, and Russia,* pp. 630–632.
[62] Truman, *Memoirs,* I, 345–346; Brynes, *Speaking Frankly,* pp. 72–73.
[63] McNeill, *America, Britain, and Russia,* pp. 612–613.
[64] Byrnes, *Speaking Frankly,* pp. 69–72; Truman, *Memoirs,* I, 352.
[65] *Ibid.,* I, 354.

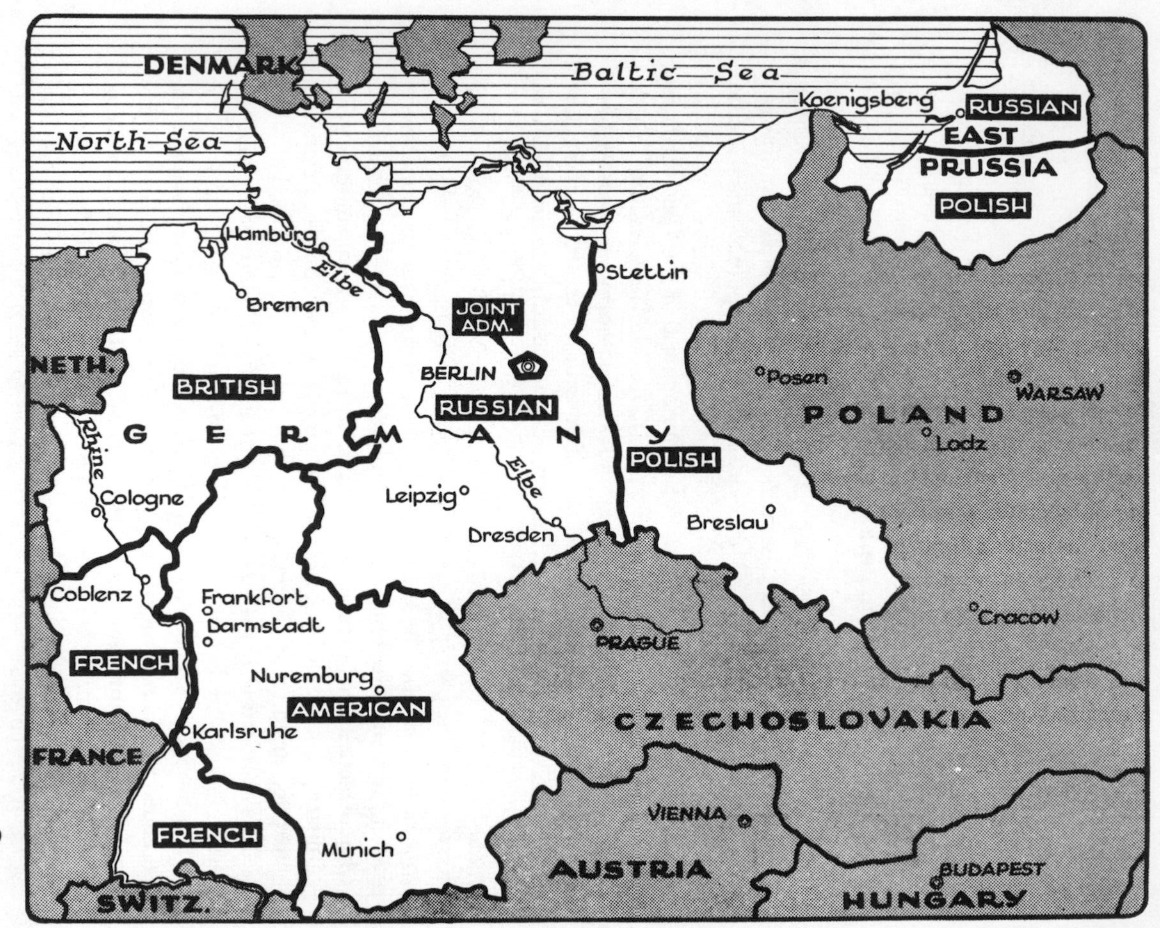

OCCUPIED GERMANY

which the Foreign Ministers were ready and they presented a formula which the conference accepted.[66]

One of the most important issues was that of German reparations. The Russians wanted huge reparations and they wanted them quickly; the British and Americans wanted to guarantee that reparations would not be so great that they would destroy German economy. This problem became so seriously deadlocked that Byrnes announced that unless the Russians came to an agreement the United States would leave the conference.[67] Since the heavy industry reparations Stalin wanted were mainly in the Western zones, Stalin had to yield to the principle that reparations payments "should leave enough resources to enable the German people to subsist without external assistance."[68] If Stalin conceded on this point, the Americans and British weakened on the matter of Poland's western border and agreed to leave to Poland on a temporary basis land which the Russians had given them and from which they were expelling Germans. The British and Americans rationalized on the ground that permanent boundaries of Poland could be written in the final treaty, but actually German hopes of regaining their land appeared slight.[69]

The Potsdam Conference settled little, and what agreements there were, were temporary in nature. Stalin, for example, reluctantly agreed to a French zone of occupation in Germany, but the French had not participated in the Potsdam discussions nor approved the principles decided upon by that conference. Many issues had been pushed into the hands of the Foreign Ministers with little possibility that they could solve them.

The Potsdam Declaration, or Ultimatum, to Japan is discussed elsewhere. It was at Potsdam that Truman heard of the successful test of the atomic bomb at Alamagordo and it was on his way home that he issued the fateful order for the use of the new weapon against Japan. Had the Japanese heeded the warning issued at Potsdam, the conference indeed might be considered of the greatest significance. Since they did not, the ultimatum must be listed with the other frustrations of the conference.

In the various international conferences from Washington in De-

[66] *Ibid.*, I, 355; McNeill, *America, Britain, and Russia,* pp. 617–618.
[67] Byrnes, *Speaking Frankly,* p. 85.
[68] Quoted in McNeill, *America, Britain, and Russia,* p. 623.
[69] *Ibid.*, pp. 624–626.

cember, 1941, to Potsdam in the summer of 1945, the Allies had solved successfully economic and military problems which led to the collapse of the enemy and they had created an international organization designed to preserve peace. They had failed, however, to reconcile divergent postwar aspirations that produced a peace continually jeopardized by suspicions and distrust.

CHAPTER 24

The Pacific War, April—November, 1944

THE Joint Chiefs of Staff's directive of March 12, 1944, had authorized continuance of the dual advance toward the Philippines; MacArthur's forces would move against Hollandia on April 15, and the Central Pacific forces would invade the Marianas on June 15.[1]

Hollandia, in Dutch New Guinea, appeared to be a desirable objective for development of both naval and air facilities. The Cyclops Mountains constitute a bulge in the northwest coast, having at each end of the protrusion a harbor, one of which, Humboldt Bay, was considered to be the only good harbor in a 450-mile stretch of New Guinea coastline. Behind the Cyclops Mountains was a lake valley or plain, in which the Japanese had begun to develop an air base. Needing an intermediate air base, U.S. forces included Aitape in the Hollandia invasion; at this spot on the coast some 125 miles southeast of Hollandia, the Japanese had completed an air strip and started two others.[2]

[1] Message, Joint Chiefs of Staff to MacArthur and Nimitz, Mar. 12, 1944, summarized in Maurice Matloff, *Strategic Planning for Coalition Warfare, 1943–1944* (*United States in World War II: The War Department*) (Washington, 1959), pp. 458–459.

[2] For accounts of the Hollandia-Aitape operation, see Robert Ross Smith, *The Approach to the Philippines* (*United States Army in World War II: The War in the Pacific*) (Washington, 1953), pp. 13–205; Samuel E. Morison, *History of United States Naval Operations in World War II* (Boston, 1953), VIII, 59–90; Robert L. Eichelberger, *Our Jungle Road to Tokyo* (New York, 1950), pp. 100–122; W. F. Craven and J. L. Cate, *The Army Air Forces in World War II* (Chicago, 1950), IV, 575–614; Walter Krueger, *From Down Under to Nippon: The Story of Sixth Army in World War II* (Washington, 1953), pp. 56–78.

The task of the Southwest Pacific forces, supported by Task Force 58, was to commence this assault on the revised date of April 22 in order to seize these areas and isolate the Japanese Eighteenth Army to the east. The task force had as its primary mission destruction or containment of Japanese naval forces that might try to interfere and a secondary mission of providing air support for the landings. Another task force (78) would support the Aitape landings and provide close support missions at Hollandia after the departure of the larger Task Force 58. General Krueger, whose Alamo Force would carry out the ground operations, had about fifty thousand troops for the total assault phase. He delegated responsibility for the landings to two task forces, code-named Reckless and Persecution; the former, under General Eichelberger, would invade Hollandia, and the latter, headed by Brigadier General Jens A. Doe, would attack Aitape.

Logistical support of the Hollandia-Aitape operation was extremely important, for this was the largest operation to date in the Southwest Pacific. Over 84,000 men would participate, of whom about 50,000 were ground combat personnel. The latter needed an average of over a ton of supplies apiece, 58,100 tons of supplies and equipment for 52,000 men. The men were to land on three separate beaches far from supply bases and they would have to rush heavy equipment for preparation of airfields. The problem of air coverage was difficult, for Hollandia lay outside the then existing range of most fighter escort planes. There were two possible solutions, to use carrier-based planes or increase the range of land-based fighter escort aircraft. Allied forces employed both solutions; carrier planes in preliminary strikes, losing twenty planes and suffering no surface ship damage, destroyed almost 150 Japanese planes, two enemy destroyers, and numerous auxiliary craft, while the U.S. Army Air Force increased the range of P-38's by installing leading-edge tanks in the wings. Raids on Hollandia itself, between March 30 and April 16, resulted in virtual elimination of its air strength, for the Japanese lost over three hundred aircraft and after April 6 had only twenty-five serviceable aircraft in the region.

After rendezvousing northwest of the Admiralties, the forces began three simultaneous landings on April 22. Forces landing at Humboldt Bay and Tanahmerah Bay at the other end of the bulge planned a pincers movement to converge on the Sentani Lake plain and secure the Hollandia airfields. The third assault was at Aitape. Under light and easily silenced fire, troops landed on Tanahmerah Bay to find im-

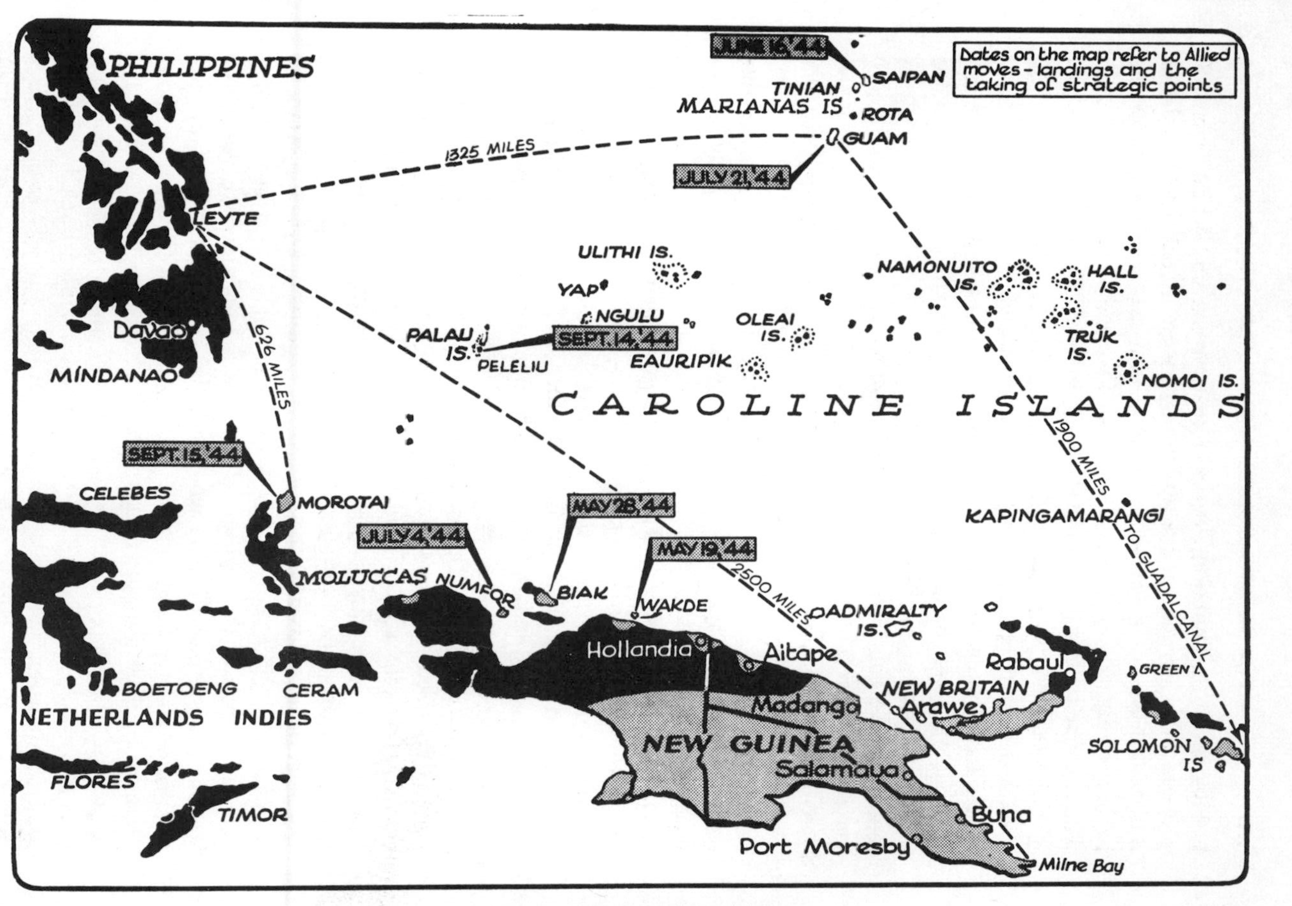

TOWARD THE PHILIPPINES

possible swampy conditions behind and between the landing beaches. The unloaded portions of the attack force were diverted to Humboldt Bay, and those already on shore began a hard march inland, hampered by heavy rain, sporadic forays with the Japanese, and a narrow trail. They reached the westernmost airfields by April 26 and seized them with little difficulty.

At Humboldt Bay the invaders effected complete surprise and then encountered mangrove swamps and heavy rain as they pushed inland. On reaching Lake Sentani, they used LVT's (amphibian tractors) for inland amphibious movements which took key points on the plain. A lone Japanese bomber made a lucky hit which destroyed more than 60 percent of the rations and ammunition landed the first two days. However, by April 26 the Humboldt force had secured its main objectives. Instead of fighting it out, some seven thousand Japanese troops started a jungle trek of 125 miles west toward Wakde-Sarmi; starvation, disease, and battle wounds proved insurmountable, and only about 7 percent reached their goal.

Total Japanese losses at Hollandia were extremely high; of eleven thousand Japanese in the area probably fewer than one thousand, including prisoners, survived the war. The Japanese high command in the area had anticipated an attack farther east, and was unprepared. Hollandia lay beyond the new defense line which the Japanese had been forced to set up as a result of Allied advances, and once the Japanese lost air strength in the area they could not and would not replace it. The disastrous losses also produced a change in command, and the commanding officer who faced the Allied invasion forces had been in Hollandia only ten days before the attacks. Japanese naval forces declined to risk the effort to relieve the garrisons.

These factors also affected the Aitape landings. One force landed in the wrong place, but by this accident found the best beach in the locality. Surprised, the enemy fled into the jungle, and with the loss of two men killed and thirteen wounded, the Americans seized the two air strips. The fighter strip went into operation on April 28, but poor drainage made it virtually useless. The bomber strip was not ready for fighter and transport plane use until May 27 and was not available for bombers until early July. Rightly expecting counterattack by the bypassed Japanese Eighteenth Army, the Americans sent in additional troops and awaited the attack, which began July 10. Heavy jungle fighting continued until General Krueger on August 25 declared the operations over. By that time the Japanese Army had ceased to be a threat to the Allies.

Difficult though this fighting had been, it was not vital to the conduct of the war. Other forces under MacArthur had been continuing their advance while the desperate engagements were taking place, and the bases near Aitape were hardly worth the cost. On the other hand, this campaign must be counted a success in the war of attrition against the enemy.

Two hundred miles northwest of Hollandia is huge Geelvink Bay, 200 miles deep into the island and 250 miles across. Numerous islands at its opening are large enough for air installations, and on one, Biak, the Japanese had begun such facilities in 1943. They also had built supply and air bases at Sarmi, on the northwest coast of New Guinea about 145 miles from Hollandia, and an air base on a small island, Wakde, about twenty miles from Sarmi. The Sarmi-Wakde area became attractive as a target because of its potentialities as a major air base, as a menace to Hollandia and an obstacle to the anticipated advance of the Allies. Furthermore, since the Hollandia bases already were proving unfeasible to develop, the U.S. forces viewed Wakde, Sarmi, and Biak as essential for the development of bomber facilities. Allied advance was leaving bomber bases in the Admiralties and at Nadzab behind.

After some revisions, the Allies set the attack date for Wakde at May 17, and for Biak, May 27, and dropped plans to take Sarmi.[3] The invaders took Wakde by landing first on the mainland nearby and then engaging in a shore-to-shore movement.[4] Even before the island was secure, engineers had begun repairs on the airfield and its facilities, and bombers were able to support the Biak operations. Seizure of Wakde proved to be only half the story; a substantial enemy force which had been by-passed tried unsuccessfully to dislodge the Americans in a campaign that lasted from May 19 to the first of September and resulted in heavy attrition of enemy troops. Wakde proved to be a valuable air base and staging site.

The next objective was Biak, one of the largest of the Schouten

[3] Aerial photographs showed that the ground around Sarmi was not suitable for development of airdromes for heavy bombers. Smith, *Approach to the Philippines,* p. 211.

[4] Accounts of the Wakde operation include Morison, *History,* VIII, 91–102; Craven and Cate, *The A.A.F. in World War II,* IV, 617–631; Smith, *The Approach to the Philippines,* pp. 206–231.

Islands lying astride the opening to Geelvink Bay.[5] This coral island has a rough terrain covered with dense rain forest and jungle undergrowth; aside from the mangrove swamps along the shore, there was little readily available water since the rain sank quickly through the coral. The Japanese had built or planned the construction of five air strips on the southern side of the island. There were about eleven thousand troops on the island, of whom some four thousand were combat troops, and their leaders decided not to contest the landings but make a stand in the hills overlooking the airfield, which they knew the invaders wanted. Steep hills, defiles, and deep caves aided the Japanese in their defense, and the length of time it would take to subdue them was for some time in doubt.

On May 9, 1944, the Japanese high command in the Southwest Pacific decided on a strategic withdrawal of the main line of resistance to Sorong, in the western part of the Vogelkop Peninsula, and Halmahera, in the Moluccas. Biak and Manokwari, east of the line, became strategic outposts which would hold out as long as possible without expecting reinforcements. When the attack started on Biak on May 27, Japanese Imperial Headquarters reconsidered the case of Biak. During this same period the Japanese Navy had been preparing for a great showdown with the U.S. Navy. The Japanese originally intended to stage this operation, called either Operation A or the A-Go Operation, near the Palaus, but they also thought it might occur off northern New Guinea or in the Marianas. On May 3, units of the Combined Fleet received orders to begin assembling for the A-Go Operation. The bulk of the fleet's striking power was organized into the 1st Task Force, divided into the Second Fleet of battleships, cruisers, and destroyers of the battle line, and the Third Fleet, centering about nine carriers and some five hundred planes. The First Air Fleet was also scheduled to take part in the operations; however, one of its flotillas was still in Japan without sufficient training, and the planes of the other were scattered among the Marianas, Palaus, and Carolines. The 23d Air Flotilla, at that time the only Naval Air Service Unit based in New Guinea, had only twelve fighters and six medium bombers when U.S. forces landed on Biak.

[5] For details of the Biak operation, see Craven and Cate, *The A.A.F. in World War II,* IV, 631–646; Smith, *The Approach to the Philippines,* 280–396; Eichelberger, *Our Jungle Road to Tokyo,* pp. 135–154; Morison, *History,* VIII, 103–135; Krueger, *From Down Under to Nippon,* pp. 93–105.

The attack of the U.S. Fifth Fleet on Marcus on May 20 convinced the Japanese that this fleet would advance in the Central Pacific into waters in which the Japanese would have the advantage, and the 1st Task Force assembled at the end of the Sulu Archipelago to be ready to leave on short notice. Knowing that they were meagerly prepared for the A-Go Operation, the Japanese decided not to send additional planes to western New Guinea in a gamble that the A-Go Operation would start before the Allies attacked Biak. News of the Allied attack on May 27 told them that they had lost and, concerned over the potential danger from Allied planes at Biak, the Japanese Navy made two moves. One was to send from one-third to one-half of its available naval land-based aircraft from the Central Pacific to support the 23d Air Flotilla. Just how many planes reached the Vogelkop Peninsula is not clear, but it appears that many of the pilots became ill with malaria and other tropical diseases and were of little help. The Navy's second step was to try to hold Biak by sending to it the Army's 2d Amphibious Brigade from the Philippines in an effort called Operation KON. Ships were detailed from the A-Go Operation to transport the brigade to its destination. Finding that they had been sighted, and receiving an erroneous report that there was a large Allied naval force lying off Biak, the Japanese turned back and called off the KON operation. When they discovered, probably through aerial reconnaissance, that there was no large fleet at Biak, they decided on a second KON operation, in which four destroyers, carrying about two hundred infantrymen apiece and towing barges carrying from thirty to fifty men each, tried to make the run in alone. Allied planes broke up the attempt, and only about a hundred men landed on the island. Despite two failures, the Japanese planned a third KON operation, which included a heavy striking force as well as transports. On June 11 and 12, the U.S. Fifth Air Force made heavy attacks on Japanese positions in the Marianas, and, convinced that the Allies were about to invade the Marianas, the Japanese called off the third KON operation. After dropping this operation, the Japanese were able to slip about eleven hundred men on barges from Manokwari by way of Noemfoor past Allied patrols to Biak.

Meanwhile, the Americans were having their difficulties on Biak. Advance was so slow that one general was relieved of his command, as the Japanese retired to caves and other strong points and desperately resisted attack. It was not until two months after the initial landings that the invaders made the island secure. The hard-won victory was a notable Allied advance, for Biak proved to be a valuable air and logistical base.

The next target was Noemfoor Island, about halfway from Biak to the Japanese base at Manokwari, at the northeastern end of Vogelkop Peninsula.[6] Noemfoor had been used by the Japanese as a staging base and had three completed or partly completed airfields, which the Allies hoped quickly to rehabilitate. Elements of the Alamo Force made the invasion, which began on July 2 and in many ways resembled the attack on Biak. There were variations; on the day after the initial landings, which had placed seven thousand men ashore, paratroopers began landing on one of the narrow airfields which ground forces had already seized. After the parachutists had suffered from 8 to 10 percent casualties from low drops or poor plane formation, the regimental commander secured permission to have the remainder of his men taken in by sea. The attackers seized the important objectives by July 5 and reduced significant opposition by the tenth, although it took until the end of August to complete mopping-up operations. In the process the Allies became aware of the inhuman treatment the Japanese had accorded the Javanese slave laborers and Formosan work troops whom they had transported to this island. Only about four hundred of the three thousand or more Javanese men, women, and children survived their terrifying ordeal. Development of Allied airfields on Noemfoor Island shortened the range of air strikes on the last major objective in New Guinea, Japanese air bases on Vogelkop Peninsula.[7]

In this instance, the Allied planners decided not to attack Japanese installations, but to seize relatively undefended positions and develop their own airfields. Careful planning coupled with lack of enemy resistance resulted in a successful landing midway between the main Japanese bases on the peninsula. Construction of airfields for medium bombers proceeded on schedule; one strip was ready for use on August 17 and another was operational on September 3. The Japanese did

[6] The Noemfoor operation is described in Craven and Cate, *The A.A.F. in World War II,* IV, 652–661; Smith, *The Approach to the Philippines,* pp. 397–424; Krueger, *From Down Under to Nippon,* pp. 106–113; Morison, *History,* VIII, 134–140.

[7] For accounts of the operations on Vogelkop Peninsula, see Smith, *The Approach to the Philippines,* pp. 425–449; Craven and Cate, *The A.A.F. in World War II,* IV, 661–670; Morison, *History,* VIII, 140–144; Krueger, *From Down Under to Nippon,* pp. 114–121.

not counterattack, and the only conflicts resulted from patrolling encounters. The Japanese were reduced to ineffectiveness on the peninsula, although they eked out an existence until the end of the war. With their achievement, the Allies had ended the long trek along the north coast of New Guinea and they made ready for the next moves toward the Philippines.

Before General MacArthur's forces had started their last jump in New Guinea, those of Admiral Nimitz had begun their move into the Marianas. The important southernmost island in this string of fifteen islands is Guam, lying about 250 miles north of the Carolines, and the chain extends over 400 miles farther north to Farallon de Pajaros, which is 350 miles south of Iwo Jima. The four largest islands, Saipan, Tinian, Rota, and Guam, lie farthest south in the group. The United States had acquired Guam as a result of the Spanish-American War, and shortly thereafter Germany had bought the remaining islands from Spain, only to lose them to Japan in World War I. By the outbreak of World War II, the Japanese outnumbered the natives by two to one and had greatly expanded the sugar industry begun by Spain and Germany. As we have seen, shortly after the war started, Japanese forces seized Guam.[8]

Then as the war progressed and U.S. forces came within range, they initiated strikes at the Marianas. The first came on February 23, 1944, and for once aviators inflicted more damage than they reported. Locating airfields whose existence they only suspected, they destroyed 168 Japanese planes and also sank two freighters and numerous small craft. In the next few days U.S. submarines exacted heavy toll from surface craft trying to escape air search.[9] This combined effort of Allied planes and submarines proved effective on numerous occasions in the Pacific war. During March, 1944, land-based aircraft replaced Task Force 58 in the harassment of the Marianas and the Carolines, as bombers from New Guinea, Bougainville, the Marshalls, and other recently acquired Allied bases made coordinated night raids.[10]

On March 12, 1944, the Joint Chiefs of Staff decided to invade the southern Marianas. As indicated earlier, the Navy wanted to establish advance bases on Guam and Saipan, and the U.S. Army Air Force

[8] O. R. Lodge, *The Recapture of Guam* (Marine Corps Monographs [12]) ([Washington] 1954), pp. 7–8.

[9] Morison, *History,* VIII, 154–155.

[10] Craven and Cate, *The A.A.F. in World War II,* IV, 676–683.

desired a base for B-29 operations against Japan. Conquest of the islands might confuse Japanese defense plans, for the Allies could move from them against the Palaus, the Philippines, Formosa, or through the Bonins toward Japan itself. Also, for sentimental reasons, since the American flag had flown over Guam and its citizens were loyal to this country, military leaders wished to regain this island.

The Marianas operation was the most ambitious yet attempted in the Pacific. It involved using some 535 vessels to transport 127,571 troops for assault landings more than a thousand miles from the nearest advance base, Eniwetok, and about 3,500 miles from Pearl Harbor. It should also be remembered that this great venture in the Pacific came during the same month as the Normandy invasion.

The leaders were no novices. Under Admiral Nimitz, who had overall command, was Vice Admiral Raymond A. Spruance, commander of the Fifth Fleet. Under him were such figures as Admiral Richmond K. Turner, in command of the Joint Expeditionary Force, and Lieutenant General Holland M. Smith, in charge of tactical command of all troops ashore. There were 66,779 assault troops assigned to seize Saipan and Tinian and 39,080 to take Guam. Primarily, the larger, the Northern Attack Force, was made up of two reinforced Marine divisions and a provisional Marine brigade composed of two regimental combat teams. Three experienced divisions were to invade Saipan, the 2d and 4th Marine Divisions and the 27th Infantry. The 3d Marine Division and other Marine units would take Guam, and the 77th Infantry Division, still in the United States, was designated Area Reserve. The Northern Attack Force assembled in Hawaii; the Southern Attack Force assembled in Guadalcanal; the combined forces staged through the Marshalls and headed for the Marianas, hearing on the way of the Normandy landings.[11]

By the time of the Marianas campaign the techniques of amphibious assault had developed greatly. Vastly improved air and submarine photography provided accurate information on beach conditions. Underwater demolition teams made close prelanding reconnaissance and prepared for destruction of underwater obstacles. Nevertheless, the Marianas presented a combination of hazards to the invader. They were large enough for defense in depth, had elevations for artillery

[11] Morison, *History,* VIII, 157–169; Philip A. Crowl, *Campaign in the Marianas* (*United States Army in World War II: The War in the Pacific*) (Washington, 1960), pp. 33–52.

sites and coral caves for protection. Preattack intelligence underestimated the number of defenders by about one-half. The 32,000 troops on Saipan, however, were not so well equipped as they wished as a result of U.S. submarine depredations on enemy shipping. Also, not realizing until 1944 that Saipan was in danger, the Japanese had done little to prepare defenses and apparently had no plan beyond the intention of destroying the invaders on the beaches.

Preliminary pounding of the objectives and surrounding Japanese bases had aleady begun;[12] the powerful Task Force 58 moved ahead of the invading armada, and planes from its fifteen carriers began a series of air strikes. Battleships approached and carried on heavy bombardment of Tinian and Saipan.[13] Although the preliminary blasting of Saipan was heavy, it was not enough, and the Japanese were waiting, not only near the shore but with carefully located and directed artillery. Nevertheless, although encountering severe fire and suffering heavy casualties, over eight thousand men landed within twenty minutes. Amphibious tractors failed in their assignment, and at the end of the first day, June 15, casualties had been high, and men and supplies were pinned to the water's edge.

During the next few days the landing force increased to about twenty thousand troops, over two thousand of whom were killed or wounded. Early on the sixteenth, Admiral Spruance received information from a submarine that Japanese naval forces were headed for the Marianas, and he reasoned that a naval battle was imminent. He canceled the attack on Guam, scheduled for the eighteenth, and after a conference with Admiral Turner and General Holland M. Smith, decided to commit the reserve, the 27th Division, immediately and use the Guam Attack Force as a floating reserve for Saipan if necessary. He then set about deploying his vessels to prepare for the naval battle and at the same time provide cover for the forces on Saipan. On that island during the night of the sixteenth, the Japanese launched a fierce counterattack of forty-four tanks. By dawn U.S. ground forces had disabled all but one, and, directed by a naval liaison officer, a destroyer obliter-

[12] Craven and Cate, *The A.A.F. in World War II,* IV, 676–690.

[13] For accounts of the Saipan operation, see Crowl, *Campaign in the Marianas,* pp. 71–266; Morison, *History,* VIII, 170–212, 322–350; Jeter A. Isely and Philip A. Crowl, *The U.S. Marines and Amphibious War: Its Theory and Its Practice in the Pacific* (Princeton, 1951), pp. 319–351; Carl W. Hoffman, *Saipan: The Beginning of the End* (Marine Corps Monographs [6]) ([Washington] 1950), *passim.*

ated the remaining tank with five-inch gunfire. The landing of artillery and tanks made it clear that the Japanese had failed to stop the Americans at the beaches.

Since October, 1943, Imperial Headquarters had determined to throw the full strength of the Japanese Fleet against the U.S. Pacific Fleet when the opportunity came to destroy it at one blow. By May, 1944, the high command felt that the propitious moment was approaching and issued orders for Operation A-Go, the purpose of which was to lure U.S. forces south into battle. By the middle of May, a sizable striking force arrived at Tawitawi, at the southwestern end of the Sulu Archipelago, near an oil supply but without an airfield and vulnerable in its approaches to submarine attacks. In addition to deploying this mobile naval force, the Japanese located 540 aircraft in the Southwest Pacific and counted heavily on land-based planes for support in the anticipated battle.[14] As we have seen, the Japanese weakened air defenses of the Marianas by trying to stop the Allied assault on Biak. Then, after incurring numerous sinkings of cargo vessels and destroyers by U.S. submarines and hearing of the attack on Saipan, the Mobile Fleet left Tawitawi and headed for the Philippine Sea to meet an augmented KON Force which had turned back from the effort to reinforce Biak.

On June 15, Admiral S. Toyoda placed Operation A-Go in action and ordered the fleet to strike enemy naval forces in the Marianas area. Sailing through the archipelago, the fleet was east of the Philippines on June 18. Although his force was inferior except for cruisers, Vice Admiral J. Ozawa felt confident of victory. He planned to fight within reach of land-based planes, his carrier planes had greater range than American naval aircraft for they were without armor or self-sealing fueling tanks, and the Admiral had the wind advantage for launching and recovering planes. Unfortunately for Ozawa, Japanese land-based planes had suffered heavy attrition, and Japanese carrier aviators were poorly trained. By 1944, the United States training program was placing aboard carriers pilots with at least two years' training experience in contrast to their Japanese counterparts, who had only two or three

[14] For accounts of the Battle of the Philippine Sea, see Morison, *History,* VIII, 213–321; E. B. Potter and Chester W. Nimitz (ed.), *The Great Sea War: The Story of Naval Action in World War II* (Englewood Cliffs, N.J., 1960), pp. 355–360; A. R. Buchanan (ed.), *The Navy's Air War: A Mission Completed* (New York and London [1946]), pp. 208–214.

months' flying experience and who were especially deficient in the use of radar.

Although he knew of the Mobile Fleet's departure from Tawitawi, Admiral Spruance carried out planned strikes against Iwo and Chichi-jima to the northwest. Then came a tense period in which each opponent sought to locate the other first. Spruance rejected an opportunity for a night surface engagement with a segment of the Japanese force. On the other hand, the Japanese discovered the U.S. main force June 18 but determined to delay attacking until the next day.

Meanwhile, the four U.S. carrier groups had rendezvoused around noon on the eighteenth. Spruance felt a dual obligation, to engage the enemy but also to protect the invading forces on Saipan, and the latter was his primary responsibility. Consequently, he issued orders to sail westward by day and eastward by night, to avoid being drawn too far away from Saipan.

The battle began shortly after 6 A.M. on June 19 when a Japanese plane eluded picket ships but failed in a bombing effort and was shot down. Between 10:00 A.M. and 2:30 P.M., the Japanese made four major attacks on the U.S. forces. The result has been called the "Marianas Turkey Shoot." Of the 69 planes sent in the first raid, 42 were shot down. On the second raid, the Japanese lost 97 out of 128 planes. Most of the participants in the third raid missed their objective and 40 out of 47 returned. In the last effort the enemy lost 73 out of 82 planes. In a single day in this "Battle of the Philippine Sea" Admiral Ozawa lost over half his planes. Meanwhile, U.S. carrier bombers blasted airfields on Guam to prevent their use and destroyed land-based planes. In the engagements of the day U.S. forces lost 29 planes in contrast to a Japanese total of about 315 land- and carrier-based planes. U.S. fighter direction was excellent, deck crews performed their functions admirably, and aviators exhibited superb training and courage. While the "Turkey Shoot" went on, U.S. submarines sank two Japanese carriers. The one flaw in American performance was failure to send out search planes, and as a result Admiral Spruance lost contact with the enemy fleet until the following afternoon. At that time, Vice Admiral Marc A. Mitscher, who was in tactical command, determined to strike again at the enemy even though U.S. planes would have to return to their carriers after dark. Two hundred and sixteen fighters, dive bombers, and torpedo bombers set out and 275 or 300 miles from their carriers encountered the enemy at about six-thirty in the evening. They sank a carrier, *Hiyo,* and exacted more toll from Japanese aircraft.

The day had been one of the most glorious in naval aviation's history; the night was one of its most hectic. Most planes returned after dark and at the end of their gas supply. Disregarding normal precautions, Admiral Mitscher ordered all the lights on, and for about two hours planes landed on or near the carriers. Loss of planes was high, but prompt rescue efforts reduced personnel losses. The slow speed of the vessels moving eastward to pick up downed airmen helped make it possible for the Japanese Fleet to escape.

The Japanese air defeat was decisive; Japanese plane losses totaled about 476, and equally significant was the loss of some 445 aviators. American losses were 130 planes, of which 80 had gone down in the wild night landings, and 76 aviators and crewmen. In spite of this victory, Admiral Spruance was criticized for letting the Japanese Fleet get away. Spruance, however, had a primary responsibility to the forces on Saipan and he chose not to risk them by drawing away in a chase after the Japanese naval forces. Furthermore, although he let the Mobile Fleet escape he rendered it impotent in the area by destroying its air arm. American control of the sea and air around the southern Marianas contributed greatly to their conquest.

Although the Battle of the Philippine Sea isolated the Japanese forces on Saipan, they continued their bitter resistance. Such place names as Death Valley and Purple Heart Ridge which parts of the island soon acquired indicate the intensity of the struggle. In the heat of the effort to force the Japanese back, Marine Lieutenant General Holland M. Smith relieved Army Major General Ralph Smith of his command and in so doing precipitated an interservice wrangle that did not terminate with the conquest of the island. Basically, the Marine Corps General acted because of his belief in the relatively poor performance of the 27th Division; he was a hard taskmaster who achieved his results by demanding what often appeared to be the impossible.[15]

Gradually, the invaders gained the higher elevations on the island and then slowly beat down the enemy. A Japanese counteroffensive broke through the U.S. lines and probably contributed to ultimate defeat, for the banzai rushes were costly to Japanese manpower. To-

[15] Hoffman, *Saipan,* pp. 45–166; Morison, *History,* VIII, 332–333; Crowl, *Campaign in the Marianas,* pp. 190–201; Isely and Crowl, *The U.S. Marines and Amphibious War,* pp. 342–347.

ward the end of the campaign, the Japanese military leaders committed suicide, and hundreds of Japanese soldiers and even civilians, including women and children, also killed themselves rather than surrender. In all nearly 24,000 Japanese died on Saipan. American forces had control of the island by July 9, and had lost almost 3,500 killed or missing in action, and more than 13,000 wounded.

There remained the conquest of Tinian and Guam. The invaders of Tinian profited by the knowledge that preliminary bombardment of Saipan had been inadequate. Ships and planes carefully and deliberately blasted enemy positions on Tinian, which was only three and a half miles from Saipan. A shore-to-shore approach was also carefully planned and effectively carried out on July 25. The first day's battle against a determined Japanese counteroffensive virtually determined the issue, although it took hard fighting for more than a week to bring the island under control. An innovation in the fighting was the jettisoning from fighter planes of tanks containing gasoline and napalm jelly, which against certain objectives seemed more effective than regular fire bombs of thermite or white phosphorus. Japanese losses on the island outnumbered those of the invaders by about thirteen to one.[16]

After the postponement of the invasion of Guam and standing by in reserve for a time, the Guam Attack Force went to Eniwetok to await orders to move again toward their target.[17] Preliminary bombardment of Guam was unusually effective and included leaflets warning friendly Guamanians to retire to the hills for safety. Bombardment knocked the big guns out of action, but, unfortunately for the attackers, the Japanese recovered and fired mortars and other artillery.

Needing the major harbor, Apra, instead of landing elsewhere and fighting to it through the jungle, the Americans prepared to land on each side of the harbor. Underwater demolition teams with hand-placed charges removed upwards of a thousand obstacles in the way and aided the assault on July 21. The Japanese poured mortar and artillery fire but could not stop the landings. The invader established a long, shallow beachhead and then had difficulty moving inland over

[16] Descriptions of the taking of Tinian include Carl W. Hoffman, *The Seizure of Tinian* (Marine Corps Monographs [8]) ([Washington] 1951), pp. 1–143; Morison, *History,* VIII, 351–370; Isely and Crowl, *The U.S. Marines and Amphibious War,* pp. 351–371; Crowl, *Campaign in the Marianas,* pp. 269–303.

[17] For accounts of the struggle for Guam, see Lodge, *The Recapture of Guam,* pp. 37–170; Morison, *History,* VIII, 371–402; Crowl, *Campaign in the Marianas,* pp. 329–437.

rugged terrain against Japanese resistance. Casualties were heavy during the first few days. The hospital ship *Solace* arrived carrying the first whole-blood bank water-borne to a force in action, a gift of one hundred pints by the Marine garrison at Eniwetok.

The Japanese fought with determination but often wasted their efforts in wild, banzai charges. One carefully planned counterattack brought out even hospital patients in the fight to turn back the enemy. By July 29, the invaders had taken much of the area around the harbor; they still had to drive the Japanese from caves and protected places throughout the rest of the island, which was by far the largest of the group. Naval gunfire, artillery, and tanks aided Marine rifle companies, which in cases suffered 50 to 75 percent casualties. U.S. infantry patrols also assisted in the desperate work of eliminating the enemy from the central and southern parts of the island. An unusual feature of communications consisted of Navajo Indians, trained as Marines, who sent important messages in their own language, a code which the Japanese could not break. The U.S. forces still had to contend with about six thousand combat troops on the northern end of Guam. Liberating Guamanians as they advanced, the Americans brought organized resistance to an end by August 10, although garrison patrolling to round up stragglers continued throughout the remainder of the year.

The seizure of Guam ended the assault campaigns in the Marianas. They were of great significance in the Pacific war, for the loss of the Marianas made responsible Japanese military officials realize that they had also lost the war, although, as in the case of the German commanders, they continued fighting long after hope of victory had gone. A sign of the trend was the fall of the Tojo government and its replacement by one more sympathetic to a negotiated peace. The loss of the Marianas was also costly in the war of attrition, for over fifty thousand Japanese died in the effort to hold the islands.[18] More important was loss of the islands themselves. Using them as bases, U.S. forces could interdict the shipment of men and supplies to by-passed Japanese garrisons. In addition, the naval base which the Americans quickly established at Guam could support a third of the Pacific Fleet and made possible rapid further penetration of the Japanese perimeter of defense. Perhaps most important of all was the fact that by its conquest of the Marianas the United States had a base which made possible B-29 raids

[18] E. B. Potter (ed.), *The United States and World Sea Power* (Englewood Cliffs, N.J., 1955), p. 800.

directly on Japan itself. On November 24, 1944, a force of one hundred superbombers left Saipan for an attack on Tokyo,[19] and the size and number of such raids increased steadily throughout the ensuing months until two B-29's from Tinian carried atomic bombs destined for Hiroshima and Nagasaki.

Both sides learned tactical lessons from the Marianas campaigns. Once again the invasion showed the dangers of insufficient and inaccurate preinvasion bombardment, and on Guam experiences showed the hazards to ground forces of poorly directed air bombing. The Japanese also learned from experience; no longer did Japanese military leaders encourage insensate banzai charges in the belief that one Japanese soldier could carry seven Americans with him in a death charge. Instead, as Americans would learn on Iwo Jima and Okinawa, the Japanese conducted a careful defense to make the utmost use of every Japanese life and concentrated more on defense in depth with underground connections for supplies and communications.[20]

About midway between Vogelkop Peninsula and Mindanao in the southern Philippines lies Halmahera, largest of the Moluccas. By the middle of July, General MacArthur decided to by-pass Halmahera and seize Morotai immediately to the north on the thesis that to try to defeat the large garrison on Halmahera would be both time-consuming and wasteful of men and materials needed for the invasion of the Philippines. Meanwhile, Admiral Nimitz prepared for the seizure of the Palaus, Yap, and Ulithi Atoll, all roughly on a line between Guam and Morotai. Late in July, the two leaders agreed on a timetable placing the invasions of Morotai and the Palaus on the same day, September 15, 1944.[21] Attacks on Yap and Ulithi would follow early in October.

For strategic air bombing of Japanese-held positions in a wide area around the two targets new bases became important. Major air installations, in particular, developed on Biak and Owi, a tiny adjacent island, and became the outstanding Allied air base in Netherlands New Guinea.[22] Strategic air support was impressive in scope and magnitude. During August, Australian and U.S. Army Air Force planes hammered

[19] Isely and Crowl, *The U.S. Marines and Amphibious War,* p. 390.

[20] For appraisals of the Marianas campaign, see Morison, *History,* VIII, 401–402; Isely and Crowl, *The U.S. Marines and Amphibious War,* pp. 390–391; Crowl, *Campaign in the Marianas,* pp. 441–447.

[21] Smith, *The Approach to the Philippines,* p. 453.

[22] Craven and Cate, *The A.A.F. in World War II,* V, 289–293.

Japanese bases in the Netherlands East Indies south and west of Morotai. The U.S. Seventh Air Force operated from Central Pacific bases to continued neutralization of the Marshalls, Carolines, and Marianas. The Pacific Fleet, centering around fast carrier task forces, began a series of long sweeps, first against the Bonin Islands. Then air strikes moved in closer toward the targets.[23]

In the Morotai landings on September 15, the invaders met little opposition from the five hundred Japanese on the island, but encountered some of the worst landing conditions in the Pacific in their initial approaches.[24] The Japanese in contrast to their custom elsewhere showed little inclination to fight, and the island was completely under control by October 5. Poor coral, however, made Morotai a disappointment as an air base.[25]

The Palaus presented a much more formidable problem than Morotai. There were over forty thousand Japanese troops in the Palaus, and the heaviest concentration was on the largest island, Babelthuap. Defense installations were particularly strong on Peleliu and Angaur. The Japanese were isolated and doomed to exist as a by-passed stronghold or if attacked fight to the death or surrender.

The Palaus invasion was the combined effort of soldiers and Marines; about 20,000 soldiers and over 24,000 Marines made the landings. The responsibility for the operation rested on Admiral Halsey, who had become Commander, U.S. Third Fleet.[26] When the Marines hit the beaches on Peleliu on September 15, they found themselves under fire from mortars, artillery, and automatic guns which preliminary shelling had failed to destroy.[27] Suffering fifteen hundred casualties, by the second day the Marines seized their first objective, the airfield, and forced the enemy into higher ground. Fighting was all the more difficult as a result of shortage of water and the intense heat, as

[23] *Ibid.,* V, 293–306.

[24] For accounts of the Morotai operation, see Morison, *History*, XII (1958), 19–29; Smith, *The Approach to the Philippines,* pp. 480–493; Krueger, *From Down Under to Nippon,* pp. 122–132. The landing force was part of Krueger's Alamo Force, and included elements of the 31st Division.

[25] Craven and Cate, *The A.A.F. in World War II,* V, 311–314; Smith, *The Approach to the Philippines,* p. 492.

[26] For a description of the organization of forces, see *ibid.,* pp. 463–467.

[27] Accounts of the taking of Peleliu include Frank O. Hough, *The Assault on Peleliu* (Marine Corps Monographs [7] ([Washington] 1950), pp. 36–106, 109–178; Smith, *The Approach to the Philippines,* pp. 494–498, 532–575; Morison, *History,* XII, 36–43.

high as 115° Fahrenheit. Major General William H. Rupertus, heading the 1st Marine Division, immobilized by a broken ankle incurred in the rehearsals, apparently did not receive a true picture of the tremendous pressure on the assault troops and did not ask for reinforcements. The higher command, thinking that developments on Peleliu were satisfactory, launched the assault on nearby Angaur September 17.[28] The 81st Infantry Division, new to battle, met little opposition in taking the southern part of Angaur with its air facilities. The General's announcement that the island was secure must have seemed premature to the soldiers, who for a month tried to dig the Japanese from their caves in the northern part of the island. Although the Japanese ultimately went to their deaths, they had successfully occupied the attention of a regiment which might have been useful on Peleliu.

Meanwhile, the Marines on Peleliu found themselves in increasing difficulty. Fortunately, troops were available after the conquest of southern Angaur and on September 23 began to replace the exhausted Marines. The Japanese also called for reinforcements from the northern Palaus; five or six hundred arrived, too few to alter the outcome, merely enough to extend the fighting. General Rupertus had predicted that the fight would be hard and that it would be over in four days.[29] His first prediction was correct, but it took two and a half months to end Japanese resistance. Of about 13,600 Japanese killed in the Palaus, more than 11,000 died on Peleliu. The cost had been high; United States forces suffered about 9,800 casualties, including almost 1,800 dead.[30]

The Palaus engagement was one of the most sanguinary of the Pacific war.[31] Admiral Halsey recommended at the time that the islands be by-passed, but he was overruled by Admiral Nimitz on the ground that possession of the islands was necessary to the Philippines invasions. Ulithi Atoll, taken without opposition, became very useful as a fleet base. Airfields in the Palaus did not prove so valuable as anticipated. A variety of factors, including construction problems and lack of ade-

[28] For descriptions of the attack on Angaur, see Hough, *The Assault on Peleliu,* pp. 106–108; Smith, *The Approach to the Philippines,* pp. 498–531; Morison, *History,* XII, 43–47.

[29] Hough, *The Assault on Peleliu,* p. 35.

[30] Smith, *The Approach to the Philippines,* p. 573.

[31] For appraisals of the Palaus operations, see Hough, *The Assault on Peleliu,* pp. 179–183; Smith, *The Approach to the Philippines,* p. 175; Morison, *History,* XII, 46–47. Ulithi Atoll was occupied with no resistance. *Ibid.,* XII, 49.

quate gasoline storage facilities, prevented use of these fields to support the Leyte landings. Later, in the Luzon phase of the campaign in the Philippines, the Angaur base was useful as a bomber base and aircraft staging point. There is a question as to whether or not in Japanese control the Palaus could have hampered the Allied advance into the Philippines. As Nimitz, MacArthur, and the Joint Chiefs of Staff viewed the situation in 1944, the islands constituted a menace, and they acted accordingly.

CHAPTER 25

The Pacific War, November, 1944—June, 1945

IN THEIR London Conference of 1944, interested in accelerating the Pacific war, the Combined Chiefs of Staff discussed by-passing the Philippines and Palaus in order to attack Formosa and even talked of by-passing Formosa to strike directly at Kyushu but could reach no agreement.[1] When queried, General MacArthur objected strongly to by-passing the Philippines and insisted that recovery of these islands was necessary not only strategically but to redeem a moral obligation to free the Filipinos.

Although, like MacArthur, Washington planners did not think it feasible to speed up the Pacific war, they saw greater military need to seize the Palaus than to invade Mindanao. By the end of June forces were engaged in amphibious operations on Biak and Saipan. Neither Army planners nor General Marshall wished to have Allied forces in the Pacific become involved in extensive land operations on the way to Japan. Responding to MacArthur, Marshall supported a study of the possibility of by-passing the Philippines and Formosa if a direct assault on Kyushu proved feasible; he noted that by-passing did not mean abandoning and he reminded MacArthur that the principal objective was to win the war.

The Joint planners noted that two courses remained open until the Mindanao operations, scheduled for November, were definitely under-

[1] For an analysis of the planning, see Maurice Matloff, *Strategic Planning for Coalition Warfare* (*United States Army in World War II: The War Department*) (Washington, 1959), pp. 479–489.

taken. One was through the Philippines, Formosa, and Ryukyus to Kyushu and Honshu; the other was by way of the Bonins to either Kyushu or Hokkaido and then to Honshu. The first route involved seizure of large land masses, was slower, and more certain of success; the second was quicker but less sure and depended on the ability of the Navy to control both the sea and the air. Both routes depended on Germany's defeat and the neutralization of the Japanese Navy. Following the principle of flexibility established earlier, the Joint planners advocated delaying a decision on the two routes until after the Palaus operation but before deciding to go into Mindanao.

As Washington planners were becoming bolder, leaders in the Pacific were more cautious. On the fourth of July, Nimitz wrote MacArthur that he thought his concept of advancing all forces, ground, land-based air, and naval, was sound. On the eighth, General MacArthur submitted a revised plan to take the Philippines (known as Reno V). This provided for an advance from Vogelkop Peninsula through Morotai to southern Mindanao on October 25. The timetable for succeeding operations was Leyte, November 15, and Lingayen Gulf on Luzon about April 1, 1945. General Kenney objected that the air planning of Reno was inadequate and did not provide for enough bases or for enough assistance from Navy planes. The Joint planners estimated that the naval requirements of the plan would tie up most of the Pacific Fleet, eliminate an opportunity to attack Formosa, and delay operations against Japan itself for a year.

Representatives of the Pacific Ocean Area and the Southwest Pacific, meeting at Pearl Harbor early in July, agreed that scheduled operations should go ahead. Nimitz concurred with MacArthur's views that the southern Philippines would have to be taken, but he thought that if the Japanese Navy received another serious blow Luzon might be by-passed in favor of Formosa. On July 27–28, President Roosevelt met MacArthur and Nimitz in Pearl Harbor.[2] This meeting undoubtedly increased the President's understanding of the Pacific war as he heard the two military leaders amicably present their views, with frequent reference to maps of the area.

In July, the last U.S. Army division designated for the Pacific war arrived in Hawaii; this made twenty-one divisions available and was

[2] For descriptions of this meeting, see S. E. Morison, *History of United States Naval Operations in World War II* (Boston, 1958), XII, 8–10; William D. Leahy, *I Was There* (New York, London, Toronto, 1950), pp. 249–252.

the peak of Army divisional deployment to the Pacific. During August, Army and Navy planners developed their respective ideas and arguments, the former for Luzon and the latter for Formosa. On August 27, General MacArthur submitted new target dates, advancing that for Lingayen Gulf from April to February 20, 1945.[3]

A critical point in the debate was over the means for accomplishing each objective. The estimate of the troop shortage for Formosa was over 100,000, and in September, for this reason, Marshall wished to defer making a decision until the outcome of the war in Europe was clear. The Joint planners made a similar suggestion in September. Admiral King, however, argued in favor of limiting MacArthur to the central Philippines and giving the next priority to Formosa. Admiral Leahy, as a compromise, suggested increasing air bombardment and sea blockade of Japan and reoccupation of the Philippines. The Joint Strategic Survey Committee, to which the matter was referred, supported taking Formosa before Luzon, but Marshall would not agree. Unable to decide between Luzon and Formosa, the Joint Chiefs of Staff on September 8 issued a directive ordering MacArthur to carry out planned preliminary operations, including attacks on Morotai, the Talaud Islands, and Mindanao, and invade Leyte on December 20.[4] At the same time they directed Nimitz to provide fleet support and assault shipping. There would also be Army air support and aid from the China-Burma-India Theater. The Joint Chiefs of Staff then went to Quebec to confer with their British counterparts in Combined Chiefs of Staff meetings during the Octagon Conference, starting September 11.

Events in the Pacific produced significant changes in the directive of September 8. Encouraged by successful carrier air strikes in the Philippines, Yap, and the Palaus, Admiral Halsey concluded that the Japanese Air Force was practically knocked out. Always an advocate of acceleration, Halsey radioed a radical recommendation to Nimitz that the Palau, Morotai, Yap, and Mindanao operations be dropped and that the forces scheduled for these invasions as well as Task Force 38 turn immediately to an invasion of Leyte. Halsey's appraisal of

[3] Message, MacArthur to Chief of Staff, Aug. 27, 1944, cited in Matloff, *Strategic Planning,* p. 485.

[4] Message from Joint Chiefs of Staff to Nimitz and MacArthur is cited in M. Hamlin Cannon, *Leyte: The Return to the Philippines* (*United States Army in World War II: The War in the Pacific*) (Washington, 1954), p. 8.

Japanese Air Forces was greatly in error. They had not struck strongly against the carrier raids; however, they were holding back in the expectation of major landings in the Philippines. Another argument against following Halsey's recommendation was the fact that Colonel William J. Ely of the Sixth Army Engineers pointed out to MacArthur's staff that weather and soil conditions on Leyte would make it difficult to construct airfields on the island during the approaching monsoon season, and subsequent actions, consequently, would be delayed.[5] Nimitz had passed Halsey's suggestion to MacArthur, who could not receive the message since he was en route to the Morotai operation and was maintaining radio silence. General Sutherland, knowing that MacArthur would approve, felt that carriers could take the place of airfields until they were constructed. Consequently, Sutherland, acting for MacArthur, told the Joint Chiefs of Staff and Nimitz on September 14 that if Halsey's recommendation was approved he would advance the date of the Leyte landings by two months, to October 20, 1944. Nimitz felt that because of the need for an air base and fleet anchorage the Palau operation should continue; otherwise he agreed with the proposal. Reviewing the proposed revision, the Joint Chiefs of Staff in Quebec quickly responded with new instructions canceling the intermediate landings on Yap, the Talaud Islands, and Mindanao and scheduling Leyte landings with a target date of October 20, 1944.[6]

No further decisions on Pacific strategy came out of the Octagon Conference. Afterward, the Joint Chiefs of Staff and other high military officers continued to consider the question of Formosa vs. Luzon. Nimitz came to feel that capture of Formosa would not be worth the time or casualties it would take and that there was still too much Japanese air strength to make Okinawa an attractive target; Luzon, therefore, seemed to be the best objective to consider after Leyte. Accordingly, he suggested an attack on Luzon to be followed by seizure of Iwo Jima, in the Bonins, and then of Okinawa. Accepting the idea, the Joint Chiefs of Staff on October 3, 1944, issued the following directive to the two leaders of the Pacific war:

> General MacArthur will liberate Luzon, starting 20 December, and establish bases there to support further operation. Admiral Nimitz will provide

[5] Morison, *History,* XII, 13–14.
[6] Cannon, *Leyte,* p. 9.

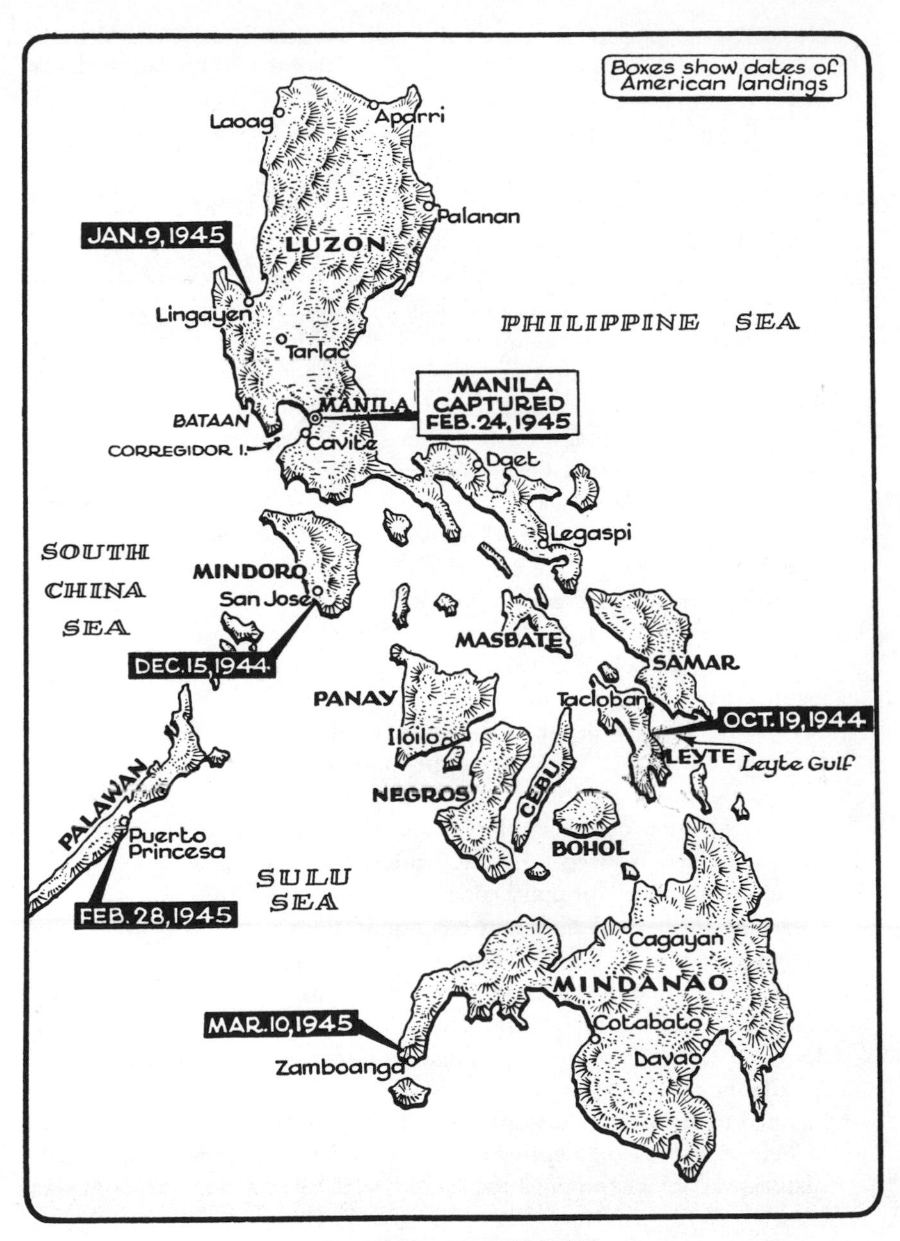

PHILIPPINES LIBERATED

fleet cover and support, occupy one or more positions in the Bonin-Volcano Island group 20 January 1945, and invade the Ryukyus, target date 1 March 1945.[7]

Leyte, one of the Visayan Islands midway in the Philippines, was a logical point of attack. Its shape, to borrow the description of a military historian, is roughly that of a molar tooth, with a crown near Samar Island to the east and roots extending southward toward Mindanao. About 115 miles in length, the island varies in width from 15 to 45 miles. The only areas of military significance are in parts of the north since the south is mountainous. Leyte Valley runs northwest from the east coast to the north shore; the main population centers were in this area, and in this region the Japanese had constructed airfields. Lying between mountains on the other side of the island, a small valley extends from the port of Ormoc only partway to the north coast. Large-scale amphibious landings were most feasible on the eastern coast since Leyte Valley was the principal objective; this coast had the advantage of easy access through Leyte Gulf, although it was exposed to heavy monsoons which periodically lashed its beaches.

Until early in 1944, the Japanese had exercised relatively light control over Leyte. The United States had encouraged resistance movements on this as well as other islands in the archipelago.[8] In January, 1944, the Japanese began to patrol against the resistance forces and deal more harshly with the civilian population.

By the summer of 1944, the Japanese anticipated Allied intentions of early invasion of the Philippines and developed plans for their defense since they realized fully the strategic threat the loss of the islands would create. Their primary concern was to hold Luzon, for with this possession they could maintain communications with Malaya and the Netherlands East Indies. The Fourteenth Area Army, headed by General Tomoyuki Yamashita, was responsible for the defense of the Philippines, and under him General Sosaku Suzuki headed the Thirty-fifth Army on Leyte. Fearing that Allied gunfire would destroy permanent installations designed to stop the enemy on the beaches, the Japanese planned to delay and cause attrition among the landing troops and also to fight a defense in depth on the island itself. Japanese Air Forces planned to attack an invading force while it was still at sea, and

[7] Quoted in Morison, *History,* XII, 18.

[8] For a description of resistance activities on Leyte, see Cannon, *Leyte,* pp. 14–17.

although weakened in air strength the Navy prepared to defend the Philippines. Loss of planes in combat and diversion of others to protect Formosa made the fleet dependent on land- rather than carrier-based planes.[9]

The Leyte operation had a complicated command organization, for there were four high commands which had no common superior under the Joint Chiefs of Staff and the President.[10] General MacArthur commanded all ground forces, some air forces, and the Seventh Fleet. Admiral Nimitz was over Halsey's Third Fleet and the Seventh Air Force. General H. H. Arnold commanded the Twentieth Air Force, the B-29's, through his deputy, Major General Curtis E. LeMay, and General Stilwell was over the Fourteenth Air Force.

Under General MacArthur, Vice Admiral Thomas C. Kinkaid, Commander, Seventh Fleet, was designated Commander, Central Philippines Attack Force, and General Walter Krueger, Commanding General, Sixth Army, was made Commander, Expeditionary Forces. There were two attack forces; the northern would land at Tacloban and the southern at Dulag, both on the Leyte Gulf side of the island. Halsey's Third Fleet would cover and support the Leyte operations as follows: October 10–13 by a strike on Okinawa; October 16–20 by a strike on Leyte and nearby islands and by support of the landings on Leyte; on and after October 21 by operating in "strategic support" of the operation by destroying enemy air and naval forces threatening the Philippines area. In the Marianas operation, it will be remembered, Admiral Spruance's primary mission had been to support the amphibious operations, and after the Battle of the Philippine Sea he had not pursued the Japanese Fleet eastward. A sentence in Admiral Nimitz' plan for Leyte read as follows: "In case opportunity for destruction of major portion of enemy fleet is offered or can be created, such destruction becomes the primary task." Halsey, therefore, had two obligations, to support and cover the Leyte operations and to hunt down and destroy the enemy fleet, and he would be the judge as to which was primary.

In the force which advanced toward Leyte there were more than 700 ships, consisting of 157 combatant ships, 420 amphibious types, 84

[9] *Ibid.*, pp. 49–54.

[10] For details of planning and preparations for the Leyte operation, see *ibid.*, pp. 21–39; W. F. Craven and J. L. Cate, *The Army Air Forces in World War II* (Chicago, 1953), V, 341–355; Walter Krueger, *From Down Under to Nippon: The Story of Sixth Army in World War II* (Washington, 1953), pp. 141–144, 148–153; Morison, *History,* XII, 54–65, 74–85.

patrol, mine-sweeping, and hydrographic types, and 73 service types. There were fewer vessels than participated in the Normandy landings, but they totaled greater striking power, and this force did not include the Third Fleet with its four great task groups.

The attacking force followed the amphibious assault doctrine which with experience and size had become increasingly effective. Army and Navy air raids in September had destroyed or made inoperable some five hundred planes, or about 57 percent of the aircraft which the Japanese had in the Philippines. On September 21, carrier-based planes struck Luzon again and destroyed almost two hundred more planes. During the first half of September, an intensive naval campaign had sunk over a hundred enemy merchant vessels in waters around the central and southern Philippines.

Next, the Third Fleet began neutralization attacks on the approaches to the Philippines. On October 12, Task Force 38 lost seventy-six planes in a raid on Formosa, but it accounted for about 280 enemy aircraft, roughly half the island's air strength. On October 13 and 14, two U.S. cruisers were badly damaged off Formosa. While having them towed to safety, Halsey decided to use them as bait to draw out the enemy and had them send out distress signals. The Japanese rose to the lure, sent out cruisers and destroyers, and then quickly retired them when their search planes discovered two U.S. task groups lying in wait. The burden of air tactical support of the Leyte landings was on the carriers of the Seventh Fleet; as soon as Halsey's ruse failed, he planned to dispatch his forces alternately to Ulithi to rest and prepare to aid in the Leyte operation.[11]

The first landings in the Leyte operations came on small islands guarding the entrance to Leyte Gulf when, on the night of October 17–18, a battalion established navigation lights to guide the armada.[12] Mine sweepers and underwater demolition teams discovered no man-made obstacles in the path. On the night of October 19–20, the American forces were in Leyte Gulf and began shelling the coastline; the next morning ships and planes resumed the preliminary bombardment.

The actual landings on two beaches near Tacloban began at ten in the morning. The Japanese let the first five waves land and then opened

[11] Third Fleet activities are described in *ibid.,* XII, 86–109.

[12] Descriptions of the landings and establishment of beachheads on Leyte include Cannon, *Leyte,* pp. 54–123; Krueger, *From Down Under to Nippon,* pp. 156–167; Morison, *History,* XII, 117–156.

fire. Casualties and destruction of landing craft delayed but did not stop movement to the beaches. By the end of the day the invaders had secured Tacloban air strip on the Cataisan Peninsula, Hill 522 overlooking the valley, and were threatening the airfield at Dulag. Although hampered by enemy fire and beach congestion, they had landed over 100,000 tons of supplies. The Japanese left forces to fight a delaying action and retired to defenses in depth. They had been warned of the landings; however, they did not know the exact time or place. Consequently, on Leyte only the local forces were present to contest the initial landings.

As soon as they heard that Allied forces were approaching Leyte, Japanese leaders put a plan (Sho-Go or Sho-1 operation) into effect. In general the plan was as follows: The Japanese Northern Force would decoy Halsey's Third Fleet north out of the way. The Central Force going through San Bernardino Strait and another going through Surigao Strait would complete a pincers movement on the amphibious and fire support ships off Leyte and destroy them. Receiving word of the approach of Japanese naval vessels, the fire-supporting group of the U.S. Seventh Fleet advanced to the southern end of Leyte Gulf and formed a battle line to challenge any effort to force Surigao Strait. The escort carriers of the Seventh Fleet cruised in three groups off the entrance to Leyte Gulf.

On October 23, two U.S. submarines sighted the Japanese Central Force on its way from North Borneo to the Philippines, sank two cruisers, including the force flagship, and seriously damaged another; moreover, they reported their contacts, and Admiral Halsey found the location of this force, whose position had been unknown since it had left Lingga Roads, near Singapore. Word came also concerning the Japanese Southern Force, and only the Northern Force had been undetected.

Three of the task groups in Task Force 38 were northeast of Samar on the twenty-third, and a fourth was headed toward Ulithi for replenishment, when a search plane sighted the Japanese Center Force and was seen by it. Admiral Halsey received information of this sighting within ten minutes and acted promptly, by-passing Admiral Mitscher and issuing orders directly to group commanders. Since San Bernardino Strait was undoubtedly mined, it was not practical to send ships through it to meet the enemy, and Halsey determined on an air attack. Recalling the group headed for Ulithi, he deployed the groups for the Battle of the Sibuyan Sea, the first of a series of engagements known collectively as the Battle for Leyte Gulf.[13]

Before the U.S. carriers got their strikes under way, land-based Japanese aircraft struck first in three separate attacks on Group 3. In general, American aircraft presented a strong defense and inflicted heavy blows on the enemy. One Japanese glide bomber, however, slipped through and so badly bombed the light carrier *Princeton* that it had to be sunk the next day. Meanwhile, U.S. carrier planes located Center Force and launched the Battle of the Sibuyan Sea, during which they made 259 sorties against the enemy. The huge battleship *Mushashi* took nineteen torpedo and seventeen bomb hits before sinking, and a heavy cruiser was forced to return to base in North Borneo. Other ships received damage but not enough to lessen speed or the ability to fight. By delaying to permit land-based planes from Luzon to attack U.S. carriers, the commander of the force did throw Sho-1 off its rather tight schedule.

The Northern Attack Force on its way south to act as a decoy on October 24 sent an air strike against Task Group 38.3; it was unsuccessful, and the planes went to bases in Luzon instead of returning to the carriers. Later in the afternoon an American plane sighted the Northern Attack Force. Admiral Halsey explained his reactions in a message to Admiral Nimitz and MacArthur sent on the night of October 25:

> Searches by my carrier planes revealed the presence of the Northern carrier force on the afternoon of 24 October, which completed the picture of all enemy naval forces. As it seemed childish to me to guard statically San Bernardino Strait, I concentrated TF38 during the night and steamed north to attack the Northern Force at Dawn. I believed that the Center Force had been so heavily damaged in the Sibuyan Sea that it could not longer be considered a serious menace to Seventh Fleet.[14]

Halsey assumed that by heading north he was chasing the more powerful of the two Japanese naval forces; in reality, by his action he permitted the stronger, the Center Force, to move unseen and unchal-

[13] For details of the Battle for Leyte Gulf, see *ibid.*, XII, 159–338; A. R. Buchanan (ed.), *The Navy's Air War: A Mission Completed* (New York [1946]), pp. 236–252; E. B. Potter and Chester W. Nimitz (ed.), *The Great Sea War: The Story of Naval Action in World War II* (Englewood Cliffs, N.J., 1960), pp. 371–400.

[14] Quoted in Morison, *History*, XII, 193.

lenged through the San Bernardino Strait. Some of Halsey's force commanders were disturbed by his move, but their comments were ignored. Halsey could have left some of his naval strength behind to guard the strait; he felt, however, that he had a chance to destroy an important part of the Japanese Fleet and that he needed all his forces for the effort.

On October 24, Admiral Kinkaid, anticipating an attempted enemy night passage through Surigao Strait south of Leyte, instructed Rear Admiral J. B. Oldendorf, commander of the Seventh Fleet's Bombardment and Fire Support Groups, to prepare to check the move. Allied forces heavily overmatched the approaching Japanese, as a battle line of six battleships and a left and right flank of cruisers waited to confront the Japanese ships if they got past the PT boats and destroyers lying in wait.

The Japanese Southern Force consisted of two groups which had no tactical connection. The first arrived at about 11 P.M. on the twenty-fourth, passed by the harassing PT boats into crippling torpedo attacks by awaiting destroyers and punishing blows by the line of cruisers and battleships. Only two Japanese ships, a heavily damaged cruiser and a destroyer, were left, and they retired through the strait. The second group ran into the PT boats, could tell that the first group was in trouble, and prudently retired. As night turned into day, U.S. ships and planes gave chase and inflicted more punishment. In the Battle of Surigao Strait, Allied forces took advantage of their superior power practically to eliminate the opposition; only a heavy cruiser and five destroyers remained at the end of the battle, which was an old-time naval engagement, for aircraft entered only in the pursuit phase.

Off Samar, Task Group 77.4 consisted of sixteen escort carriers, separated into three task units, operating from thirty to fifty miles from one another. Early on the twenty-fifth, the northern unit (Taffy 3) encountered the Japanese Center Force, which had emerged undetected from San Bernardino Strait and was headed toward Leyte Gulf. The odds were hopeless; the half-dozen slow escort carriers were vulnerable and inadequately protected by three destroyers and four destroyer escorts. Nevertheless, the forces put up a desperate, courageous struggle. Rear Admiral Thomas L. Sprague, in command, launched all the planes he had to attack and attack again with whatever they had. His ships made effective use of smoke screens to try to reach the protection of a rain squall. Enemy shells began to find their mark; many went through the carriers without exploding, but one carrier, *Gambier Bay,* received two hits and sank. At about this stage of the battle one of the other carrier task units sent a concerted air attack which put two Japanese cruisers out of action. Then, facing almost certain disaster, the U.S. destroyers and destroyer escorts made an attack which cost two destroyers and a destroyer escort. In return they not only disabled a Japanese cruiser, but so disarranged the enemy battle position that Vice Admiral T. Kurita no longer could accurately determine the course of battle, and instead of forming a battle line let each ship take its own course.

Suddenly, when the small U.S. force seemed doomed to almost certain destruction, Admiral Kurita terminated the battle and after circling for a time sailed north toward San Bernardino Strait. For one of the few times in military history, naval action reports referred to divine intervention. Admiral Sprague wrote:

> The failure of the enemy main body and encircling light forces to completely wipe out all vessels of this task unit can be attributed to our successful smoke screen, our torpedo counterattack, continuous harassment of enemy by bomb, torpedo and strafing air attacks, timely maneuvers, and the definite partiality of Almighty God.[15]

Later, Admiral Kurita stated that a principal factor which caused him to terminate the battle was the belief, gained through intercepion of Allied messages, that a large force was on its way to intercept him. He was also fearful of air attack should he enter Leyte Gulf.

After Kurita's departure, the U.S. escort carriers underwent another attack, the first organized suicide, or Kamikaze, attack of the war. Disturbed by the loss of Japanese planes and pilots, Vice Admiral Takijiro Ohnishi, commander of the First Air Fleet, with headquarters in Manila, conceived or at least put into effect a desperate plan to train special suicide attack units to crash-dive on enemy craft, especially carriers. Kamikaze, the name given the units, was that of a "Divine Wind" which according to Japanese accounts intervened to protect the Emperor from a threatened Mongol invasion in 1281. The first special attack corps was formed at an airfield near Manila in October, 1944, and on October 25 it attacked the escort carriers off Samar.[16] Flying

[15] Quoted in *ibid.,* XII, 297.

[16] For a history of the Kamikazes, see Rikihei Inoguchi, Tadashi Nakajima, Roger Pineau, *The Divine Wind: Japan's Kamikaze Force in World War II* (Annapolis, 1958), *passim.*

low to keep off radar screens, the planes arrived too unexpectedly for the combat air patrol to react, and it was up to the ships themselves to avoid being hit by suicidal pilots. Some planes were shot down by antiaircraft fire, others crash-dived, as intended, on the carriers, sinking one, the *St. Lo,* and seriously damaging others. This attack was not recognized as the beginning of a new and unorthodox way of waging war, which would deal heavy blows to the Allies before the conflict was over.

The fourth major engagement of the Battle for Leyte Gulf was the Battle off Cape Engaño between Halsey's Third Fleet and the Japanese Northern Force which successfully had drawn Halsey away from San Bernardino Strait. Vice Admiral J. Ozawa, in command of the Japanese force, later said, "My chief concern was to lure your forces farther north. We expected complete destruction." They could well expect destruction, for sixty-four combatant ships were chasing nineteen, and the disparity in planes was as great. Under Admiral Mitscher's tactical direction, six carrier air strikes sank four Japanese carriers and a destroyer. Halsey wanted to send in his battleships for the kill, but he finally yielded to urgent messages to send them south to intercept Kurita's Center Force. They arrived too late, and in the meantime the remainder of the Japanese Northern Attack Force managed to reach home in safety, in spite of surface and air craft pursuing it and submarines lying in wait.

The significance of the Battle for Leyte Gulf was that it gave control of the Pacific to the Allies. After the war, Admiral M. Yonai, Japanese Navy Minister, stated, "Our defeat at Leyte was tantamount to the loss of the Philippines. When you took the Philippines, that was the end of our resources."[17]

Leyte, of course, still had to be taken after the Battle for Leyte Gulf.[18] General Yamashita sent reinforcements from other islands, especially to Ormoc on the west coast. American planes, some from New Guinea and others from limited facilities on Leyte, exacted heavy toll; Japanese postwar estimates placed losses at 80 percent of the vessels sent to Leyte, but the Japanese landed about 45,000 additional troops and 10,000 tons of supplies.

[17] Quoted in Morison, *History,* XII, 338.

[18] For details of the struggle for Leyte, see Cannon, *Leyte,* pp. 124–370; Krueger, *From Down Under to Nippon,* pp. 168–196; Craven and Cate, *The A.A.F. in World War II,* V, 368–389.

The U.S. 96th Division, given the task of securing the southern Leyte Valley, started a slow movement inland on October 21. The troops encountered strong enemy positions, had to wade through swamps and rice paddies, and laboriously evict the enemy from protected hills. A macabre incident occurred near Dagami, when in a cemetery the Japanese evicted the deceased from stone crypts or open graves and used these places as pillboxes or foxholes. Finally six flame throwers, followed by U.S. infantrymen, marched through the cemetery and qualified the enemy for permanent occupancy. By November 2, the U.S. forces had secured the southern Leyte Valley.

Farther north other American troops seized control of the strait between Leyte and Samar and then took Tacloban, the major town of the island. General MacArthur and President Sergio Osmena of the Philippine Commonwealth came ashore, and MacArthur announced the establishment of the Philippine civil government under Osmena. Stating, "I have returned," the General called on Filipinos to rally against the enemy.

U.S. forces moved inland through the northern Leyte Valley toward the north coast against a foe that delayed but could not stop their advance. After bombarding the main town, Carigara, the Americans discovered that the enemy had skillfully withdrawn from the town to more protected positions in the mountains southeastward toward Ormoc.

The Americans then launched a drive on two fronts. The first entailed hard fighting in extremely rugged terrain southeast from Carigara. The other consisted of an unopposed movement much farther south across the island and an advance up the west coast toward Ormoc. To speed up this second move, the 77th Division made an amphibious landing near Ormoc, in which on December 7 troops landed with precision and three days later took possession of the valuable port. The move divided and isolated the enemy, although hard fighting still remained. The U.S. troops slowly brought their pincers movement to bear on the Japanese forces; the two fronts joined and pushed the enemy into the northeastern mountains of the island. The condition of the Japanese became desperate as they faced defeat and experienced starvation. As general retreat began, officers encouraged the seriously wounded to commit suicide. On December 19, Japanese headquarters in Manila told General Suzuki that thereafter his Army would have to fend for itself. On the twenty-fifth, General MacArthur announced the end of organized resistance, and on the same day General Suzuki received word that the campaign was considered lost and that some of the troops would be shifted to other areas. On March 18, the General and part of his staff left Leyte in small craft, but as they sailed from one island to another in the Visayas they found the Americans in control. Almost a month later an American plane found the wanderers and with a bomb killed the General and terminated the odyssey.

There were disappointments in the campaign, one of the most important of which was the fact that the prediction of Army engineers that swampy conditions would render Leyte Valley unsatisfactory for the development of airfields proved correct. On the other side of the ledger, Americans had seized a valuable island in the heart of the Philippines against determined opposition, and the Filipinos as guides, scouts, and civilians carrying supplies or evacuating wounded had aided in their own salvation.

On October 3, 1944, the Joint Chiefs of Staff directed General MacArthur to invade Luzon on December 20, 1944.[19] To provide additional air bases for operations against Luzon, MacArthur decided on a preliminary invasion of Mindoro, a large island south of his principal objective, since its level southwestern portions seemed preferable to the swampy lowlands of hard-won Leyte. Several factors, including the Pacific Fleet's need for rest and rehabilitation, damage of four fast carriers by suicide planes, and the exasperatingly slow progress of airfield construction on Leyte, made MacArthur reluctantly postpone the attack date of Mindoro to December 15 and that of Luzon to January 9, 1945. The delay served at least one good purpose, for it enabled Army and Navy aircraft to deplete still further Japanese air strength in the area.

Sixth Army was to make the landings on Mindoro and Luzon.[20] The convoy for Mindoro left Leyte Gulf on December 15 and ran through an increasingly fiery gantlet of Kamikaze attacks as it continued toward its objective. Planes from escort carriers from Task Force 38 and from fields in Leyte intercepted and shot down many Japanese aircraft and attacked Luzon airfields. Enemy planes which eluded interception were

[19] Message, Joint Chiefs of Staff to MacArthur and Nimitz, Oct. 3, 1944, cited in Matloff, *Strategic Planning,* p. 531.

[20] Accounts of the Mindoro operation include Krueger, *From Down Under to Nippon,* pp. 199–207; Morison, *History,* XIII (1959), 17–51; Craven and Cate, *The A.A.F. in World War II,* V, 390–412.

unable to find the convoy again until landings had begun. The coastal waters were not mined, and there was little opposition on the ground; the beachhead could expect heavy air opposition, for it lay within reach of a dozen airfields on Luzon and in the Visayas. Shortly after the landings were made, Kamikazes headed for the area; most were shot down, but two made successful crashes which sank two PT boats and most of the equipment for a projected base for such craft. Work went on ashore in spite of continued attacks, and by the twenty-second or twenty-third the San José airfield was ready for use, and Army planes no longer had to fly from Leyte to protect convoys. Raids on Mindoro convoys, some of them quite damaging, continued until the Japanese found more attractive targets moving toward Luzon. New airfields constructed on Mindoro soon demonstrated their usefulness in supporting the Luzon operations as well as the occupation of the southern Philippines.

Extensive planning was necessary for the invasion of Luzon, for on December 5 Sixth Army estimated that there were about 234,000 Japanese on the island; actually, there were almost 260,000.[21] The ground forces for the invasion would be those of the Sixth Army, covered and supported by Third Fleet, Fourteenth and Twentieth Air Forces, and Allied Air Forces, Southwest Pacific Area. In summary, the operations plan called for three phases: first, an amphibious operation to seize beachheads in the Lingayen-Damortis area of Lingayen Gulf and start establishing air and base facilities; second, to attack and destroy enemy forces north of the Agno River and secure crossings of that river; third, to destroy Japanese forces in the Central Plains area and advance to capture Manila.

In preparation for the invasion, Admiral Halsey reorganized the Third Fleet into four task groups instead of three to provide a heavier screen of fighter craft.[22] From a launching point off Luzon, the task force tried a tactical innovation, now possible with the number of planes available, of setting up an umbrella of fighter aircraft over Luzon airfields to prevent the take-off of enemy planes. From December 14 to 16, the American fighters kept planes from these fields from attacking convoys. Then the weather appeared as an enemy of the

[21] Descriptions of planning for the Luzon operation include Krueger, *From Down Under to Nippon,* pp. 211–221; Morison, *History,* XIII, 6–16.

[22] For details of Halsey's operations before the Luzon landings, see *ibid.,* XIII, 52–92.

Third Fleet. Intent on carrying out his mission against the Japanese, Halsey insisted on refueling operations, which unknown to him placed part of the fleet in the path of a small but severe typhoon. On the afternoon of December 18, the storm struck with all its fury, and under the terrific battering some 146 planes were destroyed or lost overboard. Hardest hit among the ships were the destroyers, three of which went down with heavy loss of life. The disaster forced cancellation of scheduled strikes, and after a search for survivors the fleet returned to Ulithi for repairs and replenishment. On December 30, soon to be strengthened by a night fighter group, Task Force 38 started out again from Ulithi, and on January 3 and 4 made a successful strike on Japanese installations on Formosa. No Japanese planes from Formosa attacked Allied vessels in Lingayen Gulf during the next week. Several other raids completed the fleet's direct support of the Lingayen landings.

The Luzon Attack Force, which assembled in Leyte Gulf, consisted of 164 ships, ranging from battleships to LCI gunboats.[23] The two main bodies of the force tried to set up a tight cover of carrier and Army planes, but on January 4 a Kamikaze got through practically unnoticed and so effectively crashed into an escort carrier that it had to be abandoned and sunk. Suicide planes caused added damage during that day and the following and reached a peak on the sixth, with numerous successful crashes. One plunged into the navigating bridge of the battleship *New Mexico* and killed upwards of thirty persons, including the captain of the ship, a British lieutenant general, and a correspondent for *Time* magazine. During the approach to the Lingayen landings, the Australian cruiser *Australia* was hit on four separate occasions by Kamikazes, yet stayed afloat through the ordeal. The assault forces experienced attacks from not only Kamikaze pilots but also midget submarines.

On S-day (January 9), following preliminary naval and air bombardment, two corps landed abreast, XIV Corps on the right and I Corps on the left. The landings were made without initial opposition; soon, however, the division on the extreme left came under fire. The Japanese had expected landings farther north in the gulf on beaches to which they themselves had come at the outbreak of the war. The Sixth Army had gained the element of surprise by selecting an unde-

[23] For an account of the approach and landings in Lingayen Gulf, see *ibid.*, XIII, 93–136.

sirable part of the coastline, quickly seized Lingayen airfields, and by the end of the day had established a sizable beachhead. By the sixteenth, they had a beachhead about twenty miles deep and thirty miles wide. General MacArthur, who was aboard the *Boise,* called General Krueger aboard for a conference on the twelfth. MacArthur was anxious to push ahead rapidly toward Manila; Krueger wanted to await reinforcements and feared that too rapid an advance might result in a setback. Although not enthusiastic, MacArthur did not alter Krueger's plans.[24] On the seventeenth, General Headquarters sent a message to Krueger emphasizing the need for rapid seizure of Clark Field, and Krueger decided to drive ahead with his right, XIV, Corps toward this objective. Under pressure, engineers performed extraordinarily well in opening lines of communications, and although delayed by artillery fire and mine fields, the 37th Division seized Clark Field.

On the twenty-seventh, came word that from three to five hundred American prisoners of war were in a lightly guarded stockade about twenty-five miles within enemy lines. A force selected from the 6th Ranger Battalion, guided by an Alamo Scouts team, made a successful surprise approach to the stockade and withdrew with the prisoners. A roadblock established and held by Filipino guerrillas helped the relief force evade enemy attempts at interception.

With I Corps providing a strong bulwark against Japanese counterattacks, XIV Corps began its drive toward Manila. The reinforced 1st Cavalry Division fought through enemy resistance and reached the northern outskirts of the city by February 2. On the fifth it seized Santo Tomás University and released about 3,521 Allied internees. As it neared the Pasig River, the advance slowed down before strong Japanese resistance and a demolished bridge. The 37th Infantry was also having trouble with rivers whose bridges had been destroyed by the retreating enemy. Meanwhile, I Corps had encountered stubborn points of resistance, featured by dug-in tanks, artillery, and entrenched infantry. A combination of Allied artillery, air bombardment, and the dogged advance of the foot soldier gradually wore the Japanese down and produced slow progress.

On January 29, XI Corps landed on the coast of Zambales Province

[24] The operations on Luzon are described in Krueger, *From Down Under to Nippon,* pp. 221–329; Morison, *History,* XIII, 137–156, 184–210; Craven and Cate, *The A.A.F. in World War II,* V, 413–447; Robert L. Eichelberger, *Our Jungle Road to Tokyo* (New York, 1950), pp. 188–199.

and started inland on what was hoped to be part of a pincers movement against the enemy. The Japanese did not contest the landings, which proceeded without difficulty. In another amphibious operation the 11th Airborne Division landed near Nasugbu, Batangas Province, on January 31. The purpose of this landing, which was made without much difficulty, was to provide a force which would advance toward Manila from the southwest.

In the city of Manila, the Japanese forces, three-fourths of whom were naval, were cut off from retreat and refused to surrender. The result was a bitter, month-long struggle to eliminate some twenty thousand defenders. MacArthur forbade bombing the city; artillery fire and demolitions by the Japanese, however, left much of Manila in ruins. Nichols Field fell on February 12, but forces in the city held out until March 4.

While the struggle in Manila continued, other forces sought to secure Manila Bay. Capture of Corregidor was carefully planned and executed. After heavy naval and air bombardment had forced the Japanese (approximately five thousand) on the island into tunnels and caves, paratroopers landed on the high point of the island on a small parade ground and an equally small golf course. Landing forces followed on the beaches, and together they reduced the Japanese; about twenty were captured, and the remainder were either killed outright or sealed in caves or tunnels. On the small islands in the bay, U.S. forces when unable to dislodge the Japanese burned or blasted them out with oil or TNT thrown into the pits or tunnels.

Clearing Manila of sunken ships and other obstacles was a task that ranked with that of rehabilitating Cherbourg. By May 1, some 350 sunken ships had been removed, and the harbor could berth twenty-four Liberty ships at one time.

The final amphibious landing on Luzon took place on April 1, when a combat team landed on Bicol Peninsula in the southeastern part of the island. The purpose, which was accomplished with only slight opposition, was to secure San Bernardino Strait and shorten the passage from Leyte to Manila.

Of about 170,000 Japanese troops still at large after the capture of Manila, the largest segment was in the northern part under General T. Yamashita. Second largest was a group in the mountains east and northeast of Manila; among several other pockets of resistance about thirty thousand in the Zambales Mountains were troublesome to forces at the Clark Field complex. By June 30, the Sixth Army had control of the parts of Luzon which the Allies needed for the conduct of the war, although General Yamashita and about fifty thousand soldiers held out until the end of the war and then surrendered.[25] In the campaign, which lasted from January 9 to June 30, 1945, the Sixth Army had lost 8,140 killed, 29,557 wounded, and 157 missing; Allied naval losses were in excess of 2,000. The Japanese lost through battle, starvation, and disease an estimated 240,000 in addition to 7,297 captured. On July 1, 1945, control passed from the Sixth Army to the Eighth Army.[26]

On February 1, 1945, at the Yalta Conference, General Marshall and Admiral King told the Combined Chiefs of Staff that it was not the intention for major U.S. forces to be used either in "mopping-up operations" or invading Mindanao. Instead, the Joint Chiefs of Staff hoped that the "rearmed Philippine army and guerrillas" would be able to carry out these operations.[27] General MacArthur, on the other hand, wished to liberate all the Philippines, and his forces took much more than a passive role in removing Japanese control from the archipelago. The Eighth Army and the Seventh Fleet worked together in some ten amphibious actions.[28] Most of the landings were uncontested; that on Cebu was not, and mines wreaked havoc among landing craft but did not stop the landing. The invasion of Mindanao, second largest of the Philippine Islands, consisted of several landings. About 25,000 guerrillas aided materially in the campaign, led by Colonel Wendell W. Fertig, a mining engineer before the war.

[25] General Yamashita surrendered Aug. 15, 1945. Morison, *History,* XIII, 210.

[26] Krueger, *From Down Under to Nippon,* p. 318; Morison, *History,* XIII, 210.

[27] "Meeting of the Combined Chiefs of Staff, February 1, 1945," *U.S. Foreign Relations of the United States: Diplomatic Papers: The Conferences at Malta and Yalta 1945* (Washington, 1955), pp. 519–520.

[28] For details of these operations, see Morison, *History,* XIII, 213–251; Craven and Cate, *The A.A.F. in World War II,* V, 448–464; Eichelberger, *Our Jungle Road to Tokyo,* pp. 200–231.

CHAPTER 26

The Pacific War, February—June, 1945— Iwo Jima and Okinawa

IN THE Bonin, or Volcano, group about midway between the Marianas and Japan lies the tiny island, Iwo Jima. Its strategic location is its only attraction, and for that reason alone it became one of the most bitterly contested spots in the Pacific. Slightly under five miles long, the island varies in width from two and one-half miles at the northeastern portion to less than half a mile at the other end. Mount Suribachi, an extinct volcano with an elevation of 550 feet, dominates the narrow extremity and is separated from the rocky northeastern bulk of the island by a plateau covered with deep, coarse, volcanic ash. There were no good landing sites, for surf and shifting sands made movement difficult near the plateau, and elsewhere cliffs constricted the narrow beaches. Rain caught in cisterns formed the only natural source of water on a sulphurous, chaotically rocky, porous isle.

Although the Japanese had established minor military installations on Chichi Jima, another Bonin island, Iwo Jima was the only one of the group suitable for aircraft construction, and when Saipan fell the Japanese determined to convert Iwo Jima into an impregnable fortress. Rightly anticipating that they could not prevent landings on the plateau beaches, the Japanese created semi-independent defenses around Mount Suribachi and concentrated most of their efforts on the larger portion of the island. They honeycombed it with underground passageways and prepared for defense in depth with a wide variety of weapons, from casemented coast defense guns to automatic weapons in a network of pillboxes. They planned to bring heavy enfilading fire to bear on the narrow plateau, which was the logical point of invasion; they constructed their lines of defense to profit from the difficult terrain and they abandoned the idea of wild, banzai charges in favor of a determination to wait and fight from concealment. They utilized and greatly expanded natural caves and developed underground locations varying in size from small pockets to caverns capable of holding several hundred men. Their spacious command post, reached by an underground passageway, was a concrete structure whose walls were five feet through and whose roof was double that thickness. A series of circular tunnels could conceal twelve thousand troops.[1]

Iwo Jima was an essential target for the Allies; it was one island they could not afford to by-pass, for Japanese planes were using it as a staging base for damaging raids on grounded B-29's in the Marianas or for interception of the Superfortresses attacking Japan. Iwo Jima, in Allied hands, however, could make possible fighter cover for the B-29's and furnish emergency landing facilities for B-29's in distress.[2]

As we have seen, when the Lingayen Gulf invasion was postponed, the timetable for Iwo Jima was changed to February 19 and that for Okinawa to April 1, 1945.[3] Experienced leaders headed the invasion of Iwo Jima; Admiral Raymond A. Spruance, Commander, Fifth Fleet, was in over-all command; Vice Admiral Richmond K. Turner headed the Joint Expeditionary Force; Lieutenant General Holland M. Smith became Commander, Expeditionary Troops, consisting of V Amphibious Corps.[4] This corps comprised the 3d, 4th and 5th Marine Divisions and was under Major General Harry Schmidt. Vice Admiral Marc A. Mitscher's fast carrier force (TF 58) would also support the operation.

Planners carefully studied the excellent photographs of Iwo Jima furnished by planes and submarines. Intelligence reports in many ways were good, but they underestimated the number of Japanese at from 13,000 to 14,000 instead of actual totals nearing 21,000. There were

[1] Whitman S. Bartley, *Iwo Jima: Amphibious Epic* (Marine Corps Monographs [13]) ([Washington] 1954), pp. 5–18.

[2] W. F. Craven and J. L. Cate, *The Army Air Forces in World War II* (Chicago, 1953), V, 577–587; Bartley, *Iwo Jima,* pp. 19–20.

[3] S. E. Morison, *History of United States Naval Operations in World War II* (Boston, 1960), XIV, 8.

[4] For plans and preparations for the Iwo Jima operation, see *ibid.,* XIV, 5–19; Bartley, *Iwo Jima,* pp. 5–39.

important variations in the planning, which generally resembled earlier invasions; the lack of reefs around the island made possible "palletizing" much of the equipment for more effective handling. A whole-blood distribution center was in operation at Guam, and a mobile blood bank facility would move in with the forces at Iwo Jima. This unit had refrigeration and planned to maintain its supply of blood by air transport from Guam.

Iwo Jima received the longest and most intensive preinvasion bombardment of any objective in the Pacific, but instead of destroying Japanese defenses it merely caused the enemy to dig deeper underground. Regular air raids began in August, 1944, and soon they were on a daily schedule. At night Marine medium bombers tried to prevent the Japanese from repairing damage inflicted during the day. About three weeks before D-day the tempo increased to from thirty to forty attacks daily in an effort to neutralize airfields, destroy fixed gun positions, and to expose hidden defenses. Having experienced the results of insufficient preinvasion naval gunfire, General Schmidt requested ten days of such bombardment before D-day. Naval authorities believed that air bombardment of Iwo Jima would render this many days' fire unnecessary.[5] Also, as the deadline approached, the Navy found it difficult to supply all the fire support vessels needed; some were still protecting General MacArthur's forces in the Philippines,[6] and others needed repairs after incurring recent damages. After a decision to limit preinvasion gunfire to three days, the task forces arrived and on February 16 began their attack.[7] Each vessel had an assigned part of the island as its target, but a low ceiling and intense antiaircraft fire hampered the work of spotting planes.

On the seventeenth, while moving in to cover Underwater Demolition Teams, the battleship *Tennessee* and the cruiser *Pensacola* received hits from shore guns and suffered about a hundred casualties; the gunboats supporting the teams were also hard hit. In opening fire, the Japanese made one of their few blunders on Iwo Jima; apparently

[5] Jeter A. Isely and Philip A. Crowl, *The U.S. Marines and Amphibious War* (Princeton, 1951), pp. 26–35; Bartley, *Iwo Jima,* pp. 39–49; Craven and Cate, *The A.A.F. in World War II,* V, 588–590; Holland M. Smith, *Coral and Brass* (New York, 1949), pp. 243–248; Morison, *History,* XIV, 73.

[6] General Smith charged that General MacArthur held the vessels longer than necessary. Smith, *Coral and Brass,* p. 248.

[7] For details of preliminary bombardments and the landings, see Morison, *History,* XIV, 20–46; Bartley, *Iwo Jima,* pp. 39–68; Craven and Cate, *The A.A.F. in World War II,* V, 589–592.

unable to resist the attractive targets, enemy gunners violated the general instructions to lie low. Their action cost the Japanese valuable guns, for they had exposed themselves. The *Nevada, Tennessee,* and *Idaho* went to the rescue with fourteen-inch gunfire that knocked out important defense guns which could have fired on assault troops in the ensuing landings. The battleships also made it possible for the demolition teams to complete their duties and for the gunboats to withdraw under a smoke screen. For the remaining preinvasion period heavy ship and air bombardment continued, hampered part of the time by bad weather.

Early on February 19, 1945, the assault forces began a pre-H-hour bombardment of naval gunfire, rockets, and air strikes in an effort to neutralize the beaches in a rolling barrage working inland from the shore. So effective was enemy camouflage that the attackers could not know in advance of landing the extent of their neutralizing achievements.

Some 450 vessels participated in this great amphibious assault, and Marines moved into 482 amphtracs shortly before eight in the morning. At five minutes past the hour naval gunfire gave way to a last preliminary assault of seventy-two carrier-based bombers and fighters, followed by forty-eight Navy and Marine Corps planes with napalm bombs, rockets, and machine-gun fire. At half-past eight, the first wave of assault craft headed in from the line of departure four thousand yards offshore. Thirty-two minutes later, preceded by a furious barrage of naval and plane fire, the Marines hit the beaches. The neutralization of the enemy was temporarily successful, and the 4th and 5th Marine Divisions in this and succeeding waves pushed up through the loose volcanic sand. Quickly, however, the Japanese recovered and began an increasingly heavy fire from well-prepared positions which had withstood all the preliminary bombardment. Although the defensive fire inflicted casualties and produced congestion, it did not prevent the eight assault battalions from landing by ten-thirty in the morning.

Farther south along the narrow neck of the island, the 28th Marines, 5th Marine Division, made similar landings and encountered like difficulties. From protected places on Mount Suribachi, Japanese placed the invaders under heavy mortar and artillery fire, in the face of which artillery and tank divisions made their landings. The volcanic sands of the beaches, the rough terrain behind them, and the devastating fire of a determined foe made D-day a costly one for the Marines. On the

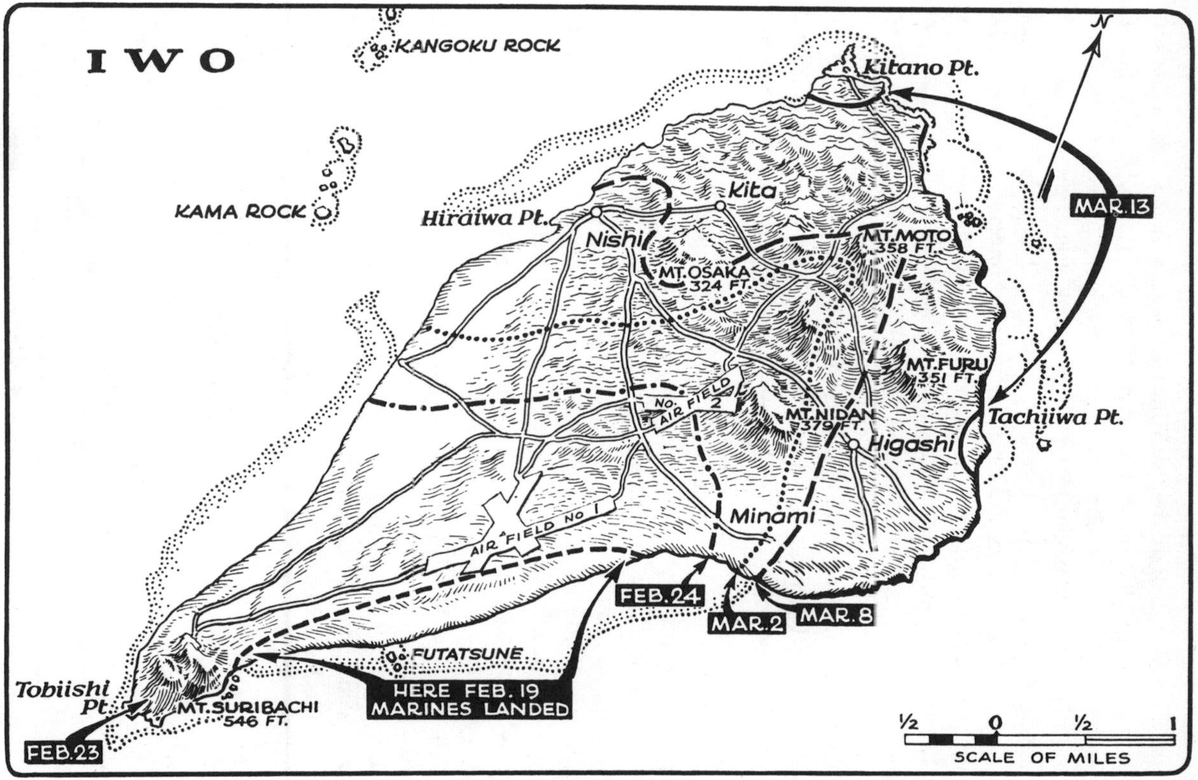

IWO
KANGOKU ROCK
KAMA ROCK
Kitano Pt.
N
MAR. 13
Kita
Hiraiwa Pt.
Nishi
MT. MOTO
358 FT.
MT. OSAKA
324 FT.
MT. FURU
351 FT.
NO. 2 AIR FIELD
MT. NIDAN
379 FT.
Tachiiwa Pt.
Higashi
Minami
AIR FIELD NO 1
FEB. 24
MAR. 2
MAR. 8
FUTATSUNE
Tobiishi Pt.
MT. SURIBACHI
546 FT.
HERE FEB. 19
MARINES LANDED
FEB. 23
½ 0 ½ 1
SCALE OF MILES

"BLOODY IWO"

first day, the Marines had pushed their way across the narrow neck of the island, although they still had to deal with by-passed pockets. They now had a dual objective, to conquer the virtually self-sufficient defenders on Mount Suribachi and reduce opposition on the rest of the island. The 28th Marines, given the first task, found enemy resistance so strong that during the forenoon of the next day they advanced a maximum of seventy yards. Until tanks could operate effectively, Marines had to move with flame throwers and explosive charges against well-concealed, protected, and lethal pillboxes. That afternoon they advanced another two hundred yards. Early the next morning, a forty-plane attack ahead of the Marines tried to soften enemy positions; tanks began to function on part of the front and aided the slow push forward. During the afternoon about fifty Japanese suicide planes sank the light carrier, *Bismarck Sea,* and damaged two other carriers and smaller surface craft.

The tortuous advance against Mount Suribachi continued; by D-plus-3-day the Marines had virtually surrounded the mountain, and about midmorning of the fourth day a small detachment followed the only possible route to the rim of the crater. At ten-twenty they raised a small flag and shortly afterward a somewhat larger flag secured from one of the naval vessels. Mr. Joe Rosenthal, an Associated Press photographer, was present, and his photograph of the second raising gave the world testimony of Marine valor. The Marines broke the resistance of the enemy remaining on the slopes and needed five days more to finish the task.[8]

The bulk of the enemy forces were on the other part of the island, whose wild surface of huge rocks, concrete fortifications, and rough hills defied mechanized approach or the heaviest bombardment.[9] In fact, aerial assault, naval gunfire, and artillery shelling merely eliminated what trails there had been and increased the volcanic rubble which blocked the invader and protected the Japanese. Inhospitable though the region and the enemy were, the Marines began to advance on a

[8] Secretary of the Navy James Forrestal was on an inspection tour and at Iwo Jima witnessed the raising of the flag. Smith, *Coral and Brass,* p. 261; James Forrestal, *The Forrestal Diaries,* edited by Walter Millis (New York, 1951), p. 30.

[9] For accounts of the ground struggle for Iwo Jima, see Bartley, *Iwo Jima,* pp. 69–210; Isely and Crowl, *The U.S. Marines and Amphibious War,* pp. 475–529; Morison, *History,* XIV, 59–75.

four-thousand-yard front. They encountered land mines, pillbox resistance, and carefully directed artillery or mortar fire. On the beaches, landing casualties and congestion increased, yet naval gunfire, aerial bombardment, and Marine pressure at the front resulted in a slow advance achieved at a cost of heavy losses.

Next came a struggle for the two completed airfields on the island, and like most of the fighting on Iwo Jima it was a strange contest in which the invaders seldom saw the enemy. Firing from concealed points, the Japanese challenged the American advance yard by yard, as they controlled numerous hills which enabled them to fire both on the front-line Marines and on the beaches. Grimly the invaders continued their costly but unrelenting advance; after heavy fighting they dislodged the enemy from elevations north of airfield Number 2 on February 27 and secured control of the air strip. It took two days more to eliminate by-passed pockets of Japanese strength.

At the end of two weeks' fighting the Marines were well enough advanced to pause for reorganization. Airfield Number 1 was taken and made operable for a Marine observation squadron and shortly afterward for air evacuation of wounded to supplement tedious and at times difficult removal by sea. A mobile blood facility was in operation on the southern end of the island, and distillation units, although they needed frequent cleaning, were providing an adequate water supply.

Although the battle was by no means won, General Smith felt that enough Marines were ashore for the task and that more would increase congestion; accordingly, he ordered the reserves to return to Guam. On the fifteenth day the Marines resumed the offensive. For the next five days forces in the north made practically no gains. Farther south the 3d Division varied the bloody routine by making a predawn assault. Although they attacked the wrong hill by mistake, they were headed in the right direction, surprised the enemy, and seized some of the strongest Japanese positions.

Gradually, the Marines brought mechanized equipment and artillery to bear on the enemy. Tanks and artillery functioned wherever possible, truck-mounted rocket launchers went into action, and air and naval support continued. One enemy strong point was Hill 362A, an escarpment honeycombed with passages and bristling with defenses; one day demolition teams blasted sixty-eight caves in its serrated sides.

Armored bulldozers in this and other regions created trails which flame tanks could follow. Then came infantrymen to wipe out the pockets of resistance. As earlier in the campaign, the enemy was seldom seen, dead or alive, for the retreating Japanese took their killed and wounded with them through the underground channels.

In the north heavy fighting took place around such places known to the participants as Hill 382, or the "Meat Grinder." Smoke screens aided withdrawals when they became necessary and covered the evacuation of wounded. Throughout the campaign loss of officers as well as enlisted men was high. In one action around Hill 382, for example, five of six officers in one company were killed or wounded, and the survivor led his force successfully through the flanking movement assigned it. Within fifteen days this company had seven commanders. As on the western front, the fight often reduced itself to combat on the platoon or small-unit level. By the end of two weeks of this type of engagement combat fatigue came to be important and coupled with loss of officers affected advance.

Progress was slow and painfully hard but it was progress. On March 8, the enemy made one of its most concerted counterattacks, which failed, although it caught the Marines off guard, and Japanese losses were high. Actually, this counterthrust was a turning point in this area, for in a great flanking movement the Marines had pressed the enemy back toward the sea. The last chapter began on March 11 with an increased speed of American advance. Five days later one of the last segments of the opposition was pushed into a small region in the northern end of the island, where, although the cause was hopeless, the Japanese fought defiantly to the end. Other final pockets resisted until eliminated; one was a force of some fifteen hundred around brigade headquarters.

By the end of the Iwo Jima campaign, most of the original Marines had been succeeded by replacements who, although fresh and strong, lacked the experience of the veterans who preceded them. This factor may have delayed but did not alter the outcome. Although a pocket of resistance still continued in the north, U.S. authorities declared the island secure March 16. The Marines made numerous efforts to induce the enemy to surrender, but propagandist leaflets and broadcasts by Japanese-speaking Americans had little effect. On March 26, the 147th Infantry arrived to assume the defense of Iwo Jima. The intensity of the earlier struggle for the island is indicated by the fact that to this date the Marines had taken only 216 prisoners. In the next two months the infantry captured 867 prisoners and killed 1,602 Japanese.[10]

The Japanese had conducted an able and determined defense of Iwo Jima. Their underground warfare with mutually supported fortifications had made each pillbox a battle. Several factors increased casualties among the invaders. The terrain was generally unsuitable for such heavy direct fire guns as the tank-mounted 75-mm. guns and the 75-mm. half-track, and artillery, air, and naval gunfire were relatively ineffective against cleverly placed and strongly fortified installations.

Throughout the campaign, problems of supply were extremely important. Marines found that steel Marston matting, designed for air strips, could be useful for traction on the beaches, and they employed armored bulldozers extensively to clear exits from beaches. As the campaign progressed, tactical air support of the ground forces improved, and throughout the campaign aerial observers were quite useful, for Marines soon noticed that enemy fire lessened when a U.S. plane was overhead. One factor working for success on Iwo Jima was close supporting arms coordination. Generally good communications made it possible for artillery, naval gunfire, and air bombardment to function well together. Walkie-talkies and other types of radio were of great value, and the small size of the island made possible rapid construction of wire communication facilities. As elsewhere in the Pacific, Navajo Indian Marines provided a baffling code for voice transmission of secret messages.[11]

The conquest of Iwo Jima cost the lives of 6,821 Americans, mostly Marines. Even before they had won the campaign, however, the assault troops saw tangible evidence of the need for the island. Less than two weeks after D-day a B-29 made an emergency landing on airfield Number 1. By the end of the war, 2,251 B-29's carrying 24,761 crewmen had landed on Iwo Jima. Even though many of these could have reached the Marianas, the saving in men, planes, and morale was significant, and the conquest of the rugged little isle was not only a heroic page in Marine Corps annals but an essential step in the Pacific war. The campaign also demonstrated that, if the need justified the losses, an amphibious assault force with control of sea and air could take any objective in the Pacific.[12]

[10] Bartley, *Iwo Jima,* pp. 190–193.
[11] *Ibid.,* p. 210.
[12] For appraisals of the Iwo Jima campaign, see Isely and Crowl, *The U.S.*

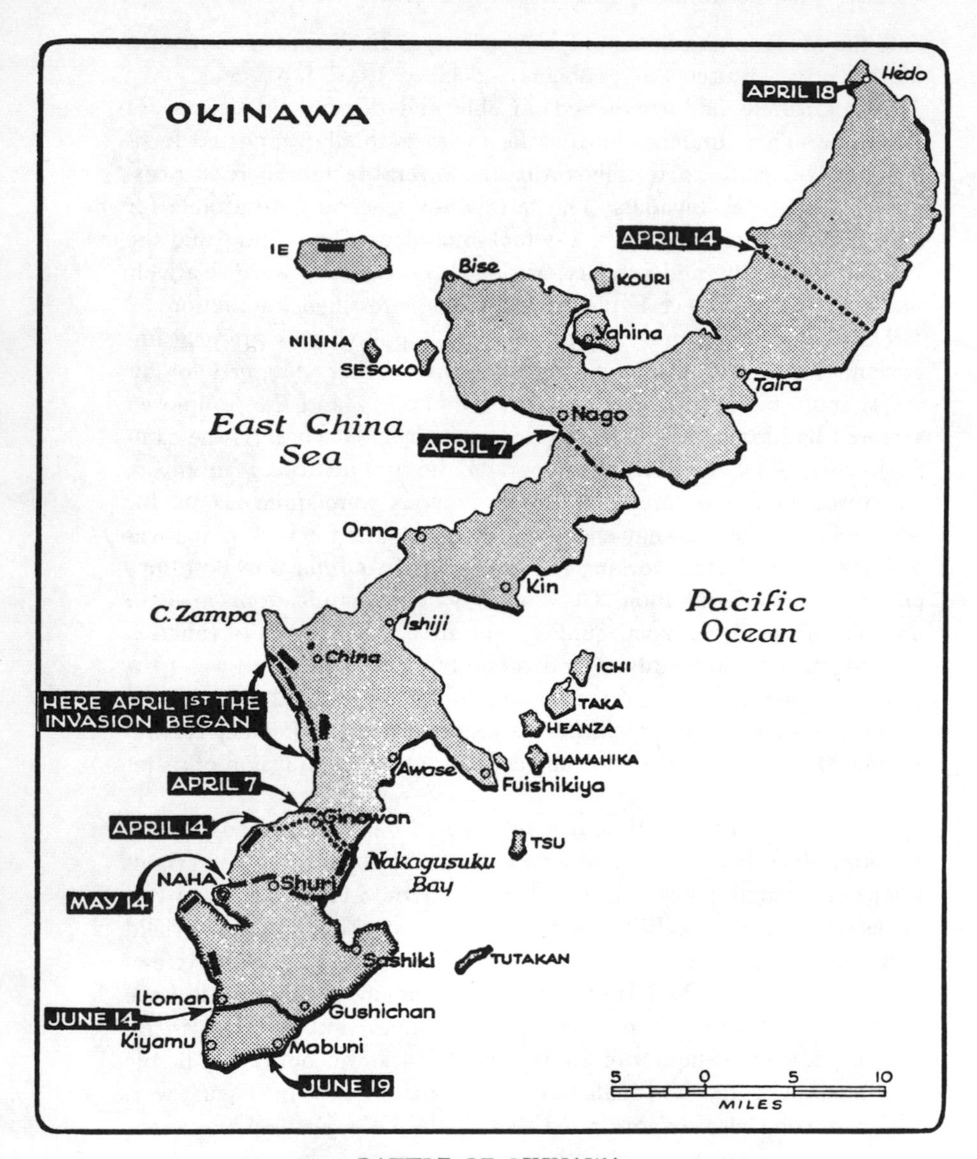

BATTLE OF OKINAWA

Okinawa is in the center of Nansei Shoto, or Ryukyus, a string of islands between Formosa and Kyushu, the most southerly of the major Japanese islands. Its possession would enable the Allies to control the East China Sea and prepare for possible assault on either the China coast or Japan itself. The military planners knew that the Japanese would defend Okinawa to their utmost and that since Okinawa was only 325 miles from southern Kyushu their effort would be substantial.

Okinawa, the largest island in the Ryukyus, is a narrow strip of land about sixty miles long, surrounded by smaller islands. Lying mainly from northeast to southwest, Okinawa is fifteen to eighteen miles wide, except for Ishikawa Isthmus, a narrow strip roughly two miles across which cuts the island into two parts, the larger being in the north. The half-million Okinawans, although controlled by Japan, were Chinese in cultural background and, generally speaking, resented but did not oppose Japanese dominance. Their young men were called to military service for the Imperial government.[13]

Lack of complete photographic information hampered Allied planning, and the campaign was half over before the invading forces had a complete map of the island.[14] They knew that the heaviest concentration of Japanese forces was in the southern portion of the island since it was less wooded and had more level area. Convinced that the Japanese would send strong air support from Kyushu, they determined that the first objective of a three-phase campaign should be the seizure of southern Okinawa and adjacent islands as the most suitable for rapid construction of port and air facilities. The second phase would be the conquest of the rest of Okinawa and of a small island, Ie Shima, off its northwest tip. Finally, the assault forces would take additional islands in the area. Subsequent developments reversed the first two and eliminated the third.[15]

The size of the Okinawa operation dictated the use of a field army.[16]

Marines and Amphibious War, pp. 529–530; Bartley, *Iwo Jima,* p. 210; Morison, *History,* XIV, 70–75; Smith, *Coral and Brass,* p. 275.

[13] Charles S. Nichols, Jr., and Henry I. Shaw, Jr., *Okinawa: Victory in the Pacific* (Marine Corps Monographs [15]) ([Washington] 1955), pp. 6–11.

[14] *Ibid.,* pp. 20–21; William F. Halsey, *Admiral Halsey's Own Story* (New York, 1947), p. 247.

[15] Nichols and Shaw, *Okinawa,* p. 23; Roy E. Appleman, James M. Burns, Russell A. Gugeler, and John Stevens, *Okinawa: The Last Battle* (*United States Army in World War II: The War in the Pacific*) (Washington, 1948), pp. 19–34.

[16] For details of the plans and preparations for the Okinawa operation, see

Lieutenant General Simon Buckner, Jr., assumed command of the Tenth Army and set up headquarters in Hawaii in September, 1944. He went to his new post from four years' command in the Alaskan Theater. The Tenth Army was a joint expeditionary force of soldiers and Marines. The XXIV Corps, headed by Major General John R. Hodge, who had fought the Japanese from Guadalcanal to Leyte, consisted of four infantry divisions. The III Amphibious Corps, under Major General Roy S. Geiger, who had led Marines at Bougainville and Guam, consisted of three Marine divisions, with an infantry division held in reserve in New Caledonia. Plans indicated landing about 172,000 combatant and 115,000 service troops in Okinawa before the end of the campaign; it was estimated that the island held about 77,000 Japanese troops.

In every way Okinawa was the largest amphibious undertaking of the Pacific war, for about 183,000 troops made ready for the assault operations. Under the strategic command of Admiral Nimitz, Admiral Raymond A. Spruance became commander of the invasion. When the amphibious phase was completed, General Buckner would assume command of forces ashore and later he would be in command of all forces in the Ryukyus, responsible to Admiral Nimitz for defense and development of bases in the area.

Preparations capitalized on past experience and differed mainly in the greatly increased size of operations. For the first time in the Pacific conflict, Allied forces would have to deal with large groups of enemy aliens, and planners not only prepared for psychological warfare to win support of Okinawans, but made ready to govern and care for the conquered people. Each combat division carried seventy thousand civilian rations, including such staples as rice, soybeans, and canned fish, as well as medical supplies. Logistical preparations for attack were necessarily extensive, and the main assembly points for men and supplies were Eniwetok, Ulithi, Saipan, and Leyte. With the exception of Leyte, whose loading facilities were inadequate, all were at least five days distant by freighter, and resupply had to come from the West Coast of the United States, over six thousand miles away.

Okinawa received its first installment of preliminary bombardment on October 10, 1944, when carrier planes of Admiral Mitscher's task force in more than thirteen hundred strikes laid waste three-fifths of

---

ibid., pp. 1–43; Nichols and Shaw, *Okinawa,* pp. 12–62. The code name for this operation was Iceberg.

Naha, the principal city, blasted military and air installations, destroyed grounded aircraft, and sank a destroyer and numerous other craft. Early in January, 1945, carrier planes hit Okinawa again, as part of a major assault on enemy aircraft on Formosa; in March, another carrier raid featured not only air bombardment but cruiser and destroyer gunfire and caused heavy damage to Japanese ships and planes. Meanwhile, Marianas-based planes had been making almost daily raids especially against shipping in the area, while submarines were also aiding materially in the interdiction campaign.[17]

On March 17, now boasting ten large and six small carriers, Task Force 58 began a heavy raid on Kyushu, the Inland Sea, and such important Japanese centers as Kobe and Hiroshima. Striking back, Japanese aircraft seriously damaged the carrier *Franklin* and other vessels, but in a five-day air battle the task force by destroying 528 enemy planes dealt a crippling blow to remaining Japanese air power and effectively checked air opposition during the first days of the Okinawa invasion. Meanwhile, B-29's had been increasing their devastating raids on Tokyo and other cities.[18] As theater commander, Admiral Nimitz exercised his right to call on the B-29's; on March 27, they struck effectively at harbors and airfields in southern Japan, and other B-29's began a mine-laying campaign designed to close the Inland Sea.[19]

U.S. leaders designated April 1, 1945, as L-day and scheduled earlier landings on Kerama Retto and Keise Shima. Kerama Retto was a group of islands ten to twenty miles west of Okinawa, which could provide suitable anchorage for a floating naval base, and Keise Shima was a small island near enough Okinawa to be used for artillery fire support of the landings.[20]

Allied invasion came as no surprise to the Japanese. Previously, the Japanese had resorted to suicidal attacks; in the Okinawa campaign self-destruction became a calculated part of tactics and even affected the strategy of defense. Lieutenant General Mitsuru Ushijima, ably assisted by an aggressive chief of staff, Lieutenant General Isamu Cho, commanded the Thirty-second Army which defended Okinawa. Two

[17] Theodore Roscoe, *United States Submarine Operations in World War II* (Annapolis, 1949), pp. 410–435.

[18] Craven and Cate, *The A.A.F. in World War II,* V, 614–632.

[19] *Ibid.,* V, 627–635.

[20] Nichols and Shaw, *Okinawa,* p. 38.

factors apparently influenced their decision not to contest the American landings; one was a healthy respect for naval gunfire and a conviction that it was impossible to prevent Allied assault troops from landing, and the other was a belief that they could destroy the invading force more easily after it moved inland. Suicide tactics would help achieve victory, for the Japanese had constructed several hundred small plywood boats equipped with depth charges to be used in a suicidal attack on enemy shipping. Also, striking from the air, Kamikazes would complete the destruction of the Allied Fleet. Then the Thirty-second Army at its leisure could annihilate the isolated assault forces by forcing them to attack strongly defended Japanese positions.[21]

On March 26, using well-tested amphibious procedures, men of the 77th Division began landings on the islands of Kerama Retto; they not only easily secured their objectives but captured and destroyed more than 350 suicide boats and effectively disrupted this phase of the enemy's defense plans. Landing forces also took Keise Shima, emplaced 155-mm. guns and began a fire on southern Okinawa that the Japanese were never able to stop. Kerama Retto served its function well as a floating naval base.[22]

U.S. leaders decided to make their assault on the Hagushi beaches on the west coast not far south of the Ishikawa Isthmus, since they offered the best prospects for landing four divisions abreast and providing full fire and logistical support. The planners also prepared for a strong feint of two divisions toward the southeastern shore.[23] Suicidal air attacks began several days before L-day and damaged half a dozen vessels. Early April 1, 1945, which happened to be both Easter and April Fool's Day, some 1,213 ships of the amphibious phase of the operation headed for the target. They escaped air attack, but Kamikazes struck at the diversionary force and drew blood from Marines not even scheduled to land.

Preliminary firing on Iwo Jima had been too brief; on Okinawa it was too long. One of the heaviest preinvasion bombardments of the Pacific war landed on an undefended and practically unoccupied Okinawan coastline. Later opinions are that much of this ammunition

[21] *Ibid.*, pp. 48–56.

[22] Accounts of the seizure of Kerama Retto and Keise Shima include *ibid.*, pp. 38–43; Appleman *et al.*, *Okinawa*, pp. 51–67; Morison, *History*, XIV, 117–129.

[23] For a description of the landings and early action on Okinawa, see Appleman *et al.*, *Okinawa*, pp. 68–137; Nichols and Shaw, *Okinawa*, pp. 63–86.

could have been used more profitably on Iwo Jima or reserved for more rewarding targets on Okinawa, but perhaps the invading forces can be excused for taking all precautions. By the end of the first day the two corps had landed about sixty thousand troops on a beachhead fifteen thousand yards long and from four to five thousand yards in depth, and the next moves were equally successful, as troops seized Yontan airfield and pushed across the narrow waist of the island against light opposition. By April 4, the Tenth Army had a beachhead fifteen miles long and from three to ten miles wide, which contained two airfields, beaches large enough to handle the great tonnage needed, and ample space for dumps and installations. As troops moved south, however, they began to encounter the real line of Japanese resistance.

On April 6, the Japanese launched one of the most extensive suicidal assaults of modern warfare. Leaving Kyushu, more than one hundred bombers and fighters set out to engage the carrier task forces, and about two hundred Kamikazes headed for the Hagushi beaches. A five-hour battle ensued in which the suicidal air fleet sank six vessels and damaged eighteen others in return for 135 Kamikaze planes destroyed. On the following day the greatest suicidal craft of them all started toward its destiny. The 69,000-ton *Yamato,* the world's largest battleship, with a covering squadron of a light cruiser and eight destroyers, left Kyushu to shell American-held beaches on Okinawa and lend support to the Kamikaze attacks. The suicidal nature of the venture is clear from the fact that the mammoth warship carried only enough fuel for a one-way trip. No more was available. U.S. submarines sighted the force within two hours after it left the harbor and notified the Fifth Fleet. Navy seaplanes tracked the squadron's progress, and at twelve-twenty on the next day two American air groups located it. In less than an hour they sank the *Yamato,* the cruiser, a destroyer, and so badly damaged another that it had to be scuttled.[24] Thus ended the Japanese surface fleet.

Having divided Okinawa with ease, the invaders decided to modify their original plans and reduce opposition in the north before turning their full strength against the Japanese Army in the south.[25] Conse-

[24] Morison, *History,* XIV, 200–209; Andrieu d'Albas, *Death of a Navy* (New York, 1957), pp. 342–348.

[25] For a description of the campaign in northern Okinawa and on Ie Shima, see Appleman *et al., Okinawa,* pp. 138–183; Nichols and Shaw, *Okinawa,* pp. 87–118.

quently, while the XXIV Corps concentrated on the Shuri defenses to the south, III Amphibious Corps advanced northward, usually against light opposition, and found coordination excellent with the naval forces along the coast. The mountainous nature of this part of the island, however, made advance tiring and complete reduction of the enemy difficult. Gunfire from the battleship *Tennessee* helped take out one of the most stubborn strongholds. Reconnaissance indicated that there were no defenses on tiny Ie Shima, which was mainly flat and coveted for use as an air base. A cautious invader, however, landed in strength; it was just as well, for some seven thousand persons were hidden on the island, and even the Okinawan women joined in a bitter six-day struggle. During the fighting a Japanese machine gunner shot and killed Ernie Pyle, one of America's most widely admired war correspondents, who had survived front-line experiences in the war in Europe.

While U.S. forces advanced to a successful conquest of northern Okinawa by the end of April, the divisions facing south came to a halt against the bulk of Japanese strength, and it became apparent that they confronted a real battle. The Japanese, using every tactic and skill developed in the long retreat across the Pacific, had taken advantage of the rougher features of the terrain to prepare and maintain defenses. Elevations which broke the generally level land were used to check advance, and around the ancient city of Shuri, inland from the modern Naha, the Japanese had created a series of defense rings which made that area the strongest Japanese position on the island.

During April, heavy fighting produced a virtual stalemate on this front.[26] Toward the end of the month, the Japanese launched a counterattack, which involved not only operations along the front but minor amphibious jumps along both coasts to place harassing forces behind the enemy. The action started on the afternoon of May 3 with Kamikaze attacks. The Japanese had been experimenting with a piloted bomb known as *Baka*, or "fool."[27] Carried near the target by a mother plane, the bomb with its live pilot attained speeds in excess of five hundred miles an hour but lacked maneuverability and usually caused little

[26] *Ibid.*, pp. 119–141.

[27] For the background of the Baka bomb, or Ohka bomb as the Japanese termed it, see Rikihei Inoguchi, Tadashi Nakajima, Roger Pineau, *The Divine Wind: Japan's Kamikaze Force in World War II* (Annapolis, 1958), pp. 140–141.

damage. On this day, however, one of them hit and seriously damaged a light mine layer. The Japanese amphibious forces were not so successful, for American troops discovered them on both coasts and cut them to pieces. After laying down a heavy barrage, the Japanese attacked along the front; they made brief gains around Tanabaru but generally failed in their counteroffensive. General Ushijima could ill afford his loss of 6,227 veterans and 59 artillery pieces, and he reorganized his army once again on a defensive basis.[28]

The U.S. force also reorganized, and General Buckner for the first time assumed direct control of operations of a two-corps front. Although heavy rains on May 7 and 8 immobilized tanks and other motorized equipment, the Tenth Army started an attack May 11. By this time the assault vessels had discharged their men and cargoes; 458 vessels had transported 193,852 men and 824,567 measurement tons of materials.[29] On the front, the III Amphibious Corps was on the right and the XXIV Corps on the left. The plan was to make an enveloping advance on both the right and the left while the center made a strong holding attack. Attrition was heavy on both sides, and the actual land gains were limited. On May 22, heavy rains began to fall, and the resultant mud made even more difficult the American advance.

The continued, though slow, American progress made Japanese leaders reappraise their situation, and they considered two possible courses of action. One was to stay and fight to the end, for they were being threatened with encirclement in an area less than a mile in diameter which was too restricted for effective use of their artillery, and they reasoned that U.S. firepower would be too great on their defenses. Consequently, General Ushijima chose to retreat toward Kiyama Peninsula, the most southerly part of the island. There such escarpments as Yaeju Dake and Yuza Dake were well equipped with natural and artificial caves large enough for the entire Japanese force. Heavy rains assisted the Thirty-second Army in its withdrawal, and holding troops checked the Americans long enough for the main force to reach the new positions.

The war of attrition, however, was beginning to go strongly against the defenders.[30] At the end of two months of fighting, U.S. forces had

[28] Nichols and Shaw, *Okinawa,* pp. 142–150.

[29] *Ibid.,* p. 172.

[30] For the struggle in southern Okinawa, see *ibid.,* pp. 176–261; Appleman *et al., Okinawa,* pp. 265–474.

killed an estimated 62,548 Japanese and had lost one man for every ten of the enemy killed, although their advance was still slow. By June 4, the enemy was established in its new defenses. Although it considered the withdrawal a success, Japanese headquarters estimated that about twenty thousand men had been lost in the move and that about thirty thousand remained for the last stand. Although the top command still remained largely intact, most of the surviving troops were untrained rear-guard personnel and Okinawans. Arms and ammunition had suffered similar attrition. The supply of hand grenades and explosives was practically gone, four-fifths of the machine guns had been lost, and the defenders had enough ammunition for only about ten days' firing of the limited artillery pieces left.

By June 11, the U.S. forces were pushing strongly against the Japanese-held ridges and escarpments. Using tanks, flame fuel, and other devices, they pressed the attack, and clearing weather made possible air bombardment and naval gunfire. Although the end was in sight, there was still fighting to do and there were still men to die. One was General Buckner, who on June 18, a few days before the end of the campaign, was killed by fragments of coral thrown up by artillery shells. General Geiger assumed command until the end of the campaign.

As inevitable defeat became apparent to Japanese soldiers, some responded to loudspeaker invitations to surrender. Others fought until killed in pockets of resistance, and still others committed suicide. Among the last were Generals Ushijima and Cho, who in the predawn hours of June 22, less than a hundred feet from unsuspecting U.S. troops, completed the prescribed rituals of hara-kiri. About seven hours later in a public ceremony, General Geiger noted the conclusion of official resistance on Okinawa. The Japanese had fought hard and with ability and they had utilized unusual and widespread suicide tactics, yet they had been able only to postpone disaster.

In the costly Okinawan campaign, the U.S. Navy had suffered its heaviest losses in history, for the enemy, mainly through Kamikaze attacks, had sunk thirty ships. None of these was larger than a destroyer, but among the 368 vessels damaged were 10 battleships, 13 fleet and escort carriers, 5 cruisers, and 67 destroyers.[31] Casualties included almost 5,000 dead and about an equal number wounded. Tenth

[31] Morison, *History,* XIV, 282; E. B. Potter (ed.), *The United States and World Sea Power* (Englewood Cliffs, N.J., 1955), p. 881. Potter gives the number of vessels sunk as thirty-six.

Army losses were greater, and of the 7,374 Americans losing their lives in the land engagements almost 3,000 were Marines. There were 31,807 wounded and 239 missing. Much higher Japanese casualties included 107,539 dead, 23,764 estimated to have been either buried by the Japanese or entombed in caves, and 10,755 who surrendered. Since these totals exceeded the armed complement on the island, Tenth Army Intelligence officers have concluded that about 42,000 Okinawans were among the casualties.[32]

The Okinawan campaign was primarily significant as a victory in the war of attrition against Japan.[33] In addition, its purpose had been to provide a last steppingstone for assault of Japan if invasion became necessary. The Joint Chiefs of Staff felt that Phase III, seizure of adjacent islands, was not necessary and aside from occupation of one small island for radar installation canceled the operation. Under adverse weather conditions, work started on airfields on Okinawa. Actually, Okinawa proved unnecessary not only as a staging ground for invasion but as an air base. The first and only B-29 mission from Okinawa did not take off for Japan until the last night of the war.[34]

[32] Nichols and Shaw, *Okinawa,* p. 260; Appleman *et al., Okinawa,* pp. 473–474.

[33] For appraisals of the Okinawa campaign, see *ibid.,* p. 473 and *passim;* Nichols and Shaw, *Okinawa,* pp. 269–275; Isely and Crowl, *The U.S. Marines and Amphibious War,* pp. 557–579; Morison, *History,* XIV, 272, 282.

[34] Appleman *et al., Okinawa,* pp. 419–421.

CHAPTER 27

The Collapse of Japan

ON JUNE 15, 1944, while Allied forces were launching their assault on Saipan, about fifty B-29's from Chinese bases struck the Imperial Iron Works at Yawata in Kyushu in the first strategic blow by the U.S. Army Air Force against Japan. A basic problem of strategic air war on Japan was distance. The acquisition of bases in Chengtu, China, and in the Marianas placed the enemy's homeland within range.

The Army Air Forces had been working since 1939 on the development of what they designated a "Very Long Range" four-engine bomber with a range above two thousand miles. Eventually one emerged which stood the test of war. The Boeing B-29 made an inauspicious start, for the second test model caught fire, crashed, and killed the test pilot, ten engineers, and several other persons. The third model appeared more satisfactory, and in an unorthodox move the War Department ordered production of 1,664 planes before the test model had been flown.[1]

The construction of a very-long-range bomber posed numerous problems and resulted in such innovations as pressurized cabins, remote-control turrets, and more powerful engines. In comparison with other aircraft of its day, the B-29 was impressive. Its span was 141 feet 3 inches, it was 99 feet long, it had an over-all height of 27 feet 9 inches and a maximum war weight of 135,000 pounds. Four Wright engines capable of developing 2,200 horsepower each at sea level turned four-

[1] The development of the "Very Long Range" project is described in W. F. Craven and J. L. Cate, *The Army Air Forces in World War II* (Chicago, 1953), V, 3–32.

bladed propellers, which could develop a maximum cruising speed of 361 miles per hour at 33,000 feet, and reach a ceiling of 38,000 feet. Combat experience demonstrated that the Superfort had a range without bombs of 4,400 miles and of 3,500 miles while carrying a four-ton bombload. When fully armed it bristled with twelve .50-caliber machine guns and a 20-mm. cannon in its tail.

Spurred on by President Roosevelt's desire to raise Chinese morale, the Army Air Force moved toward bombing raids on Japan from China, and after about a year of debate the Chiefs of Staff agreed April 10, 1944, on operations from China as a preliminary move to all-out bombing from the Marianas, which were still in enemy possession. Although the Superforts from China could not reach Tokyo or other potential targets on Honshu, they could attack important steel mills on Kyushu to the south. The XX Bomber Command, reporting directly to the Joint Chiefs of Staff, emerged as the agency to undertake this operation, known as Matterhorn, which also involved construction of advance air bases near Chengtu, in the heart of China, and of air supply from Burma or India.[2]

While the top leaders were determining the role of the B-29's, the men who were to fly and maintain them prepared for the task. Under command of Brigadier General Kenneth B. Wolfe, training fields appeared around Salina, Kansas, not far from Boeing's B-29 plant at Wichita. Wolfe combined testing and training as an unorthodox timesaving device, as in June, 1943, a few key pilots flew the first experimental plane not only to train themselves but to test the plane's flight characteristics. Modifications, such as the installation of a four-gun turret, delayed the number of planes produced; this delay in turn hampered training and postponed the departure of B-29's and their crews from Kansas.

For its B-29 rear base area in the Far East the Army Air Force selected southern Bengal and at an estimated cost of $20 million constructed five airfields some sixty miles west of Calcutta. U.S. engineers, using about 27,000 Indian contract civilian workers, built airfields, laid oil pipelines, constructed railroad connections, and installed utilities. The first four combat crews arrived at the India bases in May and June, 1944.[3]

[2] *Ibid.*, V, 17–18, 33–57; Charles F. Romanus and Riley Sunderland, *Stilwell's Command Problems* (*United States Army in World War II: China-Burma-India Theater*) (Washington, 1956), pp. 111–115.

[3] Craven and Cate, *The A.A.F. in World War II*, V, 60–65, 77.

The construction of the Chinese airfields constituted an even more difficult problem. Chengtu lay in a fertile, heavily populated delta about two hundred miles northwest of Chungking and four hundred miles from the end of the Hump at Kunming, and its isolation demanded that construction be done with Chinese labor and materials. Under American guidance, therefore, between 300,000 and 500,000 Chinese men and women built the air strips. Using primitive techniques, the workers crushed rocks with hammers, transported materials in buckets or baskets suspended from yokes, and laid the stones by hand. Despite the low wage scale of the worker, the sums poured into the top of the Chinese hierarchy were fantastic. Inflation, black markets, and other manifestations of human cupidity raised the cost of construction to an estimated $4.45 billion.[4]

Construction materials could be found in China, but supplies for maintenance of the bases and their operations had to go in from the outside. Although designed to be self-sufficient, the XX Bomber Command was forced to draw in part on supplies taken over the Hump by the Air Transport Command. Later the force received its own air transport squadrons with about sixty C-46's, and General Wolfe also made extensive use of the B-29's themselves as cargo planes. One of his first tasks was to build a stockpile of fuel and materials which would make strategic bombardment possible.[5]

Even before combat missions began it became apparent that operations from China would be secondary to those from the Marianas. Meanwhile, pilots and crews at Chengtu were gaining experience by flying over the Hump with oil supplies, but they were not getting practice in such other important matters as high-altitude formation flying, gunnery, and bombing. On June 5, 1944, B-29's made their first strike, a daylight raid on railway shops at Bangkok, which was valuable for training purposes but not especially destructive. Responding to pressure from Washington, Wolfe sent a second mission ten days later against the Imperial Iron and Steel Works at Yawata on Kyushu in Japan. Synchronizing their raid with the landings on Saipan, sixty-eight B-29's left Chengtu, and only forty-seven arrived over the target. The results were hardly indicative of later successes, for damage inflicted was

[4] *Ibid.,* V, 65–71; Romanus and Sunderland, *Stilwell's Command Problems,* p. 115.

[5] For Matterhorn logistics and operations, see Craven and Cate, *The A.A.F. in World War II,* V, 58–132.

slight, and the attack force lost seven planes, mainly from operational failures. The raid, however, gave evidence that Japan was open to heavy bomber attack.

Other raids followed at intervals dictated by the hard necessity of building up stockpiles. A ninety-six-plane mission had fair success against coke-oven installations at Anshan in Manchuria, and a few days later, on August 10–11, a double mission hit two widely separated targets, Palembang in Sumatra and Nagasaki in Kyushu. The Sumatra-bound contingent staged through Royal Air Force bases in Ceylon, on which, to meet the needs of the B-29's, the Allies expanded landing facilities at China Bay. The British also set up an elaborate air-sea rescue force to assist in emergencies that might arise from the long return flight. Damage inflicted on the Sumatran oil installations was slight, and since China Bay was not used again for heavy bombers the expenditures involved in remodeling the base seem wasteful. The night attack on Nagasaki showed improved skill, but the damage was minor. Continued B-29 raids provoked the Japanese into a counter air raid on the Chengtu bases, September 8, which was ineffective.

On August 29, Major General Curtis E. LeMay assumed command of the XX Bomber Command. An energetic and driving leader, LeMay was more of an innovator than his predecessor, and one of his ideas was "synchronous bombing." In clear weather when the bombardier could see the target he would release the bombload; otherwise he would turn the task over to the radar operator, who was also following in on the target. On September 26, 1944, General LeMay reached one of his first goals, a hundred-plane raid. Bad weather permitted only 73 of the 109 planes to reach the target and these bombed ineffectively by radar.

Throughout the entire Matterhorn operation the question of supply was critical. Reorganization and experience improved the command, but it could not procure sufficient supplies for sustained strategic warfare on Japan. Toward the end of the China operation, also, B-29's had to devote considerable time to tactical raids in China and Southeast Asia. These included strikes to support General MacArthur, raids on shipping, rail lines, and ammunition dumps for Lord Louis Mountbatten, aerial mine laying, and long-range reconnaissance, all valuable war efforts but not the strategic warfare for which the command was designed.

Two of these operations were harbingers of later developments. In

October, B-29's joined Admiral Halsey's Task Force 38 in attacks on Formosa and the Ryukyus. The task force steamed toward Okinawa, and its planes struck the island's bases, but then after a deceptive move toward Luzon Halsey turned the full power of his air force against Formosa. Anticipating such action, the Japanese had stocked Formosa with fighter planes. Their plan was to knock out the American planes and use night bombers, the so-called Typhoon Attack Force, to sink the unprotected carriers and other surface craft. The Japanese plan failed in execution rather than conception. Disparity in training and ability was too great, and starting their attack October 12 U.S. aircraft blasted enemy fighters either on the ground or in the air. Late the next day the Typhoon Force began to enter the battle and they too suffered heavily, although they torpedoed two cruisers, *Canberra* and *Houston*.

Misled by their own burning aircraft, the Japanese thought they had sunk other American vessels and they reported a great naval victory. Admiral Halsey used the situation to attempt to entrap the enemy by withdrawing the task force and leaving the stricken cruisers as decoys. Responding to the ruse, the Japanese sent carrier planes and bombers toward the crippled targets, but quickly recalled them when their search planes located the U.S. task force in the distance. One Japanese plane managed to send another torpedo into the *Houston*, but both damaged vessels made their way back to Ulithi. In this so-called "Battle off Formosa," U.S. planes had virtually eliminated Japanese fighter planes on Formosa and exacted heavy toll from other types of aircraft. Admiral Halsey claimed the destruction of 520 planes, in addition to many surface craft in the area.[6]

While the task force was reducing the enemy's planes, B-29's dealt hard blows to the aircraft installations on Formosa. On October 14, 104 Superforts reached Okayama and dropped about 650 tons of bombs on its aircraft repair and assembly plant and the adjoining air base. Succeeding raids in the next few days were less impressive, but the B-29's had practically knocked out of operation a vital air center on Formosa.

On December 18, the XX Bomber Command executed a mission

[6] William F. Halsey, *Admiral Halsey's Story* (New York, 1947), pp. 205–209; S. E. Morison, *History of United States Naval Operations in World War II* (Boston, 1958), XII, 86–109; A. R. Buchanan (ed.), *The Navy's Air War: A Mission Completed* (New York [1946]), pp. 233–234; M. Hamlin Cannon, *Leyte: The Return to the Philippines* (*United States Army in World War II: The Pacific Theater*) (Washington, 1954), pp. 43–44.

which was a prototype of later operations, when General LeMay sent his Superforts on a coordinated raid with Major General Claire L. Chennault's Fourteenth Air Force which featured fire bombs. The idea of incendiary raids on congested, inflammable cities of the Far East was not new to Air Force planners, but the successful gutting of Hankow may have influenced General LeMay's later decision to make such raids on Japan.[7]

The political situation in China affected the Matterhorn project. Lieutenant General Albert C. Wedemeyer, who had succeeded General Joseph W. Stilwell in command of U.S. Forces in China, concluded that China could not support all the military establishments within its borders and on December 4, after discussing the matter with others, recommended the withdrawal of the XX Bomber Command to release greater support for the Fourteenth Air Force and the Chinese Nationalist Army.[8] Like General Stilwell, he was highly critical of the motives and abilities of the Chinese Nationalist leaders.

From its inception, General Arnold had looked on the XX Bomber Command as a mobile organization, and early in its history one wing had been transferred to Saipan. On General Arnold's recommendation the Joint Chiefs of Staff accepted General Wedemeyer's suggestion and on January 15, 1945, ordered the command to withdraw from China to bases in India preparatory to a later move of the bulk of the force to the Marianas. General LeMay used the stay in India for tactical missions against such cities as Rangoon, Bangkok, and Singapore to improve the skill of his air crews.[9]

The Matterhorn operation from the start had been a makeshift one with little chance of success. Even Air Force leaders viewed it as secondary to anticipated strikes from the superior Marianas bases. The operation may have bolstered Chinese morale, and the tactical missions of the Command were valuable, although it is possible that if the Fourteenth Air Force could have had the funds and equipment of the XX Bomber Command it might have done even more. Possibly Matterhorn's greatest contribution was as a proving ground for both the Superforts and their crews, since the B-29 was a new plane which be-

[7] For these operations, see Craven and Cate, *The A.A.F. in World War II*, V, 137–139, 143–144.

[8] Charles F. Romanus and Riley Sunderland, *Time Runs Out in CBI* (*United States Army in World War II: China-Burma-India Theater*) (Washington, 1959), p. 161.

[9] Craven and Cate, *The A.A.F. in World War II*, V, 151–165.

came better with modifications growing out of combat experience.

Much more significant were the B-29 operations from the Marianas. In anticipation both of B-29 activities and of redeployment of men and planes from Europe, the Joint Chiefs of Staff on April 4, 1944, created the Twentieth Air Force, which was not confined to any particular theater but was under the Joint Chiefs of Staff, with General Arnold as their executive agent. In the Pacific, Lieutenant General Millard F. Harmon became Deputy Commander, Twentieth Air Force. Japanese resistance, the struggle for priorities, and adverse weather conditions delayed construction of airfields in the Marianas, but gradually work progressed, and B-29's began to arrive in the islands. Ultimately, there were two fields on Guam, one on Saipan, and two on Tinian. Iwo Jima became a staging base for B-29's and long-range fighter escorts. Subsequently, as we have seen, other B-29 bases appeared in Okinawa.[10]

The first planes and crews arrived in Saipan during October, 1944, and on November 24 the first mission took place against Tokyo.[11] From the 110 B-29's that went on this mission, the supply rose to 985 on July 31, 1945. In fact, by March, 1945, the number of planes was producing a shortage of combat crews which could not be solved quickly by expanded training programs. Critical supplies of materials also developed. The decision to concentrate on fire raids produced a shortage of incendiary bombs from March into the summer. Earlier, from November, 1944, to March, 1945, inadequate supplies of spare parts left many planes grounded. General LeMay placed maintenance on a factory basis, and although there were protests against the loss of identity with different groups, the change appreciably increased efficiency, for the handling of supplies improved, and the number of mechanical failures on missions declined.

Brigadier General Haywood S. Hansell, Jr., head of the XXI Bomber Command, flew into Saipan the first B-29, "Joltin' Josie, the Pacific Pioneer," and began the operations of his command with a training raid on Truk, October 28. After two other rather unsatisfactory attacks on this by-passed Japanese point of resistance, Hansell sent a strike against Iwo Jima, November 5, which was also hardly successful from the standpoint of damage inflicted. Truk continued to be a Superfort practice target throughout the remainder of the war.

By November, 1944, the progress of the war had altered strategic

[10] *Ibid.*, V, 512.

[11] For an account of B-29 raids on Japan, see *ibid.*, V, 546–576, 608–644.

aims. The remarkable advances made toward Japan, the virtual destruction of the Japanese Navy, and the decimation of its Air Force led to an acceleration of Allied plans and operations. Since the Joint Chiefs of Staff believed that invasion of Japan would be necessary, the Twentieth Air Force shifted priorities and replaced basic industries such as steel as targets with industries directly connected with war operations. Concentrating on air power, it gave the aircraft industry top priority.

Consequently, B-29's from the Marianas made their first Tokyo raids against an aircraft plant in the northwest part of the city. Prior to the mission, B-29's showed their versatility by engaging in photo reconnaissance. Modified as the F-13 and F-13A, these planes flew at 32,000 feet, above flak and fighters, and returned with valuable photographic information. Bad weather delayed departure of the first mission for about a week, but finally on November 11, 1944, well equipped with news correspondents, 111 B-29's got under way. Although plane losses were not excessive, damage to Tokyo was correspondingly slight. The raid, however, did show that the Japanese Air Force could not prevent the B-29's from striking at the heart of Japan.

During the next three months, following strict Army Air Force doctrine, the XXI Bomber Command concentrated on high-level precision bombing directed at aircraft industries. There were a few exceptions to the customary procedure. On January 3, 1945, ninety-seven Superforts made a test incendiary raid on Nagoya, but failure to start a general conflagration apparently lulled the Japanese into confidence in their fire-fighting equipment. The last strike under General Hansell's command was one of the most satisfactory high-altitude precision bombardments, for sixty-two planes practically demolished a twin-engine aircraft factory at Akashi, near Kobe. General Hansell, however, had adhered too inflexibly to doctrine, and the results were mounting too slowly to satisfy the higher command. On January 20, 1945, the more aggressive and less orthodox General LeMay replaced General Hansell as head of the XXI Bomber Command.

Briefly, General LeMay continued the tactics of his predecessor, but on February 3 he varied the routine with a raid on Kobe in which the emphasis was on fire bombs. Despite determined opposition by about two hundred enemy fighters, the attackers caused marked fire damage and in the process destroyed a number of war industries and shipyards. Nevertheless, high-level bombing continued in coordination with the

Iwo Jima campaign. Washington, however, was becoming increasingly convinced that this type of attack was not producing the desired results and it began to think more seriously of fire-bombing. While waiting for an increase in the B-29 force in the Marianas, General Arnold directed further tests of fire bomb raids, and on February 19, although he still gave aircraft plants first priority, he listed urban centers as secondary targets for incendiary raids.

In its effort to knock out the aircraft industry through high-altitude precision bombing the XXI Bomber Command had failed to achieve the damage sought or to diminish materially aircraft production. In one strike carrier planes had exacted more toll from the Mushashino-Tama aircraft industry in Tokyo than B-29's had been able to inflict in seven raids. From the long-range view, however, the Marianas B-29's had not failed, for like the XX Bomber Command they had gone through the pioneer stage.

The number of B-29's in the Marianas had increased to such a point that General LeMay was able to send a strike of 231 planes against Japan in support of the Iwo Jima operation. Bad weather over the primary target led to another experiment with fire bombs, which burned out about a square mile of Tokyo, and shortly thereafter the command began intensified incendiary raids. In an effort to induce surrender without invasion, the Army Air Force shifted from aircraft industries to the congested, inflammable cities and the people in them. General LeMay altered his tactics accordingly and took his B-29's down from 25,000 or 30,000 feet to 5,000 or 6,000 feet in night attacks. By sending planes in at this low altitude and practically disarming them, General LeMay increased the bombload of each plane an average of six tons.

On March 8, counting on the surprise of low-altitude night attack, General LeMay ordered a mass fire bomb raid on Tokyo. On the following day 334 bombers, carrying about two thousand tons of bombs, left bases in the Marianas. It took two and three-quarter hours merely to get the raiding force in the air. Finding the target and effecting surprise with their new tactics, the B-29's dropped their bombloads on the city. The result was one of the worst holocausts of all time. The target was a part of Tokyo into which people were crammed on an average of 103,000 to the square mile. The conflagration gutted about a fourth of the city's buildings and rendered homeless more than a million persons. Casualty lists were terrific; 83,793 persons died and 40,918 were injured. People caught in the bombed area were helpless for there

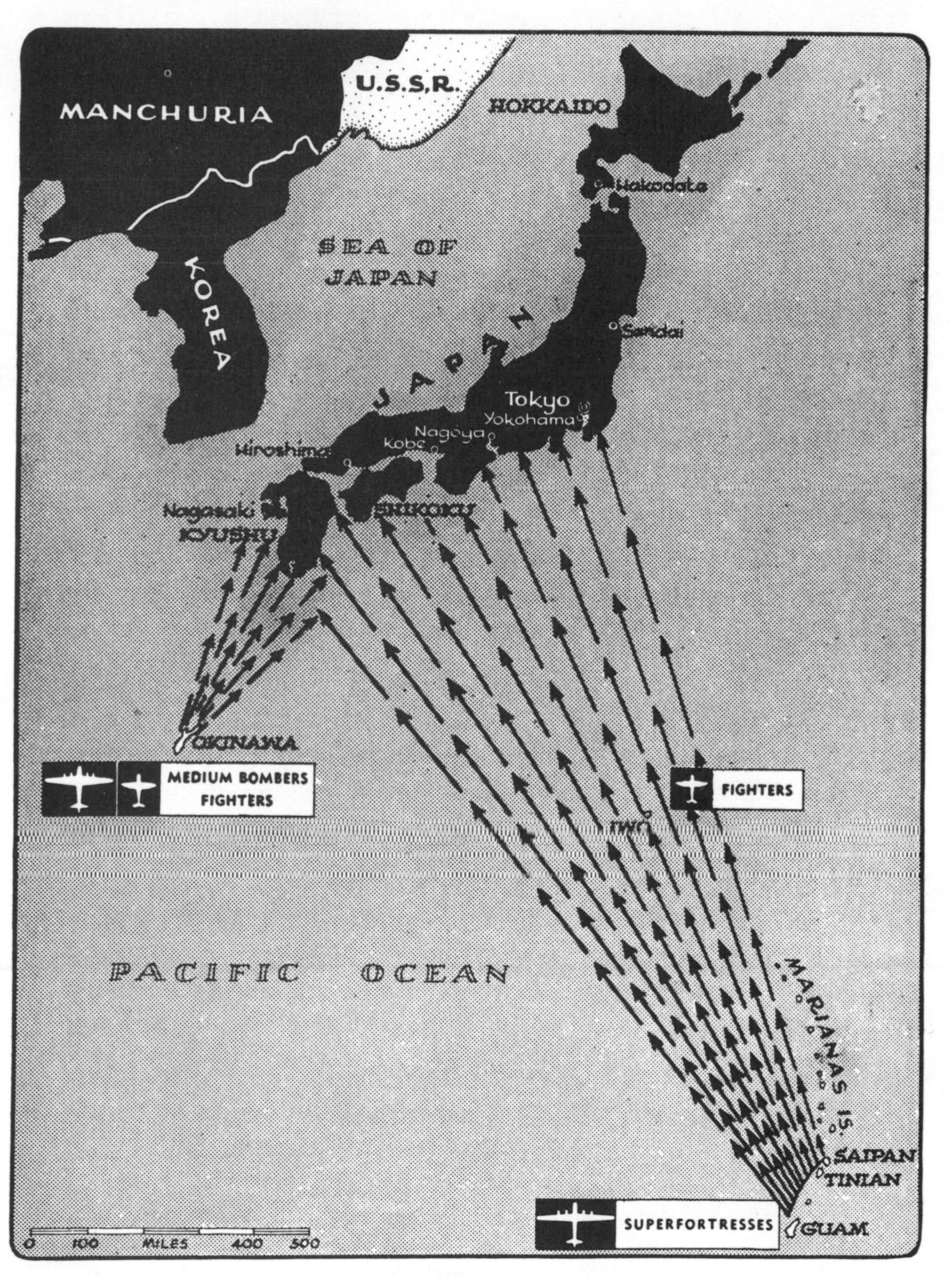

AIR ASSAULT ON JAPAN

was no place to go, and the fire-fighting equipment was utterly inadequate. Water boiled in some of the smaller canals running through the flaming city. Not excepting the later raids, the Tokyo fire raid on March 9–10, 1945, was the most destructive air raid in history.[12]

Finding the new tactics successful, the B-29's struck again. On March 11, they hit Nagoya with more bombs than had fallen on Tokyo. The results, while destructive, were much less spectacular than those in Tokyo and pointed out certain errors in bombing tactics which General LeMay corrected in subsequent raids. On March 13, Superforts laid waste more than eight square miles of Osaka, a few nights later they burned out a fifth of Kobe, and on March 19 they returned to Nagoya. The March operations definitely showed the effectiveness of the new tactics against the leading Japanese urban centers, and losses of men and planes had been lower than on the less successful high-altitude bombing attacks. The Joint Chiefs of Staff, consequently, designated some thirty-three Japanese cities for attack in addition to key industries which as yet had escaped destruction.[13]

Officially, the Army Air Force had begun its new campaign as a preliminary to invasion of Japan. Actually, a good many Air Force leaders hoped that air attack would force surrender without invasion. General LeMay had made a calculated risk in shifting tactics. Now he had to make another decision, for there were the two critical areas of crews and incendiary bombs. There simply were not enough experienced bomber crews to continue the anticipated program, and new crews could not be obtained in time. Staking success on his belief in a quick victory and securing approval from Washington, General LeMay drove his crews at a pace which, if the war had dragged on, would have carried them to exhaustion.

Although he had made his decision, General LeMay found himself forced to some diversion from strategic air bombardment. The Kamikaze threat during the Okinawa invasion was so great that even B-29's turned aside to raid Japanese air bases in an effort to check this last blow by the Japanese Air Force. Partly to aid the Okinawa operation and partly as a strategic blow, B-29's engaged also in sowing aerial

[12] For Japanese reactions to the raids, see Toshikazu Kase, *Journey to the Missouri* (New Haven, 1950), pp. 205–206; Masatake Okumiya and Jiro Horikoshi, *Zero!* (New York, 1956), pp. 276–277.

[13] For the all-out B-29 attack, see Craven and Cate, *The A.A.F. in World War II,* V, 645–675.

mines in Japanese waters. By May 11, fighters from new air strips on Okinawa and Ie Shima released B-29's from these tactical operations. Furthermore, the war in Europe had just ended, and the Allies could turn their full attention to the Pacific war. In the middle of July, therefore, General LeMay renewed intensified air war on Japan. The first high-altitude raid on Nagoya burned out more three square miles and destroyed an important aircraft engine bearing-part factory. A few nights later, low-flying Superforts destroyed by fire 3.8 more square miles of the same city. A week later, the bombers made two raids on Tokyo in which, carefully following orders to avoid the Emperor's palace, they fired more than sixteen square miles. As a result, Tokyo and Nagoya no longer needed to be considered primary targets.

By this time the enemy was increasing its defenses, and B-29 casualties mounted, although fighter aircraft from Iwo Jima were now available to escort the bombers. In the Osaka raid of June 1, these fighters ran into adverse weather conditions, and twenty-seven collided and crashed. The raid itself was successful in adding to destruction along the Japanese coast. The second intensive bombardment of Japan lasted about a month, and by June 15, B-29's had rendered useless the six leading industrial cities of Japan. The XXI Bomber Command did not limit its attacks to low-altitude night incendiary bombing. It increased its performance as well in high-level precision bombing, and the result was both flexibility and devastating power. With ever-increasing force the Army Air Force in the summer of 1945 launched attacks on individual industrial targets, incendiary raids on secondary urban centers, blows at the oil industry, and mine-laying operations against shipping.

As U.S. forces neared Japan, the problem of command became increasingly acute. General Arnold, eager for Air Force parity with the Army and Navy, favored a supreme commander with three coequal subordinates, Army, Navy, and air. Personalities made selecting such a supreme commander impracticable, for MacArthur and Nimitz were too big to be passed over, yet neither was acceptable to the other as supreme commander. On April 3, the Joint Chiefs of Staff reached a compromise solution. General MacArthur would command all Army resources in the Pacific, Admiral Nimitz would head all naval forces, and the Twentieth Air Force would continue to report directly to the Joint Chiefs of Staff. In ensuing campaigns all units would cooperate and make exchanges of units by mutual understandings.

Specifically, the directive ordered Admiral Nimitz to conclude the

Ryukyus operation, plan for an invasion of the Chinese coast, give naval support to the Army, and prepare the naval and amphibious phases of the Japanese landings. General MacArthur's task was to complete the Philippine operations, direct the occupation of North Borneo by Australian troops, and make ready for the invasion of Japan. On May 25, the Joint Chiefs of Staff agreed on the invasion of Kyushu on November 1, 1945.[14] The primary responsibility was MacArthur's, but he was to cooperate with Admiral Nimitz and the Twentieth Air Force in planning the amphibious phase of the operation. General MacArthur on May 28 issued a strategic outline for invasion of southern Kyushu on November 1, 1945, and of Honshu, March 1, 1946. For the first invasion he planned to use mainly forces already in the Pacific, and he anticipated that by the time of the second landings forces would be available from the European Theater.[15]

Meanwhile, despite command disputes among the services, air warfare against Japan continued. During July, the Seventh Air Force moved into Okinawa. The Japanese Air Force at first aggressively contested the daylight bombing raids which followed, but soon it was practically eliminated. Night-fighting P-47's and the more effective P-61's harassed the enemy to make the Allied scourge an around-the-clock affair, in which targets included railroads, bridges, shipping, and even civilians in the field. Everything was considered fair game in the effort to shorten the war and avert the need for invasion. At the same time, the Fifth and Seventh Air Forces joined the B-29's in strategic blows at industrial targets and urban centers.

Meanwhile, United States submarines had been taking increasing toll of Japanese shipping. Early in the war the offensive-minded Japanese Navy had scorned the convoy system as a defensive device. Shipping losses by the end of 1943 forced escort protection and provided a measure of security for merchant vessels, but losses, especially of tankers, continued. By the time of the Battle for Leyte Gulf, shipment of oil from the Netherlands East Indies had been drastically curtailed. The Japanese were more successful in guarding shipments from Man-

[14] *Ibid.,* V, 686; see also William D. Leahy, *I Was There* (New York, London, Toronto, 1950), p. 385.

[15] Craven and Cate, *The A.A.F. in World War II,* V, 689; Charles A. Willoughby and John Chamberlain, *MacArthur, 1941–1951* (New York, 1954), pp. 287–289.

churia and parts of the Asiatic mainland, and American submarines found it difficult to enter the heavily mined Sea of Japan. Introduction of a new electronic sonar device, FMS, which enabled submariners to identify mines, made it possible for American undersea craft to move into formerly restricted enemy waters. In early June, 1945, nine submarines, in Operation Barney, penetrated the Sea of Japan and sank a Japanese submarine and twenty-eight merchant ships, with a loss of one U.S. submarine. As a result of their sinkings during the war, American submarines helped tighten a cordon around Japan which by the summer of 1945 was reducing the Japanese people to starvation.[16]

On August 6, 1945, a B-29 dropped a bomb of devastating power on Hiroshima. The scientific background of the atomic bomb is described briefly elsewhere, but necessary also were careful military preparations as well as the political decision to drop the bomb.

Major General Leslie R. Groves, director of the Manhattan Engineer District, informed General Arnold of the bomb, and upon Arnold devolved the responsibility for preparing the aircraft to take it to the target. As early as September, 1943, it was apparently agreed that the B-29 would be the carrier, and in 1944 work began on modification of the plane and especially the bomb for actual military use. The anticipated goal was fifteen such modified aircraft.

In the summer of 1944, a carefully selected combat unit began training under Colonel Paul W. Tibbets, Jr., a pilot with an excellent record. He was the only one of the group who knew the nature of the bomb; the others were aware only that they would drop a special bomb, which they called "the gimmick." After training first at isolated Wendover Field in Utah and receiving additional personnel, the unit gained experience in high-altitude simulated missions, flying from Batista Field in Cuba, and in May and June, 1945, set up headquarters on Tinian. The mysterious nature of their functions intrigued not only others in the Marianas but the members of the 509th Bombardment Group themselves as they continued their training by dropping thousand- and five-hundred-pound bombs on by-passed islands. Toward the end of July they sent from two to six planes against relatively insignificant targets

[16] E. B. Potter and Chester W. Nimitz (ed.), *The Great Sea War: The Story of Naval Action in World War II* (Englewood Cliffs, N.J., 1960), pp. 418–424; Morison, *History,* XIV (1960), 291–293; Theodore Roscoe, *United States Submarine Operations in World War II* (Annapolis, 1949), pp. 479–482.

in Japan, and in these raids they simulated all the procedures of the real attack to come. By the end of the month the group was ready for its task.[17]

Although it seems clear that President Roosevelt anticipated the use of the atomic bomb as soon as it was available, the actual decision to drop it was made by President Truman. After the fall of Germany and in anticipation of the Potsdam Conference, an "interim committee" of civilians close to the Manhattan Project recommended use of the bomb against Japan as soon as possible. All except one member, Ralph A. Bard, of the distinguished group, which included James F. Byrnes, Vannevar Bush, Carl Compton, and James B. Conant, recommended use of the bomb without specific warning of its nature. Some of the scientists connected with the project advocated a demonstration before UN representatives of the bomb's power on a desert island, but others, including Enrico Fermi, E. O. Lawrence, and J. R. Oppenheimer, advocated direct military use of the bomb. These recommendations came before the test at Alamagordo and contemplated the possibility that the experiment might be a fiasco.[18]

While the President moved toward his decision, General Groves and General Arnold decided that the target should be a Japanese city which as yet had escaped severe punishment. Secretary of War Stimson eliminated Kyoto from consideration as too important a national shrine, and the planners narrowed the field to four cities, Hiroshima, Niigata, Kokura, and Nagasaki.[19]

Toward the middle of July, President Truman was in Europe attending the Potsdam Conference. Receiving word of the successful atomic test at Alamagordo July 16, he relayed the information to Prime Minister Churchill and Generalissimo Stalin. Churchill already knew of the project, but the Soviet leader seemed unimpressed by the event. A top secret U.S. War Department order dated July 24 set in motion the operation for the dropping of the bomb on Japan, but the final decision still rested with President Truman.[20] On July 26, Truman, Churchill,

[17] Craven and Cate, *The A.A.F. in World War II,* V, 705–709.

[18] *Ibid.,* V, 710; Arthur Holly Compton, *Atomic Quest: A Personal Narrative* (New York, 1956), pp. 233–240.

[19] Henry L. Stimson and McGeorge Bundy, *On Active Service in Peace and War* (New York, 1947), p. 625. J. Robert Oppenheimer raised the same objections to bombing Kyoto. Compton, *Atomic Quest,* p. 237.

[20] Harry S. Truman, *Memoirs* (New York, 1955), I, 415–421. Winston Churchill stated that the British had agreed in principle to the use of the bomb on July 4, and that the final decision lay with President Truman.

and Chiang Kai-shek issued the so-called Potsdam Proclamation calling on Japan to surrender. On the twenty-eighth, the Japanese Premier informed the Japanese press that his government would ignore the ultimatum. Unfortunately, the impression became widespread both in Japan and abroad that the government was not simply following a policy of delay but instead was contemptuously rejecting the proclamation.[21]

Meanwhile, the military operation started to move. The cruiser *Indianapolis* carried part of the fissionable material to Tinian, arrived July 26, and on its return trip was sunk three days later by a submarine. Air transport delivered the rest of the bomb material, and by the end of the month the bomb could have been ready for use if necessary. The orders, however, were to await favorable weather on or soon after August 3. The field orders designated Hiroshima, Japan's eighth largest city as the primary target, Kokura the secondary, and Nagasaki the third choice.[22]

Seven B-29's were involved in the mission. Shortly after midnight on August 5, three weather planes left the Marianas, one assigned to each target. At 2:45 on the morning of the sixth, three other Superforts followed. The seventh plane was on Iwo Jima for emergency use in case of the necessity of landing and reloading. Colonel Tibbets commanded the *Enola Gay,* which carried the bomb, and was one of the planes in the main force. The other two planes contained cameras, scientific instruments and civilian and military observers. By this time the crews knew that their task was to drop a single bomb with an explosive power equal to twenty thousand tons of TNT.

En route the bomb commander and his assistant completed the assembly of the bomb and rechecked it during the trip, which was without incident. The weather report of good weather over Hiroshima confirmed it as the target, and flying at 31,600 feet at a ground speed of 328 miles per hour, the *Enola Gay* reached its objective, and the bombardier Major Thomas W. Ferebee dropped the bomb. Fifty seconds later, when the plane was some fifteen "slant" miles away, the bomb

---

Churchill also stated that he believed that Truman made the right decision. Winston Churchill, *The Second World War* (Boston, 1953), VI, 639. See also Louis Morton, "The Decision to Use the Atomic Bomb," Kent R. Greenfield (ed.), *Command Decisions* (Washington, 1960), pp. 493–518.

[21] Robert J. C. Butow, *Japan's Decision to Surrender* (Stanford, Calif., 1954), pp. 142–149.

[22] Craven and Cate, *The A.A.F. in World War II,* V, 714–715.

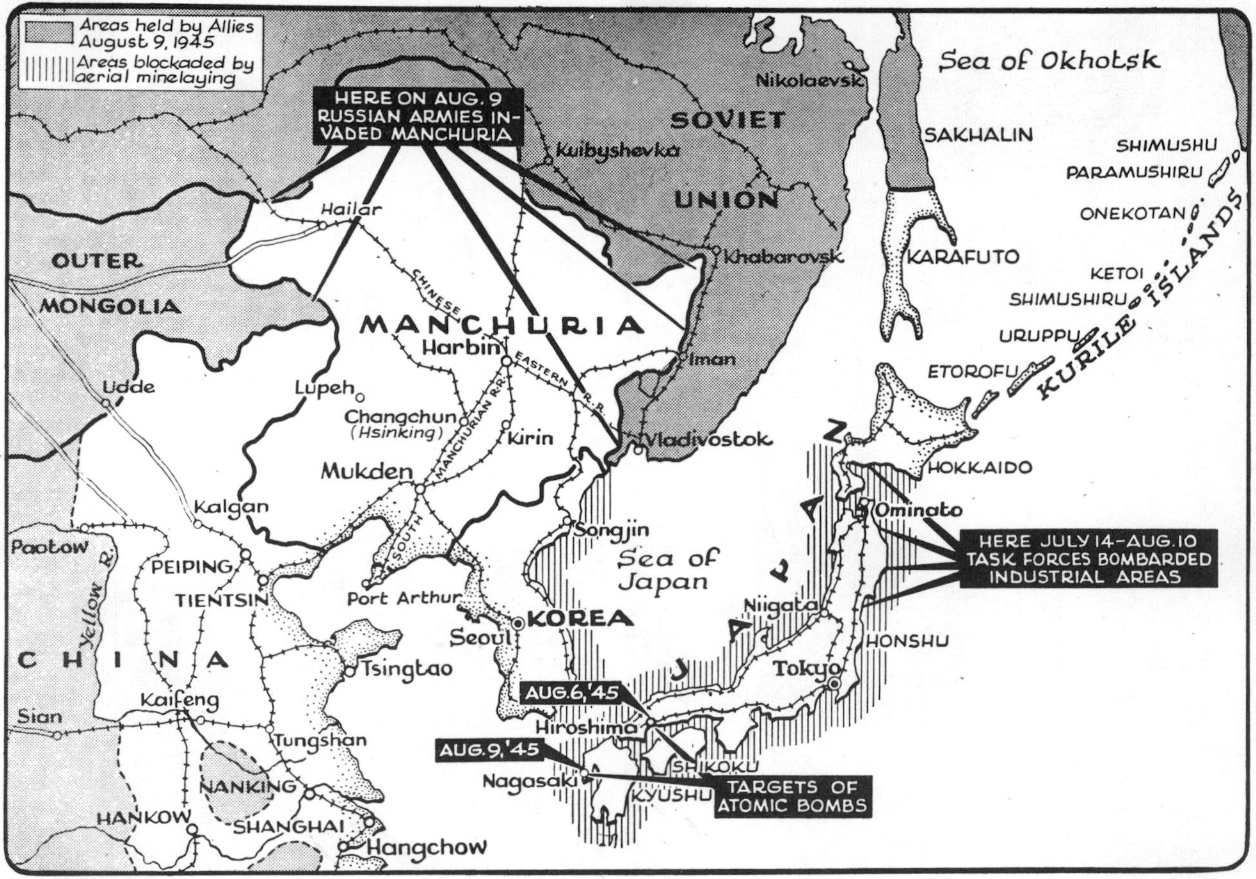

THE FINAL PHASE

exploded about two thousand feet above the doomed city. The only opposition had been mild antiaircraft fire, and after observing briefly the blast and resultant conflagration, the planes returned without difficulty to Tinian.[23]

Receiving notification of the successful completion of the mission, President Truman publicly announced the event sixteen hours after the bombing and called on Japan to surrender to avoid a "rain of ruin" from the air.[24] In the meantime, having enough material on hand for one more bomb, the Twentieth Air Force prepared for its second strike. Predictions of approaching bad weather advanced the date, and early on August 9 a striking force similar to the first one left the Marianas with a newer and more efficient bomb, although its outward characteristics made no change in bombing techniques. Good weather had doomed Hiroshima; bad weather saved Kokura, the primary target of the second mission and marked for destruction instead the secondary objective, Nagasaki. Although the operation was not quite so smooth as the first, the planes made their drop, flew to Iwo Jima for refueling, and then returned to Tinian.[25]

The effects of the two bomb explosions on Hiroshima and Nagasaki clearly indicated the terrific destructive power of the new weapon of war. Physically speaking, Hiroshima was laid waste; over 80 percent of the buildings were destroyed, and 16.7 percent were severely damaged. Although the loss of life was less than in the Tokyo fire bomb raid of March 9–10, the total casualties were higher. A single plane dropping but one bomb had killed between 70,000 and 80,000 and injured as many more. At Nagasaki destruction was not so widespread, but damage to industry was heavier. Casualties were estimated at 35,000 dead, 5,000 missing, and 60,000 injured.[26]

The forces of political power within Japan were feeling the impact of war. Although the Emperor was the titular head of the Empire and had tremendous prestige, he normally did not play an active role in government, and his customary function was to receive information of the government's policy decisions, not to make these decisions nor even

[23] *Ibid.*, V, 715–717.

[24] Truman, *Memoirs,* I, 422; Craven and Cate, *The A.A.F. in World War II,* V, 717–718.

[25] *Ibid.*, V, 719–720.

[26] *Ibid.*, V, 722–725. For a graphic account of the results at Hiroshima, see John Hersey, *Hiroshima* (New York, 1946), *passim.* This account originally appeared in *The New Yorker.*

to resolve differences among the policymakers.[27] A potentially significant figure was Marquis Koichi Kido, the Lord Keeper of the Privy Seal, whose real importance lay in the fact that he was the principal informant and adviser of the Emperor. Powerful also were the *jūshin,* or senior statesmen, a group of former premiers who without constitutional authorization or imperial decree met informally to discuss questions of the war and of Japan's future. Then there was the official Cabinet, headed by the Premier and including the various portfolios.[28] Dominating the Cabinet, however, were the militarists who had gained the ascendancy with Premier Tojo and had taken the nation into war.

As the Japanese military course changed from astounding success to slow retreat, Tojo and his Cabinet sought to increase their control over the state. Supported by a favorable and pliant House of Representatives, they placed the military element in charge of the occupied territories, reorganized the local government of Japan, and centralized industrial effort under a Munitions Ministry.[29] Continued military reverses, however, required a scapegoat, and Tojo was unable to evade the assignment. The loss of the Marianas resulted in the collapse of his ministry.[30] It furthermore appears that some eminent Japanese leaders already had reached the conclusion that Japan could not win the war and that it should be ended as soon as possible. Such was the war spirit within Japan that these men dared not express their ideas candidly even to one another. Consequently, they resorted to the use of *haragei,* which translated very roughly means the art of saying one thing while meaning another. While the motives of men who spoke by such indirection are most difficult to ascertain, scholars are inclined to feel that there were Japanese leaders who honestly sought to terminate the war.[31]

The collapse of the Tojo Cabinet did not signify the end of military control of Japan. The succeeding ministry was a copremiership, headed by General Kuniaki Koiso as Premier and Admiral Mitsumasa Yonai as Navy Minister and co-Premier, but greater power lay with the newly

[27] Butow, *Japan's Decision to Surrender,* pp. 228–230.

[28] *Ibid.,* pp. 7–17.

[29] Chitoshi Yanaga, *Japan Since Perry* (New York, 1949), pp. 605–613; F. C. Jones, *Japan's New Order in East Asia: Its Rise and Fall, 1937–45* (London, 1954), pp. 331–400.

[30] Butow, *Japan's Decision to Surrender,* pp. 27–29.

[31] *Ibid.,* pp. 58–75; Jones, *Japan's New Order in East Asia,* pp. 422–423.

created "Supreme Council for the Direction of the War." On April 5, 1945, less than a week after the Allied landings on Okinawa, the Koiso-Yonai ministry fell, and on the same day the Soviet Union announced that it would not renew its neutrality pact with Japan.[32]

Called together by the Lord Keeper of the Privy Seal, the senior statesmen, who now included ex-Premier Tojo, discussed the type of premier needed. Tojo, with some support, pleaded for one who would lead the nation to victory, but others thought of ending the war, although they were not so open in their assertions. Finally, certain points of agreement emerged; this must be the last Cabinet of the war, and the premier must have the confidence of the people and be an independent agent. The appointment went on April 5 to a man who appeared to have the necessary qualifications. Kantaro Suzuki, a retired admiral who had been seriously wounded in 1936 in an attempted assassination by a military fanatic, enjoyed considerable prestige and at the outset satisfied both extremes among the senior statesmen. As it developed, Suzuki was so adept at *haragei* that it is difficult to ascertain his real motives. The peace advocates viewed favorably his selection of Shigenori Togo as Foreign Minister, since Togo in the same post in the Tojo Cabinet had opposed launching the war. On the other hand, Suzuki during the discussions leading to his appointment had spoken only of continuing the war effort. After the war, the Admiral insisted that he would have courted assassination had he spoken otherwise. Whatever his thoughts may have been, the Premier supported a continuance of the struggle, and in his first message to the Diet, June 9, insisted that Japan had been forced into the war and must fight to the end. He had already declared that Germany's collapse would not affect Japan's determination to continue the war and at that time he predicted ultimate victory.[33]

For some time the Japanese leaders had been considering overtures to Soviet Russia to keep that government from entering the Pacific war, to gain its friendship, and to seek Soviet mediation of the war. The Kremlin's announcement of withdrawal from the Russo-Japanese nonaggression pact forced the Japanese to make definite attempts to

[32] Butow, *Japan's Decision to Surrender,* pp. 30–58.

[33] *Ibid.,* pp. 68–69, 79. Suzuki told Togo that he thought Japan could carry on the war for another two or three years. Shigenori Togo, *The Cause of Japan* (New York, 1956), p. 269.

renew the treaty and to prevent Soviet Russia's entrance into the struggle. Jacob A. Malik, the Soviet Ambassador in Japan, was uninterested and uncooperative, for the Yalta bargains had already been drawn.[34]

Despite the ominous course of the war and Foreign Minister Togo's warning that the USSR would never become Japan's ally, the Supreme Council for the Direction of the War determined that the Japanese people should resist invasion and fight to the end. The Cabinet, including Premier Suzuki, endorsed the decision, and high officials reviewed it without opposition in a conference before the Emperor, June 8, 1945.[35] Although both the Emperor and the Lord Keeper of the Privy Seal Kido had remained silent, the latter apparently sensed that the Emperor was concerned by the decision. Kido consequently appears to have begun a counterplan which involved Imperial intervention to reverse the decision which the military had dictated. On June 22, when Okinawa had fallen, the Emperor called an Imperial conference and in veiled terms requested the Cabinet or the Supreme Command to consider alternatives to the decision to fight to the conclusion. From the discussion came an agreement to approach Moscow with a view toward a negotiated peace, but the effort to make headway with Ambassador Malik failed, as the Russian diplomat first made uncooperative responses and then declined to meet the Japanese representative on the ground of illness.[36] Aware of the impending Potsdam Conference, the Japanese next sought to send Prince Konoye as a special emissary to the Kremlin. Ambassador Naotake Sato found the Soviet leaders in Moscow as unhelpful as was Malik in Japan and he was unable to secure an interview with Foreign Commissar V. M. Molotov prior to the latter's departure for Potsdam.[37] On July 18, the Soviet Vice Foreign Commissar informed Ambassador Sato that the Japanese message was too vague and the purpose of Prince Konoye's visit too indefinite for the Soviet government to reply to the message or to the suggestion of a special Japanese mission.[38] In desperation Togo made it clear that Japan sought a cessation of hostilities, although he insisted that peace must come on other terms than unconditional surrender. The Japanese

[34] Butow, *Japan's Decision to Surrender,* pp. 90–92; Kase, *Journey to the Missouri,* pp. 170–171.

[35] Butow, *Japan's Decision to Surrender,* pp. 101–102.

[36] *Ibid.,* pp. 118–123; Kase, *Journey to the Missouri,* pp. 171, 187–188.

[37] *Ibid.,* p. 194.

[38] Butow, *Japan's Decision to Surrender,* p. 126; Kase, *Journey to the Missouri,* p. 205.

government, said Togo, wished to send Prince Konoye to present Japan's concrete proposals.[39]

Japan's cause with the Soviet Union was hopeless, for the leaders in the Kremlin had secured advantages at Yalta which they could insure only by entering the war against Japan, not by interceding on the latter's behalf to terminate the war.[40] On July 28, Stalin informed President Truman of the Japanese overtures but he asserted that Japan was seeking collaboration for continuing the war.[41] The President did not need Stalin's warped revelation, for Washington was receiving and deciphering the messages which passed between Foreign Minister Togo and Ambassador Sato. Prior to the start of the Potsdam Conference the United States government knew that Japan was seeking to end the war short of unconditional surrender although it had little hope of securing Russian assistance in the effort.[42] U.S. leaders, however, apparently paid little attention to this information. Basically, lack of agreement on two important matters hampered U.S. policy decisions and consequent action. In the first place, although President Roosevelt, President Truman, and some of their advisers desired Soviet Russia's entrance into the war against Japan, other officials questioned its need or advisability.[43] Further, there was lack of accord on the implications of "unconditional surrender" as far as disposition of the Japanese Emperor was concerned. Had Washington reached the decision earlier to retain the Emperor and had it made this decision known to the Japanese, it might have accelerated surrender. In his statement of May 8, 1945, announcing the end of the European war, President Truman had made it clear that, although unconditional surrender would terminate military rule in Japan, it did not mean the "extermination or enslavement" of the Japanese people. The President did not, however, indicate the future role of the Emperor or the Empire.[44]

[39] Butow, *Japan's Decision to Surrender,* pp. 127–128.

[40] *Ibid.,* pp. 128–129.

[41] *Ibid.,* p. 129.

[42] *Ibid.,* pp. 129–130; James Forrestal, *The Forrestal Diaries,* edited by Walter Millis (New York, 1951), pp. 74–76.

[43] Butow, *Japan's Decision to Surrender,* p. 132. According to Churchill, after the atomic bomb test in New Mexico, he and President Truman felt that they no longer needed Soviet Russia's help against Japan. Churchill, *The Second World War,* VI, 640. Without indicating the effect of the atomic bomb test, Truman states that he and Churchill wanted to get Soviet Russia into the war to speed up Japanese defeat. Truman, *Memoirs,* I, 387.

[44] Butow, *Japan's Decision to Surrender,* pp. 132–141; Kase, *Journey to the Missouri,* p. 203.

On July 26, 1945, the heads of the British, Chinese, and United States governments issued what is known as the Potsdam Declaration or Proclamation, in which they called upon Japan to proclaim the "unconditional surrender of all Japanese armed forces, and to provide proper and adequate assurances of their good faith in such action." The alternative for Japan, the Proclamation warned, would be "prompt and utter destruction." The document demanded the elimination of the "self-willed militaristic advisers whose unintelligent calculations have brought the Empire of Japan to the threshold of annihilation."[45] Not included in the final Proclamation was a statement by Secretary Stimson that the Allies would not exclude the possibility of maintaining a constitutional monarchy under the present dynasty.[46] In Japan the peace advocates interpreted the Proclamation to imply that the institution of the Empire could be saved, but the militarists read in the document its threatened destruction.[47]

Minister Togo persuaded the Cabinet not to reject the Proclamation outright, and instead of replying immediately to it, the Cabinet decided to see what steps the Soviet government would take in response to continued Japanese overtures. Through an unfortunate interpretation of the Premier's words, Japan and the world gained the impression that Suzuki had contemptuously rejected the Allied Proclamation. Some critics feel that if the Potsdam Proclamation had been presented diplomatically to the Japanese government instead of openly in a public pronouncement, the Japanese might have given a favorable response.[48] Such was not the procedure, and considering the warning to have been rejected the Allies proceeded with their assault on Japan. As has already been noted, an atomic bomb fell on Hiroshima August 6, and two days later Soviet Russia entered the war against Japan. Curiously, American statesmen provided Generalissimo Stalin with the pretext for breaking the Russo-Japanese nonaggression pact, which was still in effect although Soviet Russia had announced its nonrenewal. Acting on President Truman's suggestion, the Soviet government declared war on Japan in accordance with paragraph 5 of the Moscow Pact of October, 1943, which stated that until the United Nations organization came

[45] Butow, *Japan's Decision to Surrender,* pp. 243–244.

[46] *Ibid.,* pp. 139–140; Stimson and Bundy, *On Active Service,* pp. 621–625.

[47] Butow, *Japan's Decision to Surrender,* pp. 140–141.

[48] *Ibid.,* pp. 138–141; Kase, *Journey to the Missouri,* pp. 209–211; Togo, *The Cause of Japan,* pp. 313–314.

into being the United States, the United Kingdom, the Soviet Union, and China would consult "with a view to joint action on behalf of the community of nations."[49]

The atomic bomb and the Soviet entrance into the war marked the end of military control in Japan. On August 9, the members of the Supreme Council for the Direction of the War met and deadlocked on the course of action to take. Three members, Admiral Baron Kantaro Suzuki, Premier, Shigenori Togo, Foreign Minister, and Admiral Mitsumasa Yonai, Navy Minister, favored capitulation with the sole reservation of retention of the Empire. The other three, General Korechika Anami, War Minister, General Yoshijiro Umezu, Army Chief of Staff, and Admiral Soemu Toyoda, Navy Chief of Staff, insisted that Japan had not yet reached defeat, for the Japanese could still defend the homeland. News of the atomic drop on Nagasaki interrupted the discussion but did not break the deadlock, which continued in the next day's meeting. Shortly afterward, Premier Suzuki and Foreign Minister Togo went to the Emperor and persuaded him to call an Imperial conference. This was an unprecedented move, since normally in such meetings the Emperor heard only of problems which the government already had resolved. A little before midnight on August 9, the Emperor met Japan's top military and political leaders in the underground air raid shelter adjoining the Imperial library. Once again, this time in the presence of the Emperor, the chief protagonists presented their arguments. Baron Kiichiro Hiranuma, President of the Privy Council, added his recommendation for surrender based on protection of the Emperor's prerogatives.

Finally, the Emperor gave his opinion and in a scene deep with emotion sanctioned the proposal to seek peace based on retention of the Empire. At other times the Emperor's words might have been disregarded, but Japan's desperate situation resulted in acquiescence by even the military advocates of continued struggle. Early in the morning of August 10, capitulation messages went to the Allies by way of Japanese representatives in Sweden and Switzerland.[50]

It was the Allies' turn to make a decision, and instead of accepting

[49] James F. Byrnes, *Speaking Frankly* (New York, 1947), pp. 208–209; Butow, *Japan's Decision to Surrender*, pp. 156–158.

[50] *Ibid.*, pp. 158–178. Togo told the Emperor, and he agreed, that atomic bombing made it all the more necessary to end the war. Togo, *The Cause of Japan*, pp. 315, 321.

OCCUPIED JAPAN

the capitulation as offered by Japan they responded with what has been called the Byrnes note, which stated, "From the moment of surrender the authority of the Emperor and the Japanese Government to rule the state shall be subject to the Supreme Commander of the Allied powers who will take such steps as he deems proper to effectuate the surrender terms."[51] The Byrnes note revived intense debate among the Japanese leaders, some of whom saw ultimate destruction of the Imperial government in the wording of the message.[52] Japanese officials had attempted to keep the peace messages secret, but early on August 14 they learned that U.S. planes were dropping leaflets on Japan containing the Japanese capitulation offer and the Byrnes reply. Consequently, acting on the advice of the Premier and the Lord Keeper of the Privy Seal, the Emperor called another Imperial conference. After listening to a brief discussion, the Emperor requested his ministers to accept the Allied reply. The long debate had ended, and in a few hours the world heard of the Japanese surrender.[53]

Receiving the Japanese response, the United States government ordered an immediate cessation of hostilities and directed the Japanese to send representatives to General MacArthur, who had been designated Commander in Chief of the Allied Powers and who was in Manila to arrange for formal surrender. The Japanese Emperor continued his important role by announcing the surrender to a Japanese people, who heretofore had been kept uninformed concerning developments. A few die-hards staged protest movements, but they were either killed or committed suicide; most Japanese accepted the pronouncement of their ruler.[54]

The war was over, but there were many things to do. The Japanese emissaries flew to Manila for instructions, and U.S. forces rushed to release prisoners of war or accepted the surrender of Japanese troops who had been by-passed in the advance across the Pacific. In Japan the Emperor disregarded tradition once more by selecting as the new Premier his uncle, Prince Higashikuni Naruhiko, a general with both experience and prestige.[55] The final surrender scene came Sep-

[51] Byrnes, *Speaking Frankly,* p. 209.

[52] Butow, *Japan's Decision to Surrender,* pp. 197–198.

[53] *Ibid.,* pp. 205–209; Togo, *The Cause of Japan,* pp. 334–335.

[54] Craven and Cate, *The A.A.F. in World War II,* V, 731. For developments in Japan, see Butow, *Japan's Decision to Surrender,* pp. 210–227; Kase, *Journey to the Missouri,* pp. 258–265.

[55] Butow, *Japan's Decision to Surrender,* pp. 226–227.

tember 2, 1945, in Tokyo Bay on the battleship, *Missouri,* on whose deck the Supreme Commander accepted the Japanese surrender document, signed by himself, two Japanese officials, and representatives of the victorious powers. In a brief address General MacArthur noted the end of the war and that everywhere men walked "upright in the sunlight." With his understandable expressions of pride in victory went encouragement to Japan that if it turned its talents "into constructive channels" it could "lift itself from its present deplorable state into a position of dignity."[56]

[56] Kase, *Journey to the Missouri,* pp. 11–12; Willoughby and Chamberlain, *MacArthur, 1941–1951,* pp. 294–297; Halsey, *Admiral Halsey's Story,* pp. 281–284.

Bibliography

Histories of the Armed Forces

There is a tremendous amount of material on various phases of the role of the United States in World War II. Much of this is too voluminous, detailed, and inaccessible for the person who seeks an over-all understanding of the subject. The armed services, for example, early became "history" conscious and in addition to keeping their customary records during the war developed staffs of historians who began to prepare in a variety of ways accounts of the service to which they were attached. Furthermore, every unit, from a Navy blimp squadron in the Caribbean to the Office of the Chief of Staff of the War Department, wrote its own history. Fortunately, the military leaders secured the services of skilled historians who, working either singly or in teams, have prepared specialized studies which gradually are appearing in print. One such series is the *History of United States Naval Operations in World War II* (Boston, 1947–60) by Samuel Eliot Morison. This Harvard professor, who rose to the rank of rear admiral in the Navy, headed a group of historians who during the war started the preparation of naval operational history. Although these volumes bear Morison's inimitable style and reflect his own opinions, they must be classed as at least semiofficial naval history. Similarly, two scholars, Wesley Frank Craven and James Lea Cate, with the assistance of other scholars, have produced a carefully documented and restrained history of *The Army Air Forces in World War II* (6 vols., Chicago, 1948–53). Using numerous authors, the Marine Corps is publishing a series of well-documented Marine Corps Monographs ([Washington] 1947——). Surpassing the other services in volume, the United States Army has embarked upon a multiseries account of both combat and supporting activities. (See *United States Army in World War II: Master Index* Reader's Guide I [Washington, 1955].) These publications, like the others, are thoroughly documented and carefully written. Other service accounts, issued on a more modest scale, are noted among the subject bibliographies.

The Coming of World War II—Europe

Extremely valuable are documents from captured German archives being published jointly by the American, British, and French governments. *Documents on German Foreign Policy,* well along in publication, cover the period from January 30, 1933, to December, 1941. Another important volume of documents published by the U.S. State Department is *Nazi-Soviet Relations, 1939–1941* (Washington, 1948). Among the many memoirs and biographies are Neville Chamberlain, *In Search of Peace* (New York, 1939); Maxime Weygand, *Recalled to Service* (Melbourne, London, Toronto, 1952); Frank Owen, *Tempestuous Journey: Lloyd George His Life and Times* (New York, Toronto, London, 1955); G. M. Young, *Stanley Baldwin* (London, 1952); Keith Feiling, *The Life of Neville Chamberlain* (London, 1947). Winston Churchill, *The Second World War* (6 vols., Boston, 1949–53), is indispensable for many aspects of the war. An important study of Germany and the peoples under German control during the war is Arnold Toynbee and Veronica Toynbee (ed.), *Hitler's Europe* (*Survey of International Affairs, 1939–1946*) (London, 1954). Materials on the course of the war in Europe prior to American entrance include J. F. C. Fuller, *The Second World War, 1939–1945: A Strategical and Tactical History* (New York, 1949). General Fuller, a prominent British military historian, is generally critical of Allied air warfare. General Wladyslaw Anders, a Pole who fought against the Germans in Italy and elsewhere, has written an interpretive account of *Hitler's Defeat in Russia* (Chicago, 1953). The British government has begun publication of an extensive *History of the Second World War: United Kingdom Military Series,* edited by J. R. M. Butler. The authors have had full access to official documents, but unlike the United States military accounts the British volumes are not documented. Useful volumes in the series for this period are L. F. Ellis, *The War in France and Flanders, 1939–1940* (London, 1953), and Basil Collier, *The Defence of the United Kingdom* (London, 1957). German accounts include Friedrich Ruge, *Sea Warfare, 1939–1945: A German Viewpoint* (London, 1957), and Siegfried Westphal, *The German Army in the West* (London, 1951).

The Coming of World War II—The Far East

The materials on the entrance of the United States into the war are staggering in proportion. A brief description of the nature of public documents, memoirs, and other source materials on this subject is in the preface to William L. Langer and S. Everett Gleason, *The Challenge to Isolation, 1937–1940* (New York, 1952). Among the most important published documents are those in the State Department series, *Foreign Relations of the United States,* its *Documents on German Foreign Policy,* and the *Pearl Harbor Attack,* thirty-nine volumes and a *Report* of the Joint Committee on the Investigation of the Pearl Harbor Attack, 79th Cong., 1st Sess. (Washington, 1946). Historians and other writers have been endeavoring to winnow the essential truth from this mass of materials, but since the causes of war are controversial the results have varied widely. A critical study of writings on this subject is Wayne S. Cole, "American Entry into World War II: A Historical Appraisal," the *Mississippi Valley Historical Review,* XLIII (1957), 595–617. Probably among the most objective and certainly among the most carefully documented volumes are those by William L. Langer and S. Everett Gleason, *The Challenge to Isolation, 1937–1940,* and *The Undeclared War, 1940–1941* (New York, 1953). Another thoughtful study is Donald F. Drummond, *The Passing of American Neutrality, 1937–1941* (Ann Arbor, 1955). One of the best monographs on the coming of the war in the Pacific is Herbert Feis, *The Road to Pearl Harbor: The Coming of the War between the United States and Japan* (Princeton, 1950). Highly critical of the Roosevelt administration are Charles A. Beard, *President Roosevelt and the Coming of the War: A Study in Appearances and Realities* (New Haven, 1948); Charles C. Tansill, *Back Door to War: The Roosevelt Foreign Policy, 1933–1941* (Chicago, 1952); Robert A. Theobald, *The Final Secret of Pearl Harbor* (New York, 1954). One of the most readable accounts is Walter Millis, *This Is Pearl! The United States and Japan* (New York, 1947).

Accounts dealing with participants are helpful. Robert E. Sherwood, *Roosevelt and Hopkins: An Intimate History* (New York, 1948), is a significant work on a key figure in the Roosevelt administration. Other personal accounts include Cordell Hull, *The Memoirs of Cordell Hull* (2 vols., New York, 1948); Henry L. Stimson and McGeorge Bundy, *On Active Service in Peace and War* (New York, 1947, 1948); Sumner Welles, *The Time for Decision* (New York, 1944), "Roosevelt and the Far East," *Harper's Magazine,* Vol. 202 (Feb., 1951), 27–38. A definitive study of Roosevelt for the war years remains to be written, but Samuel I. Rosenman has edited *The Public Papers and Addresses of Franklin D. Roosevelt* (13 vols., New York, 1938–50). Roosevelt's letters for the period are in *F. D. R., His Personal Letters, 1928–1945* (Vol. II, New York, 1950). A brief biography is James MacGregor Burns, *Roosevelt: The Lion and the Fox* (New York, 1956).

The coming war and American politics are discussed in H. Bradford Westerfield, *Foreign Policy and Party Politics: Pearl Harbor to Korea* (New Haven, 1955). Important aspects of the background of war in the Far East are in Morison, *History of United States Naval Operations in World War II,* Vol. II. Other works dealing with Japan in the prewar period include A. Whitney Griswold, *The Far Eastern Policy of the United States* (New York,

1938); Chitoshi Yanaga, *Japan Since Perry* (New York, 1949); Hugh Borton, *Japan's Modern Century* (New York, 1955); F. C. Jones, *Japan's New Order in East Asia: Its Rise and Fall, 1937–45* (New York, 1954); Paul W. Schroeder, *The Axis Alliance and Japanese-American Relations* (Ithaca, N.Y., 1958). A careful defense by the Japanese Foreign Minister is Togo Shigenori, *The Cause of Japan* (New York, 1956). Useful volumes in the British Military Series are S. Woodburn Kirby, *The War Against Japan* (Vol. I, London, 1957) and J. R. M. Butler, *Grand Strategy* (Vol. II, London, 1957). Other U.S. military accounts, in addition to Morison, include Richard M. Leighton and Robert W. Coakley, *Global Logistics and Strategy, 1940–1943* (*United States Army in World War II: The War Department*) (Washington, 1955); George Raynor Thompson, Dixie R. Harris, Pauline M. Oakes, and Dulaney Terrett, *The Signal Corps: The Test* (*December 1941–July 1943*) (*United States Army in World War II: The Technical Services*) (Washington, 1957); and A. R. Buchanan (ed.), *The Navy's Air War: A Mission Completed* (New York [1946]), produced by the Naval Aviation History Unit from naval records.

War Plans and the Start of the War in the Pacific

The outstanding documentary source is the *Pearl Harbor Attack.* The best single account of Japanese preparations and of the attack on Pearl Harbor is in Morison, *History of United States Naval Operations,* Vol. III. Other works dealing with the attack on Hawaii include Craven and Cate, *The Army Air Forces in World War II,* Vol. I; Buchanan (ed.), *The Navy's Air War;* Thompson *et al., The Signal Corps: The Test* (*December 1941–July 1943*). Japanese versions are in Andrieu d'Albas, *Death of a Navy: Japanese Naval Action in World War II* (New York, 1957); Masatake Okumiya and Jiro Horikoshi, *Zero!* (New York, 1956).

Japanese Conquest of the Philippines

The outstanding work on the attack on the Philippines is Louis Morton, *The Fall of the Philippines* (*United States Army in World War II: The War in the Pacific*) (Washington, 1953). Valuable also are Craven and Cate, *The Army Air Forces in World War II,* Vol. I, and Morison, *History of United States Naval Operations,* Vol. III. The novelist Walter D. Edmonds in his *They Fought with What They Had* (Boston, 1951) tells the story from the point of view of the Army Air Forces. Color and personal accounts in the Philippines, as well as throughout the rest of the war, are in Walter Karig, *et al., Battle Report* (4 vols.. New York, Toronto, 1944–48).

The War in the Atlantic

The standard account of United States naval action in the Atlantic is Morison, *History of United States Naval Operations,* Vols. I and X. A shorter but still good treatment is in the volume written by members of the staff of the United States Naval Academy, E. B. Potter (ed.), *The United States and World Sea Power* (Englewood Cliffs, N.J., 1955). More specialized accounts include Theodore Roscoe, *United States Submarine Operations in World War II* (Annapolis, 1949), and Theodore Roscoe, *United States Destroyer Operations in World War II* (Annapolis, 1953). The official British account is S. W. Roskill, *The War at Sea, 1939–1945* (3 vols., London, 1954–61). Useful is another volume of the United Kingdom Military History Series, J. R. M. Butler, *Grand Strategy* (London, 1957), Vol. II.

Important works on the development of American maritime policy include Langer and Gleason, *The Undeclared War,* and Mark S. Watson, *Chief of Staff: Prewar Plans and Preparations* (*United States Army in World War II: The War Department*) (Washington, 1950).

Material on scientific advances in the naval war is in James Phinney Baxter III, *Scientists Against Time* (Boston, 1952); Basil Collier, *The Defence of the United Kingdom;* Buchanan (ed.), *The Navy's Air War.*

Democracy's Arsenal

Valuable summaries of military preparations are in war reports of top American military leaders, *The War Reports of General of the Army George C. Marshall, Chief-of-Staff, General of the Army H. H. Arnold, Commanding General, Army Air Forces, Fleet Admiral Ernest J. King, Commander-in-Chief, United States Fleet and Chief of Naval Operations* (Philadelphia and New York, 1947). Among the specialized accounts of military organization and training are Kent Robert Greenfield, Robert R. Palmer, and Bell I. Wiley, *The Organization of Ground Combat Troops* (*United States Army in World War II: The Army Ground Forces*) (Washington, 1947); Robert R. Palmer, Bell I. Wiley, and William R. Keast, *The Procurement and Training of Ground Combat Troops* (*United States Army in World War II: The Army Ground Forces*) (Washington, 1948); Craven and Cate, *The Army Air Forces in World War II,* Vol. VI.

One of the best books on science and the war is Baxter's *Scientists Against Time,* which is a history of the Office of Scientific Research and Development. Another account of the work of this organization is Lincoln R. Thiesmeyer and John E. Burchard, *Combat Scientists* (*Science in World War II: Office of Scientific Research and Development*) (Boston, 1947). Developments in Army communications are described in Thompson *et al., The Signal Corps: The Test* (*December 1941—July 1943*), and advances in ordnance are recounted in Constance McLaughlin Green, Harry C. Thomson, and Peter C. Roots, *The Ordnance Department: Planning Munitions for War* (*United States Army in World War II: The Technical Services*) (Washington, 1955). There are numerous accounts of the development of the atomic bomb. The official version is Henry DeWolf Smyth, *Atomic Energy for Mil-*

itary Purposes: The Official Report on the Development of the Atomic Bomb under the Auspices of the United States Government, 1940–1945 (Princeton, 1945.) More personal accounts include Arthur Holly Compton, *Atomic Quest: A Personal Narrative* (New York, 1956), and Robert Jungk, *Brighter Than a Thousand Suns: A Personal History of the Atomic Scientists* (New York, 1958). Useful information is in Stimson and Bundy, *On Active Service in Peace and War,* and Harry S. Truman, *Memoirs by Harry S. Truman* (Garden City, N.Y., 1955), Volume I.

An excellent treatment of government controls of production is David Novik, Melvin Anshen, and W. C. Truppner, *Wartime Production Controls* (New York, 1949). A good treatment of politics and war is Roland Young, *Congressional Politics in the Second World War* (New York, 1956). A history of production by one of the government leaders is Donald M. Nelson, *Arsenal of Democracy: The Story of American War Production* (New York, 1946). Lawrence Sullivan, *Bureaucracy Runs Amuck* (Indianapolis, New York, 1944), is highly critical of the Roosevelt administration's conduct of the war. Marshall B. Clinard has made a careful study of *The Black Market: A Study of White Collar Crime* (New York, 1952). A good study of labor at war is Joel Seidman, *American Labor from Defense to Reconversion* (Chicago, 1953). Additional information is in Foster Rhea Dulles, *Labor in America: A History* (New York, 1949); Seymour E. Harris, *Inflation and the American Economy* (New York, 1945); Merle Fainsod and Lincoln Gordon, *Government and the American Economy* (New York, 1948). The best brief source on agriculture is Murray R. Benedict, *Farm Policies of the United States, 1790–1950: A Study of Their Origins and Development* (New York, 1953). Rainer Schickele, *Agricultural Policy: Farm Programs and National Welfare* (New York, 1954), has some information on government policy toward agriculture in wartime.

North Africa

Material on the strategic decision to invade North Africa is in numerous sources already cited. These include Sherwood, *Roosevelt and Hopkins;* Churchill, *The Second World War,* Vol. III; Morison, *History of United States Naval Operations,* Vol. II; Leighton and Coakley, *Global Logistics and Strategy, 1940–1943;* Stimson and Bundy, *On Active Service in Peace and War.* Other volumes in the Army series useful for this subject are George F. Howe, *Northwest Africa: Seizing the Initiative in the West* (*United States Army in World War II: The Mediterranean Theater of Operations*) (Washington, 1957); Maurice Matloff and Edwin M. Snell, *Strategic Planning for Coalition Warfare, 1941–1942* (*United States Army in World War II: The War Department*) (Washington, 1953); and Gordon A. Harrison, *Cross-Channel Attack* (*United States Army in World War II: The European The-*

ater of Operations) (Washington, 1951). Several autobiographical accounts are significant. Among the best are Dwight D. Eisenhower, *Crusade in Europe* (New York, 1948); Mark W. Clark, *Calculated Risk* (New York, 1950); Omar N. Bradley, *A Soldier's Story* (New York, 1951). The personal side of Eisenhower's life is described by his naval aide, Harry C. Butcher, *My Three Years with Eisenhower* (New York, 1946).

Accounts of the approaches and landings are in Morison, *History of United States Naval Operations,* Vol. II; Karig *et al., Battle Report,* Vol. II; Roskill, *The War at Sea,* Vol. II. A good divisional history has been published—George F. Howe, *The Battle History of the 1st Armored Division "Old Ironsides"* (Washington, 1954).

Good treatments of the invasion of Tunisia are in Eisenhower, *Crusade in Europe;* Bradley, *A Soldier's Story;* and Howe's history of the 1st Armored Division. *War As I Knew It,* by George S. Patton, Jr., although drawn from the General's letters and diary, is disappointing, especially on the North African campaign. There are several popular accounts of Patton's life, including James Wellard, *General George S. Patton, Jr., Man Under Mars* (New York, 1956) and William Bancroft Mellor, *Patton: Fighting Man* (New York, 1946). The usual good accounts of naval operations are in Morison, *History of United States Naval Operations,* Vol. II, and of air operations in Craven and Cate, *The Army Air Forces in World War II,* Vol. II. Political aspects of the North African campaign are discussed in William Hardy McNeill, *America, Britain, and Russia: Their Co-operation and Conflict, 1941–1946* (*Survey of International Affairs, 1939–1946* (London, 1953).

Sicily and Italy

Materials on the Casablanca Conference include Sherwood, *Roosevelt and Hopkins;* Leighton and Coakley, *Global Logistics and Strategy, 1940–1943;* Harrison, *Cross-Channel Attack;* Herbert Feis, *Churchill, Roosevelt, Stalin: The War They Waged and the Peace They Won* (Princeton, 1957), a careful analysis by a recognized scholar. British views are in Churchill, *The Second World War,* Vol. IV; John Slessor, *The Central Blue: The Autobiography of Sir John Slessor, Marshal of the RAF* (New York, 1957).

Accounts of the invasion of Sicily are given from different points of view in Bradley, *A Soldier's Story;* Eisenhower, *Crusade in Europe;* Bernard L. Montgomery, *The Memoirs of Field-Marshal the Viscount Montgomery of Alamein, K. G.* (Cleveland and New York, 1958); Craven and Cate, *The Army Air Forces in World War II,* Vol. II; Morison, *History of United States Naval Operations,* Vol. IX; G. W. L. Nicholson, *The Canadians in Italy, 1943–1945* (*Official History of the Canadian Army in the Second World War,* Vol. II) (Ottawa, 1957). The case of "Major William Martin" is in Ewen Montagu, *The Man Who Never Was* (Philadelphia, 1954).

An excellent account of the relations of the Allies with Italy is Norman Kogan, *Italy and the Allies* (Cambridge, 1956). Additional information on this subject is in Toynbee and Toynbee, *Hitler's Europe;* McNeill, *America, Britain, and Russia;* Butcher, *My Three Years with Eisenhower;* Churchill, *The Second World War;* and the works of Bradley and Eisenhower cited above.

Military aspects of the war in Italy are recounted in Clark, *Calculated Risk,* Morison, *History of United States Naval Operations,* Vol. IX; Craven and Cate, *The Army Air Forces in World War II,* Vol. II; Howe, *The Battle History of the 1st Armored Division "Old Ironsides"; Anzio Beachhead (22 January—25 May, 1944)* (Historical Division Department of the Army) (Washington, 1947); Nicholson, *The Canadians in Italy, 1943–1945.* An excellent detailed study of the break-through in northern Italy is in Charles B. MacDonald and Sidney T. Mathews, *Three Battles: Arnaville, Altuzzo,* and *Schmidt* (*United States Army in World War II*) (Washington, 1952). A good account of Japanese-Americans in the Italian campaign is Thomas D. Murphy, *Ambassadors in Arms* (Honolulu, 1954). German views are in Erwin Rommel, *The Rommel Papers,* edited by B. H. Liddell Hart (London, 1953) and Siegfried Westphal, *The German Army in the West* (London, 1951).

Works dealing with the role of the Italian campaign in the strategy of the Allies include the works of the following persons cited above: Churchill, Sherwood, Morison, Clark, and Eisenhower. Valuable for British strategy during the war, as well as for candid appraisals of some of the leading figures on the Allied side, is Arthur Bryant, *The Turn of the Tide: A History of the War Years Based on the Diaries of Field-Marshal Lord Alanbrooke, Chief of the Imperial General Staff* (Garden City, N.Y., 1957). Useful also is John Ehrman, *Grand Strategy* (Vol. V, London, 1956).

Strategic Air Warfare

The basic source for America's role in the strategic air war is Craven and Cate, *The Army Air Forces in World War II,* Vols. I and II. Several volumes in the Army series which are valuable as supplementary reading are Watson, *Chief of Staff: Prewar Plans and Preparations;* Harrison, *Cross-Channel Attack;* Forrest C. Pogue, *The Supreme Command* (*United States Army in World War II: The European Theater of Operations*) (Washington, 1954). British accounts include *Royal Air Force, 1939–1945,* Vol. II, *The Fight Avails,* by Denis Richards and Hilary St. George Saunders (London, 1954); *Royal Air Force, 1939–1945,* Vol. III, *The Fight Is Won,* by Hilary St. George Saunders (London, 1954); Collier, *The Defence of the United Kingdom;* and Slessor, *The Central Blue.* An interesting German source is Adolf Galland, *The First and the Last: The Rise and Fall of the German Fighter Forces, 1938–1945* (New York, 1954).

The Pacific War: Plans and Objectives

There are good sources available on this subject from the various American fighting forces in the Pacific. The leading account of naval operations is Morison, *History of United States Naval Operations,* Vol. IV. See the following Army publications: Louis Morton, *Strategy and Command: The First Two Years* (*United States Army in World War II: The War in the Pacific*) (Washington, 1962); Leighton and Coakley, *Global Logistics and Strategy;* Matloff and Snell, *Strategic Planning for Coalition Warfare, 1941–1942;* and Samuel Milner, *Victory in Papua* (*United States Army in World War II: The War in the Pacific*) (Washington, 1957). The standard work for the Army Air Forces is Craven and Cate, *The Army Air Forces in World War II,* Vols. I and II. Marine Corps publications include Robert D. Heinl, Jr., *The Defense of Wake* (Marine Corps Monographs [1]) ([Washington] 1947); Robert D. Heinl, Jr., *Marines at Midway* (Marine Corps Monographs [3]) ([Washington] 1948); John N. Rentz, *Marines in the Central Solomons* (Marine Corps Monographs [11]) ([Washington] 1952).

Guadalcanal and Papua

Military accounts are good for the Guadalcanal campaign. The outstanding volumes are Morison, *History of United States Naval Operations,* Vol. V; John Miller, Jr., *Guadalcanal: The First Offensive* (*United States Army in World War II: The War in the Pacific*) (Washington, 1949): John L. Zimmerman, *The Guadalcanal Campaign* (Marine Corps Monographs [5]) ([Washington] 1949). Jeter A. Isely and Philip A. Crowl, *The U.S. Marines and Amphibious War: Its Theory and Its Practice in the Pacific* (Princeton, 1951), is an important history of the development of amphibious warfare and a valuable interpretive account of the war in the Pacific. The best coverage of Army Air Force operations is again in Craven and Cate, *The Army Air Forces in World War II,* Vol. IV. Among the specialized accounts are Roscoe, *United States Destroyer Operations in World War II* and Roscoe, *United States Submarine Operations in World War II.* A popular wartime account was Richard Tregaskis, *Guadalcanal Diary* (New York, 1943).

Background material on Papua is in Linden A. Mander, *Some Dependent Peoples of the South Pacific* (New York, 1954), published under the auspices of the Institute of Pacific Relations. Other background sources are W. E. H. Stanner, *The South Seas in Transition: A Study of Post-War Rehabilitation and Reconstruction in Three British Pacific Dependencies* (Sydney, 1953), and Kenneth B. Cumberland, *Southwest Pacific* (New York and Christchurch, 1956).

Military sources include Matloff and Snell, *Strategic Planning for Coalition Warfare, 1941–1942;* Rentz, *Marines in the Central Solomons;* Milner, *Victory in Papua;* Morison, *History of United States Naval Operations,* Vol.

VI; Craven and Cate, *The Army Air Forces in World War II;* Isely and Crowl, *The U.S. Marines and Amphibious War;* Robert L. Eichelberger, *Our Jungle Road to Tokyo* (New York, 1950); George C. Kenney, *General Kenney Reports: A Personal History of the Pacific War* (New York, 1949).

The Pacific War—1943

Accounts for this phase of the Pacific war include Maurice Matloff, *Strategic Planning for Coalition Warfare, 1943–1944* (*United States Army in World War II: The War Department*) (Washington, 1959); John Miller, Jr., *Cartwheel: The Reduction of Rabaul* (*United States Army in World War II: The War in the Pacific*) (Washington, 1959); Craven and Cate, *The Army Air Forces in World War II,* Vol. IV; Morison, *History of United States Naval Operations,* Vols. VI and VII. For other works on phases of the subject, see Kenney, *General Kenney Reports;* John N. Rentz, *Bougainville and the Northern Solomons* (Marine Corps Monographs [4]) ([Washington] 1948); Frank O. Hough and John A. Crown, *The Campaign on New Britain* (Marine Corps Monographs [10] ([Washington] 1952); George Odgers, *Air War Against Japan, 1943–1945* (*Australia in the War of 1939–1945,* Ser. 3, Vol. II) (Canberra, 1957).

The Pacific War, November, 1943—May, 1944

For materials dealing with planning, see Matloff, *Coalition Planning for Strategic Warfare, 1943–1944;* Ray S. Cline, *Washington Command Post: The Operations Division* (*United States Army in World War II: The War Department*) (Washington, 1951); Albert C. Wedemeyer, *Wedemeyer Reports!* (New York, 1958); H. H. Arnold, *Global Mission* (New York, 1949).

Accounts of operations include Philip A. Crowl and Edmund G. Love, *Seizure of the Gilberts and Marshalls* (*United States Army in World War II: The War in the Pacific*) (Washington, 1955); Morison, *History of United States Naval Operations in World War II,* Vol. VII; Robert D. Heinl and John A. Crown, *The Marshalls: Increasing the Tempo* (Marine Corps Monographs [14]) ([Washington] 1954); Craven and Cate, *The Army Air Forces in World War II,* Vol. IV; James R. Stockman, *The Battle for Tarawa* (Marine Corps Monographs [2]) ([Washington] 1947); Miller, *Cartwheel: The Reduction of Rabaul;* Walter Krueger, *From Down Under to Nippon: The Story of Sixth Army in World War II* (Washington, 1953).

The Statesmen at War

Important Army publications dealing with aspects of wartime diplomacy include Matloff and Snell, *Strategic Planning for Coalition Warfare, 1941–1942;* Matloff, *Strategic Planning for Coalition Warfare, 1943–1944;* Leighton and Coakley, *Global Logistics and Strategy, 1940–1943;* Harrison, *Cross-*

Channel Attack; Cline, *Washington Command Post;* Charles F. Romanus and Riley Sunderland, *Stilwell's Command Problems* (*United States Army in World War II: China-Burma-India Theater*) (Washington, 1956); Pogue, *The Supreme Command.* Among the personal accounts are, Hull, *Memoirs,* Vol. II; Churchill, *The Second World War,* Vol. III; Sherwood, *Roosevelt and Hopkins;* Edward R. Stettinius, Jr., *Lend-Lease: Weapon for Victory* (New York, 1944); Eisenhower, *Crusade in Europe;* John R. Deane, *The Strange Alliance: The Story of Our Efforts at Wartime Cooperation with Russia* (New York, 1947). Other accounts include Feis, *Churchill, Roosevelt, Stalin;* Herbert Feis, *The China Tangle: The American Effort in China from Pearl Harbor to the Marshall Mission* (Princeton, 1953); McNeill, *America, Britain, and Russia: Their Cooperation and Conflict, 1941–1943;* H. Bradford Westerfield, *Foreign Policy and Party Politics: Pearl Harbor to Korea* (New Haven, 1955).

The Home Front

There are no satisfactory single accounts of this subject, and the picture must be drawn from a variety of sources. Such newspapers and periodicals as *The New York Times* and *Time* are most useful, and the *Britannica Book of the Year* and the *Social Work Yearbook* have important information. Works bearing on sociological problems include M. H. Newmeyer, *Juvenile Delinquency in Modern Society* (New York, 1949); Alfred M. Lee and N. D. Humphrey, *Race Riot* (New York, 1943); Earl Brown, "The Truth about the Detroit Riot," *Harper's Magazine* (Nov., 1943); W. F. Ogburn and M. F. Nimkoff, *Sociology* (Cambridge, Mass., 1950); Ray E. Baber, *Marriage and the Family* (2nd ed.) (New York, 1953).

Problems connected with labor and the war are discussed in Irving Bernstein, "The Growth of American Unions," *The American Economic Review* (June, 1954); Seidman, *American Labor from Defense to Reconversion;* L. C. Kesselman, *The Social Politics of FEPC: A Study in Reform Pressure Movements* (Chapel Hill, N.C., 1948); Louis Ruchames, *Race, Jobs, and Politics: The Story of FEPC* (New York, 1953); D. W. Wynn, *The N. A. A. C. P. Versus Negro Revolutionary Protest: A Comparative Study of the Effectiveness of Each Movement* (New York, 1955); Robert C. Weaver, *Negro Labor: A National Problem* (New York, 1946); E. Franklin Frazier, *The Negro in the United States* (New York, 1949). Benedict, *Farm Policies of the United States, 1790–1950,* gives a good brief summary of agricultural labor problems. Calvin B. Hoover and B. U. Ratchford, *Economic Resources and Policies of the South* (New York, 1951), is useful for this area. Carey McWilliams, *North from Mexico: the Spanish-speaking People of the United States* (Philadelphia and New York, 1949), criticizes the treatment of Mexican labor.

Most of the works dealing with Japanese-Americans during the war are strongly critical of government actions. The following are detailed treatments: D. S. Thomas and R. S. Nishimoto, *The Spoilage: Japanese American Evacuation and Resettlement* (Berkeley and Los Angeles, 1946); Jacobus ten Broek, Edward N. Barnhart, and Floyd W. Matson, *Prejudice, War and the Constitution: Japanese American Evacuation and Resettlement* (Berkeley and Los Angeles, 1954); Morton Grodzins, *Americans Betrayed: Politics and the Japanese Evacuation* (Chicago, 1949). There are two good studies of Japanese-Americans in Hawaii, A. W. Lind, *Hawaii's Japanese* (Princeton, 1946), and Murphy, *Ambassadors in Arms.*

Build-up for D-day

Among the numerous important military accounts of the preparations for D-day are the following: Harrison, *Cross-Channel Attack;* Matloff and Snell, *Strategic Planning for Coalition Warfare, 1941–1942;* Leighton and Coakley, *Global Logistics and Strategy, 1940–1943;* Cline, *Washington Command Post;* Pogue, *The Supreme Command;* Roland G. Ruppenthal, *Logistical Support of the Armies* (*United States Army in World War II: The European Theater of Operation*) (Washington, 1953), Vol. I. Morison, *History of United States Naval Operations in World War II,* Vol. XI, is valuable for naval preparations. Several personal accounts by Americans which have pertinent information are Stimson and Bundy, *On Active Service in Peace and War;* Sherwood, *Roosevelt and Hopkins;* Bradley, *A Soldier's Story;* Eisenhower, *Crusade in Europe;* Walter Bedell Smith, *Eisenhower's Six Great Decisions: Europe, 1944–1945* (New York, London, Toronto, 1956). Very helpful for the work of Cossac are the memoirs of its head, Frederick Morgan, *Overture to Overlord* (New York, 1950). Other significant British sources are Churchill, *The Second World War,* Vol. V, and Bryant, *The Turn of the Tide.* An account of Mulberry Operation by one of its leaders is Alfred B. Stanford, *Force MULBERRY: The Planning and Installation of the Artificial Harbor off U.S. Normandy Beaches in World War II* (New York, 1951). German defense preparations are described in Hans Speidel, *Invasion 1944: Rommel and the Normandy Campaign* (Chicago, 1950), and Rommel, *The Rommel Papers.* Wilmot, *The Struggle for Europe,* is a readable summary from the British point of view.

Cross-Channel Assault and the Capture of Cherbourg

The outstanding military accounts are Harrison, *Cross-Channel Attack;* Morison, *History of United States Naval Operations in World War II,* Vol. XI; Craven and Cate, *The Army Air Forces in World War II,* Vol. III. Other important military sources include Ruppenthal, *Logistical Support of the Armies,* Vol. I; Joseph Bykofsky and Harold Larson, *The Transportation Corps* (*United States Army in World War II: The Technical Services*) (Washington, 1957); *Utah Beach to Cherbourg (6 June to 27 June 1944) (American Forces in Action Series)* (Washington, 1947). Among the significant personal accounts are Bradley, *A Soldier's Story;* Eisenhower, *Crusade in Europe;* Bernard L. Montgomery, *Normandy to the Baltic* (Boston, 1948); Bernard L. Montgomery, *Memoirs.* Stanford, *Force MULBERRY,* continues the account of the artificial beaches. Light on German operations is thrown by Speidel, *Invasion 1944: Rommel and the Normandy Campaign,* and Rommel, *The Rommel Papers.*

Breakout and Advance to the Seine

Many of the sources dealing with the cross-Channel assault continue to be useful for Allied operations in Europe. These include: Craven and Cate, *The Army Air Forces in World War II,* Vol. II; Bradley, *A Soldier's Story;* Eisenhower, *Crusade in Europe;* Montgomery's *Normandy to the Baltic* and his later *Memoirs.* Pogue, *The Supreme Command,* is especially good for the command problem. Willy Ley, *Rockets, Missiles, and Space Travel* (revised and enlarged edition, New York, 1958), has useful information on the German V-1 and V-2. An excellent account of British defense is in Collier, *The Defence of the United Kingdom.* German operations receive continued treatment in Speidel, *Invasion 1944,* and Rommel, *The Rommel Papers.* The following works deal with the attempt to assassinate Hitler: Constantine FitzGibbon, *20 July* (New York, 1956); John W. Wheeler-Bennett, *The Nemesis of Power: The German Army in Politics, 1918–1945* (New York, 1954); Wilhelm von Schramm, *Conspiracy among Generals* (London [1956]).

Advance Across France

Military publications and memoirs continue to be the best sources of information. Among the former, Pogue, *The Supreme Command;* Ruppenthal, *Logistical Support of the Armies,* Vol. I; and Craven and Cate, *The Army Air Forces in World War II,* Vol. III, are valuable, and among the latter, Eisenhower, *Crusade in Europe,* and Bradley, *A Soldier's Story,* are important. The debate over the invasion of southern France is discussed from different viewpoints in Eisenhower, *Crusade in Europe;* Pogue, *The Supreme Command;* Morison, *History of United States Naval Operations,* Vol. XI; Feis, *Churchill, Roosevelt, Stalin;* Churchill, *The Second World War,* Vol. VI; John Ehrman, *Grand Strategy* (London, 1956). The following works deal with the actual invasion of southern France: Morison, *History of United States Naval Operations,* Vol. XI; Craven and Cate, *The Army Air Forces in World War II,* Vol. III; Jean de Lattre de Tassigny, *The History of the French First Army* (London, 1952); Guy Salisbury-Jones, *So Full a Glory: A Biography of Marshal de Lattre de Tassigny* (London, 1954). The Arnhem operation receives treatment in *Royal Air Force, 1939–1945,* Vol. III, *The Fight Is Won,* by

Hilary St. George Saunders (London, 1954); Craven and Cate, *The Army Air Forces in World War II,* Vol. III; Montgomery, *Normandy to the Baltic;* Montgomery, *Memoirs;* Bradley, *A Soldier's Story;* Wilmot, *The Struggle for Europe.* Excellent treatments of logistical problems in France are in Ruppenthal, *Logistical Support of the Armies,* Vol. I; Bykofsky and Larson, *The Transportation Corps: Operations Overseas.* Also helpful are Erna Risch, *The Quartermaster Corps: Organization, Supply and Services* (*United States Army in World War II: The Technical Services*) (Washington, 1953), and C. M. Green, H. C. Thompson, and P. C. Roots, *The Ordnance Department: Planning Munitions for War* (*United States Army in World War II: The Technical Services*) (Washington, 1955).

Fall Deadlock and the Battle of the Bulge

There are some excellent specialized accounts, including H. M. Cole, *The Lorraine Campaign* (*United States Army in World War II: The European Theater of Operations* (Washington, 1950), and MacDonald and Mathews, *Three Battles: Arnaville, Altuzzo* and *Schmidt.* Valuable also are Bradley, *A Soldier's Story;* Eisenhower, *Crusade in Europe;* Craven and Cate, *The Army Air Forces in World War II,* Vol. III; Pogue, *The Supreme Command.* French military participation is described in de Lattre de Tassigny, *The History of the French First Army,* and Salisbury-Jones, *So Full a Glory: A Biography of Marshal de Lattre de Tassigny.* The British side is covered in Montgomery, *Normandy to the Baltic;* Montgomery, *Memoirs;* Wilmot, *The Struggle for Europe.* The war from the German view is seen in Speidel, *Invasion 1944: Rommel and the Normandy Campaign;* Rommel, *The Rommel Papers;* F. W. von Mellenthin, *Panzer Battles, 1939–1945* (2nd. ed.) (London, 1956); Westphal, *The German Army in the West.* Other works include Smith, *Eisenhower's Six Great Decisions;* Patton, *War As I Knew It;* Charles R. Codman, *Drive* (Boston, 1957); Wellard, *General George S. Patton, Jr., Man Under Mars;* Milton Shulman, *Defeat in the West* (New York, 1948). A good summary account is that of Robert E. Merriam, *Dark December: The Full Account of the Battle of the Bulge* (Chicago, New York, 1947).

The Collapse of Germany

The U.S. Army has not yet published extensively on this period of the war, but Pogue, *The Supreme Command,* is an important summary. Memoirs again are helpful, although they sometimes reveal personal bias. These include Eisenhower, *Crusade in Europe;* Bradley, *A Soldier's Story;* Montgomery, *Normandy to the Baltic;* Montgomery, *Memoirs;* Churchill, *The Second World War,* Vol. VI. Essential, respectively, for the role of air and sea operations are Craven and Cate, *The Army Air Forces in World War II,* Vol. III, and Morison, *History of United States Naval Operations,* Vol. XI. Parts of the German side are in Westphal, *The German Army in the West;* Mellenthin, *Panzer Battles, 1939–1945;* Heinz Guderian, *Panzer Leader* (London, 1952). A standard account of Hitler's death is H. R. Trevor-Roper, *The Last Days of Hitler* (New York, 1947). An interpretive treatment of German and other surrenders in World War II is Paul Kecskemeti, *Strategic Surrender: The Politics of Victory and Defeat* (Stanford, Calif., 1958). A leading study of American military government in Germany is Carl J. Friedrich and Associates, *American Experiences in Military Government in World War II* (New York, 1948).

China, Burma, India

The best sources of information for this theater are three volumes in the Army series written by Charles F. Romanus and Riley Sunderland, *Stilwell's Mission to China* (*United States Army in World War II: China-Burma-India Theater*) (Washington, 1953); *Stilwell's Command Problems* (*United States Army in World War II: China-Burma-India Theater*) (Washington, 1956); *Time Runs Out in CBI* (*United States Army in World War II: China-Burma-India Theater*) (Washington, 1959). Other useful works in the series are Leighton and Coakley, *Global Logistics and Strategy, 1940–1943,* and Cline, *Washington Command Post: The Operations Division.* Craven and Cate, *The Army Air Forces in World War II* is valuable. Joseph W. Stilwell, *The Stilwell Papers* (New York, 1948), is helpful for the views of this controversial figure. A critical British opinion of Stilwell is expressed in John Ehrman, *Grand Strategy* (London, 1956), Vol. V. See also Claire Lee Chennault, *Way of a Fighter: The Memoirs of Claire Lee Chennault* (New York, 1949); Wedemeyer, *Wedemeyer Reports!*

The Statesmen Face the Peace

Materials dealing with the Quebec Conference and the Morgenthau Plan include Sherwood, *Roosevelt and Hopkins;* McNeill, *America, Britain, and Russia;* Churchill, *The Second World War,* Vol. VI; Henry Morgenthau, Jr., "Post-war Treatment of Germany," American Academy of Political and Social Science, *Annals,* Vol. 246 (July, 1946), 125–129; James Forrestal, *The Forrestal Diaries,* edited by Walter Millis (New York, 1951); John L. Chase, "The Development of the Morgenthau Plan through the Quebec Conference," *Journal of Politics,* XVI (May, 1954), 324–359; Stimson and Bundy, *On Active Service in Peace and War;* Hull, *Memoirs.* Additional bibliographical references on the Morgenthau plan are in John L. Snell (ed.), *The Meaning of Yalta* (Baton Rouge, La., 1956).

Among the works dealing with the Yalta Conference are *Foreign Relations of the United States: Diplomatic Papers: The Conferences at Malta and Yalta 1945* (84th Cong., 1st Sess., House Document No. 154) (Washington,

1955); Snell (ed.), *The Meaning of Yalta;* Feis, *Churchill, Roosevelt, Stalin;* Edward R. Stettinius, *Roosevelt and the Russians: the Yalta Conference* (New York, 1949); James F. Byrnes, *Speaking Frankly* (New York, 1947).

The following sources have information on Roosevelt's death and Truman's assumption of the presidency: Ross T. McIntire, *White House Physician* (New York, 1946); Truman, *Memoirs,* Vol. I; Jonathan Daniels, *The Man of Independence* (Philadelphia, 1950).

Among the numerous works treating the San Francisco Conference are McNeill, *America, Britain, and Russia;* Arthur H. Vandenberg, *The Private Papers of Senator Vandenberg,* edited by Arthur H. Vandenberg, Jr. (Boston, 1952); Truman, *Memoirs,* Vol. I; Westerfield, *Foreign Policy and Party Politics.*

Information on the Potsdam Conference and the question of Russian entrance into the Far Eastern war is in Truman, *Memoirs;* Deane, *The Strange Alliance;* Byrnes, *Speaking Frankly;* Cline, *Washington Command Post: The Operations Division;* McNeill, *America, Britain, and Russia;* Craven and Cate, *The Army Air Forces in World War II,* Vol. V.

The Pacific War, April–November, 1944

A principal Army account is Robert Ross Smith, *The Approach to the Philippines* (*United States Army in World War II: The War in the Pacific*) (Washington, 1953). The main Marine Corps monographs are Carl W. Hoffman, *Saipan: The Beginning of the End* (Marine Corps Monographs [6]) ([Washington] 1950); Carl W. Hoffman, *The Seizure of Tinian* (Marine Corps Monographs [8]) ([Washington] 1951); O. R. Lodge, *The Recapture of Guam* (Marine Corps Monographs [12]) ([Washington] 1954); Frank O. Hough, *The Assault on Peleliu* (Marine Corps Monographs [7]) ([Washington] 1950). Essential also are Morison, *History of United States Naval Operations,* Vol. VIII; Craven and Cate, *The Army Air Forces in World War II,* Vol. IV. Pertinent memoirs include Holland M. Smith, *Coral and Brass* (New York, 1949), and William F. Halsey, *Admiral Halsey's Story* (New York, 1947).

The Pacific War, November, 1944—June, 1945

For the planning, see Matloff, *Strategic Planning for Coalition Warfare, 1943–1944.* There is good coverage for the Leyte operation in M. Hamlin Cannon, *Leyte: The Return to the Philippines* (*United States Army in World War II: The War in the Pacific*) (Washington, 1954); Craven and Cate, *The Army Air Forces in World War II,* Vol. V; Morison, *History of United States Naval Operations in World War II,* Vols. XII, XIII. There are fewer military sources on the remainder of the campaign in the Philippines. Helpful, however, are Charles W. Boggs, Jr., *Marine Aviation in the Philippines* (Marine Corps Monographs [9]) ([Washington] 1951); Walter Krueger, *From Down Under to Nippon: The Story of Sixth Army in World War II* (Washington, 1953); Craven and Cate, *The Army Air Forces in World War II,* Vol. V; Potter (ed.), *The United States and World Sea Power;* Buchanan (ed.), *The Navy's Air War;* Eichelberger, *Our Jungle Road to Tokyo;* C. A. Willoughby and John Chamberlain, *MacArthur, 1941–1951* (New York, 1954). See also Robert Ross Smith, *Triumph in The Philippines* (*United States Army in World War II: The War in the Pacific*) (Washington, 1963).

The Pacific War, February–June, 1945—Iwo Jima and Okinawa

There are excellent military accounts of both the Iwo Jima and the Okinawa operations. Among the best for Iwo Jima are Whitman S. Bartley, *Iwo Jima: Amphibious Epic* (Marine Corps Monographs [13]) ([Washington] 1954); Craven and Cate, *The Army Air Forces in World War II,* Vol. V; Morison, *History of United States Naval Operations in World War II,* Vol. XIV. See also Holland M. Smith, *Coral and Brass,* and Isely and Crowl, *The U.S. Marines and Amphibious War.*

The leading studies of the Okinawa campaign are Charles S. Nichols and Henry I. Shaw, Jr., *Okinawa: Victory in the Pacific* (Marine Corps Monographs [15]) ([Washington] 1955); Roy E. Appleman, James M. Burns, Russell A. Gugeler, and John Stevens, *Okinawa: The Last Battle* (*United States Army in World War II: The War in the Pacific*) (Washington, 1948). Valuable also are Craven and Cate, *The Army Air Forces in World War II,* Vol. V; Halsey, *Halsey's Own Story;* Morison, *History of United States Naval Operations in World War II,* Vol. XIV.

The Collapse of Japan

The best account of the strategic air war against Japan is Craven and Cate, *The Army Air Forces in World War II,* Vol. V. Romanus and Sunderland, *Stilwell's Command Problems,* is valuable for operations from China. Naval and naval air operations are dealt with in Halsey, *Admiral Halsey's Story;* Potter (ed.), *The United States and World Sea Power;* Buchanan (ed.), *The Navy's Air War;* Roscoe, *United States Destroyer Operations in World War II;* Roscoe, *United States Submarine Operations in World War II.*

Japanese reactions to air raids are in Toshikazu Kase, *Journey to the Missouri* (New Haven, 1950) and Masatake Okumiya and Jiro Horikoshi, *Zero!*

Preparations for possible invasion of Japan are discussed in Cline, *Washington Command Post: The Operations Division;* Craven and Cate, *The Army Air Forces in World War II,* Vol. V; Willoughby and Chamberlain, *MacArthur, 1941–1951.*

Materials dealing with planning and dropping the atomic bombs are in Craven and Cate, *The Army Air Forces in World War II,* Vol. V. Additional information is in Stimson and Bundy, *On Active Service in Peace and War;* Compton, *Atomic Quest;* Truman, *Memoirs,* Vol. I; Churchill, *The Second World War,* Vol. VI. John Hersey, *Hiroshima* (New York, 1946), is a graphic account of the effects of the bombing.

An excellent study of the collapse of the Japanese government is Robert J. C. Butow, *Japan's Decision to Surrender* (Stanford, Calif., 1954). Japanese sources include Kase, *Journey to the Missouri,* and Shigenori Togo, *The Cause of Japan* (New York, 1956). Other information is in Jones, *Japan's New Order in East Asia.* Matters relating to the surrender are in Byrnes, *Speaking Frankly;* Craven and Case, *The Army Air Forces in World War II,* Vol. V; Butow, *Japan's Decision to Surrender;* Kase, *Journey to the Missouri;* Willoughby and Chamberlain, *MacArthur, 1941–1951;* Halsey, *Admiral Halsey's Story;* Togo, *The Cause of Japan.*

Index

940.5397 BUCH
Buchanan, Albert Russell, 1906-
The United States and World War II
V. 2